New Ways of
Looking at Old Texts, IV

Papers of the
Renaissance English Text Society
2002–2006

MEDIEVAL AND RENAISSANCE
TEXTS AND STUDIES
VOLUME 345

RENAISSANCE ENGLISH TEXT SOCIETY
SEVENTH SERIES
SPECIAL PUBLICATION

NEW WAYS OF
LOOKING AT OLD TEXTS, IV

PAPERS OF THE
RENAISSANCE ENGLISH TEXT SOCIETY
2002–2006

Edited by
MICHAEL DENBO

ACMRS
(Arizona Center for Medieval and Renaissance Studies)
Tempe, Arizona
in conjunction with
Renaissance English Text Society
2008

Library of Congress Cataloging-in-Publication Data

New ways of looking at old texts. IV : papers of the Renaissance English Text
Society, 2002-2006 / edited by Michael Denbo.
    p. cm. -- (Medieval and Renaissance texts and studies ; v. 345)
  Includes bibliographical references and index.
  ISBN 978-0-86698-393-8 (alk. paper)
  1. English literature--Early modern, 1500-1700--Criticism, Textual. 2. Trans-
mission of texts--England--History--16th century. 3. Transmission of texts--
England--History--17th century. 4. Manuscripts, Renaissance--England--
Editing. 5. Manuscripts, English--Editing. 6. Renaissance--England.
7. Paleography, English. I. Denbo, Michael Roy. II. Renaissance English Text
Society.

PR418.T48N4945 2008
820.9'003--dc22

                                            2008050828

∞
This book is made to last.
It is set in Adobe Minion Pro,
smyth-sewn and printed on acid-free paper
to library specifications.
Printed in the United States of America

Contents

John Foxe: *The Acts and Monuments*

Manuscript Studies

In Memoriam—David Freeman

David Freeman was for many years until the time of his death one of the most learned, generous, and beloved members of the Executive Council of the Renaissance English Text Society. His expertise was in the study of classics and of the ancient languages, concepts, and tropes by which much Renaissance English writing was formulated and which offered rules and models for imitation. Yet he shared his knowledge with instantaneous willingness and enthusiasm and with a remarkable and memorable modesty. His ranging intellect, combined with great good humor and what seemed limitless patience, made him the ideal chair of editorial teams supervising and certifying a number of volumes published by the Society.

From boyhood, David developed the inborn empathy and the widely ranging and exacting mind which would lead him to his vocation of scholar and humanist. He was born in 1936 at Harpenden, Hertfordshire, England. His grandfather was in charge of German prisoners during World War II, and many of them were brought to the Freeman home in Piggottshill Lane along with evacuees from London and other soldiers billeted there during the war. It was during these years that David became interested in people of other nationalities and that began his life-long love of travel. He first won a much-coveted scholarship to St.

Alban's Abbey School and subsequently an open scholarship to Wadham College, Oxford, to read English, graduating in 1955. He attended the University of Leicester where in June 1959 he was awarded the Graduate Certificate in Education with distinction; a year later, he was named Assistant English Master for the City of Leicester Boys School.

David's yearning for travel and for a more exotic culture than his own was fulfilled when the British Council recruited him in September 1960 to teach English in Rasht, northern Iran, to Iranian teachers of English. There he mastered the Farsi language, and during his travels also picked up a reading knowledge of Arabic. In Iran too he met and married his wife Nina. In 1962 he took up the post of Lecturer in English at Memorial University of Newfoundland in St. Johns, Canada, and served successively as secretary and president of the St. John's branch of the Humanities Association of Canada and as a member of the National Executive of the Association. In 1969 he returned to England to earn the Ph.D. at Birkbeck College, University of London, where he prepared for his thesis a critical edition of Francis Quarles' heroic romance *Argalus and Parthenia* (1629), drawn from Sir Philip Sidney's prose romance *The Countess of Pembrokes Arcadia*. As he was the first to acknowledge gratefully, he was helped in this by a number of scholars, most notably by the distinguished Renaissance and Shakespearean scholar Dr. Harold Brooks, a good friend to him and the supervisor of his doctoral dissertation. This text was later published by the Renaissance English Text Society and brought him onto the Society's Executive Council.

In the fall of 1975 David was asked to create the English Department of a new college later named Sir Wilfred Grenfell College—on the west coast of Newfoundland where he spent the remainder of his career. There he built a warm community of faculty and students punctuated by annual Christmas readings which he arranged, Valentine's Day performances, special celebrations of Shakespeare's birthday, and the honoring of Remembrance Day, many of them broadcast on radio and television. He was also much involved in the annual World Championship of Horseshoes on the Humber River, contested by the PH.D. All Stars (People for Horseshoe Democracy) and the world champion members of the English Department. David, together with other distinguished scholars such as Adrian Fowler, played a pivotal role in creating a hospitable and fertile atmosphere for writers, and in this milieu a number thrived: Al Pittman, perhaps the outstanding poet and dramatist of his generation in Newfoundland; John Steffler, who has recently been chosen Parliamentary Poet Laureate of Canada; and Randall Maggs, who with his poetic sequence *Night Work* has received acclaim from the Atlantic to the Pacific.

Winters he taught a range of courses including Chaucer, Shakespeare, and works of the English seventeenth century. At Corner Brook he also performed Shakespeare, taking the roles of Theseus, Sir Toby Belch, Holofernes, Adam, and Gloucester in *King Lear*. Summers he taught, even after retirement, a summer course for American students at Corpus Christi College, Oxford, while returning to stay at Wadham. In June 2006, he planned another idyllic summer in England. On June 22 he flew with two Grenfell colleagues to England, and left them about midnight. The next morning he collapsed outside his Gatwick hotel and died before he could journey to Oxford.

He was a noted member of his faculty, "warmly supportive, deeply intelligent, unfailingly cheerful, and often very funny." He was buried with his family in Harpenden while in Newfoundland "there was a moving and fitting memorial service with an academic procession, a full choir, music by a string quartet, a number of tributes, strong hymns." The Council of the Renaissance English Text Society voted to dedicate this collection of essays it has sponsored over the past five years in his memory, privileged to be a part of his legacy too.

ARTHUR F. KINNEY, PRESIDENT
FOR THE RENAISSANCE ENGLISH TEXT SOCIETY

Editor's Note

Since this is the first volume of *New Ways of Looking at Old Texts: Papers of the Renaissance English Text Society* that I have edited, I think a few words are in order. Before his passing, Speed Hill, former president of RETS and creator of this archive, asked me to take up the editorship. It is not a job I had ever envisioned for myself, but Speed was quite encouraging and convinced me that I was up to the task. I hope he was right. Editing *New Ways IV* has been far different than I anticipated, much more complicated, but also very rewarding. I am grateful to all the writers who contributed to the volume. Their work—both collectively and individually—speaks for the entire RETS project, and I think no one should be surprised by the breadth of scholarship and attention to detail that this volume demonstrates.

The reader will see some changes to this volume of *New Ways*: I have altered its organization. Rather than organize by session, I have arranged by theme. There were a number of reasons for this: several articles were not available to me when I became editor, and one essay, for a variety of reasons, had been omitted from the previous volume. So rather than present truncated panels from various meetings (some of which would have had serious omissions), we have a new format, one that I hope will make *New Ways* more user-friendly to readers looking to explore specific aspects of Renaissance textual studies. I think even a cursory examination of the table of contents will explain my thinking on this. However, for clarity, a roster of panels is included at the conclusion of this volume. Readers will also notice that *New Ways IV* adds two RETS panels held in the spring of 2007. Since papers delivered at these two sessions were part of a larger series on early modern women's manuscripts, they are included in order to maintain the integrity of the series. *New Ways V* will start with MLA 2007.

Also, I would like to add a personal note on David Freeman. David passed away about a year before Speed, so the plan to dedicate this volume to him was made between these two losses that RETS suffered. David was a dedicated scholar, a fine gentleman, and a wonderful friend. Although I was never his student, it is not hard to imagine what type of teacher he was. Everything was bright and warmly humorous to him: he loved literature, art, and music, anything that brought out the best in us. Oddly, I can remember no time sitting down with both David and Speed, but clearly, from their comments, each had high regard for the other and must have enjoyed the other's company. I miss them both.

Finally, on the volume itself, there is much for the reader who wants to pick and choose, but having been through all the essays, I can assure anyone that there are many rewards to a sequential reading. Themes will emerge of their own volition, and I think this volume is a treasure trove for students and scholars looking for new areas to consider in Renaissance studies. RETS is a unique organization, and if you are interested, you are welcome to join us.

MICHAEL DENBO
EDITOR, *NEW WAYS IV*

John Foxe: *The Acts and Monuments*

Print Reformation or Print Revolution?
John Foxe and the History of Books

JESSE M. LANDER

He who first shortened the labor of Copyists by device of *Movable Types* was disbanding hired Armies, and cashiering most Kings and Senates, and creating a whole new Democratic world: he had invented the Art of Printing. —Carlyle

The invention of the printing press and the Reformation are and shall remain Central Europe's two most sublime contributions to humanity. —Mann

THE APPEARANCE OF THE *VARIORUM EDITION ONLINE* OF *ACTS AND Monuments* is an occasion for extravagant happiness among all those with an interest in early modern culture and the history of books.[1] It is also an occasion for reflection. The transformation of one of the most imposing of physical books manufactured in sixteenth-century England into bytes and pixels is astounding. Whether we confront this new development with unalloyed jubilation or with an optimism tempered by anxiety and nostalgia, the fact of change seems inescapable. And this inescapable fact throws into relief the narratives that we have used to order our understanding of the history of books. In particular, I want to focus on two key terms that have long served to mark major historical transformations: *reformation* and *revolution*.

---

[1] This paper was originally delivered at the 2003 MLA convention in San Diego, CA, at a panel entitled "The Josephine A. Roberts Forum: Twenty-First Century Foxe—The Online Genetic Edition of John Foxe's *Book of Martyrs*" (http://www.hrionline.ac.uk/johnfoxe/), John N. King, Ohio State University, presiding. I would like to thank Professor King for inviting me to participate. In preparing this paper for publication, I have added footnotes and excised a few verbal infelicities; otherwise, the text stands as delivered.

The print revolution, a once potent concept, has lost its teeth. The decisive emergence of print technology in early modern Europe no longer appears so decisive. Moreover, the imagined cultural consequences of the press are said to have been grossly exaggerated. Indeed, the once common notion of a "print culture" has come under withering attack. Skepticism about a print revolution is not a new thing, but recently critiques of the idea have achieved the status of conventional wisdom. There are three versions of the argument that I want to look at briefly: a definitional argument that claims that the revolution metaphor significantly misdescribes conditions on the ground; a theoretical argument that identifies the print revolution as an unacceptable version of technological determinism; and lastly an historical argument that dissolves print into the *longue durée* of the codex.[2]

Definitional arguments focus on the ways in which the terms associated with print revolution fail to accurately portray the historical phenomena. These arguments invariably include an empirical component because they draw attention to phenomena inadequately rendered by the vocabulary of revolution. Thus a more finely focused attention to historical detail has revealed many of the generalizations associated with the print revolution paradigm to be vulnerable, but in some cases these arguments appear trivial. For example, the well-established fact that no two copies of a book in the handpress period were identical has been invoked to counter the claim that print was uniquely able to produce identical copies.[3] A more promising line of attack has been pursued by scholars such as Harold Love, who have so successfully described the vitality of scribal production in a post-print world and thus put paid to any argument suggesting that print simply displaced other modes of communication.[4] Coming from a different chronological direction, Paul Saenger's claim that private, silent reading preceded the discovery of print undermines the notion that print brought about a reading revolution.[5]

---

[2] This division is in some senses arbitrary and makes no claim to exhaustiveness. In addition, it should be pointed out that many scholars deploy all three types of argument and some particular arguments combine elements of the three. The taxonomy is merely a heuristic device intended to highlight the logic underlying several of the more successful critiques of print revolution.

[3] For examples, see Michael Warner, *The Letters of the Republic: Publication and the Public Sphere in Eighteenth-Century America* (Cambridge, MA: Harvard Univ. Press, 1990); Adrian Johns, *The Nature of the Book: Print and Knowledge in the Making* (Chicago: Univ. of Chicago Press, 1998).

[4] Harold Love, *The Culture and Commerce of Texts: Scribal Publication in Seventeenth-Century England* (Amherst: Univ. of Massachusetts Press, 1998).

[5] Paul Saenger, "Silent Reading: Its Impact on Late Medieval Script and Society," *Viator* 13 (1982): 367–414.

Thus the model of revolutionary overturning gives way to a vision of gradual change in which oral, written, and print forms were in complex suspension; recalcitrant facts, in all their local particularity, prove resistant to the synthetic impulses of the print revolution paradigm.

The theoretical argument that interests me here construes print revolution as an unacceptable version of technological determinism and offers in its place an argument about the social and cultural construction of technology. Two recent and important examples are provided by the work of Michael Warner and Adrian Johns. In 1990, Warner observed that historians attempting to trace the effects of the press overlook "the political and symbolic constitution of print" (6). In a bid to recover the political and symbolic dimension of print, Warner emphatically rejects the notion that "technology has an ontological status prior to culture" (7)—a doctrine that he associates with Jack Goody, Marshall McLuhan, Elizabeth Eisenstein, and other "technodeterminists."[6] The question of "ontological priority" may strike the uninitiated as a superfluous bit of metaphysical jargon. Who, after all, makes the argument that any technology is prior, anterior, or outside culture? What produces Warner's metaphysical turn is, in fact, his sense that his antagonists have themselves invested print with metaphysical attributes: "What have historically become the characteristics of printing have been projected backward as its natural, essential logic" (9). Warner's basic point—that technology does not come from outside history and that its meanings are invariably structured by local culture—is cogent, and yet it comes very close to dissolving technology altogether. Technology, according to Warner, comprises "practices and structured labors"—and these are, in turn, inseparable from their political meaning.[7] Technology, dissolved in the dimension of culture, loses its specificity and assumes an extreme plasticity. One need not advocate a simplistic equation between technology and the physical machine in order to feel as though Warner's account is etiolated.[8] By focusing insistently on the dimension of culture, Warner excludes the concrete aspect of the printing press and thus leaves very little room

---

[6] "Technodeterminism" and "technodeterminist" may well be Warner's own neologisms. In any case, they fulfill an important polemical function in his argument.

[7] Warner writes: "The cultural constitution of a medium (in this case printing) is a set of political conditions of discourse. Those conditions include the practices and structured labors that we call technology. But I shall suppose that the latter have no ontological privilege over and at no point can be distinguished from their political meaning; that the practices of technology, in other words, are always structured, and that their meaningful structure is the dimension of culture" (9–10).

[8] Warner's "practices and structured labors" can be usefully compared to Alex Roland's definition of technology as "systematic, purposeful manipulation of the material world." Roland, however, adds that technology is comprised of four components: "materials, technique,

for the notion that technology makes demands upon its users, that it is something that must be accommodated.

Adrian Johns offers a similar argument. He too draws attention to the social construction of print, but his position is not as extreme as Warner's. "What we often regard as essential elements and necessary concomitants of print are," in Johns' estimate, "in fact rather more contingent than generally acknowledged"(2). Like Warner, Johns attacks the metaphysicians of print: "The very identity of print had to be *made*." Print has no essential identity, and our modern understanding of it is the result of a long and arduous process. Despite his emphasis on the contingent nature of print, Johns avoids dissolving print technology entirely into the cultural. Indeed, despite the polemical stance at the beginning of his introduction, he soon concedes that technology must remain part of the equation: "The sources of print culture are therefore to be sought in civility as much as in technology, and in historical labors as much as in cause and effect. The 'printing revolution,' if there was one, consisted of changes in the conventions of handling and investing credit in textual materials as much as in transformations in their manufacture" (35–36). These arguments attack the causal claim implicit in print revolution by insisting that it is an unacceptable form of technological determinism.[9]

The third argument has been put forward by Roger Chartier. In an essay that first appeared in *Common Knowledge*, Chartier resituated print within a long-running culture of the book. In this history, the two decisive developments were the shift from the roll to the codex occurring at the beginning of the Christian era, and the shift from book to electronic media happening as we speak. Chartier does not here dispense with the language of revolution nor does he reject the force of technology. The technology of the codex is of enormous cultural consequence: "The reader was liberated by the codex."[10] "With the codex," according

---

power, and tools or machines." See Alex Roland, "Theories and Models of Technological Change: Semantics and Substance," *Science, Technology, & Human Values* 17 (1992): 79–100.

[9] The accusation of technological determinism is not, of course, new. In 1974, Perry Anderson found the work of Elizabeth Eisenstein "audacious," but "marred by the monomania familiar in historians of technology": *Lineages of the Absolutist State* (London: Verso, 1974), 22. In a volume originally published in 1983, Benedict Anderson observed that Eisenstein and S. H. Steinberg "come close to theomorphizing 'print' *qua* print as the genius of modern history": *Imagined Communities: Reflections on the Origin and Spread of Nationalism*, rev. ed. (London: Verso, 1991), 44. While there is not space here to address the issue, it is striking that talk of technological determinism invariably assumes, rather than demonstrates, that it is not an intellectually respectable position.

[10] Roger Chartier, *Forms and Meanings: Texts, Performances, and Audiences from Codex to Computer* (Philadelphia: Univ. of Pennsylvania Press, 1995). The initial version is Roger Chartier, "From Codex to Screen: Trajectories of the Written Word," *Common Knowledge* 2.3 (1993): 160–71.

to Chartier, "came the invention of a formal typology that associated formats and genres, types of books and categories of discourse, so initiating a grid for the identifying and categorizing books that the printing press would inherit and that we still possess today" (20). Chartier is explicit about the value of this retrospective: "understanding and mastering the electronic revolution of tomorrow (or today) very much depends on properly situating it within history over the *longue durée*" (20). Chartier acknowledges the possibility of a revolution in the technology of communication that has cultural consequences, but he demotes the invention of print to the status of a minor event in the history of the codex.[11]

"Print revolution" may finally involve too much conceptual obscurity to be a useful historical term.[12] It functions as an intensifier—proclaiming print very important and very consequential—and an honorific. But sorting out degrees of importance and the range of consequences requires language that is more finely calibrated. Dissatisfaction with the sweeping claims for the print revolution has encouraged work on the interaction between print and various departments of knowledge and culture such as philosophy, science, literature, and religion. The print reformation is one discrete area in which the importance of print can be traced. However, the notion of a print reformation has, like print revolution, fallen into disrepair. In part this is because the print reformation is often understood as an early version of the technological triumphalism that would eventually emerge as the print revolution; there is a continuous tradition, running from the early reformers through the Enlightenment *philosophes* and their contemporary champions, that celebrates print as essentially emancipatory. Increased skepticism about whiggish history has certainly taken its toll. After all, the alliance between print and Protestantism has the now dubious imprimatur of Lord Macaulay: "The fulness of time was now come. The clergy were no longer the sole or the chief depositories of knowledge. The invention of printing had furnished

---

[11] Chartier's argument here bears some resemblance to Henri-Jean Martin, *The History and Power of Writing*, trans. Lydia G. Cochrane (Chicago: Univ. of Chicago Press, 1994). Martin, who collaborated with Lucien Febvre on the groundbreaking *L'apparition du livre* (1958), here provides a sweeping history of the technologies of writing that also downplays the invention of print. However, unlike Chartier, Martin is happy to punctuate his *longue durée* with revolutions of various sorts. In his account even the typewriter is a revolution (464).

[12] For a short and helpful overview, see John Dunn, "Revolution," in *Political Innovation and Conceptual Change*, ed. Terence Ball, James Farr, and Russell L. Hanson (Cambridge: Cambridge Univ. Press, 1989), 333–56. Dunn concludes that "If revolution is left simply as a term of common speech the extreme promiscuity of its modern usage now precludes its being judged to express a single clear concept" (345).

the assailants of the Church with a mighty weapon which had been wanting to their predecessors."[13]

Skepticism about the connection has come less from historians of the book than from historians of religion. In particular a variety of revisionist work on the English reformation has tended to cast doubt on the alliance—a slow and political Reformation hardly seems a promising example of the radical consequences of the new technology in alliance with a powerful set of ideas. As revisionist historians have disaggregated the Reformation into a sequence or set of disparate and chronologically and geographically limited reformations, it has been harder to see a robust connection. In addition, scholars have successfully shown that post-Tridentine Catholicism was a vital force capable of effectively using the press to proselytize.[14]

A recent work assessing the connection between print and Protestantism in an English context, Ian Green's massive and learned book, cautiously endorses the reciprocal relationship between Protestantism and print but with a revisionist spin.[15] Rather than focusing on the particularities obscured by the word *print*, Green argues that print worked to create three distinctive sorts of Protestants. Green's taxonomy—an orthodox Protestantism that maintained *sola fides*; an elite Protestantism influenced by Renaissance humanism that balanced faith with works; and a demotic Protestantism that combined semi-Pelagianism with anti-popery—reveals the degree to which the godly minority's hopes for the evangelical utility of print were frustrated. At the same time, the diffusion of the other two types of Protestantism suggests that print played a major role in creating a multihued religious identity for those in England who rejected Roman Catholicism.

A similar stance is adopted by Jean-François Gilmont in his recent work on the book and Protestant religion. An essay on "Protestant Reformations and Reading" rejects as simplistic the idea that Protestantism promoted reading and

---

[13] Thomas Babington Macaulay, *The Works of Lord Macaulay* (London: Longmans, Green, and Co., 1898; rpt. New York: AMS Press, 1980), 1: 448.

[14] For a typical example of the view that Catholicism was somehow antithetical to print, see J. W. Martin, "The Marian Regime's Failure to Understand the Importance of Printing," *Huntington Library Quarterly* 44 (1980–1981): 231–47. Rejoinders to this argument can be found in Eamon Duffy, *The Stripping of the Altars: Traditional Religion in England 1400–1580* (New Haven: Yale Univ. Press, 1992); Christopher Haigh, *English Reformations: Religion, Politics, and Society under the Tudors* (Oxford: Clarendon Press, 1993); Alexandra Walsham, "'Domme Preachers'? Post-Reformation English Catholicism and the Culture of Print," *Past & Present* 168 (2000): 72–123.

[15] Ian Green, *Print and Protestantism in Early Modern England* (Oxford: Oxford Univ. Press, 2000).

concludes, "Perhaps it would be more accurate to speak of an interplay in reciprocal influences among societies and religions."[16] The collection of essays edited
by Gilmont conform to this description by offering a series of local investiga-
tions of the intersection between a local book trade and a specific set of religious
beliefs and practices, and yet in his conclusion Gilmont is willing to venture a
few generalizations. Acknowledging that attitudes toward printed books must be
broken down in generic terms, Gilmont observes that Protestants "were innova-
tors in the field of religious polemic."[17] In contrast, Catholic exploitation of the
press for liturgical and devotional works preceded the Reformation and continued uninterrupted in its wake. Bible printing was associated with Protestantism,
but the "unenthusiastic Catholic attitude was not monolithic." "The generalized
practice of censorship" suggests that Catholic authorities were deeply suspicious
of the book, and yet "every civil and ecclesiastical power sought to control more
or less closely the output of the presses" (487). Gilmont, finally, feels comfortable
asserting that "Protestantism clearly felt more confident about printing," but he
warns that this should not lead us to conclude that all Catholics "rejected the new
technique" (488). On the influence of the Reformation on the book, Gilmont is
more guarded.

The Reformation was responsible, in the short term, for an acceleration in
the printing of not only polemic, but also Bibles and other devotional books. In
addition, Gilmont claims that vernacularization was "largely due to the Reformation" (490). But these matters do not, it seems, amount to "a real division between
Protestants and Catholics in terms of their relations with printing." However, if
one adopts a long-term perspective things look slightly different. Without en-
dorsing the claim that these phenomena are subject to a "religious explanation,"
Gilmont points to "the present-day gap between countries with a Protestant tradition and Catholic ones regarding books and reading."

Though a nervousness about whiggish history has led to a chastening of the
claims for a special relationship between print and Protestantism, the idea still
finds support. And it may be that a carefully articulated account of the relationship between print and Protestantism in turn gives support to the hoary notion
of the print revolution itself. The two different ideas have a historical relationship—the print Reformation secularized becomes the print revolution. All our
accounts of revolution bear the impress of 1789—the French Revolution is the

---

[16] Jean-François Gilmont, "Protestant Reformations and Reading," in *A History of Reading in the West*, ed. Guglielmo Cavallo and Roger Chartier (Amherst, Mass.: Univ. of Massachusetts Press, 1999), 213–37.

[17] Jean-Francois Gilmont, ed., *The Reformation and the Book* (Aldershot: Ashgate, 1998),
487.

implicit model, often unrecognized and unacknowledged, according to which subsequent and prior revolutions are understood. According to Reinhart Koselleck, the fundamental divide marked by the modern notion of revolution is the transit to modernity itself. [18] The formulation *print revolution* clearly exploits this meaning: advocates of the print revolution invariably stress the ways in which print technology helps to inaugurate modernity. [19] While the language of revolution may be too freighted to serve in a careful historical analysis of print and its consequences, the rejection of the term is frequently accompanied by a general diminishment of the novelty of print. Print did not, as Francis Bacon suggested, change "the whole face and state of things throughout the world," [20] but that Bacon and many of his contemporaries saw the printing press as an enormously important invention should make us sensitive to the experience and perception of change.

One of the best pieces of evidence for the massive consequence of the intersection of print and Protestantism in England is the *Book of Martyrs* in all its various forms. The *Variorum Edition Online* will furnish scholars with a significant resource for the investigation of early modern English history in all its aspects. The most important feature of the *Variorum Edition Online* is its inclusion of all four texts published in Foxe's lifetime (1563, 1570, 1576, and 1583). Having these texts available for comparative analysis—a task greatly facilitated by a split-screen function—will only increase our already growing appreciation for the many ways in which *Acts and Monuments* remained a work in progress. Too frequently, the book is cited for its monumentality with little or no appreciation of the ways in which it shifted over time. In large part this is due to the fact that scholars have had the unfortunate habit of citing the multi-volume Victorian editions that almost entirely obscure the differences among the various early editions. [21] The ability to compare sections of successive editions will also improve our understanding of the way in which Foxe and his collaborators responded to changing circumstances and to hostile criticism. Finally, it is to be hoped that the accessibility of the *Variorum Edition Online* will encourage scholars to explore in detail that ways in which this massive work was taken up by its many readers. Exaggerated claims for the ubiquity of the original editions of *Acts*

---

[18] Reinhart Koselleck, "Historical Criteria of the Modern Concept of Revolution," in idem, *Futures Past: On the Semantics of Historical Time* (Cambridge, MA: The MIT Press, 1985), 39–54.

[19] See for example Benedict Anderson's invocation of "print-capitalism."

[20] Francis Bacon, *The Works of Francis Bacon*, ed. Robert Leslie Ellis, James Spedding, and Douglas Denon Heath (London: Longmans, 1870), vol. 4, 114.

[21] On this point, see Thomas Freeman, "Texts, Lies, and Microfilm: Reading and Misreading Foxe's 'Book of Martyrs,'" *Sixteenth Century Journal* 30 (1999): 23–46.

and Monuments have been decisively rejected—and yet we still lack a careful account of all the various channels—such as abridgements, stage plays, sermons, and chronicle histories—that enabled the transmission of Foxe's material. It is too early to make definitive pronouncements, but even now it is possible to say that the emergence of electronic archives—such as EEBO, LION, and the *Variorum Edition*—are changing the way we do scholarship. Such archives not only enable new work on lexical history, they also promise to enhance our ability to track the diffusion of particular texts or ideas. We are unlikely to arrive at a definitive account of the place of *Acts and Monuments* in Elizabethan culture, but the accounts we are able to offer will be greatly enriched by the appearance of the *Variorum Edition Online.*

UNIVERSITY OF NOTRE DAME

From Manuscript to Codex to E-Book: The Interactive Foxe

SUSAN WABUDA

S IR WALTER MILDMAY, THE GREAT ELIZABETHAN PRIVY COUNCILOR AND chancellor of the exchequer, entrusted several bundles of assorted letters to Emmanuel College, Cambridge soon after he founded it in 1584. Even though many of them had already been printed and were readily available to a wide readership, as manuscripts their prestige remained remarkably high, as the symbolic tokens of the recent past and indeed the entire history of the Christian Church. For Mildmay had endowed his college with the autograph letters of some of the foremost leaders of the Reformation in England, of those who had died during the reign of Queen Mary some thirty years earlier as witnesses for their faith, including John Hooper, Nicholas Ridley, John Philpot, and John Careless. Mildmay's gift was a vast epistolary outpouring, framed in conscious imitation of the letters of St Paul, meant when they were written in the 1550s,

---

This paper was delivered at the 2003 MLA convention in San Diego, CA at a panel entitled "Twenty-First Century Foxe—The Online Genetic Edition of John Foxe's *Book of Martyrs*," John N. King, Ohio State University, presiding. I am grateful to the Folger Shakespeare Library for the short-term fellowship I enjoyed there recently. The late Frank Stubbings of Emmanuel College Library deserves great thanks for the helpfulness he offered to my work over many years. As usual, I wish my paper was a better reflection of the advice I have received from Professor Patrick Collinson. The last time I saw the manuscripts, they were bound in three volumes and known as Emmanuel College Library (ECL), Cambridge, MSS 260, 261, and 262. See also ECL, MS BUR 8.1, pp. 14 (the rebinding of the manuscripts for 16 d. in October 1598), 191 (library inventory of 1597); and two of the original bindings from ECL, BOX LIB, 10.5. Also, Gilbert Burnet, *The History of the Reformation of the Church of England*, ed. Nicholas Pocock (Oxford, 1865), vol. 2, 457.

and for all time, to edify their readers. They conveyed an automatic, incontestable authority, a sense of close connection with those men and women who had been killed, they who had helped to form that vast procession of martyrs which stretched back over time from recent memory to the earliest junctures of the Primitive Church of the Apostles. Suitably rebound in the late 1590s (after Mildmay's death) as the "LETTERS OF HOLY MIRTYRS," the "6. bookes of monumentes of Martyrs" were not placed with the other volumes in Emmanuel's first library, but rather were preserved in a special position, among its furnishings. Thus they were treated not only as the particular legacy of its founder, with whom they have been associated to the present day, but they were also recognized as Protestant relics of particular mystique, almost as Puritan talismans, like the name of the College ("God with us") itself.[1]

If we create our own myths and place ourselves inside the stories we tell, then Mildmay associated his foundation with the most ambitious perspectives of reformed theology and mission. For every preacher trained by Emmanuel College was to be the living voice of St. Stephen the proto-martyr, in the proclamation of the truth of Christ, and with this sensibility, Emmanuel's sons came to New England and the new Jerusalem they wished to establish in Massachusetts.[2] The symbiosis of the godly community with manuscript text, and printed text, is at the center of my essay, as we stand near the beginning of a whole new round of creation, now that John Foxe's *Actes and Monuments* is available on the internet. I wish to revisit how several complementary goals were developed as the original manuscripts were transformed into the culture of print in the sixteenth century, and what its on-line availability might suggest for the future. This is a delicate moment for the transfer of well-known texts to their electronic form. Much may

---

[1] Susan Wabuda, "Henry Bull, Miles Coverdale, and the Making of Foxe's *Book of Martyrs*," in *Martyrs and Martyrologies*, ed. Diana Wood, Studies in Church History, 30,(Oxford: Blackwell, 1993), 245–58; Patrick Collinson, "The Foundation and Beginnings," in *A History of Emmanuel College, Cambridge*, by Sarah Bendall, Christopher Brooke, and Patrick Collinson (Woodbridge, Suffolk: Boydell Press, 1999), 1, 22, 43–44. See also David Cressy, "Books as Totems in Seventeenth-Century England and New England," *Journal of Library History* 21 (1986): 92–106; Alexandra Walsham, "*Vox Piscis or the Book Fish*: Providence and the Uses of the Reformation Past in Caroline Cambridge," *English Historical Review* 114 (1999): 574–606.

[2] Collinson, "Foundation and Beginnings," 13–55, "Puritan Emmanuel," 177–226, and "Emmanuel, New England and Harvard," 227–39, in *Emmanuel College*; Francis J. Bremer, *John Winthrop: America's Forgotten Founding Father* (Oxford: Oxford Univ. Press, 2003), 48, 80, 131; also John King, "Fiction and Fact in Foxe's *Book of Martyrs*," in *John Foxe and the English Reformation*, ed. David Loades (Aldershot: Scolar Press, 1997), 12–35; Susan Wabuda, *Preaching during the English Reformation* (Cambridge: Cambridge Univ. Press, 2002), 80–99.

change in the time ahead, but at least for the moment we can draw some conclusions from past experience as we consider what the future may bring.[3]

Mildmay's gift represents the fruit of several well-coordinated efforts of finding, amassing, preserving, and printing the writings of the martyrs. The bishops who were imprisoned in Oxford and London during the reign of Queen Mary had been frequently "sent to" by confused and frightened Protestant men and women who were desperate for advice on how to conduct themselves once the Latin Mass and other ceremonies of the Roman Church were re-instituted.[4] The prisoners contrived to have ink, pens, and paper, and smuggled what they could to friends outside their prison walls. Towards the end of his life, Archbishop Thomas Cranmer was watched too closely to correspond, though Nicholas Ridley wrote prodigiously from prison, and many of his exhortations came into the hands of his chaplain, Edmund Grindal, who had reached safety in Strasbourg. In May 1555, Hugh Latimer managed to send (through his loyal Swiss servant, Augustine Bernher) missives of advice and comfort to friends and to "all the unfeigned lovers of God's truth," that urged patience under persecution. "Because you be God's sheep, prepare yourselves to the slaughter, always knowing, that in the sight of God our death is precious."[5] John Careless, Latimer's associate from Coventry, was a prolific copyist in his cells. Until his death in 1556, the polemics he transcribed for his prison-mates (including Philpot) were sent overseas for foreign presses, to be printed and smuggled back into England.[6]

---

[3] The first English edition of the *Book of Martyrs* is John Foxe, *Actes and Monuments* (London: John Day, 1563; STC 11222). The 1583 edition promises to become the standard study edition: John Foxe, *Actes and Monuments* (London: John Day, 1583; STC 11225). For further information about the British Academy John Foxe Project see http://www.hrionline. ac.uk/johnfoxe/edition.html.

[4] Maria Dowling and Joy Shakespeare, "Religion and Politics in Mid-Tudor England through the Eyes of an English Protestant Woman: The Recollections of Rose Hickman," *Bulletin of the Institute of Historical Research* 55 (1982): 94–102, at 100. See also Thomas Freeman, "'The Good Ministrye of Godlye and Vertuouse Women': The Elizabethan Martyrologists and the Female Supporters of the Marian Martyrs," *Journal of British Studies* 39 (2000): 8–33; Susan Wabuda, "Sanctified by the Believing Spouse: Women, Men and the Marital Yoke in the Early Reformation," in *The Beginnings of English Protestantism*, eds Peter Marshall and Alec Ryrie (Cambridge: Cambridge Univ. Press, 2002), 111–28.

[5] ECL, MS 262, fols. 175r–180r, printed in Hugh Latimer, *Sermons and Remains*, ed. George Elwes Corrie, Parker Society (Cambridge: Cambridge Univ. Press, 1845), 435–44, p. 442 (and see also my biographies of Latimer and Ridley in *The Oxford Dictionary of National Biography*); Diarmaid MacCulloch, *Thomas Cranmer: A Life* (New Haven: Yale Univ. Press, 1996), 569–74 (and his last letter of 1555 to Peter Martyr Vermigli, plate 39).

[6] See a letter from Philpot to Robert Harrington that explains that he had left a copy of St Ambrose against the Arians with Careless to copy: ECL, MS 260, fols. 65r–65v; and *The examinacion of the constaunt Martir of Christ, John Philpot*, prt. with *An Apologie of Johan*

John Foxe began his great venture in print in 1554 while he was in Stras-bourg, before the worst of the burnings started,[7] and he followed this first Latin effort with another embryonic edition, printed in Basle. Fine organization and a prudent exploitation of their connections abroad meant that many of the reform-ers' letters and testimonies reached continental presses with what we may rec-ognize as remarkable speed, and that same urgency was the hallmark of Foxe's partnership with John Day in London, as they printed ever-larger and more in-clusive editions of the *Actes and Monuments* at regular intervals, in 1563, 1570, 1576, and 1583. Mildmay presented the precious bundles of manuscripts to his new college in 1584, the same year that Day died.[8] Although Foxe's name was on the title page, it was never his project alone. Just as his great ecclesiastical history was never meant to be closed, his was a common book, the product of a godly "textual community," whose full scope is still not completely understood for the sixteenth and seventeenth centuries,[9] and it has created many textual communi-ties over the intervening centuries, whose latest manifestations are only now un-der development today in its new electronic guises.

From the beginning, Foxe's vision, as inspired by Grindal, was not only am-bitious but multi-faceted. First in Strasbourg, and continuing after Foxe moved to Basle, their aim was to build up a vast ecclesiastical history without losing sight

Philpot written for spitting vpon an Arrian [Emden: Egidius van der Erve, 1556?; *STC* 19892]; John Foxe, *Rervm in Ecclesia Gestarum . . .* 2 vols. (Basle: Nicolavm Brylingervm et Joannem Oporinum, [1559]–1563), 543–631; Wabuda, "The Making of Foxe's *Book of Martyrs*," 251–52 (see ns. 27, 32–33); Thomas Freeman, "Dissenters from a Dissenting Church: The Challenge of the Freewillers, 1550–1558," in *The Beginnings of English Protestantism*, 129–56, and the same author's "Publish and Perish: The Scribal Culture of the Marian Martyrs," in *The Uses of Script and Print, 1300–1700*, ed. Julia Crick and Alexandra Walsham (Cambridge: Cambridge Univ. Press, 2004), 235–54; Andrew Pettegree, "The Latin Polemic of the Marian Exiles," in *Marian Protestantism: Six Essays* (Aldershot: Scolar Press, 1996), 118–28.

[7] Patrick Collinson, "Truth and Legend: The Veracity of John Foxe's *Book of Martyrs*," in *Elizabethan Essays* (London: Hambledon Press, 1994), 151–77.

[8] Elizabeth Evenden and Thomas S. Freeman, "John Foxe, John Day and the Printing of the *Book of Martyrs*," in *Lives in Print: Biography and the Book Trade from the Middle Ages to the 21st Century*, ed. Robin Myers, Michael Harris, and Giles Mandelbrote (London: British Li-brary, 2002), 23–54; and by the same authors, "Print, Profit and Propaganda: The Elizabethan Privy Council and the 1570 Edition of Foxe's *Book of Martyrs*," *English Historical Review* 119 (2004): 1288–1307.

[9] Susan Felch, "Shaping the Reader in the *Acts and Monuments*," in *Foxe and the Eng-lish Reformation*, 52–65; Patrick Collinson, "John Foxe and National Consciousness," in *John Foxe and His World*, ed. Christopher Highley and John N. King (Aldershot: Ashgate, 2002), 10–34; and see also Brian Stock, *The Implications of Literacy: Written Language and Models of Interpretation in the Eleventh and Twelfth Centuries* (Princeton: Princeton Univ. Press, 1983), 88–240.

of the particular. We can see the outlines of their plans in their early correspondence. In May 1556, only six weeks after Cranmer's execution, Foxe wrote Grindal to ask for his help in bringing to the press an account of the archbishop's life and death. In 1557, as the second Latin edition was being prepared, Grindal could describe Foxe's project as "the history of the Martyrs" ("De Martyrum Historia quod scribes"), and recommend that his "tedious work" on Cranmer (which had been amplified by additional information from a friend of Peter Martyr) should not completely distract him from the larger goal of completing another volume of his "Ecclesiastical History."[10] "I wish by all means in my power to promote your undertaking," Grindal wrote, for many friends shared the desire to have "the history of this English persecution."[11]

As the larger aims were being pursued, Grindal could also encourage the more limited and piecemeal approach. He recommended that documents be printed independently, in short, self-contained versions, and that these could be reprinted in the larger work, as necessary. In 1556, he advised Foxe: "And perhaps even if you should publish Philpot's examinations separately, the same may be again inserted in the great work among the Acts."[12] Later, when they were able to return to England, and Grindal was bishop of London, their partnership continued in the same vein. As Foxe produced expanded editions of his ecclesiastical history, Grindal remained a patron to the shorter efforts that now could be printed in light of the fresh manuscript discoveries that were being made by their friends, including Henry Bull. Not every letter that had come from the pens of the Marian martyrs had left England. Inevitably many writings had gone astray, or were hidden, until it was safer to share. Even now, it is still possible to discover manuscript material that has escaped serious attention, for a few years ago I located a previously-unknown short set of documents in New York, including a 1553 tract by Hooper, "Whether Christian faithe maie be kept secret in the hert without confession Therof openlie to the worlde," written into the back pages of

---

[10] "Gaudeo te tandem opus illud Domini Cantuariensis ad exitum perduxisse. Longum opus fuit, et in quo necesse erat multis cum difficultatibus luctari," and later, Grindal wished that Foxe would finish "alterum tomum ecclesiae tuae historiae": *The Remains of Edmund Grindal*, ed. William Nicholson, Parker Society (PS) (Cambridge: Cambridge Univ. Press, 1843), Letter III, 224–28. Grindal's correspondence with Foxe: Letters I–VII, from BL, Harleian MS 417.

[11] "Cupio equidem omnibus modis quibus potero institutum tuum promovere, ut hujus Anglicanae persecutionis historiam ad exitum qualem optamus perducere possis": Grindal, *Remains*, Letter IV (1557), 228–30; Patrick Collinson, *Archbishop Grindal, 1519–83* (London: Jonathan Cape, 1983), 80–81.

[12] "Ac fortassis, etiamsi separatim Philpotti examinationes emittas, poterunt eadem denuo magno operi inter acta inseri": Grindal, *Remains*, Letter II, 221–24.

a printed volume in the Burke Library, Union Theological Seminary, New York City.[13] In 1562, a year before the first English edition of the *Actes and Monuments* appeared, Grindal encouraged Bull to print another essay by Hooper, with letters that had newly come to light, whose originals survive among the Emmanuel manuscripts. Bull pleaded with his readers to bring any such writings to the world, to be "set abroad in printe to the commodity of many," on "behalfe of the churche of God."[14] The books that Grindal sponsored were subsidiaries that fed Foxe's larger work, but one goal served the other. The success of Bull's request for more material is plain from Mildmay's gift.

The manuscripts were brought to John Day's printing house at Aldersgate, or to his shop at the west door of St Paul's Cathedral. They were carried in as they were discovered. "Peruse this boke well for letters" reads a small slip stuck between the leaves of one of the Emmanuel manuscripts.[15] They were shared out among Foxe's friends, and brought back again when they were needed for casting off the next edition of the *Actes and Monuments* or its supplements. Hooper's letters are marked with the printer's notations. "I will further see to the correction herof at the printers handes," Bull added. "Restore this to mr fox," Bull wrote on another Emmanuel document. And again, he noted: "Mr Dayes wrytings wherein are letters of Careles & other."[16]

Something of the breathtaking rate at which Foxe and Day could accommodate fresh information is revealed by Julian Roberts's painstaking study of irregularities that can be discerned in the 1563 and 1570 editions. Not only did Foxe use copy from many different sources, but he and Day did not hesitate to add or remove material at the last moment when the type was being set, or, more startling, to make substantial changes even after many sheets had been printed. In 1563, when more material suddenly became available on Cranmer, they added it even though a leaf had to be reset. Unexpected finds of this kind meant that Day ran out of paper for the 1570 edition, and had to use slip-cancels to paste

---

[13] I discussed this find in "Measuring the *Monuments*: A Further Look at Foxeian Manuscript Sources," a paper delivered at the John Foxe and His World Interdisciplinary Colloquium at The Ohio State University (1999), and look forward to its future publication.

[14] Hooper's manuscripts: ECL, MS 261, fols. 1r–14r; Bull's printed version: *An apologye made by the reuerende father and constante Martyr of Christe John Hooper*, ed. Henry Bull (London: John Tisdale and Thomas Hacket; 1562, *STC* 13742); Wabuda, "Making of Foxe's *Book of Martyrs*," 252–54 (esp. n. 39).

[15] ECL, MS 262, between fol. 213v and fol. 214r.

[16] ECL, MS 261, fols. 12r–14r, 87v; Wabuda, "Making of Foxe's *Book of Martyrs*," 245–58.

corrections over already-printed pieces of text. "The labour involved" in making so many changes so late "can only be imagined."[17]

Challenging though the production of each edition of the *Actes and Monuments* was, the other dimension of the project was always maintained. Between edition and edition of the ever-larger ecclesiastical history, Day also printed an impressive array of the particular, supplementary volumes which were part of the entire vision. Bull's edition of a lengthy collection of *Certain most godly, fruitful, and comfortable letters . . . of Martyrs* appeared in 1564, only a year after the first English edition of the *Actes and Monuments*.[18] Thus *The Book of Martyrs* was accompanied by a retinue of smaller, shorter books on discrete subjects, such as the tribulations of a single sufferer, or batches of letters arranged by author. Just as the fresh discoveries that ultimately enriched the pages of the *Actes and Monuments* would not have been possible without the extensive network of wealthy friends and supporters who, as Brett Usher has revealed, were a considerable element in the spread of English Protestantism,[19] so too the *Book of Martyrs* needed its accompaniments. For they also, like the "little foxes" that David Scott Kastan has described, provided shorter, cheaper, and more direct approaches to the work as a whole, and they served to promote the same culture of godliness.[20]

What does the historical background of the interweaving connections between the original manuscripts and the earliest print editions mean as we confront the availability of the facsimile version of the 1583 edition of the *Actes and Monuments* on CD-Rom?[21] Or what will it mean to scholars to have all of Day's books on their desktops through EEBO, the Early English Books Online project (the successor of all of those endless reels of microfilm that many of us have had to consult when we could not reach a major rare book library)? Or the new electronic version of the *Actes and Monuments* that is emerging from the British

---

[17] See the impressive remark "The 1570 edition is the most bibliographically complex book I have ever encountered": Julian Roberts, "Bibliographical Aspects: John Foxe," in *Foxe and the English Reformation*, 36–51 (the quotations appear at pp. 43, 45).

[18] Miles Coverdale [and Henry Bull], comps., *Certain most godly, fruitful, and comfortable letters of such true Saintes and holy Martyrs of God . . .* (London: John Day, 1564; *STC* 5886); Wabuda, "Making of Foxe's *Book of Martyrs*," 245–58.

[19] Brett Usher, "Backing Protestantism: The London Godly, the Exchequer and the Foxe Circle," in *John Foxe: An Historical Perspective*, ed. David Loades (Aldershot: Ashgate, 1999), 105–34; and the same author's "'In a Time of Persecution': New Light on the Secret Protestant Congregation in Marian London," in *Foxe and the English Reformation*, 233–51.

[20] David Scott Kastan, "Little Foxes," in *Foxe and His World*, 117–29; Collinson, "Foxe and National Consciousness," 10–34.

[21] *Facsimile of John Foxe's Book of Martyrs: Actes and Monuments of Matters Most Speciall and Memorable, 1583*, ed. David G. Newcombe with Michael Pidd (British Academy by Oxford Univ. Press), version 1.0.

Academy John Foxe Project, hosted by the Humanities Research Institute at the University of Sheffield, which is in the process of presenting the same material from different editions side-by-side for the ease of comparison?[22] If Brett Usher could speak recently of Foxe's documents as "telephone messages" left on a cultural answering machine,[23] then surely it is not too fanciful to think too of the *Book of Martyrs* and its manuscripts as an early interactive effort, a vast slow-motion web of dialogue and exchange. It created its own textual communities from the very beginning, and the rate of creation is about to increase, and grow more diverse, now that it is available to anyone with a computer. Foxe's great work hardly represents a coherent collection, any more than the various books of the Old and New Testaments represent one unified story. Different (and sometimes conflicting) points of view have always been apparent in its pages. If one types "John Foxe" into a search engine, one is likely to find that diversity reflected in web-pages that range from the purely academic, or the informative, to others with particular theological or polemical stances to defend.

As the past keeps shifting its boundaries, we find that the *Actes and Monuments* has accommodated many interpretive strategies. What fresh myths will Foxe help us to create in the new electronic media? Much is promising, but some choices may well give us pause. Patrick Collinson reminds us, "We can no more rewrite Foxe than the Gospels in the New Testament and Foxe is no less indispensable." All of those "desperately important" details will make us see the Reformation as Foxe willed us to see it, like Latimer following Ridley to the stake "in a poor Bristol frieze frock all worn," even if we now know from Thomas Freeman's work that the most moving element of the account, Latimer's stirring words: "Be of good comfort, master Ridley, and play the man," was incorporated at a late stage, and was perhaps a symbolic reference to the sacrifice of the martyr Polycarp from the pages of Eusebius, rather than a literal account of the event as it occurred in Oxford.[24]

Death, Miri Rubin reminds us, creates a debt, and "every martyr beckons another."[25] As Latimer preached at Friar John Forest's burning, so he too went

[22] The address is: http://www.hrionline.ac.uk/johnfoxe/edition.html.

[23] Usher, "Backing Protestantism," 124.

[24] John Foxe, *Actes and Monuments* (London: John Day, 1563; *STC* 11222), 1377; Collinson, "Veracity," 177; Thomas Freeman, "Texts, Lies, and Microfilm: Reading and Misreading Foxe's 'Book of Martyrs,'" *Sixteenth Century Journal* 30 (1999): 23–46.

[25] Miri Rubin, "Choosing Death? Experiences of Martyrdom in Late Medieval Europe," in *Martyrs and Martyrologies*, 153–83, at 182.

to the flames.[26] Were the deaths of John Fisher and Thomas More revenged by killing Ridley and the other bishops? For this idea was preached by Henry Cole before Cranmer's burning.[27] Perhaps our discussions in the future will move further towards explaining how the type of martyrdom Foxe and Day exalted can serve to inform us, if it can, with the type of nihilistic terrorism that appears every day in the news under the name of martyrdom. Now is perhaps a good time to remind ourselves that the debts of death need not be cancelled with further bloodshed, and that the seeds of toleration can be found in the pages of Foxe too.[28]

Let me conclude by citing an early twentieth-century prayer that is inscribed in Westminster Abbey at the resting place of queens: "Near the tomb of Mary and Elizabeth, remember before God all those who, divided at the Reformation by different convictions, laid down their lives for Christ and conscience sake."[29]

     ～   ～   ～

Author's Note: When I wrote the entry for Nicholas Ridley for *The Oxford Dictionary of National Biography* just after the attacks of September 11ᵗʰ (which I had managed to put off until then because the specter of that Broad Street burning was dispiriting, though alas, it suddenly fit all too well with the caliber of the times), I asked myself with increased urgency if the stories of the deaths of Latimer and Ridley (among the rest) kept the worst aspects of the hatreds of the Reformation alive. P. D. James remembers that in her Cranmer-soaked

---

[26] Peter Marshall, "Papist as Heretic: The Burning of Friar John Forest, 1538," *Historical Journal* 41 (1998): 351–74; rptd. in *Religious Identities in Henry VIII's England* (Aldershot: Ashgate, 2006), 199–226.

[27] I wish to thank Maria Dowling for discussion on this point, and her *Fisher of Men: A Life of John Fisher, 1469–1535* (London: Macmillan, 1999). See also MacCulloch, *Cranmer*, 600–1; and the Townsend edition of *Acts and Monuments*, vol. 8, 85–86. See also John Jewel's criticism of Cole for his noisy rudeness when he disputed with Cranmer in Oxford in *The Trve copies of the Letters between the reuerend father in God Iohn Bisshop of Sarum and D. Cole . . .* (London: John Day, 1560; *STC* 14613), fol. 46r.

[28] Patrick Collinson, "Cranbrook and the Fletchers: Popular and Unpopular Religion in the Kentish Weald," in *Reformation Principle and Practice: Essays in Honour of Arthur Geoffrey Dickens*, ed. Peter Newman Brooks (London: Scholar Press, 1980), 171–202 (rptd. in *Godly People: Essays on English Protestantism and Puritanism* [London: Hambledon Press, 1983], 399–428); Alexandra Walsham, *Charitable Hatred: Tolerance and Intolerance in England, 1500–1700* (Manchester: Univ. of Manchester Press, 2006).

[29] Peter Sherlock, "The Monuments of Elizabeth Tudor and Mary Stuart: King James and the Manipulation of Memory," *Journal of British Studies* 46 (2007): 263–89.

childhood, one of her Sunday School teachers in the late 1920s "spent little time in telling us Bible stories, but did recount the more lurid examples from Foxe's *Book of Martyrs*, which both thrilled and half-terrified us."[30] Such reminders convey a small echo of the idea that as a divinely-inspired text, Foxe's book has a talismanic power to repel what was once perceived (into the seventeenth century and later) as a potent Catholic threat.[31]

FORDHAM UNIVERSITY

---

[30] P. D. James, *Time to Be in Earnest: A Fragment of Autobiography* (New York: Alfred A. Knopf, 2000), 85–86.

[31] Damian Nussbaum, "Appropriating Martyrdom: Fears of Renewed Persecution and the 1632 Edition of *Acts and Monuments*," in *Foxe and the English Reformation*, 178–91.

Saints, Martyrs, Murderers:
Text and Context of Foxe's Images

MARGARET ASTON

THE IMAGES AT THE HEART OF THIS PAPER ARE SOME OF THE SMALL single-column woodcuts that were added to *The Acts and Monuments* in the second edition of 1570. Small though they were, and subject in many cases to frequent re-use (sometimes with what seems a blithe disregard for accurate representation of the text they illustrated), the role of these twenty-five small blocks should not be underestimated. Ruth Luborsky, who helpfully analysed their several styles as well as their content, pointed out that for all the 'icon-like' character of these illustrations, they included some that had narrative content and which were not devoted to scenes of burning.[1] However, it is also clear that the series of small woodcuts as a whole *did* significantly contribute to the pictorial impact of martyrs being burned at the stake, and that they were not seen by the makers of the book as different in kind from the larger narrative cuts.

This paper was first delivered at the 2004 Annual Meeting of the Renaissance Society of America, New York, NY, at a panel entitled "Text and Image in Foxe's *Book of Martyrs*," Carolyn Kent, RETS, presiding. The British Academy supported by attendance at this meeting.

[1] Ruth Samson Luborsky, "The Illustrations: Their Pattern and Plan," in *John Foxe: An Historical Perspective*, ed. David Loades (Brookfield, VT: Ashgate, 1999), 67–84, at 70, 76. For further comment on these woodcuts see the online edition of *The Acts and Monuments*, and on Foxe's illustrations James A. Knapp, *Illustrating the Past in Early Modern England* (Aldershot and Burlington, VT: Ashgate, 2003), 129–35. On the theme of 'gallows literature' and images of martyrdom created by English Catholics, see Anne Dillon, *The Construction of Martyrdom in the English Catholic Community, 1535–1603* (Aldershot and Burlington, VT: Ashgate, 2002), chaps. 3–5. For a helpful discussion of depictions (both Catholic and Protestant) of the *Auto da fé*, see Francisco Bethencourt, "The *Auto da Fé*: Ritual and Imagery," *Journal of the Warburg and Courtauld Institutes* 55 (1992): 155–68.

This can be demonstrated numerically, by comparing the presence of flame and fire in the larger narrative cuts and the small woodcuts. Of the twenty-nine large woodcuts in the last three books, only half (fifteen) are of executions.[2] The other fourteen are devoted to depictions of other kinds of suffering inflicted on the persecuted, some directly related to the martyrdoms. Among the small cuts, on the other hand, there is only a handful in the work as a whole which do not represent death on the pyre in some form, and of the forty-five such repeating images that crowded the pages on Marian burnings, only one did not focus on the martyr or martyrs in the fire, and nearly all are of flaming pyres.[3] This too is in contrast to the larger woodcuts, where the majority (nine out of fifteen) of the pictures of burnings depict the moments (dramatic enough in themselves) before the fire was lit.[4] Interestingly, it is the small woodcuts that deliver the repeating images of figures in flames, the heroic martyrs in the fire, perhaps with a focus that their size renders the more intense. It is their presence in particular that makes it possible to imagine how lasting retinal images of martyrs encircled by flames could have dented the memories of contemporary readers (or viewers) of Foxe's book, as well as those of Victorians.[5]

At the same time we should notice the differences governing the relationships between text and image of the small and large woodcuts. The single-column cuts, like the wide double-column ones, had identifying headings, and also additional explicatory information in the marginal annotation. But these, set in the same typeface as the text itself, were necessarily less eye-catching than those in large type that accompanied the bigger images. Another difference was that, with a few exceptions (on one of which more shortly), there was no print in the form of names or speech scrolls integrated into the depiction, which were such an important part of the grander woodcuts. These features, which show the small images both embedded in the text, while themselves in a sense atextual, perhaps have some bearing on how they were received by those who read or scanned the book.

We should also observe that some of the small woodcuts were perhaps as much individual character studies as those of more famous martyrs. This might

---

[2] This figure does not include the burning of Bucer's and Fagius's bones.

[3] See the discussion and analysis in the online edition at http://www.hrionline.ac.uk/foxe/apparatus/astonimagelist.html. The exception is "The Description of a Popish Priest"; *Acts and Monuments* (hereafter *A&M*), 1583, p. 1561. On the small cuts in earlier books, which included scenes of penance and punishment, see Luborsky, "The Illustrations," 78–79.

[4] This is a count of the double-column woodcuts, which omits the odd-man-out misfit of the Norwich man and woman (Alexander Gouch and Driver's wife), *A&M* (1583), 2049.

[5] For a nineteenth-century figurine of Cranmer in the flames see *Cranmer, Primate of all England*, Catalogue of a Quincentenary Exhibition (London: British Library, 1989), and my review, *Renaissance Studies* 4 (1990): 346–54.

be the case with the small cuts of three women burned at the stake: Margery Polley (Figure 1), Cicelie Ormes (Figure 9), and the woman of Exeter ('Prestes wyfe', Figure 2).[6] Each of these is illustrated by a woodcut with very distinct individualised features. None of these images was reused, convenient and economical though it would have been to resort to repetition, about which there often seems to have been small scruple.[7] If this tells us something about the author's respect for the martyrs thus honoured, it also suggests that some of the small tailor-made woodcuts aimed, within their limits, at individual portraits.

Martyrdom by fire of course had earlier precedents, though it was not that common in medieval hagiography and iconography. Foxe himself made use of the example of the "Martyr of Christ," St Laurence, in his survey of the first ten persecutions of the primitive church, and the depiction of the saint in the huge woodcut of this topic is quite traditional in its iconography.[8] We have to look elsewhere for the prototype of the bonfire martyr. The image of the single martyr standing erect in the pyre was a direct take-over of depictions of medieval heretics, part of the reformers' historiographical revolution, as they drafted earlier critics and outcasts of the Church of Rome into the family tree of their faith, adopting as spiritual ancestors those whose beliefs had been proscribed. The figure of John Hus at the stake, as portrayed in Ulrich Richental's fifteenth-century chronicle, appropriated by Flaccius Illyricus in 1558, and a few years later by Foxe, was the prototype for the new-style martyr.[9] Bohemian reformers were naturally at the forefront of this process of arrogating heretic and death by fire into the ancestral line of their reformed church. The *Gradual of Malá Strana* of 1572 contains a marginal illumination showing the descent of reform from Wycliffe to Hus and Luther, respectively lighting spark, holding candle, and bearing torch, combined with a vivid scene of Hus's burning.[10]

From such models Foxe's illustrators embarked on producing their long series of new-style martyrs at the stake. An early example is that of William Sawtry, the first Wycliffite to be burned in England (though not the first to be threatened

---

[6] *A&M* (1583), 1679, 2023, 2052. On Cicelie Ormes see below.

[7] On the reuse of the woodcuts, sometimes with obvious disregard for the text being illustrated, see my contribution on the illustrations in the online edition.

[8] For Foxe on St Laurence see *A&M* (1570), 101–2, (1583), 71–72. St Laurence survived in the Church of England calendar. On his significance at Little Gidding, and the image in the Ten Persecutions woodcut, see my "Moving Pictures: Foxe's Martyrs and Little Gidding," in *Agent of Change: Print Culture Studies After Elizabeth L. Eisenstein*, ed. Sabrina A. Baron, Eric H. Lindquist, and Eleanor F. Shevlin (Amherst: Univ. of Massachusetts Press, 2007), 82–104.

[9] For these examples see M. Aston and Elizabeth Ingram, "The Iconography of the *Acts and Monuments*," in *John Foxe and the English Reformation*, ed. David Loades (London and Brookfield, VT: Scolar Press, 1997), 66–142, at 90–98.

[10] Prague University Library, MS XVII A 3, fol. 363a, reproduced in A. G. Dickens, *Reformation and Society in Sixteenth-Century Europe* (London: Thames and Hudson, 1966), 13.

Figure 1. The martyrdom of Margery Polley. John Foxe, *Actes and monuments* (1583), 2:1679. Courtesy of the British Academy John Foxe Project.

Figure 2. The cruel burning of a woman at Exeter. John Foxe, *Actes and monuments* (1583), 2:2052. Courtesy of the British Academy John Foxe Project.

Figure 3. The burning of William Sawtry. John Foxe, *Actes and monuments* (1563), 142. Courtesy of Lambeth Palace Library.

Figure 4. The burning of William Sawtry. John Foxe, *Actes and monuments* (1570), 1:618. Courtesy of Lambeth Palace Library.

with this fate) in 1401, when the statute enacting this punishment was about to be passed, having probably already been decided on.[11] We can see from the peculiar layout of the pages of *The Acts and Monuments* both in the first edition of 1563 and still in 1570, when the woodcut frame was trimmed to accommodate the illustration—which was only headed with an identifying label in this second edition—that readers could have been impressed by this image (Figures 3 and 4) even without the vivid colouring supplied in the two copies of the 1570 edition that survive in Cambridge.[12] However, its self-evident awkwardness led to its banishment in 1576. The misfitting Sawtry woodblock was jettisoned and in its place one of the existing smaller woodcuts was drafted in from the 1570 series, where it aptly represented the martyrdom of the bearded old man, Rawlins White.[13]

Punishment of death by burning was meted out not only to heretics. Well before the passage of the statute *De heretico comburendo*, which legalized its application to Lollards in England, execution by fire became the penalty for a particular form of treason. It applied only to women. The killing of a husband by a wife was defined as petty treason by the 1352 Statute of Treason, and carried the penalty of execution by fire. (This was only for wives; spouse-killing husbands were hanged, not burned.) John Stow laconically chronicled the cases of two women burned at Smithfield in the 1590s for poisoning and murdering their husbands, and his continuator reported likewise the fate of a poor woman of Westminster burned at Smithfield in July 1628 for stabbing her husband to death.[14] There are records throughout the eighteenth century of women who suffered the penalty of death by burning for petty treason, until 1790, when this offence was reduced to

---

[11] See the recent evaluation of the passage of this legislation by A. K. McHardy, "*De Heretico Comburendo*, 1401," in *Lollardy and the Gentry in The Later Middle Ages*, ed. M. Aston and Colin Richmond (Thrupp, Stroud, Gloucs: Sutton Publishing, and New York: St Martin's Press, 1997), 112–26.

[12] *A&M* (1563), 142, (1570), 618.

[13] Foxe, *A&M* (1576), 501. For "the burning of Raulins, Martyr," see *A&M* (1570), 1728, (1576) 1476, (1583) 1559. On changes in the 1576 edition, and Richard Day's initiatives, see Elizabeth Evenden and Thomas Freeman, *Religion and the Book in Early Modern England: The Making of Foxe's "Book of Martyrs"* (forthcoming).

[14] John Stow, *The Annales, or Generall Chronicle of England* (London, 1615), 764; continued by E. Howes (1631), 765, 767. One of Stow's cases (no names recorded), of June 1592, was that considered below of Anne Welles and the murder of John Brewen, goldsmith. On the burning of Margaret Ferneseed in St George's Field (1609), see J. A. Sharpe, "'Last Dying Speeches': Religion, Ideology and Public Execution in Seventeenth-Century England," *Past and Present* 107 (1985): 144–67, at 153, and *The Araignement and burning of Margaret Ferneseede* (London, 1609). In Kent, women who had murdered their husbands appear to have suffered the penalty of burning in 1591, 1608, and 1692: J. S. Cockburn, "Patterns of Violence in English Society: Homicide in Kent 1560–1985," *Past and Present* 130 (1991): 70–106, at 99.

ordinary murder, and a ballad was written about the last woman to be burned at the stake (for the high treason of counterfeiting the coinage) in 1789.[15]

Such popular recording of the legal punishment bears directly on the question of the reception of Foxe's images. We now leave the *Book of Martyrs* to look at some ballad literature. It's well recognised that Foxe's text spilled over into ballads. Stories from the martyrology were recounted in ballad form. There was the ballad of Anne Askewe ("I am a woman poor and blind"), and *The most rare and excellent history of the Dutchesse of Suffolkes calamity* (c. 1602). Thomas Nashe refers (in 1596) to "the godly ballet of John Carelesse" who filled so many pages in the *Book of Martyrs*. But if Anne Askewe's ballad is (as Tessa Watt puts it) "the musical equivalent of the woodcuts which illustrated *The Actes and Monuments*," with its repeating images of martyrs in flames, what of these images themselves?[16] Do they, like the verbal accounts of Marian heroism, find their way into other quarters?

Images derived from the *Book of Martyrs* do appear in ballads, though not in those I've just mentioned. The 1616 ballad, *Anne Wallens Lamentation*, told (in the confessional words of the murderess) the story of a woman of Smithfield who had wounded her husband John Wallen, a turner, in the stomach with his own chisel (see Figure 5), after a drunken argument. He died next day.[17] *A warning for all desperate Women* of 1628 was also presented as a first-person repentance narrative, in this case the "moane ... unto the world" lamenting her crime being that of Alice Davis, a woman of good repute who lived in Westminster (the case mentioned in the continuation of Stow's *Chronicle*). She had knifed her husband (a smith) in the heart in a quarrel over money, resulting in his immediate death. Both women were convicted and burned at Smithfield, and the same woodcut was used in both ballads to illustrate the execution (see Figure 6)[18]. The scene of burning represented here, generic as it is, echoes, even if it does not specifically recall, the many small woodcuts of its kind in *The Acts and Monuments*. Was it

---

[15] Ruth Campbell, "Sentence of Death by Burning for Women," *Journal of Legal History* 5 (1984): 44–59; Cockburn, "Patterns of Violence," 100; Sheila O'Connell, *The Popular Print in England 1550–1850* (London: British Museum Press, 1999), 96, 229, n. 60. The sentence of burning was ended by statute: 30 George III, cap. 48.

[16] Tessa Watt, *Cheap Print and Popular Piety, 1550–1640* (Cambridge: Cambridge Univ. Press, 1991), 90–96, at 94, 335–36, nos. 21, 29. It is pointed out here (90) that the women in Foxe's martyrs are over-represented in the ballads. On the "balade" that Anne Askew wrote herself while in Newgate see Brad S. Gregory, *Salvation at Stake: Christian Martyrdom in Early Modern Europe* (Cambridge, MA: Harvard Univ. Press, 1999), 160–61.

[17] *The Pepys Ballads*, ed. W. G. Day, 5 vols. (Cambridge: Brewer, 1987), 1:124–25.

[18] Day, *Ballads*, 1:120–21.

Anne VVallens Lamentation,

For the Murthering of her husband *Iohn Wallen* a Turner in Cow-lane neere Smithfield; done by his owne wife, on satterday the 22 of Iune. 1616.
who was burnt in Smithfield the first of Iuly following.
To the tune of Fortune my foe.

Great God that sées al things that here are don
  kéeping thy Court with thy celestiall Son;
Héere her complaint that hath so sore offended,
Forgiue my fact before my life is ended.

Ah me the shame vnto all women kinde,
To harbour such a thought within my minde:
That now hath made me to the world a scorne,
And makes me curse the time that I was borne.

O would to God my mothers haples wombe,
Before my birth had béene my happy tombe:
Or would to God when first I did take breath,
That I had suffered any painefull death.

If euer dyed a true repentant soule,
Then I am she, whose déedes are blacke and foule:
Then take héed wiues be to your husbands kinde,
And beare this lesson truely in your minde,

Let not your tongus ore-sway true reasons bounds,
Which in your rage your vtmost rancour sounds:
A woman that is wise should seldome speake,
Vnlesse discréetly she her words repeat

Oh would that I had thought of this before,
Which now to thinke on makes my heart full sore:
Then should I not haue done this déed so foule,
The which hath stained my immortall soule.

Tis not to dye that thus doth cause me grieue,
I am more willing far to die then liue;
But tis for blood which mounteth to the skies,
And to the Lord reuenge, reuenge, it cries.

My dearest husband did I wound to death,
And was the cause he lost his swéetest breath,
But yet I trust his soule in heauen doth dwell,
And mine without Gods mercy sinkes to hell.

In London néere to smithfield did I dwell,
And mongst my neighbours was beloued well:
Till that the Deuill wrought me this same spight,
That all their loues are turnd to hatred quight.

Iohn Wallen was my louing husbands name,
Which long hath liu'd in London in good fame.
His trade a Turner, as was knowne full well,
My name An Wallen, dolefull tale to tell.

Figure 6. A warning for all desperate Women. Courtesy of the Pepys Library, Magdalene College, Cambridge.

derived from there? If no sure answer can be given to that question, it is worth considering another example.

A warning for wives of 1629[19] follows the same pattern of heinous murder and punishment, with woodcuts (as in the earlier cases) illustrating respectively the murder with the tool that accomplished it, and the killer's execution. Katherine Francis, alias Stoke, of Cow Cross near Smithfield Bars, whose marriage had long been a cat and dog affair, succeeded in despatching her hated husband with a pair of scissors. The woodcut seems less accurate here in its depiction of the murder weapon, but graphically correct as to the neck wound inflicted, after a day of drinking, on the night of 8 April 1629.[20] Mrs Francis was burned at Clerkenwell two weeks later—a warning to "all good wives . . . in country and in city."

This time the moral address is emphasized by a refrain "Oh women, / Murderous women / whereon are your minds?" It was to be sung to the lost tune of Bragandary.[21] The ballad text dwells on the "cruel death" by burning which reduced Katherine Francis to ashes. It stood as the warning to all wives with such barbarous hearts, who should "thinke how they shall at a stake / be burned without pitty." The woodcut adds to this message (Figure 7). It is very distinctive, and one certainly would not know it was of a woman. In its first appearance, it wasn't. As we have seen, this image was used in the first and second editions of *The Acts and Monuments* to illustrate the death of William Sawtry. Neither Martin Parker (the probable author of this ballad, which bears the initials MP) nor the publisher, Francis Grove (whose publishing career began in the 1620s), specialized in ballads on religious or godly issues. But someone had spotted the value of the superannuated woodcut ousted from the *Book of Martyrs*, and drafted it into new service some fifty years after its use in that work. In the intervening period the woodblock itself might have been part of some printer's stock, and the

---

[19] *STC* 19280, s.n. Martin Parker.

[20] Day, *Ballads*, 1:118–19.

[21] As both Tessa Watt and Christopher Marsh have made clear, the meaning of a printed ballad depended to a large degree on the tune to which it was sung, which is named in all these three examples—something that was becoming commoner in the early seventeenth century, though less than half of the named melodies have survived. One that has is "Fortune my foe," prescribed for "Anne Wallens Lamentation," a very successful tune with strong associations with disaster and death, which would have reinforced the doleful message represented by the figure in the flames. On this important aural aspect of ballad literature see Watt, *Cheap Print*, 33, 35, 57–66 (more at 65), 79–80, 328–29; Christopher Marsh, "The Sound of Print in Early Modern England: The Broadside Ballad as Song," in *The Uses of Script and Print, 1300–1700*, ed. Julia Crick and Alexandra Walsham (Cambridge: Cambridge Univ. Press, 2004), 171–90, at 180–81 and following on how the tune could affect, alter, even subvert the meaning of the words. The author's forthcoming book on popular music in early modern England will enlighten us further on this topic.

The second part   To the same tune.

Figure 7. A warning for wives. Courtesy of the Pepys Library, Magdalene College, Cambridge.

remade copy which did duty for Katherine Francis remains (though cruder) close to Foxe's original, while removing the speech-scroll with its "Jesu have mercy" prayer (Figures 3 and 4).

Foxe's vivid images of martyrs on their terrible pyres clearly had uses beyond the covers of *The Acts and Monuments* where they were immortalized. My final example proves this in what seems a rather surprising way. It takes us back to the late sixteenth century. In 1592, five years after John Foxe's death, a murder pamphlet of six pages of a very racy and gripping kind was printed by John Kyd for sale by Edward White at the sign of the gun by the north door of St Paul's.[22] The title summarizes the page-turning contents, which are framed by a minimal amount of religious moralizing on the heinousness of the crime and its proper punishment: *The trueth of the most wicked and secret murthering of John Brewen, Goldsmith of London, committed by his owne wife, through the provocation of one John Parker whom she loved: for which fact she was burned, and he hanged in Smithfield, on wednesday, the 28 of June, 1592, two yeares after the murther was committed*[23] (Figure 8). The woodcut of the murderer on the title page is lifted straight from the *Book of Martyrs*, where it represented "The burnyng of Cicelie Ormes at Norwich" on 13 September 1557, as one of the small woodcuts of individual martyrs added to the work in 1570[24] (Figure 9). It remained in place in Foxe's lifetime. But then it disappeared. Someone seems to have taken advantage of the disputes and rearrangements over the printing of the *Book of Martyrs* which took place after the deaths of both Foxe and his printer John Day in the 1580s to make off with a conveniently useful block.[25]

---

[22] On murder pamphlets, which had their own moralizing agenda, see Peter Lake, "Deeds against Nature: Cheap Print, Protestantism and Murder in Early Seventeenth-Century England," in *Culture and Politics in Early Stuart England*, ed. Kevin Sharpe and Peter Lake (Basingstoke: Macmillan, 1994), 257–83; idem, "Popular Form, Puritan Content? Two Puritan Appropriations of the Murder Pamphlet from Mid-seventeenth-century London," in *Religion, Culture and Society in Early Modern Britain*, ed. Anthony Fletcher and Peter Roberts (Cambridge: Cambridge Univ. Press, 1994), 313–34. On murder pamphlets and their title-pages (including this one) in chapter 5 of Peter Lake and Michael Questier, *The Antichrist's Lewd Hat: Protestants, Papists and Players in Post-Reformation England* (New Haven and London: Yale Univ. Press, 2002), see Patrick Collinson, "Saints on Sundays, Devils All the Week After," *London Review of Books*, 19 Sept. 2002, 15–16.

[23] *STC* 15095 lists the work under Thomas Kyd, pointing out that it was anonymous, and not by him. The sole surviving copy is at Lambeth.

[24] *A&M* (1570), 2219; (1576), 1916; (1583), 2023.

[25] On the litigation that followed John Day's death in 1584 and the changes that took place before the 1596 edition see C. L. Oastler, *John Day, the Elizabethan Printer* (Oxford: Oxford Bibliographical Society, 1975), 28; Julian Roberts, "Bibliographical Aspects of John Foxe," in Loades (ed.), *Foxe and the Reformation*, 36–51, at 48–51; Elizabeth Evenden and Thomas S. Freeman, "John Foxe, John Day and the Printing of the 'Book of Martyrs'," in *Lives in Print:*

Figure 8. The trueth of the . . . murthering of John Brewen, title page. Courtesy of Lambeth Palace Libray, 1594.16.

Figure 9. The burning of Cicelie Ormes. John Foxe, *Actes and monuments* (1583), 2:2023. Courtesy of the British Academy John Foxe Project.

The next edition (the fifth, of 1596) was the work of a syndicate of ten stationers, acting as assigns of Richard Day (John's son). In both that edition and the following one of 1610 Cicely Ormes' martyrdom had to be represented by repeating "the Martyrdom of Margery Polley," who was burned at Tunbridge in July 1555 (Figure 1). The Ormes woodblock had apparently gone irretrievably missing.

These murder-pamphlet and ballad images with their resonances of Foxe's martyrs raise questions about the viewing of such pictures. If readers and users of these lurid stories were attracted by the graphic scenes of death and punishment (however crudely depicted), was the figure of the murderer in the fire divorced from those repeating images in the martyrology? Executions for petty treason, though they continued through the period, were rare, newsworthy events, and it is no coincidence that two of the publications considered here were about cases that were chronicled at the time. Such a death was obviously always horrific, but Foxe made sure that its terrible frequency as spiritual punishment in the time of Mary Tudor was engraved in popular memory. Were there not likely associations here which could have affected people who saw the woodcuts—let alone

Biography and the Book Trade from the Middle Ages to the 21st Century, ed. Robin Myers, Michael Harris, and Giles Mandelbrote (London: British Library, 2002), 23–54, at 45–46.

those who witnessed the events? Even if—given the large size and expense of *The Acts and Monuments*—most contemporaries' first-hand knowledge of these great volumes was through hearing or seeing them in churches or clerical houses, we have quite early comments suggesting that non-readers enjoyed looking at the pictures. Robert Parsons, early in the seventeenth century, remarked (by way of criticism) that "the . . . spectacle and representation of martyrdomes (as they are called) delighteth many to gaze on, who cannot read."[26] Of all the many pictures in Foxe's book, it was the iconic depictions of martyr-figures standing, alone or in groups, erect in the flames that were perhaps the most memorable. This was the emblem of papistry and Romish prelacy, witness John Bunyan in whose *Holy War* (1682), the scutcheon of Captain Pope (a commander of the Bloodmen attacking Mansoul) was "the stake, the flame, and the good man in it."[27]

Was it possible to reproduce such an image without some recall of the commemorated Marian martyrs? After all, as late as the 1630s corrections of Foxe's account derived from living memory were still reaching his heirs. One John Deighton, who wrote—seemingly to the martyrologist's son Simeon Foxe—to explain that there were errors in the account of the martyrdom of Edward (not John) Horne, had been to Newent in Gloucestershire and talked with witnesses who had seen this burning, which took place about eight weeks before the death of Queen Mary in 1558. They were able to provide graphic details, and Deighton sent the correction of this "smale error," some time between 1631 and 1637, out of reverence for the memory of John Foxe and his works.[28] Even after two generations, living memory was still contributing to the *Book of Martyrs*. Foxe himself, anxious to "stop the mouthes of . . . carping cavillers" of his time, knew

---

[26] Robert Parsons, *A Treatise of Three Conversions of England* ([St Omer], 1603–4), Pt. 3, *The last six monethes*, 400, cited in Aston and Ingram, "The Iconography," 70. Watt, *Cheap Print*, 90, comments: "The horrifying human image of the martyr was worth a thousand abstract arguments in the task of embedding anti-Catholic feeling in popular consciousness."

[27] John Bunyan, *The Holy War*, ed. Roger Sharrock and James F. Forrest (Oxford: Clarendon Press, 1980), 229; cited Thomas S. Freeman, "A Library in Three Volumes: Foxe's 'Book of Martyrs' in the Writings of John Bunyan," *Bunyan Studies* 5 (1994): 47–59, at 54. For a contemporary image of such an envisaged popish event, with four martyrs at the stake in a Foxean scene of burning, see the 1681 print delineating the *Prospect of a Popish Successor*, reproduced in John Miller, *Religion in the Popular Prints 1600–1832* (Cambridge: Chadwick-Healey, 1986), 120–21, no. 30. On the propaganda prints at the time of the Popish Plot see Antony Griffiths, *The Print in Stuart Britain 1603–1689* (London: British Museum, 1989), chap. 12.

[28] *Narratives of the Days of the Reformation*, ed. John Gough Nichols, Camden Society, First Series 77 (London: Camden Society, 1859), 69–70; J. F. Mozley, *John Foxe and his Book* (London: SPCK, 1940), 186–87; Thomas Freeman, "Texts, Lies and Microfilm: Reading and Misreading Foxe's 'Book of Martyrs'," *Sixteenth Century Journal* 30 (1999): 23–46, at 38 (dating the letter on internal evidence).

from experience that men and women were still alive to bear factual witness to a burning they had witnessed in Amersham more than six decades earlier.[29] Pictured figures standing in flames were attached to this experience, and might be consciously shifted out of it to instruct those who inherited these memories. If so, were the ballad-writers and printers who used this imagery deliberately exploiting a pool of Protestant image-associations for their own commercial ends? Or could contemporaries keep death by burning at the stake for murder and for religious conviction in separate categories of their minds? Or did nobody bother too much about the pictures decorating popular ballads?

So we have here a kind of iconographic circle. The image of the sufferer in the pyre, having first represented the condign punishment that dispatched the heretic to eternal fire, was drafted into a reversed celebration of victoriously attested faith, only to return thereafter to the humiliation of an age-old public secular execution. The single image is serially transformed by the text in which it is placed. Was an image then only as much as its text and context made it? Have we been mistaken to suppose that Foxe's images, informing and supporting his famous book, became memorable in their own right, indelibly lodged in people's heads and inscribed in popular memory of Marian martyrdoms, with the teaching of the *Book of Martyrs*? Or was thrill at the gruesome and macabre, the lure of the public execution and morbid details of death and dying, always more powerful than the moral message? After all, Foxe himself was quite ready to advertise his work as concerned with the "bloudy" and "horrible."[30] And images of people on pyres always spoke with immediate, painful directness, with inescapable thoughts of everlasting fire. Perhaps murder pamphlet and martyr story were more nearly allied than we have supposed.

CASTLE HOUSE
CHIPPING ONGAR, ESSEX

---

[29] Foxe, *A&M* (1583), 774 (on William Tilsworth, Martyr). I am grateful to Tom Freeman for this reference.

[30] The title page of the *A&M* in 1583 referred to "the bloudy times, horrible troubles, and great persecutions agaynst the true Martyrs of Christ," whereas in 1570 the words were "persecutions, horrible troubles, the sufferyng of Martyrs."

Text and Image in Foxe's Book of Martyrs

JOHN N. KING

OHN FOXE'S *BOOK OF MARTYRS* IS THE LARGEST, MOST COMPLICATED, AND best illustrated English book of the early modern era.[1] Not only do the woodcuts constitute an integral part of this massive text, which provides many narratives that complement the illustrations, but many of the pictures also contain a significant amount of text. The repertoire of woodcuts underwent change in each of the four increasingly large editions produced during the lifetimes of Foxe and his publisher, John Day. In its most profusely illustrated form, this book contained 105 woodcuts in 158 occurrences. About two-thirds of these pictures were large narrative scenes that illustrated specific segments of text.[2] The remaining one-third of these cuts consisted of small non-narrative scenes, which the compositors used repeatedly to illustrate different sections of text. Unlike permanent xylographic inscriptions carved into a few woodblocks, whose lettering

---

This paper was delivered at the 2004 Annual Meeting of the Renaissance Society of America, New York, NY, at a panel entitled "Texts and Images in Foxe's *Book of Martyrs*," Carolyn Kent, Renaissance English Text Society, presiding.

[1] Although this essay refers to early editions of Foxe's *Acts and Monuments* by the popular title of the *Book of Martyrs*, notes employ the abbreviation *A&M*.

[2] For a census of the woodcuts, see Ruth Samson Luborsky and Elizabeth Ingram, *A Guide to English Illustrated Books, 1536–1603* (Tempe: MRTS, 1998), nos. 11222–25. The overall count of woodcuts is corrected by reference to Mark Rankin, "Complete Set of Woodcut Illustrations from the First Four English Editions of John Foxe's *Actes and Monuments* (the 'Book of Martyrs'), with Selected Images from the 1554 and 1559 Latin Editions," at The American Theological Library Association Cooperative Digital Resources Initiative. <http://www.atla.com/digitalresources/>. October 2005. Contractions are expanded in quotations from early printed books. For books that contain copy-specific information, references contain library shelf numbers. The abbreviation OSU refers to the Rare Book and Manuscript Library at The Ohio State University.

is confined wholly, or almost wholly, to unframed captions that identify persons or objects, drop-in typesettings generally fill banderoles that create a boundary between speeches and the images within which they appear. The windblown banderoles and gesticulating figures that we encounter in Day's woodcuts and those of other London printers conform to the northern European style of book illustration, as opposed to the restrained classicism of Italian book illustration. Banderoles invariably contain verbal utterances attributed to specific individuals, whereas cartouches (or tablets) typically contain scriptural texts, captions, or other forms of "silent" commentary.

Testimonials uttered by martyrs prior to being burnt alive fill virtually all of the many banderoles in the narrative woodcuts. Clustering thickly during the reign of Mary I, who is commonly remembered by the unforgettable epithet of "Bloody Mary," they appear in four-fifths of the large illustrations for the intense burst of persecution that transpired during three years of her reign. The piety of dying speeches accords with the widespread belief that last words should command attention because individuals on the verge of death rarely fail to tell the truth. It seems likely that many readers experienced an entertaining *frisson* as an accompaniment to the religious instruction afforded by these affective declarations. These moments of high drama culminate stories about the *acts* of martyrs, which are filled with anecdotal detail, rather than their *monuments* (i.e., treatises, letters, and other textual vestiges). Abounding in aphorisms and maxims, these cartoonlike distillations of narrative provide vivid moments of human interest within stories that make up a relatively small component of a collection teeming with prolix documents. These epigrammatic speeches include some of the most memorable wording in the collection. Although they sometimes contain direct quotations from the text *per se*, they more often constitute formulaic responses to persecution. The provision of speeches in woodcuts is typically posterior to the reading of narrative texts that they illustrate.

The variability of drop-in typesettings for dying petitions exemplifies the status of banderoles more as signs for formulaic utterance than as frames for verbatim transcriptions of verifiable words spoken by the martyrs. Such is the case in the depiction of the execution of William Gardiner, an English merchant resident in Portugal, the cutting off of whose hands preceded his auto-da-fé in Lisbon during 1552. An executioner intensifies Gardiner's torture by raising and lowering his body in the flames over which it is suspended from a gallows by means of a pulley. Like banderoles in William Caxton's *Mirror of the World* and *Golden Legend,* this one is devoid of wording. This empty space invites filling in by readers, however, as is the case in a copy of the 1576 edition that contains the following inscription in a seventeenth-century hand: "Lord rec[e]ave my sole"

Figure 1. The Martyrdom of William Gardiner. John Foxe, *Acts and Monuments* (1576), p. 1316.

Figure 2. The Martyrdom of William Gardiner. John Foxe, *Acts and Monuments* (1563), p. 879.

(Figure 1).[3] This speech is altogether appropriate, but it does *not* occur in the narrative, which recounts the victim's recitation of the Latin version of Psalm 43 as a prayer for vindication against injustice. The inscription instead invokes a prayer uttered by Saint Stephen as a mob stoned him to death, according to the Acts of the Apostles (7:59). An inscription in another copy assigns quite different wording to Gardiner: "I Suffer for the Truth" (Figure 2).[4] In other copies, different readers respectively attribute to Gardiner a strident attack in the manner of an Old Testament prophet: "O you wicked People,"[5] and a painfully pathetic appeal, "Pitty, Pitty."[6]

Because Saint Stephen supplies the model for martyrdom in the New Testament, this inscription confers a typological cast on Gardiner's experience. Indeed, these final words are appropriate to the execution of any martyr. As such, they recur more often than any other dying prayer within banderoles in the *Book of Martyrs*. The woodcut of John Rogers is the most notable example, because Foxe asserts that he was a latter-day Stephen when he calls him the "first

---

[3] OSU BR1600 .F6 1576, copy 2, p. 1316.

[4] OSU BR1600 .F6 1563, p. 879.

[5] OSU BR1600 .F6 1583, copy 1, p. 1366.

[6] Folger Shakespeare Library, *STC* 11223, p. 1544.

protomartyr of all the blessed company that suffered in Queen Mary's time."
After all, this saint was *the* martyr who led the way for all Christian martyrs who
followed. As a zealous proselytizer during the early days of the church according
to chapters 6 and 7 of the Book of Acts, he supplied a mirror in which preachers
such as Rogers could see themselves as agents of the religious renewal. It is worthy
of note, then, that these words appear only in the woodcut, but not in the text
of Rogers's martyrology (Figure 3).[7] Stephen's own allusion to the last words of
Christ on the Cross—"Father, into thy hands I commend my spirit"—supplies
a further resonance (Luke 23:46). Because condemned Protestants were known
to have rehearsed their comportment at the point of death, we have no reason to
doubt that these woodcuts represent martyrdom as an imitation of both Christ
and St. Stephen. The reader encounters this formulaic prayer in portrayals of
the burnings of John Hooper, Rowland Taylor, William Flower, Thomas Haukes,
and Thomas Cranmer.[8] A host of martyrs model their dying testimonials upon
St. Stephen.

In other instances, drop-in typesettings extract dramatic speeches from utterances attributed to martyrs. John Lambert exclaims "None but Christ, none
but Christ" as flames consume him at Smithfield in 1538, whereas John Philpot,
Archdeacon at Winchester Cathedral, declares "I will pay my vowes in thee, O
Smithfield" upon his arrival at the most frequently used execution site in England. In a similar vein, John Bradford adopts a prophetic voice in his attempt to
rouse his compatriots with this appeal: "Repent England."[9] Perhaps the most notable example is the perhaps apocryphal prayer attributed to William Tyndale,
which functions as a clarion call for universal access to the Bible by every kind
of reader: "Lord ope[n] the king of Englands eies" (Figure 4).[10] The execution
scene portrays Tyndale chained to the stake as the executioner garrotes him before igniting the pyre. The crowd surrounding the scaffold includes jeering friars
conventional in Foxean woodcuts in addition to soldiers, officials, and towns-
people.

The coexistence of English and Latin text within a few woodcuts in the *Book
of Martyrs* indicates that the planner(s) presumably designed them for a tiered
audience whose members included learned *literati*, who could read Latin; *illiterati*, who could only read the English vernacular; and unlettered individuals
who looked at the pictures as they heard communal readings. The Latin wording
would have mystified vernacular readers unless an individual literate in Latin

---

[7] *A&M* (1563), p. 1037.

[8] E.g., Luborsky and Ingram, *Guide*, nos. 11222/25, 26, 29, 31, 44.

[9] Ibid., nos. 11222/18, 19, 41, 34.

[10] *A&M* (1563), p. 519.

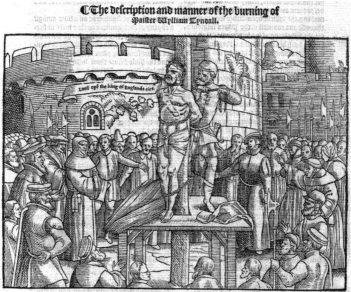

Figure 3. The Burning of John Rogers. John Foxe, *Acts and Monuments* (1563), p. 1037.

Figure 4. The Execution of William Tyndale. John Foxe, *Acts and Monuments* (1563), p. 519.

translated the speeches. (The introduction of English translations following Latin passages in the 1570 revision would have enabled *illiterati* to search the printed text for vernacular versions of Latin speeches.) We encounter a good example in what may be the best remembered depiction of martyrdom in the whole of the *Book of Martyrs*. Within a complicated portrayal of a double execution (Figure 5), Hugh Latimer delivers a final petition ("Father of heue[n] receue my soule") in tandem with Nicholas Ridley's recitation of a prayer in Latin ("In man*us* tuas domine"). Alluding respectively to the dying words of St. Stephen and Jesus Christ, speeches that they are reputed to have delivered undergo truncation in order to fit the aperture available for drop-in typesetting. Not only are Ridley's words inaccessible to *illiterati* incapable of understanding Latin, but they would make sense only to *literati* able to expand an abbreviation and move from picture to text in order to translate the unabridged quotation of the last words of Jesus Christ: "In manus tuas domine commendo spiritum meum."

The scenario typifies John Day's house style, because Dr. Richard Smith speaks from a portable wooden pulpit set up within the multitude that encircles the martyrs in front of the cityscape in the background. A banderole contains an abbreviated version of the Latin text of 1 Corinthians 13:3, on which Dr. Smith preaches: "And though I give my body, that I be burned, and have not love, it profiteth me nothing." In addition to the prominent use of Latin, banderoles contain drop-in typesettings for English speeches in addition to xylographic captions that identify "Latimer," "Ridley," "Cranmar," "Smith," and "L. Willia*m*s" (i.e., Sir John Williams, Lord of Thame). This official sits beside a companion who reads from a manuscript as he utters this promise: "Master Ridley I wil remember your suite." From atop Bocardo Prison, Cranmer prays: "O Lord strengthen them."[11] The horse at the lower right is a recurrent feature symbolic of persecution that recurs in many woodcuts in the *Book of Martyrs*. Smith's delivery of a "wicked sermon" before an audience centered upon the two martyrs inverts the dynamics of the preceding depiction of Latimer preaching to Edward VI and his courtiers from an elaborate outdoor pulpit erected in the privy gardens at Whitehall Palace (Figure 6). In accordance with the obituary pattern observed by Foxe, the earlier picture functions as an illustration not of the history of Edward VI's reign, but of the biography of Latimer that precedes the account of his martyrdom.[12]

Does this inclusion of Latin text provide evidence in support of the conclusion that the woodcuts were accessible only to literate observers? Must we therefore reject the alternative view that they "spoke also to the non-reading public"? A

---

[11] Ibid., pp. 1378–79. Printed on a separate piece of paper, this woodcut is typically tipped in at this location.

[12] Ibid., p. 1353.

Figure 5. The Burning of Nicholas Ridley and Hugh Latimer at Oxford. John Foxe, *Acts and Monuments* (1563), tipped in between pp. 1378 and 1379.

Figure 6. Hugh Latimer Preaching Before King Edward VI. John Foxe, *Acts and Monuments* (1563), p. 1353.

recent study dismisses the latter claim in attempting to set straight what it terms "three longstanding misconceptions" concerning the intended audience and reception of the woodcuts in the *Book of Martyrs*: 1) that the devisers planned the woodcuts in order to broaden the book's audience, 2) that the pictures instructed unlettered individuals, and 3) that the images were accessible to all potential viewers. Rightly noting that provision of illustrations tended to lessen the popularity of books by driving up prices, this argument interrogates the longstanding belief attributed to Pope Gregory I (the Great) that religious pictures functioned as "books" for the instruction of illiterate lay people.[13]

As appealing as this counter-intuitive argument may seem, book illustration was inseparable from a circuit of communication that encompasses reading and speaking by literate individuals in addition to hearing and seeing by both the literate and illiterate. Protestant ideology did embrace an ideal of universal literacy in accordance with the doctrine of *sola scriptura*. In the spirit of this belief, no scholar has lodged the claim that Foxe and his publisher, John Day, planned for the pictures to supplant textual instruction nor that they were so received. The *Book of Martyrs* was accessible not only to the *literati* and *illiterati* for whom they choreographed its typography, but also to illiterate individuals who relied on readers in order to gain access to written documents. This is the view of Robert Parsons, a Jesuit propagandist who charges that "the foresaid spectacle and representation of martyrdomes (as they are called) delighteth many to gaze on, *who cannot read*." He criticizes the pictures as a "pleasant (or rather peevish) invention, to entertayne the eyes of the simple readers *and lookers on*, & to make pastime for fooles."[14]

Despite the fact that the woodcuts served the needs of literate readers, no evidence compels us to conclude that Foxe and his associates planned to exclude illiterate individuals. Sir John Harington explains, on the one hand, that the pictures function as an *aide-mémoire* to more learned readers: "The use of the picture is evident, which is that (having read over the booke) you may reade it (as it were againe) in the very picture."[15] On the other hand, illiterate individuals could have been responsible for the presence of doodling and the inking-in of features of woodcuts, which we encounter in many copies of the *Book of Martyrs*. The provision of at least one copy for reading as an accompaniment to the drinking

---

[13] James A. Knapp, *Illustrating the Past in Early Modern England: The Representation of History in Printed Books* (Aldershot: Ashgate, 2003), 124–28.

[14] Robert Parsons (under the pseudonym of N. D), *A Treatise of Three Conversions from Paganism to Christian Religion* (St. Omer: François Bellet, 1603–1604), 3.400–401.

[15] Ludovico Ariosto, *Orlando Furioso, Translated into English Heroical Verse by Sir John Harington (1591)*, ed. Robert McNulty (Oxford: Clarendon Press, 1972), 17.

of ale at a public house suggests that this book was accessible for reading, hearing, *and seeing* by literate and illiterate individuals at all social levels.[16] We should recall that literacy, orality, and visuality were porous categories during the early modern era. In the case of Rawlins White, for example, an "illiterate" fisherman is reputed to have memorized the whole of the English Bible after he arranged for the education of his son in order to allow him to read the text aloud to him. The father's remarkable memory enabled him to travel about as an itinerant evangelist who expounded scriptural texts that he recited. His ability to preach demonstrates that early modern "literacy" encompassed not only silent reading, but also reading aloud, aural reception, and the seeing of pictures filled with banderoles that contained the dying speeches of martyrs.

THE OHIO STATE UNIVERSITY

---

[16] Norfolk Record Office, INV 19/145B. I am indebted to John Craig for this transcription.

Watching Women in
The Acts and Monuments

DEBORAH G. BURKS

THIS PAPER OBSERVES THE NUMEROUS AND VARIED WAYS IN WHICH THE woodcuts of John Foxe's *The Acts and Monuments* manipulate conventional strategies for the representation of femininity. In a significant— and now much studied—minority of the woodcuts, women figure as martyrs at the center of the action; in others, they stand as spectators on the margins of an illustrated scene and at the periphery of a viewer's attention. In a great many of these illustrations, the woodcut artist has used gender as a crucial constituent element of the work's valorization of the Protestant faithful and its simultaneous villainization of the Marian church and state. To a variety of complementary ends, the woodcuts mobilize popular assumptions about gender—about masculinity as well as femininity—in order to heighten sympathy for the work's protagonists.

Among the woodcuts portraying female martyrs, Rose Allin's is notable for its narrative detail (Figure 1).[1] The artist shows Allin as a compassionate daughter, fetching a drink for her bedridden mother (seen in the top left of the illustration); the artist emphasizes Allin's bravery and asserts her readiness for

---

This paper was first delivered at the 2004 Annual Meeting of the Renaissance Society of America at a panel entitled "Text and Image in Foxe's *Book of Martyrs*," Carolyn Kent, Renaissance English Text Society, presiding.

[1] John Foxe, *The Acts and Monuments of these latter and perillous dayes, touching matters of the Church, wherein ar comprehended and described the great persecutions & horrible troubles, that haue bene wrought and practiced by the Romishe Prelates, speciallye in this Realme of England and Scotlande* (Imprinted at London by John Day, dwellyng ouer Aldersgate, [1563]). Unless otherwise noted, all references to *The Acts and Monuments* will be to the 1563 first edition.

Figure 1. Rose Allin. *A&M* (1563), p. 1706. By permission of The Ohio State University Libraries.

Figure 2. Thomas Tomkyns. *A&M* (1570), p. 1710. By permission of The Ohio State University Libraries.

martyrdom by depicting her fearless submission to Sir Edmund Tiryll's licensed bullying as he burns her hand with a candle. She is a decidedly feminine figure, surrounded and dwarfed by the four armed men, who have intruded on the domestic scene. They seem to have taken her in her shift: her state of semi-dress contrasts with the many layers of Tiryll's gentlemanly apparel, which add girth, height, and authority to the man. (The feather in his cap underscores the irony of his ungentle treatment of the girl.) Like the male martyrs, Thomas Tomkyns and Thomas Bilney (Figures 2, 10), Allin does not flinch from the small-scale damage of a candle's flame, and she does not need to be restrained, though there are men enough to do the job had they been necessary.[2] Instead, she seems to have offered her right hand to be tortured, while in her left, she holds the means to end her torment: her water jug (full, presumably, as she appears to be returning from her errand) has not spilled either in self-defense or in fear. The artist scores a point with these details: Rose Allin, though only a girl, possesses a martyr's readiness for the all-consuming fire that awaits her. Just over her shoulder, in fact, the artist has inset a picture of that future; there, as though through a window, the viewer glimpses a group of martyrs burning at the stake. Meanwhile, in the foreground and in the present moment of the illustration, Allin remains undistracted by that scene of horror; she is busy with her current task—the artist's most immediate task in this illustration—outfacing her oppressors and putting to shame their intimidation tactics.

A similar point is made by the artist who crafted the busy depiction of "the burning of thirteen persons at Stratford the Bowe near London, whereof the two women went in among them to the stake untied." In this cut, several of the prisoners, including one of the women, extend their arms back towards the men and women who have come to witness their burning (Figure 3), but their gestures suggest neither reluctance nor fear. The martyrs' gestures of farewell, prayer, and exhortation have a profound effect on the crowd, which is filled with figures in motion, many of them reaching in towards the martyrs, some grappling with officers, some climbing over an embankment above the rest, as though they might leap down and disrupt the proceedings. This crowd threatens to overwhelm the armed officials carrying out the execution. The contrast is striking: it is only the crowd and their armed antagonists who display agitation, outrage, and fear: in the center, those who are on the point of death remain steadfast. Of course, the men have been chained to the stakes so they cannot escape, but the women—

---

[2] I have reproduced the woodcut depicting Tomkyns and Bishop Bonner from the 1570 second edition of *The Acts and Monuments* not because it differs in any way from the 1563 edition, but because this image has been defaced in the copy held in the Ohio State University collection. The particular defacement is interesting: Bonner's face has been gouged out of the image.

Figure 3. The burning
of thirteen persons at
Stratford the Bowe.
A&M (1563), p. 1524.
By permission of The
Ohio State University
Libraries.

Figure 4. "The cruell
burnyng of a man and
a woman at Norwich."
A&M (1563), p. 1603.
By permission of The
Ohio State University
Libraries.

especially, the cheerful girl who waves farewell as she skips barefoot in amongst the faggots—the women prove the point.

It is these willingly martyred women who demonstrate the miraculous fortitude of Protestant martyrs. By transcending the behaviors expected of women, they embody the martyrologist's claim that those who die for faith do not suffer, or, if they suffer, it does not cause them to waver. Foxe makes a particularly explicit statement of this view in his description of John Frith's execution:

> When he was tied unto the stake, there it suffyciently appeared wyth what constancy and courage he suffred death, for when as the faggottes and fyre were caste into him, he willinglye embraced the same, thereby declaringe wyth what upryghtnesse of minde, he suffered hys deathe for Christes sake and the true doctrine, where of that daye he confirmed with his bloude a perfecte and firme Testament. The winde made hys death somewhat the more longer, whych bare away the flame from him unto hys felowe that was tied to his backe, but he had so establyshed hys minde with such pacience, God geuynge hym strength, that euen as thoughe he had felte no paine in that long torment, he seemed rather to reioyse for hys felow, then to be careful for hys selfe.
>
> Thys truely is the power and strengthe of Christe striuinge and vanquishinge in his sainctes, which may sanctify us together with them, and directe us to the glorye of his holye name. Amen. (1563 ed.: 504–5)

Foxe and his illustrators would have their reader/viewers believe that true martyrs, strengthened by God, are so committed to using the spectacle of their dying as a witness to their sanctification that they suffer burning without any of the fear or frenzy one might expect of human creatures. To the sixteenth-century view, such fortitude, which had to be taken as miraculous in men, was infinitely more amazing when displayed by women. It could only be attributed to "the power and strengthe of Christe striuing and vanquishinge in his sainctes." In the Stratford le Bowe woodcut, then, the reader/viewer of *The Acts and Monuments* sees in the crowd a reminder of what normal human behavior looks like in the face of violent persecution; meanwhile, the martyrs at its center calmly demonstrate how faith transforms human weakness, even feminine frailty.

Where the previous woodcuts portray female martyrs as divinely-enabled super-women, the small cut of "the cruell burnyng of a man [Simon Myller] and a woman [Elizabeth Cooper] at Norwych" and its extended narrative caption use women's assumed physical and moral fragility in a more conventional way (Figure 4). Its caption reports of Elizabeth Cooper that thys good woman beynge condemned, & at the stake with Symon Myller to bee burnte, when the fyre came unto her, she a lytle shranke thereat wyth a crying voice, once ha. When the sayd mayster Myller heard the same, he put hys hande behinde him toward her, and willed her to bee stronge, and of good chere, for good sister (sayd he) we shal haue a ioyful and a sweete supper. Whereat shee being as it semed thereby strengthned, stoode as styll and as quiet, as one moste glad to fynysh the good worke which before most happely she had begonne. So in fine she ended her lyfe with her companion ioyfully, committing her soule into the hands of almighty God, Unto whose mercye I commit the good Reader. Amen. (1563 ed.: 1603)

This woman is merely a woman. She does not at first behave with the schooled quietude of a Rose Allin or the bravery of those women who went to the stake "untied" at Stratford le Bow. On the contrary, when the fire draws near, Elizabeth Cooper cannot hide her fear: she shrinks away from it and cries out. In short, she reacts as Foxe's readers must have expected, and her reaction serves a purpose. It capitalizes on the normative sixteenth-century view of woman as the weaker vessel, offering a logical argument aimed especially at male reader/viewers of *The Acts and Monuments*:

> *Proposition 1:* Burning is a fearful thing; it induces suffering that is beyond the human capacity to withstand.
> *Proposition 2:* The only reason that any of the martyrs who were burned at the stake could have gone calmly to that terrible death is that God answered their faith with divine care, taking away their fear and their pain.
> *Proposition 3:* This woman who flinched was an exception, but she was merely a woman, after all, and if any martyr *were* to flinch, it would, of course, *be* a woman.
> *Conclusion:* Although a mere woman, Elizabeth Cooper responded to her male companion's encouragement, and with that reminder of God's good care, she controlled her fear and embraced her death joyfully.
> *Corollary:* The reader/viewer should hope to behave as well as Elizabeth Cooper did, if (God forbid) *he* were ever to find himself in similar straits.

Thus, Elizabeth Cooper, despite her initial and instructive flinching, joins the ranks of Foxe's amazing heroines: in the end and in the woodcut, she stands "as styll and as quiet, as one moste glad to fynysh the good worke which before most happely she had begonne." Ending her life "with her companion joyfully," Elizabeth Cooper joins Anne Askew, who encouraged her *male* companions in their suffering, and the two women at Stratford le Bowe, who went unchained to their

Figure 5. The burning of three women and an infant. *A&M* (1563), p. 1542. By permission of The Ohio State University Libraries.

deaths with eleven bound men, and Rose Allin, who was as brave as Thomas Tomkyns or Thomas Bilney. All of these women challenge the male reader/viewer to test his own faith lest he be outdone by a girl.

Figure 5 could be read in much the same manner. Like the others, it features the instructive suffering of three of God's weaker creatures, but there is obviously more to this illustration of the death of three women from the Isle of Guernsey. The sensationalism of this picture outstrips anything the previous examples offer: here a pregnant woman's womb explodes and a bishop catches her child, then callously tosses it back into the fire to die with its mother. Unsurprisingly, the mother (the central figure) appears dismayed, her arms akimbo, her torso lurching sideways, her guts spilling out.[3]

---

[3] I have offered fuller readings of this woodcut elsewhere. See Deborah G. Burks, *Horrid Spectacle: Violation in the Theater of Early Modern England* (Pittsburgh, PA: Duquesne Univ. Press, 2004) and "Polemical Potency: The Witness of Word and Woodcut," in *John Foxe and His World*, ed. Christopher Highley and John N. King (Brookfield, VT: Ashgate, 2001), 263–76.

At first glance, her companions appear to have been drawn in more conventional poses of martyrdom: like Elizabeth Cooper, the woman on the right
is calm, if fervent, as she stands with her hands raised and pressed together in a
gesture of prayer. We see only the back and raised left hand of the third woman,
but she, too, stands erect, not off-balance or flailing like the exploding woman.
It is possible that this third woman is exhorting the crowd or that she is defying
the flames in the manner of John Rogers (Figure 8) or (most famously) Thomas Cranmer, but the artist has done something more with her: he has made her
beautiful, even sexy.[4] We see her with her long hair curled over her right shoulder, revealing the nape of her neck to our view: for this figure, the artist drew on
traditional representations which paradoxically depict both maidens and female
penitents with their hair tumbling loose. (Mary Magdalen is, perhaps, the most
familiar example of the latter.) Thus, the artist mobilizes a set of conventions
which simultaneously asserted either a woman's sinfulness or her nubile potential, and which exploited feminine attractiveness even while elevating women as
examples of redemption and piety. This third woman in the woodcut has been
coded as vulnerable, desirable, and maidenly—her long hair and uncovered head
point to her lack of masculine protection.

The nakedness of the women in this illustration demands our attention, both
in what the artist details and in what he distorts or omits. We see, for instance,
the navel of the woman on the right, but not her breasts. We see the same woman's flank and, of course, the writhing entrails of the woman in the center, but
nothing else below the waist of any of the figures, thanks to the obscuring screen
of smoke and flame. That is not to say that this picture is uniformly "sexsation-
alized": the sexy bits pale in significance beside (and they are *beside*) the central woman's agony. In addition to her gaping belly, we see the central woman's
splayed fingers and the bulging muscle of her forearm. We even see her breasts,
though these are strangely malformed, perhaps as an artistic means of articulat-
ing her agony. In any case, this woodcut uses its women as more than models for
and challenges to the faith and comportment of Foxe's reader/viewers; *this* woodcut uses its women to arouse its viewers—to outrage, to horror, to compassion.

In all the pictures we have seen, women are decidedly objects for the viewer
to behold. Sometimes these artfully constructed women appeal to the viewer's
pity or terror; sometimes they demand her or his admiration; and sometimes the

---

[4] In deference to printing costs, I have not reproduced the Cranmer illustration. Surely
it is famous enough that its caption alone will invoke its relevant feature: "The burning of
Tharchbishop of Cant[erbury] D[octor] Tho[mas] Cranmer in the town dich at Oxford with
his hand first thrust into the fyre wherwith he subscribed before": *The Acts and Monuments*,
p. 1503.

artist uses them to flirt with other responses as well, as when he draws on artistic tropes of the beautiful penitent (with the third Guernsey woman) or the submissive maiden (in Rose Allin) or even the unsophisticated sexuality of the peasant girl (which I would offer as an explanation for the gratuitous bare foot of the young woman shown stepping in amongst the faggots at Stratford le Bow). However, the women in *The Acts and Monuments* are not always martyrs, and I want now to shift gears from those maids, wives, and widows, who walk center stage in the *Book of Martyrs*, to take note of some other roles played by women and the artistic conventions used in representing them.

Women appear as members of crowds in many of the woodcuts (as in Figures 6, 7, and 8). Their evident distress as they witness an execution helps define the grievous circumstances of the Marian Counter-Reformation for Foxe's reader/ viewers who witnessed those events from the safety of a later time. This is true of the various and expressive postures of grieving prayer shown in the four women occupying central positions in Figure 6, the "order and maner of burying in the fieldes such as died in prisons," and it is true of the gently weeping woman who stands to the right of John Hooper in Figure 7. A commonly repeated element in Foxe's crowd scenes is the woman restrained by a masculine arm from behind; one such woman appears in the foreground of the cut depicting John Rogers' execution (Figure 8). As this woman illustrates, the woodcut artists made strategic use of female figures to convey the unruly, resistant energies of the crowds. In the altogether more chaotic Stratford le Bowe woodcut, there are likewise women in the foreground whose postures telegraph distress verging towards rebellion (Figure 3). In both of these woodcuts, the women provide an important context and buffer for the masculine figures of agitation. In the foreground of Figure 3, for instance, there is a man (to the right of center in the nearest plane of the picture) depicted as though he is rushing forwards into the scene with his arms spread wide and his cloak flapping behind him; his posture and his lack of decorum are exactly mirrored by a woman in the corresponding position to the left of center. Similarly, the man just in front and to the right of him, who seems a mere half-step from actually throwing himself into conflict with the guards (surely a foolish and impotently emotional action), has been upstaged by a woman who is both half again as close to confrontation and twice as agitated as he (she flails two hands to his one). The men do not become antic caricatures of citizen buffoonery because the women are more emotive still, lending a proportional sense of measure or merit to the men's behavior. This balancing effect plays an even greater role in Figure 8, where the man behind and to the left of John Rogers escapes looking like a Bedlamite because he is not the only one with frantic hands raised in grief; there is a woman further to the left, just rushing into the scene,

Figure 6. "The order and maner of burying in the fieldes such as died in prisons." *A&M* (1563), p. 1387. By permission of The Ohio State University Libraries.

Figure 7. John Hooper. *A&M* (1563), p. 1064. By permission of The Ohio State University Libraries.

Figure 8. John Rogers. *A&M* (1563), p. 1037. By permission of The Ohio State University Libraries.

who matches his gesture, and there is the mixed group of agitated onlookers in
the foreground, whose more moderate expressions define his behavior as belonging to a continuum of grief.

A quite different set of woodcuts places women in congregations of believers
at worship (Figure 9).[5] In these scenes, the female figures do not define emotional
distress or disruptive action; instead, they bear witness to the good order of
Protestant preaching by manifesting that even the weaker vessel can be brought
to sanctity through study and preaching of God's word in the vernacular. In
certain important regards, the illustration of Thomas Bilney's preaching mirrors
the structure of the Rogers, Hooper, and Stratford le Bow woodcuts: here, the
distressed crowd has been exchanged for an attentive congregation, and in this
case, the chaotic figures, whose arms reach and whose faces contort, are not an
assemblage of horrified witnesses, but are instead a pair of friars portrayed in the

---

[5] A similar congregational scene occurs in the woodcut of "Bishop Latimer preaching
before King Edward VI." It also makes a point of including a pious woman among those in attendance; she sits quietly on the steps of the pulpit, reading her Bible while Latimer delivers
his sermon; her presence is wholly unobtrusive in the context of the action, but the artist has
placed her pointedly in the center of the scene: *The Acts and Monuments,* p. 1353.

Figure 9. Thomas Bilney being pulled from the pulpit. *A&M* (1563), p. 474 (misnumbered). By permission of The Ohio State University Libraries.

Figure 10. Thomas Bilney awaiting martydom in his cell. *A&M* (1563), p. 478. By permission of The Ohio State University Libraries.

act of arresting (assaulting) Bilney as he preaches. There's nothing subtle about this ironic reversal: it asserts that even women and children are well ordered by Protestant discipline, whereas Roman Catholic authority figures are shown to be guilty of the most outrageous disorder. A host of visual cues reinforce this contrast. Bilney's congregation consists of calm, thin, vertically-aligned people. (Even the seated women are straight-backed save for the one [left rear], whose head is bowed over her Bible.) The friars, on the other hand, are fat, hook-nosed, and squint-eyed. The artist captures them in a moment of violence: snarling, they rush at Bilney with long strides, their bodies angled forward and their arms outstretched with fingers grasping or fist clenched. They are also comically short: Thomas Bilney was famous for his littleness, but these blokes—especially the nasty little piece of work in the front—cannot even match "little Bilney's" stature.[6]

This illustration joins others in *The Acts and Monuments* in critiquing the masculinity of the friars, priests, and bishops of the Roman Catholic church: here, the slight stature, the lack of restraint, and (most importantly) the hairless faces of the friars contrast with the beards and behavior of "real" men—and with the decorous behavior and fair faces of the women, whom the friars resemble in their beardlessness, though they fall far short of the women's humble piety. John Bale called such men the "shorn sorcerers of that sodomitical kingdom," and the woodcuts in *The Acts and Monuments* make the tonsured crown and shaven chin of the Papist a visual sign of his doctrinal error and his moral corruption.

Despite the fact that Thomas Bilney did not have perfect Protestant credentials, John Foxe and his printer-collaborator, John Day, were attracted to Bilney's bold anti-clericalism—so much so that they devoted many pages and two narrative woodcuts to his case. I've mentioned the other cut once already (Figure 10): in it, Thomas Bilney burns off the first joint of a finger in the flame of his candle. I said earlier that this illustration belongs in a set of pictures showing martyrs testing their fortitude (or being forced to this test) by burning a hand, but there is more to the Bilney illustration than a martyr's calm readiness for execution. In fact, that is only a supporting point of this picture's argument.

---

[6] Latimer uses this phrase to describe Bilney in a sermon on facing death's terrors: "I knewe a man my selfe Bilney, little Bilney, that blessed martyr of God, what tyme he had borne his fagott, and was come agayne to Cambridge, had suche conflyctes within hymselfe, beholdynge this ymage of deathe, that hys friendes were afrayde to lette hym be alone: ... yet afterward, for al this he was reuiued and toke his deathe paciently, and died well against the tyrannicall sea of Rome": Hugh Latimer, "The Seuenth Sermon of Maister Hugh Latymer, which he preached before king Edward, the.19.day of Aprill [1549]," in *27 Sermons preached by the ryght Reuerende father in God and constant ma[r]tir of Jesus Christe, Maister Hugh Latimer* (London: John Day, 1562), fol. 82–82v.

An illustration of one of Foxe's anecdotes about Bilney's time in prison, this woodcut's thesis is that Roman Catholicism is slack, luxuriant, and based on flawed doctrine, which even its best scholars cannot convincingly defend. The artist has represented the Catholic position in the recumbent figure of Dr. Stokes, one of two scholars hand-picked to debate with Bilney after he challenged the Bishop of Norwich to send the "best doctors they had, to confound hym if they could, and to shew a better truth then he had to shew for him[self] by the word of God" (478, misnumbered). Bilney converted one of these scholars, and the other, Dr. Stokes, "lay with him in prison in disputation till the writ came" for Bilney's execution. Stokes, Foxe writes, "remained obdurate and doth to this day, whose hart also the lord, if it be his wil, convert, & open [th]e eies of his age, [tha]t he may forsake [th]e former blindnes of his youth" (478, misnumbered). The wood-cut artist portrays Bilney as the good disciple who watches through the night, sit-ting or kneeling at his desk, praying and reading the Bible, disciplining body and mind, while the doctor lies behind him in the soft bed, trying to distract Bilney with his chatter and seduce Bilney from the light.

Three significant pictorial traditions stand behind this illustration, two of them religious, the other secular. The first and most obvious precursor is the medieval convention depicting saints at a prie-dieu and evangelists at a writ-ing table.[7] This prop appears so often in medieval illuminations that it needn't even be in use in order to convey its message that the subject of the illustration is pious and well-disciplined in her or his observance of the hours of prayer and study. Significantly, this convention had already been adapted by Reformed art-ists well before *The Acts and Monuments*, most influentially in engravings by Lucas Cranach and Hans Sebald Beham, of Martin Luther as evangelist, sitting, pen in hand, at his desk with a crucifix before him and the dove of the Holy Spirit descending upon his head.[8] Clearly, we are to see Bilney as a man sanctified and

---

[7] The two pieces of furniture are nearly interchangeable in this iconography: the prie-dieu is not always a kneeler and sometimes has a flat rather than a sloped surface to hold the prayer book, while the evangelist's desk is often depicted as a place for devotion, providing both a crucifix for contemplation and implements for writing. See, for instance, "Evangelist Luke" from the Da Costa Book of Hours (Bruges, ca. 1515), Pierpont Morgan Library MS M.399, fol. 113v (viewable online at Corsair, the Pierpont Morgan Library's catalog and im-age base: http://utu.morganlibrary.org/medren/single_image2.cfm?imagename=m399.113v. jpg&page=ICA000114926); "Annunciation," *Book of Hours for the Use of Paris* (Paris, ca. 1485–1490), Pierpont Morgan Library. MS M.231, fol. 31r. (http://utu.morganlibrary org/medren/ single_image2.cfm? imagename=m231.031ra.jpg&page=ICA000150492).

[8] F. W. H. Hollstein, *German Engravings, Etchings and Woodcuts, ca. 1400–1700, Volume III: Hans Sebald Beham* (Amsterdam: Menno Hertzberger, 1954), 210. I owe thanks to Chris-tiane Andersson for this reference and for her helpful comments on this paper when it was first delivered.

set apart by his faith. That he looks up from his Bible and into the candle's light rather than at a crucifix denotes the particular character of the text's Protestant- ism. In any case, he seems to embody "Sola Scriptura," the Reformation motto which insisted on the primacy and sufficiency of scripture while rejecting papal pronouncement and institutional doctrine. The two halves of this illustration are utterly separate: though his companion, Dr. Stokes, bends his attention on Bilney, the committed Protestant appears utterly impervious to his interlocutor's speech.

In fact, the bilateral arrangement of the woodcut is another of its conven- tional strategies: the artist draws from medieval and Renaissance Christian art a spatial symbolism that places the saved at God's right hand and the damned at God's left. *The Acts and Monuments'* title page (Figure 12) is a full-scale elabo- ration of this trope, helpfully clarifying the key to this schema: God's right is the viewer's left. The woodcut artist depends on the reader/viewer to notice that the Bilney illustration has been divided into two halves according to this same geometry of salvation. Bilney, with his beard, his Bible, and his candle sits with the saved at what is understood to represent God's right hand, while the clean- shaven doctor luxuriates in worldly comfort on the side of the damned. It may be worth mention that in medieval depictions of the Last Judgment, Hell Mouth of- ten yawns in the position occupied in this illustration by the bed with its curtains drawn to reveal Doctor Stokes within its gaping interior.

The third representational tradition to which this woodcut alludes is the sec- ular genre that came to be known as the "pillow sermon" or "curtain lecture," a scene familiar in English literature from the middle ages in which wives overturn their husbands' authority by waiting for bedtime to express their opinions, to beg and wheedle for expensive new clothes, or to deliver harangues on the husbands' failings.[9] One notable medieval example occurs in Chaucer's Wife of Bath's tale, which turns on just such a speech delivered by the aged and unlovely but magi- cal heroine, who has saved the young rapist from his just punishment and then lectures him into submission on their wedding night. Similar scenes litter the comic narratives of Tudor literature, all of them depicting women as "the cause of all this evil, of all the cares, griefs, and thoughts which perplex and torture" a poor husband trapped by his wife's stratagem to hold him hostage at bedtime un- til he consents to whatever demand she has in hand.[10] In *The Bachelor's Banquet* (1603), an entirely representative example of this genre, the narrator informs his

---

[9] The *OED* dates "curtain sermon" to John Speed's 1611 *The History of Great Britain*, but it may well already have been a cliché.

[10] Faith Gildenhuys, ed., *The Bachelor's Banquet*, MRTS 109 (Binghamton, NY: Medieval & Renaissance Texts & Studies, 1993), 48.

Figure 11. Richard Brathwaite. *Art Asleepe Husband? A Boulster Lecture.* London: Printed by R. Bishop for R[ichard] B[est] or his assignes, 1640. By permission of the Bodleian Library, Oxford University.

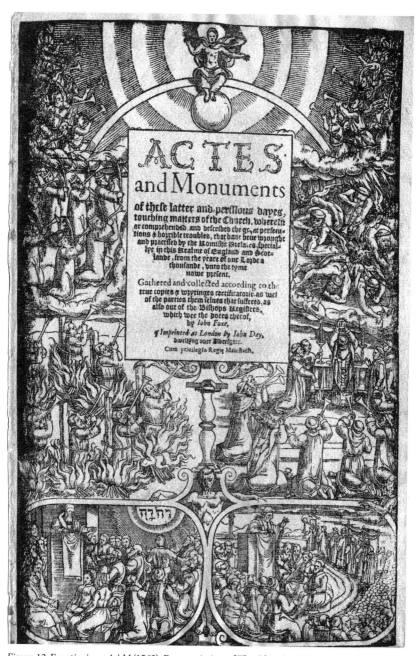

Figure 12. Frontispiece. *A&M* (1563). By permission of The Ohio State University Libraries.

reader that when a wife wants something from her husband, she will take care in choosing her venue, making "such choice that when she speaks she will be sure to speed, observing her opportunity when she might take her husband at the most advantage, which is commonly in bed, the garden of love, the state of marriage delights and the life wherein the weaker sex have ever the better" (48–49). The scene goes on to demonstrate how the clever wife overcomes whatever rhetorical mastery her husband might possess through her superior verbal endurance.

The bed in the Bilney illustration comes right out of the "bolster lecture" tradition. (Note the opened curtains, the bench and chamber pot, the table and candle.) When he depicted Dr. Stokes with his nightcap and his gender-ambiguous face, with his head propped on one hand and his mouth open, the artist invited viewers to associate this Papist scholar with the noisy matrons of popular lore, and to dismiss Stokes' false doctrine as they would the ill-informed yammering of women. While it is true that Foxe's work predates the two best known English woodcuts illustrating this genre (title page illustrations to Thomas Heywood's 1637 *A Curtaine Lecture* and Richard Brathwaite's 1640 *Art Asleepe Husband? A Boulster Lecture*),[11] the visual elements of the genre belong to a tradition stretching back at least as far as its literary examples. Medieval manuscript illuminators were fond of depicting hapless men in bed with machinating women. Manuscripts of the Arthurian cycles contain numerous illuminations of Lancelot (and occasionally Arthur or one of the wounded "fisher kings") in bed with women who get the better of them.[12] In similar straits are the foolish husbands illustrated in many of the manuscripts of *Roman de la Rose*, though in that instance it is the husbands'

---

[11] Thomas Heywood, *A Curtaine Lecture* (London: Printed by Robert Young for John Aston, 1637); Richard Brathwaite, *Art Asleepe Husband? A Boulster Lecture* (London: Printed by R. Bishop for R[ichard]. B[est]. or his assignes, 1640).

[12] See, for instance, the illumination from the Saint Graal of "King Mordrains, the wounded contemporary of Joseph of Arimathea, in bed with a woman, sighing and crying" (British Library Additional MS 10292, fol. 21v, viewable online: http://www.imagesonline. bl.uk/britishlibrary/controller/textsearch?text=10436). Of course, there are also the men who barely escape, as Joseph does in the many illustrations of his entanglement with Potiphar's wife, and as Lynceus does in illustrations of Ovid's *Heroide* XIV where Hypermnestra, alone of all her sisters, refuses her father's order to kill her husband on their wedding night. If one includes the Jaels and Judiths, the list of medieval bedroom scenes turned upside down grows impressively long. It also reveals a set of representational conventions: the beds are almost always viewed from their right side with the dominant partner (here, the female aggressor) posed above and behind/beyond the submissive or dominated partner. Only the illustrations of Joseph and Potiphar's wife regularly resist this pattern—because he is depicted escaping from her clutches.

talk that gets them into trouble as they confide too much in wives, who, because of their gender, are incapable of keeping a confidence.[13]

In art, the scene conventionally depicted a four-poster bed with its curtains drawn apart on the viewer's side (the bed's right from the perspective of one lying in it) to reveal two figures: on the near side, an agonized man and to his left, his babbling, badgering, opinionated wife (Figure 11). Strikingly similar to the seventeenth-century depictions of the "bolster lecture" or "curtain sermon" is the illustration of the foolish, confiding husband found in the manuscript of *Roman de la Rose* known as Douce 195: it positions the wife on the far side of her husband, her torso raised and partly turned towards him (and thus towards the viewer). She is, therefore, positioned as though "on top."[14] She reaches across him to grip his left wrist in a controlling rather than solicitous gesture, while he turns his head away from her, cradling his temple with his right hand as though it aches. He looks remarkably like his successors in the "curtain lecture" genre.

---

[13] See for instance, Morgan 948, fol. 162v (Pierpont Morgan Library, NY); Walters 143, fol. 105v (Walters Art Museum, Baltimore, MD); and Douce 195, fol. 118r (Bodleian Library, Oxford). The latter (Douce 195) is viewable online at http://image.ox.ac.uk/show?collection= bodleian&manuscript=msdouce195; the first two illuminations are also available online, but require a password (available on request) from 'Roman de la Rose: Digital Surrogates of Medieval Manuscripts' (Johns Hopkins University and the Pierpont Morgan Library): http://rose. mse.jhu.edu.

[14] Medieval representations were very precise in linking the masculine authority and female submission expected in social and marital relations to the spatial symbolism of top and bottom positions in bed: the normative position for women was on the bottom (and thus in the near ground of the illustration), face to face with the man who lies above her. Reversal or other disruptions of this positional geometry communicates something amiss with one or both partners, as, for instance, in an illumination depicting "the legend of the Saracen Malaquin who instructed a woman to seduce a hermit" where the woman in question has crept through the bed curtains and crawled atop the hapless holy man (Gautier de Coinsi, *Les miracles de Notre Dame. Les vies des Peres*, Den Haag, KB, 71 A 24, fol. 129r; viewable at www.mnemosyne.org). The normative posture receives explicit definition in two manuscript treatises on health and physiology, titled *Tacuinum sanitatis,* which are preserved in the collection of the Bibliothèque Nationale de France; both contain a section on sleep and problems with sleep that culminates with an illustration of "coytus," showing it to be properly performed face to face with the man atop the woman. (BnF, *Tacuinum sanitatis,* "Nouvelle acquisition latine 1673, fol. 100, Couple dans un lit"; *Tacuinum sanitatis,* "Latin 9333, fol. 99, "Couple dans un lit"; viewable online at Mandragore, bases iconographique du departement des Manuscrits: http://mandragore.bnf. fr.html/accueil.html) Like the other bedroom scenes I've described, both of these illustrations situate their action in a bed seen from its right side through its frame. These medieval illustrations—those depicting normative sex as well as those depicting aberrations—are remarkably similar in their material details of furnishing and scene-framing to the later "curtaine lecture" illustration and to the woodcut of Dr. Stokes in Thomas Bilney's bed.

It seems to me that the artist charged with illustrating Thomas Bilney's final period of imprisonment was deliberately playing with the conventions of the curtain lecture. Thus, even without including a single woman in this woodcut, the artist has used women—or the history of their representation in art—to bolster Foxe's Protestant agenda. John Foxe and the printer John Day gave prominent attention to female martyrs, placing them in key positions within the text and featuring them in a remarkable number of its illustrations. Given the historical realities of women's position within English culture, even during the lengthy reign of a powerful queen, these two men lent much more space and attention to women's history than one might expect. Their reasons were pragmatic, and in each instance, they made effective use of age, status, appearance, behavior, words, gestures—all strategically mobilized in relation to normative codes of femininity—in order to heighten, add texture, or lend poignancy to the collective portrait of English Protestantism that is *The Acts and Monuments of these latter and perilous days.*

THE OHIO STATE UNIVERSITY, LIMA CAMPUS

Manuscript Studies

Humphrey Coningsby and the Personal Anthologizing of Verse in Elizabethan England

ARTHUR F. MAROTTI

THE REVIVED FIELD OF EARLY MODERN MANUSCRIPT STUDIES HAS CHANGED some of our notions of literary history. The account of early modern English literature that is largely based on the products of print culture and on the modern emphasis on the individual (known) author, especially the canonical one, now seems inadequate to define the larger body of writing whose contours are, perhaps, best discerned through the scattered and various manuscript remains from the period, documents in which the elite and the popular, the serious and the trivial, the named and the anonymous are co-mingled. We now know that some of the assumptions of a developed print culture and of the literary institution defined within its context—for example, authorial autonomy, the separateness of "literature" from the larger field of writing, and the historically transcendent character of the literary—do not adequately represent the actual status and functions of literary texts in the transitional period during which Western culture experienced the last great media shift (simultaneously from oral to written culture, and from manuscript to print). Our current media shift from print culture to electronic communication has certainly encouraged us to try to understand such large-scale changes, as the forward-thinking Marshall McLuhan urged almost a half-century ago, to analyze the ways that the means

---

This paper was first presented at the 2004 MLA convention, Philadelphia, PA, at a panel entitled "English Renaissance Manuscript Miscellanies," Steven W. May, Georgetown College, presiding.

of communication defined the communicative message, its status as intellectual property, and the relationships of the communicators.[1]

In my study, *Manuscript, Print and the English Renaissance Lyric*,[2] I examined over 300 manuscripts—collections of loose papers and quires as well as commonplace book miscellanies and poetical anthologies. I did so in order to develop some sense of the socioliterary functioning of lyric poetry in the manuscript system that persisted in England at least two centuries into the post-Gutenberg era, discovering that in this system literary works looked different than in the context of print culture: they were textually more malleable than they were in a developed print culture, more open to revision, reader-emendation, competitive answers, parodies, and paraphrase or imitation. Authorship, or the "author-function," was, consequently, less sharply defined and more dispersed. Anonymity was common, but also texts were often misattributed to famous individuals, such as Sir Walter Ralegh and John Donne, whose names had high cultural visibility. Particular poems appeared more closely tied to specific occasions and ephemeral circumstances, signaling their place in particular social relationships and their usefulness as well in later, changed contexts. At the same time, the increasing number of publications of lyric verse in poetic anthologies and single-author editions caused the manuscript system to register the increase in the sociocultural prestige of authors and the historical durability of their texts, both consequences of print culture: the fact that lyrics by respected and well-known poets were treated as valued commodities in printed anthologies, and single-author editions encouraged individual collectors to be more self-conscious about their anthologizing activities and to treat the texts they preserved in their manuscripts with a greater sense of their being part of a larger literary culture.

Although many manuscript collections of poetry were assembled by groups of individuals in such environments as the University, the Court, the Inns of Court, and aristocratic households, the majority of these surviving documents were the product of a single individual's efforts: one person keeping a commonplace book for the purpose of either creating a personal poetic anthology or inserting a small or large selection of poems in a miscellaneous collection of texts that might include such other material as personal journals, medical receipts, household accounts, and prose passages from their reading. For example, a large and rich sixteenth-century collection of verse was assembled by John Harington of Stepney and his

---

[1] Especially valuable are *The Gutenberg Galaxy: The Making of Typographic Man* (Toronto: Univ. of Toronto Press, 1962) and *Understanding Media: The Extensions of Man* (New York: McGraw Hill, 1965).

[2] Ithaca and London: Cornell Univ. Press, 1995.

son John Harington of Kelston.[3] Other anthologies were compiled by John Finet, both as student at Cambridge and as member of the Elizabethan royal court (Bodleian MS Rawlinson Poetical 85);[4] by John Lilliat, an Elizabethan cathedral musician (Bodleian MS Rawlinson Poetical 148);[5] by Henry Stanford, a tutor in aristocratic households (Cambridge University Library MS Dd.5.75);[6] by Peter Calfe, a London apothecary, and his son of the same name (British Library MS Harley 6917–18); by Constance Aston Fowler, a Catholic gentlewoman at the heart of a familial social network (Huntington Library MS HM 904);[7] and by Nicholas Burghe, who was a royalist captain in the Civil Wars (Bodleian MS Ashmole 38).

I am currently researching and writing a study of practices of personal anthologizing of poetry in manuscript in sixteenth- and seventeenth-century England. The collectors on whom I focus come from a variety of backgrounds and often personalized their anthologies by including poems of their own and pieces written by close friends and associates. Such personal anthologizing of poetry in manuscript developed over time in the early modern period, sometimes bearing the marks of an individual compiler's movement from one environment to another—for example, from the University to the Court or to the Inns of Court and London. Anthologizing practices also registered changes in literary tastes and fashions: this is especially true in the case of such Elizabethan anthologies as those of the Haringtons and of Finet. The seventeenth-century collections also demonstrate a consciousness of literary history and tradition: the older verse of Ralegh, Donne, and Jonson is mixed with the work of younger writers such as Carew, Strode, Corbett, and Herrick. Anthologizing practices in print culture, from the time of Tottel's *Miscellany* (1557) and the other Elizabethan collections through the mid-seventeenth-century witty compilations of verse and of verse fragments, also had an impact on the behavior of individual collectors.

---

[3] See Ruth Hughey, ed., *The Arundel Harington Manuscript of Tudor Poetry*, 2 vols. (Columbus: Ohio State Univ. Press, 1960).

[4] See Laurence Cummings, ed., "John Finet's Miscellany" (Diss., Washington University, 1960).

[5] See Edward Doughtie, ed., *Liber Lilliati: Elizabethan Verse and Song (Bodleian MS Rawlinson Poetry 148)* (Newark, DE: Univ. of Delaware Press and London and Toronto: Associated Univ. Presses, 1985).

[6] See Steven W. May, ed., *Henry Stanford's Anthology: An Edition of Cambridge University Manuscript Dd.5.75* (New York and London: Garland Publishing, 1988).

[7] See Deborah Aldrich-Larson, ed., *The Verse Miscellany of Constance Aston Fowler: A Diplomatic Edition* MRTS 210 (Tempe: Renaissance English Text Society and Arizona Center for Medieval and Renaissance Studies, 2000). Another example is that of Nicholas Oldisworth's miscellany, edited by John Gouws (Tempe: RETS and ACMRS, forthcoming).

In this essay, I would like to discuss a late-Elizabethan manuscript compilation, British Library MS Harley 7392 (2), a poetry anthology that seems to have
been assembled for the most part by Humphrey Coningsby, a man who moved
from Oxford to London and whose family was connected with the Sidneys.[8] On
the recto side of the first folio, in the center of the page is a Latin motto "Cavendo
tutus" ("safe by being wary") with the name "Coningsbye" written beneath it.[9]
The other writing on the page is associated with the antiquary St. Loe Kniveton,
whose name is transcribed twice after a Latin quatrain and a Latin distich, and
the name "Ed. Evans" is written beneath a one-line Latin saying ("Si potest as-
siduo falle labore diem").[10] After the first item, with the Kniveton subscription,
there is what looks like an English translation subscribed "H C." On the verso of
the first folio of the poetry collection Coningsby's initials or abbreviated name
appear three times.[11] There is an interesting combination of hands on fol. 61r in
space available below the transcription of one of the poems. What follows is a
Latin distich transcribed in an italic hand that looks similar to that of Coningsby
on the first page of the anthology. Below this is a translation in a secretary hand

---

   [8] L. G. Black, "Studies in Some Related Manuscript Poetic Miscellanies of the 1580s," 2
vols. (Diss., Oxford University, 1971), 1:47–54, and H. R. Woudhuysen, *Sir Philip Sidney and
the Circulation of Manuscripts 1558–1640* (Oxford: Clarendon Press, 1996), 278–86. Woudhuysen (279), who has examined examples of Knyveton's writing in other manuscripts, does
not see his as the main hand(s) in this one—except in the "distinctive italic and secretary
hands . . . [in which] he signed his name three times and wrote three Latin distichs . . . on
what is now the first page of the anthology. . . ." He thinks a hand other than Knyveton's wrote
"Saintlowe Kynuetonne" on fol. 61r. There has been some dispute about the identity of the
compiler/transcriber. Steven May claims "the chief compiler of this manuscript was the antiquarian, St. Loe Knyveton": May, *Henry Stanford's Anthology*, xlv, claims "possibly the secretary hand which appears in the last ten folios of the collection is not his, but the majority of the
entries on ff. 11–68 are, to judge from his signatures on ff. 11 and 61." He says there may have
been "a few additions by the compiler's friends, Robert Allot and Humphrey Coningsby." Peter Beal also states that the manuscript was Kniveton's. Laurence Cummings, who has edited
the closely related manuscript anthology, Bodleian Library MS Rawlinson Poetical 85, also
believes Kniveton to have been the main compiler, as did Bernard Wagner, "New Poems by Sir
Edward Dyer," *RES* 11 (1935): 466n.
   [9] Woudhuysen, *Sidney*, 279, discusses these features and concludes Coningsby is the
main compiler, as well as the scribe of the collection up to fol. 62r. He does perceive Coningsby
using both secretary and italic hands.
   [10] Woudhuysen, *Sidney*, 283, identifies Evans as a student from Shropshire who began
his studies at Christ Church, Oxford in August 1583. Presumably he is related to the "Charles
Evans" whose name is deleted on fol. 61r.
   [11] The saying at the top of the page "Opportunyty/ Importunyty" is subscribed "H.
Conn." The next poem, a couplet, is subscribed "w. hill." The third item, a six-line poem, is
subscribed "H. Con" with two ascending decorative letters that may represent the rest of his
name. This is followed by a Latin distich headed "My nativytye" and subscribed "H C."

that is not the main hand of the collection, subscribed "Saintlowe Knyuetone." This is followed by another translation in an italic hand subscribed "Charles Evans," a name that was later deleted. This activity seems to have taken place (as, perhaps, a game played in a social circle) after the original sequence of poems had been transcribed.[12] Late in the manuscript (fols. 77r–78r) there are several poems subscribed "Robert Allott" (or "R Allott" or "R A"), written in three hands that differ from the dominant hand of the collection.[13]

As H. R. Woudhuysen notes, Humphrey Coningsby, who came from Shropshire, began his studies at Christ Church, Oxford in November 1581, "the same year in which Robert Allott of Driby, Lincolnshire, matriculated at Corpus . . . so that the two men whose hands are most evident in the miscellany were at Oxford at the same time. Allott entered the Inner Temple in November 1584; St Loe Kniveton had entered Gray's Inn in May 1584, and in February of the same year Humphrey Coningsby's cousin, Sidney's traveling companion, Thomas Coningsby, entered the same Inn as an honorary member."[14] Woudhuysen states, then, that "[i]t is reasonable to suppose . . . that Harley circulated first at Oxford in the early 1580s between Humphrey Coningsby and Robert Allott and later in the decade at London around the Inns of Court where Allott, St Loe Kniveton and Humphrey Coningsby's kinsman Thomas all were."[15] The evidence Woudhuysen offers of Coningsby's ties to the Sidney family and circle accounts for the significant presence of lyrics by both Sidney and Dyer in the anthology.[16]

---

[12] Black, "Studies," 2:367, points out that an English translation of the poem was printed in Abraham Fraunce's *Arcadian Rhetoric*, E1v—one that differs from the versions that appear in Harley 7392, Rawlinson Poetical 85 (fol. 83v), Marsh's Library, Dublin MS Z3.5.31 (fol. 20), and Folger MS V.a.276 (fol. 3v). He also notes the Latin poem appears with French translations in Tabourot's *Les Bigarrures* (Paris, 1583), R3.

[13] These include: "Unfriendly leavest thou me in such a sort" (fol. 77r); "Fancies they are that trouble my mind" (fol. 77v); "O Mildred if thou dost returne" (fol. 77v); "Ad Apollinem et musas ode" ("Thou sacred monarche of that holy traine" [fol. 78r]): and, in the same hand, "In everything my love & love agre" (fol. 77v). Steven W. May and William A. Ringler, Jr., eds., *Elizabethan Poetry: A Bibliography and First-line Index of English Verse, 1559–1603* (London and New York: Thoemmes Continuum, 2004), EV 17388, state that the third of these is an epistle to Mildred Cecil, Lady Burghley, written by Catherine Killigrew. It also appears in CUL MS Ff.5.14, fol. 107. Woudhuysen, *Sidney*, 279, claims Coningsby's transcriptions run up to fol. 62r of the manuscript and that other scribes complete the collection. I disagree, since the hand seems to continue beyond this point, except for the poem "The state of france" and the pieces signed by Allott.

[14] Woudhuysen, *Sidney*, 282.

[15] Ibid., 282–83.

[16] Ibid., 281–82, connecting Humphrey Coningsby's relative, Thomas Coningsby, with the Sidneys by marriage. He also notes Sidney's old college was Christ Church, Oxford and that Coningsby, "born and buried in Nene Sollers in Shropshire, came from the same part of

I choose this manuscript for discussion for two main reasons. First, as one of the few rich manuscripts of late Elizabethan verse, it is closely related in its contents to such other important contemporary manuscript anthologies as John Finet's Bodleian MS Rawlinson Poetical 85, Henry Stanford's Cambridge University Library MS Dd.5.75, an anonymous Yorkshire compiler's Marsh's Library Dublin MS Z3.5.21, and Ann Cornwallis's Folger Shakespeare Library MS V.a.89: for example, the Harley manuscript shares forty-five poems with Finet's collection, including eight poems by Sir Edward Dyer, four by Sir Philip Sidney, and five by the Earl of Oxford.[17] Like them, it reflects changing tastes for poetry occurring in the late Elizabethan period, particularly in response to the work of Sir Philip Sidney.[18] Second, it contains a large number of unique manuscript copies of poems—some attributable to familiar authors, most anonymous and apt to remain so. I emphasize the second of these topics, partly because I wish to broaden our sense of the field of writing and partly because the works that have remained in the shadows ought to be allowed to modify our conception of literary history.

Coningsby's anthology is the second part of a three-part vellum-bound manuscript, a section using different paper stock from the other two parts: when bound the pages were trimmed and some portions of text consequently lost.[19] Single or double ruling of the left margin is used on fols. 12r–61v, along with two sets of double lines framing a majuscule "FINIS" at the end of almost all of the poems on these folia (though the distinctive "FINIS" follows poems up through fol. 75r). The first part of Harley 7392 contains a text of Morris's "Wasps," a collection of epigrammatic poems. The third part contains Italian burlesque poems.[20] The verse anthology in the central section of the manuscript (fols. 11r–78r) has a collection of poems numbered 1 through 127—but, since poem 5 is the third stanza of a poem transcribed in full as poem 13, poem 18 is actually

---

the country as Arthur Ottley, who may have compiled the Ottley Manuscript: neither lived far from Ludlow, Sir Henry Sidney's residence as Lord President of the Marches" (284).

[17] See the chart in Randall Anderson, "'The Merit of a Manuscript Poem': The Case for Bodleian MS Rawlinson Poet. 85," in Arthur F. Marotti and Michael Bristol, eds., *Print, Manuscript and Performance: The Changing Relations of the Media in Early Modern England* (Columbus: Ohio State Univ. Press, 2000), 127–71, here 154–59. Cummings, "Miscellany," 60, however, counts forty-seven poems the two manuscripts share.

[18] It also has contents that overlap with such other surviving collections from the period as Cambridge University Library MS Dd.5.75, Marsh's Library Dublin MS Z3.5.21, and British Library MS Harley 6910.

[19] The manuscript has been rebound. Most of the sheets in the central section are separate, but some bifolia are present: fols. 21–22, 29–30, 36–37, 44–45, 52–53, 60–61, 68–69, 76–77. On fol. 31, the right edge of the page reveals the loss of some of the transcribed text and some folios lose part of their transcription at the bottom edge (e.g. fols. 39, 41, 42, 43, and 65).

[20] Cummings, "Miscellany," 60.

a continuation of poem 75, and poem 60 consists of three couplet-epigrams, the total remains 127;[21] there are, in addition, some thirty-one unnumbered pieces interspersed through the collection, including six at the end, following poem 127: the total number of pieces is 156, an approximate number, since it is not clear how one should count some of the items that are made up of separate parts— Latin poems with their translations, for example.[22]

The main hand in the collection is a secretary one, but there are at least two other hands that appear. The first, an italic one, distinguished by some features that separate it from the main hand,[23] often appears in poems that look like they were entered into the manuscript to fill in available spaces at the bottoms of pages—in some cases for poems that were not given numbers. This hand subscribes some of the poems with the initials "H C," with the left ascending line of the "H" topped by a leftward swooping flourish that is found in what looks like Humphrey Coningsby's abbreviated signature on the first page of the collection.

---

[21] At the end of poem 75 (fol. 47r), the last line is the first line of 18 and there is a reference to the (original number of) the folio on which the poem's continuation is found.

[22] I do not count the first four lines of Sir Arthur Gorges's poem, "Would I were changed into that golden showre," which is transcribed, then crossed out on fol. 27v, before the poem is copied in full on fol. 36v, but I do count the final couplet of Sir Walter Ralegh's "Farewell false love," which appears alone on fol. 28r as an excerpt that can stand on its own. There are also some pieces, such as the three couplets on fol. 72r, that are scribbled through and illegible. Woudhuysen, *Sidney*, 283, analyzes the structure of the poetical collection in this manuscript and draws some conclusions about its change of venue from the University to London and the Inns of Court:

> ... I think its pages were filled more or less sequentially. There are four groups of courtier verse. The first is at the beginning of the manuscript from fos. 12r–39r; there is then a sequence of poems which cannot be attached to any known authors and may indeed be unique to this manuscript; the following leaves (fos. 48v–53r) contain further courtly poems. Around this point the miscellany may have come to London, for the long poem attributed internally to Stephen Vallenger on fos. 54v–58v is followed immediately by the poem relating to the Duttons and the gentlemen from the Inns of Court. This London period is also marked by the appearance of St Loe Kniveton in the manuscript on fo. 61r and the popular political poem of 1585, 'The French Primero' on fo. 62v. Written in the same distinctive black ink fos. 53v–61r seem to belong together; fos. 61v–62r are written in a much paler ink. The ruled frames to the pages change on fo. 62v and the third group of courtier poems begins on fo. 63r and lasts with some interruptions ... until fo. 71r, which has Sidney's Attributed Poems 12. There is a final group of poems associated with the court on fos. 74r–76v at the very end of the manuscript before Allott copied some of his verses into it.

[23] These include an ascending swoop over the letter "e," ligatured "sh," "st," "ct" and, sometimes, "ch," a larger minuscule "v," a markedly more leftward leaning ascender for the minuscule "d." I differ with Woudhuysen about this hand, which he does not distinguish from the main hand of the collection.

Woudhuysen thinks that the same hand that transcribed Coningsby's initials and abbreviated signature on the first folio of the anthology is "identical with the hand in which almost all the poems in the miscellany have been copied."[24] This may be so, and the main hand may simply be another hand that Coningsby used—a not unusual phenomenon in a period in which professional and amateur scribes could use more than one style. There are other hands, late in the collection, representing, perhaps, additions to the main collection some time after its completion.

We can, with varying degrees of confidence, ascribe many of the poems in this anthology to such known authors as Sir Philip Sidney ("SY.," "Syd.," "Sr. P. Syd.," "Sr. Ph. Syd."), Sir Edward Dyer ("Dyer," "Dier," DY") Sir Walter Ralegh ("Raley," "RA"), and the Earl of Oxford ("therle of Ox.," "Lo. Ox.," "l. Ox."); there are also poems subscribed "A[nn] Vavasoare" (62v) and "Robert Allott" (or "R. Allott" or "R A"); for other individuals we only have initials or abbreviated names, some of whom we can identify ("H. C." [Humphrey Coningsby], "N. S.," "I. I.," "I. F." [John Finet?] "R. P.," "Ro. Poo.," "AN.," "E. E.," "H. W.,"[25] "EN," "R W," "h. o.," "Ty. S." or "TY. SO.," "I. E.," "I. Ed." or "Ioh. Ed.," "EL," "Regina," or "ELY." [Queen Elizabeth)], "L. Coun. de H. & L." and someone identified only by a last name, "Russell").[26] There are four poems by Sir Arthur Gorges (three misascribed to other authors),[27] Anthony Munday, Barnaby Rich, Thomas Churchyard, Humphrey Gifford, Thomas Whythorne, Thomas Campion, Nicholas Breton, George Peele, John Thorn,[28] and Catherine Killigrew.

With four poems from the *Old Arcadia* (50, 104, 112, and U22 [see Appendix I]), five from *Certaine Sonnets* (15, 41, 51, 52, and 116), plus four other poems probably by him (48, 49, 78 and 105), Sir Philip Sidney is a strong presence in this manuscript—all of the pieces probably transcribed before they appeared in print.[29] Sidney's close friend, Sir Edward Dyer, is represented by six pieces (1, 2, 8, 38, 39, and 83). Sir Walter Ralegh has four poems (44, 45, 46, 47, and 103)

---

[24] Woudhuysen, *Sidney,* 279.

[25] This may be Henry Wigley, whom May and Ringler, EV 15989, mention as owner of a book on the flyleaf of which is written "No plague to pride, no woe to want, no grief to luckless love."

[26] Poem 84.

[27] For example, poem 45 ("Would I were changed into that goulden Shower" [fol. 36v]) is attributed to "RA" (Ralegh), poem 100 ("The gentle season of the yeare" [fols. 63v–64r]) to Sidney, and poem 106 ("her fface, her Tonge, Her Wytte" [fol. 66v]) to "Raley." Poem 21 ("But this and then nor more is my laste and all" [fol. 27v–28r]) is properly ascribed ("FYNIS. GOR.").

[28] Poem 120.

[29] See Woudhuysen, *Sidney,* 278, who also notes the presence of one poem possibly by Sidney, "The darte, the beames, the stringe so stronge I prove," and four poems which have been attributed to him.

and the Earl of Oxford seven (3, 34, 40, 82, 85, 117, and 126). This verse reveals the interest of late-Elizabethan collectors (as well as of publishers) in the poetry of "courtly makers." The largest number of poems in Coningsby's anthology found also in a contemporary printed volume is six (for *The Paradise of Dainty Devices* [1576]), but there are over twenty other poems that appear in such works as George Whetstone's *An Heptameron of Civil Discourses* (1582), Thomas Watson's *Hekatompathia* (1582), *A Pleasaunte Laborinth Called Churchyards Chance* (1580), William Byrd's *Psalms, Songs and Sonnets* (1588), *Brittons Bower of Devices* (1591), *The Phoenix Nest* (1593), *England's Helicon* (1600), Barclay's *New Book of Tablature* (1596), *The Arbor of Amorous Devices* (1597), and *A Poetical Rapsody* (1602).[30] Comparison of the texts of Harley 7392 with those of the printed versions, however, leads to the conclusion that the compiler neither copied from printed editions (as did the maker of BL MS Harley 6910),[31] nor did he use manuscripts close to those on which the printed texts were based.

Of the 156 poems in the collection, fifty-five seem to be unique copies (see Appendix II).[32] This is a high percentage, but one that is not so unusual in collections of this kind: for example, one-third of the miscellaneous poems in Ann Cornwallis's miscellany (Folger MS V.a.89), nine of twenty-seven poems, are apparently unique copies,[33] and a seventeenth-century Christ Church, Oxford collection I have studied (Folger MS V.a.345) has some ninety-one of its 515 poems in apparently unique copies—although, it must be noted, there is no reliable data base of first-lines for poetry after 1603 comparable to the indexes produced by William Ringler and Steven May.[34] Many of the unique poems in the Harley manuscript are short couplets or quatrains apparently placed at the bottom of

---

[30] This information is drawn from Margaret Crum, ed., *First-Line Index of English Poetry 1500–1800 in Manuscripts of the Bodleian Library Oxford*, 2 vols. (New York: Modern Language Association, 1969).

[31] See Katherine K. Gottschalk, "Discoveries Concerning British Library MS Harley 6910," *Modern Philology* 77 (1979–80): 121–31.

[32] I am grateful to Steven May, who checked the first lines of some of the poems in Harley 7392 against the database of Elizabethan poetry that was subsequently published as *Elizabethan Poetry: A Bibliography and First-line Index of English Verse, 1559–1603*.

[33] See my essay, "The Cultural and Textual Importance of Folger MS V.a.89," in *Manuscripts and their Makers in the English Renaissance*, ed. Peter Beal and Grace Ioppolo, *English Manuscript Studies 1100–1700* 11 (London: The British Library, 2002), 70–92.

[34] In addition to Ringler's and May's index of Elizabethan verse, see William A. Ringler, Jr., *Bibliography and Index of English Verse in Manuscript, 1501–1558*, completed by Michael Rudick and Susan J. Ringler (London and New York: Mansell, 1992) and William A. Ringler, Jr., *Bibliography and Index of English Verse Printed 1476–1558* (London and New York: Mansell, 1988). For 1603 and later, it is useful to consult Margaret Crum's *First-Line Index of Manuscript Poetry in the Bodleian Library* as well as the handwritten first-line index of manuscript poetry in the British Library, Hilton Kelliher's typed index of manuscript poetry in British

pages in order to take advantage of available space in the manuscript, either to insert a poem in the numbered sequence that can fit the space available or, in the case of some unnumbered pieces interspersed in the series of 127 numbered poems, to use the space left after the initial transcription of verse.[35] The following poems are examples of this practice:

> Thine only owne while lyfe Doth last,
>   Till Breath be gon, & Sence is past.
>   (fol. 33v; poem 35)

> The silly Bird, the Bee, the Horse,
>   The oxe, that tilles and delves,
> They build, bringe hony, beare & draw,
>   ffor others, not themselves.
>   (fol. 38r; poem 49)

> Pushe Lady pushe what push may that be?
>   The best that may be yow may cheapen [sic] of me.
> Yf that be not as good as ever was bought,
>   Try them of free Cost, returne them for nought.
> A Rushe for those pushes that push but in Jeste,
>   One pushe to the purpose, is worth all the reste.
>   (fol. 60r; unnumbered poem)

> I Love a Lyfe to Lyve in Love
>   You so I Have Decreede

Library manuscripts purchased after the handwritten index was prepared, and the first-line indices of poetry found in the Folger Shakespeare Library and other archives.

[35] It is interesting, nevertheless, to note that there is still three-quarters of a page of space on fol. 29r, following the transcription of poem 24; fol. 50r has one-quarter of a page of space following the transcription of poem 80, ascribed to Queen Elizabeth ("Regina"), "Now leave & let me rest"; fol. 53v has about one-quarter of a page of space following the transcription of poem 85, the Earl of Oxford's "Wingde with Desire I seke to mount on hy"; fol. 62v has one-third of a page of space following the transcription of poem 98 ("The state of france"); fol. 64r has one-third of a page of space following the transcription of poem 100, Gorges's "The gentle season of the year"; fol. 64v has a little less than one-quarter of a page of space after poem 101 ("I wyll forget that ere I saw thy Face").

> I Cannot Lyve except I Love,
>   Is Lyfe indeed.
>   (fol. 62r; unnumbered poem)

> The Parson of Stanlake, hath stopt up my Watergap;
> With two stones & a Stake, Helpe Lordes for Gods sake.
>   (fol. 65v; unnumbered poem)

> Yf Busse bee Fetor, and Bess bee fetyt,
> I will not Buss Bess if I Remember itt.
>   (fol. 71r; unnumbered poem)

> Hic Jacet Andreas
> Qui Lapidavit eas.

> Here Lies old Andrew Hee,
> That stoned many a Shee.
>   (fol. 72r; unnumbered poem)

> In everything my love and love agre
> Save that love gentle is but cruell she
>   (fol. 77r; unnumbered poem)[36]

Sixteen of the unique poems in this manuscript are subscribed "H C," nine of them with the initials partly or wholly deleted. Woudhuysen claimed Coningsby "tried to subscribe authorship where he could, but otherwise he signed poems with his own initials or with 'H. Con.' It is unlikely he meant this to imply he was their author; rather, he was identifying himself as their collector or transcriber."[37]

---

[36] In my transcriptions I modernize u/v and i/j (except, in the latter case, for initials), change the thorn ("y") to "th," and expand contractions. I use angle-brackets to indicate deleted material and regular brackets to indicate illegible material.

[37] Woudhuysen, *Sidney,* 280. In a note Woudhuysen states: "The order in which these re-attributions was performed is made clear on, for example, fos. 33r, 33v, and 34r, where the initials H C in brown ink have been deleted by the black ink. The first reattribution in this black ink is on fo. 25r and, following that, many of Coningsby's ascriptions to himself have been deleted, some reassigned, and new ones given to others. The sole exception to his process seems to be the ascription to Dyer of 'The man whose thought*es* against him do co*n*spire', which may be in a rather later hand." Cummings, "Miscellany," 723, however claims that the "H. C." and "H. Con." subscriptions were used by St. Loe Kniveton and "the Coningsby [attributions] are well nigh worthless; Knyveton himself has gone back though his MS removing these initials

Although, certainly, some of the poems subscribed "H C" are not Coningsby's, there are others that probably are. Underneath a number of the poems in the collection the initials "H C" appear, including some where the initials are deleted. Although after one poem in the collection there is a subscription "GEVEN H E" (probably indicating the source of the copy that was transcribed), the subscription "H C" may indicate authorship, the act of scribal recording of a particular item, or the source of a poem that was copied. I believe it was probably used for the first two purposes. There is an example of this subscription at the foot of a folio in a "filler" poem that looks like it is not just a piece collected for the anthology, but a message to a female acquaintance. This posy at the bottom of fol. 60v is accompanied by a drawing of two hearts pierced by a single arrow:

> Behold the force of Hotte Desier,
> Two Hartes in one, that wold be Nyer.

Though the initials are deleted, there are two poems not simply subscribed "H C,"[38] but also identified by their addressee. Poem 86, which is headed "Being asked how he lyked, he wrote," is subscribed "H. C. to Q. R.":[39]

> To lodge Delight on Fancies single sight
>   Or builde my Hope on Bewties synking Sandes
> Were to submit my Mynde to fortunes spight
>   And snare my selfe with Cares in Cupids bandes,
> And what althoghe dame Bewty bid do soe?
>   Vertue forbids, & bids such baytes forgoe.

---

after many of the poems, sometimes offering no replacement." This would make Kniveton the main compiler.

   [38] There are eighteen poems in this manuscript associated with these initials or with "H. Con." Poem 80 ("Now leave & let me rest" [fols. 49v–50r]) has the initials deleted and "Regina" as a correction—Leicester Bradner, ed., *The Poems of Queen Elizabeth I* (Providence, Rhode Island: Brown Univ. Press, 1964), 7, has this among the "doubtful" poems of Queen Elizabeth, while Leah S. Marcus, Janel Mueller, and Mary Beth Rose, eds., *Elizabeth I: Collected Works* (Chicago and London: Univ. of Chicago Press, 2000), 305, accept it as a poem by her. It also appears (unattributed) in CUL MS Dd.5.75, fol. 42v and the Arundel Harington MS, 242 in Ruth Hughey's edition. The unnumbered poem beginning "When first of all Dame Nature thought" (fol. 11v) also appears in Marsh's Library MS Z.3.5.21 with the author identified as "H. C." Poem 30 ("Myne eye Bewrayes" [fol 33r]), which has the subscription "H C" deleted, also appears in Bod. MS Rawl. Poet. 85, fol. 116v.

   [39] It appears, however, that the "Q R" is written over the deletion marks, perhaps representing the reassignment of the poem from Coningsby to someone else.

Let Venus vawnt of all hyr gallant Gloze;
    Hir fairest face, hyr Grace and semely Shape.
Yea hyr on whom Dan Paris did repose
    Hys Hope and Hart, & made at laste his Rape,
Helen of hew was fayre I must confesse,
    A hoorishe Hart she bare yet naytheles.

Wheron but vayne can Venus make her Vaunt?
    Alluringe lookes ar all but triflying toyes.
Such symple Showes no wyse mans Hart can daunt
    Bables for Fooles & Mayegames made for Boyes.
Not every one that lyst to loke dothe Lyke,
    Some smile to see that bredes theyr most mislyke.

Forme [sic] Nulla Fides.
<H. C. to Q. R.>
(fol. 53v)

This poem, like the one following, "Care is the Gate that openeth to my Hart" (fol. 54r) (subscribed "H. C. to C. G.,"[40] then deleted) is transcribed in an italic hand. Both poems are crossed out.[41] Why the poems and the ascriptions were scored through is unknown, but it is unlikely that Coningsby would have put his initials to two poems whose addressees are also identified by initials simply to note his role as collector.

Of the other unique poems subscribed with Coningsby's initials, only one escapes deletion:

What thinge can be more fond,
    Then lyve as Cupids thrall?
To serve, to sue, to live, to dy,
    At every becke and call?
And whoso Doth not these,
    And more, when Love gives charge,
Must shrowd himself from venus sight,
    Or lyve els where at large.
(fol. 36r)

---

[40] The additional majuscule letters "RDTFOT" follow.

[41] I discuss both these poems in *Manuscript, Print, and the English Renaissance Lyric*, 179–81. One additional poem, with the "H C" subscription deleted is "Babes, that be borne adventure strypes for play" (61r).

Written in old-fashioned poulter's measure (with each six- or seven-foot line split in two), this piece is a throw-back to a mid-Elizabethan poetic idiom. So too are two other unique poems from which the "H C" subscription has been deleted: poem 42 ("Worke minde into the Skyes, thy Body taketh stand" [fols. 35v–36r]) and poem 74 ("Yf Care inforce Complaint, why do I hide my woe" [fols. 46v–47r])—only the long lines of poulter's measure are retained in them.

By contrast, there is a sonnet subscribed "H C" (with the initials deleted) that obviously responds to a newer poetic fashion:

> Who takes in hand to till the barren soyle
>   Or lokes for grapes to grow on bushy thorn,
> Or who doth seke in Sand for sweetest oyle,
>   At length his labor turnes but to a scorn.
> Even so who layes goodwill in thanckles lap,
>   And sues for service, wher ther is no gayne,
> And leapes the hedge, & never to gap,
>   In troth Desarves his labor for his payne.
> And sith such slight reward to him is Due
>   That's redy for to runne at every whistle,
> The proverb seemes in him for to be true,
>   He blessing wants, that bowes to every thistle.
> Wherfore the man deserves but <drosse> losse,
>   That leaves fine gould, and playes with drosse.
>   (fol. 41v)

On fol. 34r of the manuscript, there are two poems associated with "H C"—the first (poem 36) a unique copy of a piece ("When shall I joy, whose Joyes are over-throwne") (with the initials deleted), the second ("Lo how for whom, & whose I lyve"), for which an alternate first line is offered ("Lo whose I am, Judge whose I lyve"), a poem that also appears in Bodleian MS Rawlinson Poetical 172 (fol. 7). Since at least one poem associated with Coningsby ("When first of all Dame Na-ture" [fol. 11v], subscribed "H. Con") appears in three other manuscripts,[42] it is possible that Coningsby was the author of this second piece and that it was copied by another compiler.

There are six poems in the collection that are associated with a writer whose name is abbreviated or given in initials, "I. E.," "I. Ed.," and "Ioh. Ed.": poems 101, 102, 108, 121, 125, and the unnumbered translation beginning "Leonell of

---

[42] Ringler and May, EV 29354, list Marsh's Lib. MS Z3.5.21, fol. 1v; BL MS Harl. 6910, fol. 158r; and Bod. MS Rawl. Poet. 85, fol. 105v.

Eyes the Lefte, had given for bodily light" (fol. 72r). Of these, only one appears elsewhere.[43] Three are translations of Latin poems.[44] This activity of translating Latin verse is found throughout the anthology, as is the use of a Latin thematic heading for particular poems. For example, there is a Latin distich (Pentadius, Epigram 10) that is followed by two different translations, in two different hands, one poem subscribed with Knyveton's name, the second with the name of another, later deleted:

> Pastor, arator, eques, pavi, colui, superavi,
> Capras, rus, hostes, fronde, ligone, manu.

I sheppard	I plowman	I horseman light
Have fedd	have plowed	have put to flight
My goates	my groundes	my foes in field
With bowes	with plowes	with speare & shield
	Saintlowe Knyvetone	

A hearde	a swaine	a noble knight
I fed	I tild	I did subdue
My goates	my growndes	my foes by fighte
With bowes	with plowes	these hands them slue.
	<Charles Evans>	
	(fol. 61r)	

Woudhuysen points out that the Latin distich was usually published in the appendices of sixteenth-century editions of Virgil.[45] What this kind of translation activity suggests is the academic practice of composing English versions of Latin literary texts as well as the competitive sport of composing poetry on set themes. These pieces probably belong to the university environment, and Coningsby while at Oxford was likely to have engaged in poetic exchange with some of his fellow students, as did John Finet at Cambridge.[46]

---

[43] Poem 101, "I wyll forget that ere I saw thy Face" (fols. 64v–65r), was printed in *Brittons Bowre of Delights* (1591), F2.

[44] "Leonell of Eyes the Lefte, had given for bodily Light," and poems 121 ("Pallas, Juno, Venus on bushy Ida mounte" [fol. 72r]) and 125[.2] ("In face the fairest Goddes Lyke" [fol. 73v]).

[45] Woudhuysen, *Sidney,* 285.

[46] See the discussion of Finet's poetic exchanges with James Reshoulde and George Mills in Cummings, "Miscellany," 33–39.

Of the other poems unique to Harley 7392 there are many that are skill-fully done, examples of mid-to-late Elizabethan styles, mainly of love complaint. Some interesting pieces include: three poems in rime royal ("The rufull state, the straunge and wretched lyfe"[fol. 40v]; "Luld by Conceipte, when Fancy clozde myne Eyes" [fol. 61v], with the header "Somnium Affectionale"; and "When yonger yeres could not my mind acquaint" [fols. 74v–75r], a bawdy poem spoken by a virgin who has just discovered sexual pleasure);[47] one in hexameter ("O that I knew, or that I could forget" [fol. 41r]), three in poulter's measure ("Desire hath no rest" [fol. 43v]; "My hope doth waite for Hap" [fol. 44r], subscribed "AN"; "Oh sorow cease Good Love Begyn" [fol. 69r]), a combined hexameter-trimeter piece ("Yf that the inward Grief, which festereth in my Hart" [fols. 47v–48r]), and one sonnet subscribed "EN":

> Yf painfull nature bent with redy will,
>> Should seke to shape in finest sort & fframe,
> A comly creature by her cunninge skill,
>> Bedeckt with giftes of due deserving fame;
> Indude with Vertues most abundantly,
>> Like to my ffram yet could she never bee.
> Psiches the fairest wight that ever wend
>> In Earthly mould, & bravest in her dayes,
> Would yeld her flag of fame unto my frend,
>> Eke reverently adorne her golden rayes,
> Leave of you Lovers in your vauntinge verse
> Your Ladies halfe usurped praise texpresse
> ffor sure my ffrend doth passe them all so farre
> As doth the Sonne excel the darkest Starre.
>> (fol. 73r)

This sonnet and the rime royal poems reflect the newer fashions of poetry.

In his study of Elizabethan manuscript miscellanies, L. G. Black says that "the poems in MS Harl. 7392 have moved out of the world of the college into

---

[47] Several other poems in the anthology have female speakers, some possibly by female authors. For example, poem 27 ("I live in Blysse yet tast no Joy" [fols. 31v–32r]) is subscribed "L. Coun. de H. & L."; the unnumbered poem that begins "O Mildred, if thou dost return to me thy spouse again" (fol. 77v) has been attributed to Catherine Killigrew (I am grateful to Steven May for this identification. The poem also appears in CUL MS Ff.5.14, fol. 107, subscribed "Theyse verses were written by Mris Kyllygrewe to my Lady Cycyll."); poems 54, "an unworthy beloved, to her approved" ("Until the ffatal Day" [fol. 39v]) and 55 ("We silly Dames, that false Suspect do feare" [fol. 40r]) have female speakers.

that of the court, from student ribaldry and Ovidian imitation to the elaborately mannered graces and protestations of the Petrarchan situation, with its hints of actual liaisons veiled by the standard love conceits. They give the appearance of poems by young men about town with connections at court, imitating courtly makers of the day."[48] This is certainly the impression created by many of the poems subscribed "H C" and by a number of the unique anonymous pieces.

Before I leave off discussing the unique poems in this collection, I want to call attention to a twenty-two-line lyric, "Come Sorrow com Sitte down & morne with mee" (28, fol. 32). This piece shares its first six lines with a poem found both in Henry Stanford's anthology and in a printed songbook, Thomas Morley's *First Book of Ayres* (1600).[49] But, because the last sixteen of the twenty-two lines in the Harley text are not found in either of the other versions, the piece is, in effect, a different poem:

> Come Sorrow com Sitte down & morne with mee,
>> Enclyne thy head, upon the Balefull Breste,
> That careless pleasure may, conceave and see,
>> How heavy hartes, repose in little reste.
> Unfould thyne Armes and wring thy wretched handes,
>> To show the state wherin poore Sorrow standes.
> ffor lo the Sequels of my lyfe & love,
>> Ar sorrowes all encombred with myschaunce
> My hopes deceave: my purposes misprove
>> No trust in Time my fortune to advaunce.
> Yet this I joy, although I lyve forlorne
>> My Griefes (thoghe great) wer ever secret borne.
> ffor most my griefes ar of so straunge a sorte
>> As houldes no meane unlesse they be conceald
> Which makes me vow to kepe them from reporte
>> Els with each care his Cause should be reveald,

---

[48] Black, "Studies," 1:353–54.

[49] Steven May points out in his edition of CUL MS Dd.5.75 (277), the Harleian version of this poem "resembles the Dd.5.75 version through the first six lines . . . the remainder of the Harleian poem is so different from Stanford's that collation would be meaningless." The Dd.5.75 version (fol. 26) resembles that printed in Morley's *The First Book of Ayres* (1600) (see Edward Doughtie, ed., *Lyrics from English Airs, 1596–1622* [Cambridge, MA: Harvard Univ. Press, 1970], 143–44). May, *Henry Stanford's Anthology*, 277, suggests that the compiler of the Dd.5.75 probably copied the poem "before the late '80's . . . probably before 1585." May also notes the possible reference to the poem in Shakespeare's *Love's Labour's Lost* 4.3.

I tell to much thoughe chiefest pointes I hyde
And more He knows, which hath like Sorowes tryde.
But sithe my lucke allowes no better happe,
    Wher grief & feare < >all comfort shall expel
Tyll lyef of love, hath felt thextremest power,
And love of lyfe hath seen the latest hower.
                                          Fynys. q^d R. P.[50]

The R. P. to whom this poem is ascribed is probably Robert Pooley, the notorious double or triple agent who worked for Sir Francis Walsingham in the late 1580s and who had been placed by his Catholic friends[51] in Walsingham's house as a servant of Sir Philip Sidney in 1583 when Sidney and his teenage bride were living there. He was imprisoned in the Tower in the aftermath of the Babington Plot, and, later, was with his fellow spy, Christopher Marlowe, when the playwright was murdered in a tavern fight in 1593. Pooley matriculated at Clare College, Cambridge in 1568, served Lord North in 1578, then Sir Christopher Blunt (brother of Lord Mountjoy, and convert to Catholicism), before serving Sidney and Walsingham.[52] Sidney and Sir Edward Dyer, Sidney's close friend, have a prominent place in the anthology. The fourth numbered poem in the collection, following two Dyer poems and one by the Earl of Oxford, "Yf ffortune may enforce, the carefull hurt to try" (fols. 18r–20v), is a long poem subscribed "RO. POO," a version of which was published in that much reprinted Elizabethan poetical miscellany, *The Paradise of Dainty Devices* (1576 ff.). On the title page of the first edition of that miscellany, there is a list of the poets represented in its contents, the last of whom is identified as "M[aster]. Yloop," an unlikely name some scholars (since Malone) have suggested represented "Pooly" spelled

---

[50] May's collation of the first six lines demonstrates considerable differences between the Harley version and that of the Cambridge manuscript:

2 Enclyne] hang down the] thie
3 careless pleasure may conceave and] god & man & all the world may
4 How] our repose in] lie at
5 Unfould] enfold

Mary Hobbs, ed., *The Stoughton Manuscript: A Manuscript Miscellany of Poems by Henry King and his Circle, circa 1636* (Aldershot: Scolar Press, 1990), xviii, points to a possible later example of one poet's adding to a poem written by another, Carew's poem "Come thou gentle Western wind," which, she suggests, "may deliberately have expanded an eighteen-line version by someone else into a 32-line poem."

[51] These were people in the Morgan-Paget faction, who worked on behalf of Mary, Queen of Scots.

[52] Franz Boas, *Christopher Marlowe: A Biographical and Critical Study* (Oxford: Clarendon Press, 1953), 116–19.

backwards.[53] By the late 1580s Pooley was certainly a known, if not notorious, figure in Elizabethan London. Given Coningsby's association with the Sidney family, it is possible that the verse of someone in Sidney's service would fall into his hands. The textual variants in Harley 7392 from the text(s) printed in the successive editions of *The Paradise of Dainty Devices* are considerable enough to lead us to conclude that the Harley version is either a memorial transcription of the poem (after all, the pieces in *The Paradise* were meant to be sung) or a different text copied from a now-lost manuscript source.

There are some important poems for which Harley 7392 provides the best or, in some cases, the only texts. Steven May claims this manuscript has the best text of the much-copied piece by the Earl of Oxford, "When werte thow borne desire."[54] I would argue that it also has the best text of a poem ascribed to Shakespeare, "When that thine Eye has chose the Dame" (fol. 43r–v)—a piece that appears in two other manuscripts and in two editions of *The Passionate Pilgrim*.[55] Sir Edward Dyer's poem, "Before I dy faire Dame of me receave my last adew" (fols. 22v–23r), an extract of which appears in George Puttenham's *The Arte of English Poesie*, would have been lost were it not for this manuscript.[56] Harley's unique copy of the lyric, "Sweet are the thoughtes, wher Hope perswadeth Happe" (fol. 36r), is ascribed to Sir Walter Ralegh ("FINIS RA"). In his edition of Ralegh's verse, Michael Rudick puts the poem in the category of those pieces that are "possible" Ralegh poems: whether or not Ralegh authored it, it is a fine Elizabethan lyric.[57] Finally, two rare poems composed by Sidney, omitted from

---

[53] Hyder Rollins, ed., *The Paradise of Dainty Devices (1576–1606)* (Cambridge, MA: Harvard Univ. Press, 1927), lxv.

[54] Steven W. May, ed., *The Poems of Edward DeVere, Seventeenth Earl of Oxford and of Robert Devereux, Second Earl of Essex*, Studies in Philology, Texts and Studies 87 (Chapel Hill: Univ. of North Carolina Press, 1980), 74, claims this poem is in the hand of St. Loe Knyveton, who also transcribed a bad text of it in BL MS Harley 4286.

[55] See my discussion of this poem in my essay, "The Cultural and Textual Importance of Folger MS V.a.89," 74–79.

[56] See Steven W. May, *The Elizabethan Courtier Poets: The Poems and Their Contexts* (Columbia, MO: Univ. of Missouri Press, 1991), 295–96.

[57] Michael Rudick, ed., *The Poems of Sir Walter Ralegh: An Historical Edition*, MRTS 209 (Tempe: Arizona Center for Medieval and Renaissance Studies in conjunction with Renaissance English Text Society, 1999), 142, refers to Steven W. May, "Companion Poems in the Ralegh Canon," *ELR* 13 (1983): 260–73, which notes that this lyric is either a response to or a source for a stanza by George Whetstone found in *The Rocke of Regarde* (1576), M3. Rudick also notes that a portion of the first line of the poem, "Hope persuadeth Happe," appears in John Bodenham's *Belvedere or the Garden of the Muses* (1600), N5v. In Harley 7392 this poem is followed by three others attributed to "RA": "Would I were changed, into that goulden Shower," "Callinge to minde, mine ey went long abowte," and "ffarewell false Love, thou Oracle of Lyes."

the 1598 folio collection of his works, "Singe neighbours singe, here yow not Say" (fols. 37v–38r) and "Philisedes, the Shepherd good & true" (fols. 48v–49r), appear here, but are found in only one other manuscript.[58]

Harley 7392 is a valuable late-Elizabethan literary document: first, for its unique copies of poems that would otherwise have been lost, especially pieces by poets, such as Sidney, Oxford, Dyer, and Ralegh, who worked wholly in the manuscript system of literary production and reception; second, for its importance as an example of early anthologizing practices; third, for its registering the change from mid- to late-Elizabethan poetic styles, especially in response to the poetry of Sidney, with whose influence through print culture in the 1590s and beyond we are more familiar. From Tottel's *Miscellany* (1557) through *A Poetical Rhapsody* (1602), printed poetical miscellanies from the period present us with one picture of evolving literary tastes. As the Harley manuscript and related manuscript anthologies of the period demonstrate, we get a different sense of poetic production and reception from the manuscript anthologies: even when we are frustrated by trying to discern the marks of ownership, of personal interactions, and of social and institutional contexts in them, we get from such collections a feel for the social embeddedness of literary texts, their writers, and their readers and of a fundamentally different attitude toward textuality itself.

WAYNE STATE UNIVERSITY

---

[58] These poems are found in the National Library of Wales Ottley Papers, fol. 4r–v. Having originally put them in the category of "Attributed Poems" in his edition of Sidney's poetry, William Ringler, "The Text of *The Poems of Sidney* Twenty-five Years After," in *Sir Philip Sidney's Achievements*, ed. M. J. B. Allen, Dominic Baker-Smith, Arthur F. Kinney, and Margaret M. Sullivan (New York: AMS Press, 1990), 137, subsequently placed them in the category of poems probably by Sidney.

Appendix I

Contents of Harley 7392: Numbered Poems and Unnumbered Poems (U)

U1 Who's <   > Fancy fawnes on many (fol. 11r) ("H C," but "S. Knyveton" to right of poem)[59]

U2 Quis sapiens blandis non misceat oscula verbis (fol. 11r) ("S. Knyveton") (Ovid, *Ars Amatoria* 1. 663–66)

U3 "Repentant thoughtes, for overpassed Mayes" (fol. 11v) ("H.C." "RDTFOF" and "w.hill." [?])

U4 "When first of all Dame Nature <   > thought [in margin]" (fol. 11v) ("H. Con.")

U5 "Largus, amans, hilaris, ridens, rubeique, coloris" (fol. 11v) (headed "My nativitye")

U6 "Crine ruber, niger ore, brevis pede, lumine luscus" (fol. 11v) ("Mart.") (Martial, *Epigrams* 12. 54)

1 "He that his mirthe hathe loste" (fol. 12r) ("FYNYS qd Dyer")

2 "Amaryllys was full fayre" (fol. 15r) ("FINIS Dyer")

3 "When wert thow borne Desyre" (fol. 18v) (Oxford)

4 "Yf ffortune may enforce, the carefull hurt to try" (fol. 19r) ("fynis RO[bert]. POO[ly]") ("ball[et]." in margin)

5 "Her wyll be done but I have sworne to love" (fol. 20v) ("fynis Ti. So.") (the third stanza of poem 13)

5 (second poem with this number) "What is desire which doth approve" (fol. 21r) ("Fynis Ewph[ues].")

6 "When I was fayre & yonge then favour graced me" (fol. 21v) ("FINIS. ELY.") (ascribed to Queen Elizabeth I)

7 "an end (quoth shee) for feare of afterclappes" (fol. 21v) (some writing trimmed off at bottom of page)

8 "ffayne would I but I dare not" (fol. 22r) (headed "Ferenda Natura") ("Dy[er]")[60]

9 "Before I dy faire Dame of me receave my last adew" (fol. 22v) ("Fynis DY[er]")

10 "As rare to heare, as seldome to be seene" (fol. 23r) ("fynys DY[er].")

11 "I would it were not as it ys" (fol. 23v) ("FYNIS DY[er]")

12 "I faynt with feare, I blushe for shame" (fol. 24v) ("FYNIS TY.S.")

---

[59] This poem is preceded by a two-line Latin saying: "Praeterit, et non revocabilis [ ] vel hora / labitur hoc subito praeterit illa cito."

[60] May, *Elizabethan Courtier Poets*, 313–15 says this is in the category of "possible" poems "possibly" by Dyer.

13 "Hence burninge sighes, which sparkle from Desire" (fol. 24v) ("FYNIS <TY
   SO>"; "Incerti Autoris" added in different hand)[61]

14 "Prometheus when first from heaven hye" (fol. 25r) ("FYNIS DY[er]")

15 "A Satyre once did runne away for Dreade" (fol. 25r) ("FYNIS SY[dney]")

16 "Yf tales be trew, & Poets tell no Lyes" (fol. 25v) ("FYNIS qd N.S.")

17 "I sayd, and swore that I would never Love" (fol. 26r) ("FYNIS qd. N.S.")[62]

18 "Twixt halfe asleepe and half awake in slumber late I lay" (fol. 26v) (headed
   "Futuris   gaudeo, presentia contemno") ("FYNYS. Qd. N.S.") (continuation of poem 75 [fol. 47r])

19 "Come Charon come wythe speed" (fol. 27r) (headed "Futuris gaudeo, presentia contemno")[63]

20 "The doubte of future ffoes exiles my present Joy" (fol. 27v) ("FINIS.
   EL[izabeth].")

[Between 20 and 21 a deleted four-line stanza of a poem transcribed in full on fol.
   36v "Would I were changed into that golden showre"]

21 "But this and then no more it is my laste and all" (fol. 27v) ("FYNIS.
   GOR[ges].")

22 "I lived once lovde & swam in sweete delighte" (fol. 28r)

U7 "ffalse Love, Desire and Bewty fraile. Adiew" (fol. 28r) [64]

23 "More then most faire full of the living fyre" (fol. 28r) [Spenser][65]

24 "Dy, dy, desire and bidde Delighte adew" (fol. 28v) (headed "Himself being
   sick he pleadeth his desire to dy discovering the indirect procernings [?]
   and passages of Love") (marginal comments to left of poem)[66]

25 "Behould the blaste that blowes" (fol. 30v) ("FINIS R. N.")[67]

---

[61] This poem appears in George Whetstone's *An Heptameron of Civil Discourses* (1582).
See May and Ringler, EV 8770.

[62] Black, "Studies," 2: 411, notes that this poem also appears in Bod. MS Rawl. Poet. 85,
fol. 93 and Rawl. Poet. 172, fol. 7, as well as in Folger MS V.a.89, fol. 18.

[63] This poem also appears, with variants, in *The Arbor of Amorous Devises* (1597), D3.
See May and Ringler, EV 4765.

[64] May and Ringler, EV 6246, point out that this is a part of the poem "Farewell false
love."

[65] This poem is printed in Edmund Spenser's *Amoretti* (1595), A5v. It also appears in
several other manuscripts, including Bod. MS Rawl. Poet. 85, fol. 7r ascribed to "Mr Dier."
See Lawrence Cummungs, "Spenser's *Amoretti VIII*: New Manuscript Versions," *SEL* 4 (1964):
125–35. See May and Ringler, EV 3608.

[66] May and Ringler, EV 5347, cite the following other manuscript copies: Marsh Libr.
Z.3.5.21, fol. 23; BL MSS Harl. 391, fol. 24v and 6910, fol. 165; Bod. MS English Poetry d.3, fols
2, 36.

[67] This poem appears as the fifth poem in *The Paradise of Dainty Devices* (1576), ascribed
in the first edition to "D. S." and in subsequent editions to William Hunnis.

26 "My lyttle sweet Darling my comfort & Joy: Sing lullaby" (fol. 31r)[68]
27 "I lyve in Blysse yet tast no Joy" (fol. 31v) ("finys finis finis L. Coun. de H. & L.")
28 "Come Sorrow com Sitte down & morne with mee" (fol. 32r) ("fynys. qd. R.P.") (Thomas Morley)[69]
29 "My curious Eyes (whose wary sighte)" (fol. 32v)
30 "Myne eye Bewrayes" (fol. 33r) ("FINIS <H C>")[70]
31 "Small rule in Reasons wante" (fol. 32r)[71]
32 "Now ready is the barke that lokes for lucky wynde" (fol. 32v)
33 "In Tyme I may the ffruycte assay" (fol. 33v)
34 "Yf woman could be fayre, & yet not fond" (fol. 33v) ("FINIS R.N.")[72]
35 "Thine only owne while lyfe Doth last" (fol. 33v)
36 "When shall I joy, whose Joyes are overthrowne" (fol. 34r) ("<H C>")
37 "Lo how for whom, & whose I lyve, (or," (fol. 34r) ("<H C>")
38 "The man whose <thas> thoughts against him do conspire" (fol. 34v) ("Fynis. Dyer")
39 "When sturdy stormes of strife be past" (fol. 34v)
40 "Wher as the <arte> Art of Tennis play, & men to gamming fall" (fol. 35r) ("FINIS therle of Ox[ford")
41 "Ringe forth your Belles, let morninge tunes be spred" (fol. 35v) ("FINIS qd Sr. Ph. Syd[ney]")
42 "Worke minde into the Skyes, thy Body taketh stand" (fol. 35v) ("FINIS H.<C.>")
43 "What thinge can be more fond <then live>" (fol. 36v) ("FINIS H. C.")
44 "Sweet ar the thoughtes, wher Hope persuadeth Happe" (fol. 36v) ("FINIS RA[legh]")
45 "Would I wer changed into that goulden Shower" ("FINIS RA[legh]")[73]

---

[68] May and Ringler, EV 15292, cite three musical manuscripts with copies of this song.
[69] May and Ringler, EV 4868, attribute the poem to Morley and cite another copy in CUL MS Dd.5.75, fol. 126.
[70] This also appears in Bod. MS Rawl. Poet. 85, fol. 116v (see Cummings, "John Finet's Miscellany," 2: 792).
[71] May and Ringler, EV 20509, note that this poem also appears in Bod. MS Rawl. Poet. 85, fol. 116v and Folger MS V.a.89, fol. 18v (the latter in a six-line version).
[72] May, *Elizabethan Courtier Poets*, 284, puts this piece, which appears in three other manuscripts and three printed books, in the category of poems "possibly" by the Earl of Oxford.
[73] This poem, derived from Ronsard's *Amours de Cassandre* 20, is by Sir Arthur Gorges. See Helen Estabrook Sandison, ed., *The Poems of Sir Arthur Gorges* (Oxford: Clarendon Press, 1953), xxxviii–ix and Rudick, *Ralegh,* 142–43.

46 "Callinge to minde, mine ey went longe abowte" (fol. 36v) ("FINIS
RA[legh]")

47 "ffarewell false Love, thou Oracle of Lyes" (fol. 37r) ("FINIS RA")

48 "Singe neighbours singe, here yow not Say" (fol. 37v) (headed "[ ] habent secul-
ta [?] sepulchrum") ("FYNIS Sr. P. Sy[dney].")[74]

49 "The silly Bird, the Bee, the Horse" (fol. 38r) ("FINIS./ frustra sapit qui sibi
non sapit") ("FINIS / frustra sapit qui sibi non sapit.") (Sidney?)[75]

50 "Locke up fayre lyddes, the treasure of my harte" (fol. 38v) ("FINIS.
Syd[ney].")

51 "If I could thinke how these my thoughtes to leave" (fol. 39r) ("FINIS
Sy[dney].")

52 "The ffire to see my wronges, for anger burnethe" (fol. 39r) ("FINIS Sr. P.
Sy[dney].")

53 "We till to sow, we sow to reape" (fol. 39r) (headed "Omnia tempus")—short
for "Omnia tempus habent" (Ecclesiastes 3:1)

54 "Until the ffatal Day" (fol. 39v) (headed "an unworthye beloved, to her
approved")[76]

55 "We silly Dames, that false Suspect do feare" (fol. 40r) ("FINIS <H.W.>
Ball[et]")[77]

56 "The Coulte did pipe a cherefull round" (fol. 40r)

57 "No plage to pride, no wo to want; no grief to luckles love;" (fol. 40r)[78]

58 "The ruful state, the straunge and wretched lyfe" (fol. 40v)

59 "O that I knew, or that I could forgette" (fol. 41r)

60[.1] "As women have faces, to set men on fyre" (fol. 41r)[79]

60[.2] "The flering Fyshe, that swims secure, misdeeming no deceyte" (fol. 41r)

---

[74] William Ringler, who earlier rejected the attribution of this poem to Sidney, in "The
Text of *The Poems of Sidney*," 137, because of the confirmatory attribution in the Ottley Manuscript, put the poem in the category of those "probably by Sidney."

[75] Woudhuysen, *Sidney*, 284, says this poem is Sidney's. He notes (284–85) that the motto
is ascribed to Virgil in editions of his works and that "Sidney used the tag for Musidorus' *im-
presa* expressing his love for Pamela in the *Old Arcadia*, and some of his followers wore the
comparable motto 'Sic Nos non nobis' in the Four Foster Children of Desire tilt of 1581."

[76] May and Ringler, EV 27840, cite an incomplete thirty-one line version of this poem in
BL MS Harl. 5115, fol. 150.

[77] This piece is the last two stanzas of "Though I seem strange," a poem attributed to Ann
Vavasour. See May and Ringler, EV 26287.

[78] May and Ringler, EV 15989, note a version of this poem associated with the name Hen-
rie Wigley found on the end flyleaf of a 1566 edition of *The Warkis of the Famous and Worthie
Knicht, Schir David Lyndesay*.

[79] May and Ringler, EV 3041, note other copies in CUL MS Dd.5.75., fol. 63v, and Bod.
MS Rawl. Poet. 108, fol. 1v.

60[.3] "Fylled they may be satisfied never" (fol. 41r) (at bottom of page: "Futuris gaudeo / Presentia contemno")

61 "Who takes in hand to till the barren soyle" (fol. 41v) ("FINIS <H C>")

62 "The Bird, which is restrained" (fol. 41v) ("FINIS <H W>")[80]

63 "Adew Desire and be contente" (fol. 42r)

64 "I heard a Heardman once compare" (fol. 42r) ("FYNIS [ ]")[81]

65 "When dreadfull deathe, with his sharp piercing Darte" (fol. 42v)[82]

66 "When that thine Eye hath chose the Dame" (fol. 43r) ("FINIS < > R P") (Shakespeare?)[83]

67 "Desier hath no rest in some Desired thinges" (fol. 43v)

68 "My hope doth waite for Hap" (fol. 44r) (headed "Tempo inderno perso pyango") ("FINIS AN.")

69 "Amongst the wilfull wayward sorte" (fol. 44v) ("FINIS <H C>")

70 "Like Tantalus my payne doth last like Etna mount I burn" (fol. 45v)

71 "The Eye doth finde the Hart Doth choose" (fol. 45v) (Thomas Whythorne)[84]

72 "The choyse that I have chosen" (fol. 45v)

73 "The mountaynes highe whose lofty toppe" (fol. 46r) (headed "ballet")[85]

74 "Yf Care inforce Complaint, why do I hide my woe" (fol. 46v) ("FINIS <H C>"])

75 "Once musing as I lay within my loathed Bed" (fol. 47r) (Headed "Ictus Sapio") ("FINIS H C")

76 "Who Princkles feares, to plucke the lovely Rose" (fol. 47r)[86]

77 "Yf that the inward Grief, which festereth in my Hart" (fol. 47v)

---

[80] The initials "H W" are written over what looks like an original "H C." May and Ringler, EV 21898, identify this piece as Lucilla's verses translated by either Lodowick Brisket or Barnaby Rich, a poem found in *Riche his Farewell to Militarie Profession* (1581).

[81] The trimming of the bottom of the page makes the ascription unrecognizable. May and Ringler, EV 9859, allude to the poem in BL MS Egerton 2642, fol. 264v, beginning "I heard a shepherd once compare."

[82] May and Ringler, EV 29307, citing Humphrey Gifford's *A Poesie of Gilloflowers* (1580), where the poem is titled "A Will or Testament," attribute the poem to Gifford.

[83] See above, n. 55.

[84] May and Ringler, EV 22356, citing Bod. MS Eng. Misc.. C.330, fol. 57, quote Thomas Whythorne on this ring posy: "I wrot in a pees of paper the verses that I kawzed to be graven in her ring sumwhat altered az thus. . . ."

[85] This poem appears in *The Paradise of Dainty Devices* as poem 62, ascribed to Richard Edwards. The two texts, however, differ considerably. May and Ringler, EV 23531, also cite a copy in Bod. MS Douce e.16, fol. 81.

[86] With some variants, this poem appears in George Whetstone's *Heptameron of Civil Discourses* (1582). See May and Ringler, EV 30920.

78 "Philisides, the Shepherd good & true" (fol. 47v) ("FINIS < > P. Sidney")[87]

79 "The Trojane Prince that Priam hight" (fol. 49r) ("FINIS E. E.")

80 "Now leave & let me rest" (fol. 49v) ("FINIS <H C> Regina")[88]

81 "When griping griefes the hart wold wound" (fol. 50v) ("FINIS balle[t]") (Richard Edwards)[89]

82 "In Pescod time when hownd to horne gives care while Bucke is kild" (fol. 51r) ("FINIS l[ord]. Ox[ford].") (Thomas Churchyard?)[90]

83 "ffancy farwell, that fed my fond delight," (fol. 51v) ("FINIS H O" and "Dyer" [in different hand])[91]

84 "My harte Doth pant for sorrow," (fol. 51v) (headed "Nec una, nec altera") ("FINIS and Russell" [in different hand])

85 "Wingde with Desire I seke to mount on hy" (fol. 52r) (headed "Cuius Iussui negare nefas est") ("FINIS Lo[rd]. Ox[ford].")

86 "To lodge Delighte on fancies single sight" (fol. 53v) (headed "Being asked how he lyked, he wrote") [whole page crossed out] (subsc. "Forme [sic] Nulla Fides"; "<H. C. to Q. R.>"

87 "Care is the Gate that openeth to my Hart" (fol. 54r) [whole page crossed out] (headed "In Passione Melancholica") ("<H C to C G>" and "RDTFOF") (following the text: "Contra fatum niti fatuum")

88 "I am a post in haste with speede" (fol. 54v) (headed "Cambridge Libell") [a poem in   boxed stanzas with identifications of personages inserted in the left margin][92]

89 "The fyeld a fart durty, a Gybbet crosse corded" (fol. 59r) [Between 88 and 89 a boxed prose note serving to introduce this poem][93]

---

[87] Ringler, "The Text of *The Poems of Sidney*," 137, accepts this as Sidney's.

[88] Marcus, Mueller, and Rose, *Elizabeth I*, 305, ascribe this piece to Queen Elizabeth. May and Ringler, EV 16437, note there is a copy of the piece in CUL MS Dd.5.75, fol. 44v.

[89] This is poem 57 in *The Paradise of Dainty Devices* (1576), ascribed to Richard Edwards. The manuscript version splits the fourteener couplets into four lines (4/3, 4/3), as do the editions of *Paradise* from 1578 on forward.

[90] May, *Elizabethan Courtier Poets*, 284–85, includes this piece in a collection of poems "possibly by Oxford." It was printed in *A Pleasaunte Laborinth called Churchyards Chance* (1580) and, ascribed to "Ignoto," in *England's Helicon* (1600).

[91] May, *Elizabethan Courtier Poets*, 312–13, placing this poem among those "possibly by Dyer," calls attention to five texts of it, only two of which are full versions.

[92] This poem, minus the first five stanzas, appears in the Arundel Harington manuscript (poem 180 in Hughey's edition; see her discussion, *Manuscript*, 2: 261–76).

[93] "The Duttons and theyr fellow players forsaking the Erle of Warwycke, theyr master became followers of the Erle of Oxford & wrot themselves hys Comedians; which certayne gentlemen altered & made Camelions. The Duttons angry with that compared themselves to any Gentleman therefore these Armes were devised for them."

90 "The Russet for the Travelors weare" (fol. 59v) (headed "COLORES")

U8 "He that spareth for to speake, oft wanteth his intente" (fol. 59r)[94]

91 "Methought of late in slepe I saw a Dame" (fol. 60r)

U9 "Pushe Lady pushe what push may that be?" (fol. 60r)

92 "If ever honest mynde might gayne [ ]" (fol. 60v) ("FINIS I. F.") (John Finet?)

93 "Seinge the altryinge facions of our tyme" (fol. 60v) ("Fynis <Mrs L N>")[95]

U10 "Behold the force of Hotte Desier" (fol. 60v)

94 "Babes, that be borne adventure strypes for play" (fol. 61r) ("FINIS < >") [whole poem crossed out]

U11 "Pastor, arator, eques, pavi, colui, superavi" (fol. 61r)

U12 "I sheppard I plowman I horseman light" (fol. 61r) [translation of U11]

U13 "A hearde a swaine a noble knight" (fol. 61r) [another translation of U11][96]

95 "Luld by Conceipt when Fancy clozd myne Eyes" (fol. 61v) (headed "Somnium Affectionale") ("FINIS geven H E")

96 "The more yow desire her" (fol. 62r) (motto at end: "Pro. est.")[97]

97 "I love a Lyfe to Lyve in Love" (fol. 62r)

98 "The state of france as now yt standes" (fol. 62v)[98]

99 "Syttynge alone upon my thought in Melancholy moode" (fol. 63r) ("Finis A. Vavasoare")[99]

100 "The gentle season of the yeare" (fol. 63v) ("FYNYS Sr. P. Sidney") (Gorges)

---

[94] May and Ringler, EV 8598, suggest the poem may be by John Harington of Stepney and note it appears in BL MSS Egerton 2642, fol. 256v, and Additional 38823, fol. 48, as well as in National Library of Wales MS 23202B, fol. 171v.

[95] Black, "Studies," 2: 429, says this is an unfinished translation of a French sonnet, whose text is in BL MS Additional 38823, fol. 30.

[96] Black, "Studies," 2: 367, points out that there is a version printed in Abraham Fraunce's *Arcadian Rhetorick*, E1v:

A goteheard, plowman, knight, my goates, my fields, my foes,

I fed, I tild, I kild, with bowes, with plowes, with blowes.

Woudhuysen, *Sidney*, 285, notes that the Latin poem appears in appendixes to sixteenth-century editions of Virgil.

[97] Black, "Studies," 2: 442, notes that this poem appears as 302 in Hughey's edition of the Arundel Harington manuscript.

[98] For a discussion of this much-transcribed poem, known as "The French Primero," see Steven W. May, "'The French Primero': A Study in Renaissance Textual Transmission and Taste," *English Language Notes* 9 (1971): 102–8.

[99] There is a gap between the introductory section and the echo poem that begins "Oh Heavens (qd She who was the first that wrought in me thys Fevere) Echo Vere." The whole piece has been put by May, *Elizabethan Courtier Poets*, 282–83, in the category of "Poems Possibly by Oxford." Ann Cornwallis's miscellany (Folger MS V.a.89, p. 13) ascribes the piece to "Vavaser."

101 "I wyll forget that ere I saw thy Face" (fol. 64v) ("FINIS I. Ed.")[100]

102 "To Death no no Unto eternall Lyfe" (fol. 65r) ("I. Ed.")[101]

103 "Lady farwell whom I in Sylence serve" (fol. 65v) (Ralegh)[102]

U14 "The Parson of Stanlake, hath stopt up my Watergap" (fol. 65v)

104 "Vertue, bewty, speech, dyd Stryke wound charme" (fol. 66r) (Sidney)

105 "The Dart the Beames, the String, so strong I prove" (fol. 66r) (Sidney?)[103]

106 "Her fface, her Tonge Her Wytte" (fol. 66v) ("Raley" [in different hand]) (Gorges)[104]

107 "The Lyvely Larke stretcht forth her wynge" (fol. 67r) (Oxford)

108 "In Verse to vaunt my Ladies Grace" (fol.w 67r) ("FINIS Ioh. Ed." [in different hand])

109 "I Herd a voice & wished for a Sighte" (fol. 67v)[105]

110 "My wayning Joyes, my still encreasing Greef" (fol. 67v)

111 "What thing is Love? A vayne Concept of mynde" (fol. 68r)[106]

112 "My trewlove hath my hart, & I have his" (fol. 68r) (Sidney)

113 "The Ayre with Sweet my Sences Doth Delight" (fol. 68v) (Nicholas Breton?)[107]

114 "Oh Sorow cease Good Love Begyn" (fol. 69r)

U16 "What Thynge is Love? for sure Love is a thinge" (fol. 69r) (George Peele)[108]

115 "Devyde my Tymes, and Rate my wretched Howres" (fol. 69v) ("Dier" [in different hand])

---

[100] May and Ringler, EV 10462, note that this poem is also found in *Brittons Bowre of Delights* (1591 and 1597), F2.

[101] May and Ringler, EV 26955, refer to another manuscript copy in BL MS Sloane 2497, fol. 33, and to a printed version in Anthony Munday's *The Paine of Pleasure* (1580), H1v, where it is introduced: "Verses which the sayd Gentleman writ with his owne hand, an houre before he departed this life."

[102] See Rudick, *Ralegh*, 15–16. In one manuscript this poem is entitled "A Poem put into my lady Laitons Pocket by Sir W: Rawleigh" (16).

[103] William Ringler, ed., *The Poems of Sir Philip Sidney* (Oxford: Clarendon Press, 1962), 344–45, includes this poem in the section of "Poems Possibly by Sidney."

[104] This is poem 79 in Sandison's edition of Gorges.

[105] Black, "Studies," 2: 410, cites copies of the poem in Bod. MS Rawl. Poet. 148, fol. 67v, Arundel Harington MS 187 (in Hughey), and in Bateson's *Second Set of Madrigals* (1618), xviii.

[106] May and Ringler, EV 28987, note this poem is also found in Bod. MS Rawl. Poet. 85, fol. 13v.

[107] May and Ringler, EV 21768, note that this poem is found in four other manuscripts, as well as in *Brittons Bowre of Delights* (1591 and 1597), G3.

[108] Black, "Studies," 2:445, notes the poem is ascribed to Peele in Bod. MS Rawl. Poet. 85, fol. 13, that it is found in Bod. MS Rawl. Poet. 172, fol. 2v and *The Wisdom of Doctor Dodypoll* (1600). Lines 12–20 and 25–26 appear in Peele's *The Hunting of Cupid* (1591).

116 "Who hath his ffancy pleased with ffruites of happy Sight" (fol. 70v) (Sidney)

117 "Who taught the first to sighe alas my Harte" (fol. 70v) ("Ball[et]") (Oxford)

118 "How can the ffeeble fforte but yeld at Laste" (fol. 71r)[109]

U17 "Yf Busse bee Fetor, and Bess bee fetyt" (fol. 71r)

119 "Who knows his Cause of Greef" (fol. 71v)[110]

120 "The sturdy Rocke for all his strengthe" (fol. 72r) (John Thorn?)[111] [There are three deleted couplets or epigrams between 120 and U18.]

U18 "Hic Jacet Andreas" (fol. 72r)

U19 "Here Lies old Andrew Hee" (fol. 72r) (translation of previous item)

121 "Pallas, Juno, Venus on bushy Ida mounte" (fol. 72r) (headed "A new yeres Gift with a golden Ball") ("Subject only to yourself/ I. Ed.")[112]

U20 "Lumine Acon dextro, capra est Leonella sinistro" (fol. 72v)[113]

U21 "Leonell of Eyes the Lefte, had given for bodily Light" (fol. 72v) ("FINIS I. E.") [translation of previous item]

122 "Yf painfull nature bent with redy will" (fol. 73r) ("FINIS EN")

123 "Short is my rest whose Toyle is overlonge" (fol. 73r) ("FINIS Ball[et].")[114]

124 "Juno now at Samos must not stay" (fol. 73v) ("FINIS I. E.")

125[.1] "Est Venus in Vultu, doctor tibi Pallas in ore" (fol. 73v)[115]

125[.2] "In face the fairest Goddes Lyke" (fol. 73v) ("FINIS I. E.") [translation of previous poem]

126 "My mind to me a kingdom is, such perfect Joy therin I find" (fol. 73v) ("FINIS BALL[et]") (Oxford)

---

[109] Anderson, "'The Merit'," 149–50, who points to the ascription in Bod. MS Rawl. Poet 85, fol 114, to "Mrs M: R:," says this poem was written by a woman.

[110] May and Ringler, EV 30802, note the copy of this poem in *Brittons Bowre of Delights* (1591 and 1597), G 1.

[111] Black, "Studies," 2: 440, points out that this poem appears as 20 in *The Paradise of Dainty Devices* (1576) ascribed to "M[aster].T." and speculates that it was written by John Thorn. There are some nine textual variants from the *Paradise* version in the Harley version. May and Ringler, EV 24341, also note copies of this poem in Folger MS V.a.149, fol. 18 and Bod. MS Douce e.16, fol. 27.

[112] Black, "Studies," 2: 384, refers to the Latin poem by John Woodford in *Musa Hospitalis Ecclesia Christi* (1605), D4.

[113] In his "Essay on Pope" (1772), 1: 299, Warton called this anonymous epigram the "most celebrated of modern epigrams." See *Notes and Queries*, 3rd ser., 2 (6 Dec. 1862): 451.

[114] Black, "Studies," 2: 430, notes that the poem is ascribed to "A.H." in Bod. MS Rawl. Poet. 85, fol. 50v, that it appears in BL MS Harl. 6910, fol. 148 and Arundel Harington 193, as well as in print in *The Phoenix Nest* (1593), N2v, and Barley's *New Book of Tabliture* (1596), vi.

[115] Woudhuysen, *Sidney*, 285, notes the Latin lines "are Walter Haddon's, but had been quoted by Gabriel Harvey in *Gratulationes Valdienses* (1578), sig. A1v."

127 "When yonger yeres could not my mind acquaint" (fol. 74v)

U22 "What length of verse may serve brave Mopsa's grace to showe" (fol. 75r) ("Sr Phyll. Sydney")

U23 "The Souldier worne with wars Delightes in Peace" (fol. 75v) (Thomas Watson)[116]

U24 "Some men will say there is a kynde of Muse" (fol. 76v) (Nicholas Breton)[117]

U25 "Unfriendly leavest thou me in such a sort" (fol. 77r) (headed "A Passion") ("R Allott")

U26 "Fancies they are that trouble my mind" (fol. 77v) ("R A")

U27 "O Mildred if thou dost return to me thy spouse again" (fol. 77v) ("R Allott") (in margin: "Incerti Authoris") (Catherine Killigrew)

U28 "In everything my love & love agre" (fol. 77v)

U29 "Thou sacred monarche of that holy traine" (fol. 78r) (headed "Ad Apollinem et musas ode" ("Robert Allott")

U30 "Who sittes in lady fortunes lappe" (fol. 78v) ("I. I.")

U31 "A day, a nyght, An houre of sweet" (fol. 78v) ("I. I.") (Thomas Campion)[118]

---

[116] Black, "Studies," 2: 439, points out that this poem was printed in both Watson's *Hekatompathia* (1582), L3, and *A Poetical Rapsody* (1608 edition), D3v.

[117] Black, "Studies," 2: 432, cites copies of this poem in three other manuscripts and in *Brittons Bowre of Delights* (1591), D1, and *The Phoenix Nest* (1593), I4, in the latter of which it is headed "A most excellent passion set downe by N. B. Gent."

[118] This poem, entitled "Canto Quinto," appears in the 1591 (augmented) edition of Sidney's *Astrophel and Stella* in a section of poems by other authors. It appears in BL MS Harl. 6910, fol. 156v, minus lines three and four, and Harley 7392 has only the first of the poem's three stanzas. Collated against the text in *Astrophel and Stella*, the version in Harley 7392 has the following variants (I use the line numbers of the printed version):

3 Ungentle fates] Unequall Gods

6 Joy] blisse

Appendix II
Unique Poems in Harley 7392

Adew Desire and be contente (fol. 42r) (May and Ringler, EV 1174)
Amongst the wilfull wayward sorte (fols. 44v–45r) (EV 1988)
Babes, that be borne adventure strypes for play (fol. 61r) (EV 3287)
Before I dy faire Dame of me receave my last adew (fols. 22v–23r) (EV 3510)[119]
Behold the force of Hotte Desier (fol. 60v) (EV 3620)
Care is the Gate that openeth to my Hart (fol. 54r) (EV 4495)
Desier hath no rest in some Desired thinges (fol. 43v) (EV 5280)
Fancies they are that trouble my mind (fol. 77v) (EV 6217)
Here Lies old Andrew Hee (fol. 72r) (EV 8951)
I faint with feare, I blushe for shame (fol. 24v) (EV 9732)
I live in Blysse yet tast no Joy (fol. 31v) (EV 9964)
I lived once, loved & swam in sweete delight (fol. 28r) (EV 9973)
I love a Lyfe to Lyve in Love (fol. 62r) (EV 9990)
If ever honest mynde might gayne (fol. 60v) (EV 10722)
In everything my love & love agre (fol. 77v) (EV 11858)
In face the fairest Goddes Lyke (fol. 73v) (EV 11859)
In Tyme I may the ffruycte asay (fol. 33v) (EV 12384)
In Verse to Vaunt my Ladies Grace (fol. 67r) (EV 12436)
Juno now at Samos must not stay (fol. 73v) (EV 13013)
Leonell of Eyes the Lefte, had given for bodily Light (fol. 72v) (EV 13306)
Like Tantalus my payne doth last like Etna mount I burn (fol. 45v) (EV 13731)
Luld by Conceipte when Fancy clozd myne Eyes (fol. 61v) (EV 14286)
My curious Eyes (whose wary sighte) (fol. 32v) (EV 15067)
My harte Doth pant for sorrow (fol. 51v) (EV 15200)
My hope doth waite for Hap (fol. 44r) (EV 15243)
Now ready is the Barke that lokes for lucky wynde (fol. 32v–33r) (EV 16500)
O that I knew, or that I could forgette (fol. 41r) (EV 17609)
Oh Sorow cease Good Love Begyn (fol. 69r) (EV 17573)
Once musinge as I lay within my loathed Bed (fol. 47r) (EV 18381)
Pallas, Juno, Venus on bushy Ida mounte (fol. 72v) (EV 18706)
Pushe Lady pushe what push may that be? (fol. 60r) (EV 19186)
Sweet ar the thoughtes, wher Hope perswadeth Happe (fol. 36r) (EV 21200.6)
The choyse that I have chosen (fol. 45v) (EV 22047)
The Coulte did pipe a cherefull round (fol. 40r) (EV 22080)

---

[119] May, *Elizabethan Courtier Poets*, 296, points out that an extract of this poem (ll. 9–10) is printed in George Puttenham's *Arte of English Poesie*.

The Parson of Stanlake, hath stopt up my Watergap (fol. 65v) (EV 23681)
The rueful state, the straunge and wretched lyfe (fol. 40v) (EV 24020)
The Russet for the Travelors weare (fol. 59v) (EV 24031)
The silly Bird, the Bee, the Horse (fol. 38r) (EV 24167)
The Trojane Prince that Priam hight (fol. 49r) (EV 24529)
Thine only owne while lyfe Doth last (fol. 33v) (EV 25328)
Thou sacred monarche of that holy traine (fol. 76r) (EV 26071)
To lodge Delighte on fancies single sight (fol. 53v) (EV 27097)
Unfriendly leavest thou me in such a sort (fol. 77r) (EV 27773)
We till to sow, we sow to reape (fol. 39r) (EV 28300)
What thinge can be more fond (fol. 36r) (EV 28981)
When shall I joy, whose Joyes are overthrowne (fol. 34r) (EV 29825)
When yonger yeres could not my mind acquaint (fol. 74v) (EV 30101)
Who sittes in ladye fortunes lappe (fol. 78v) (EV 30983)
Who takes in hand to till the barren soyle (fol. 41v) (EV 30997)
Worke minde into the Skyes, thy Body taketh stand (fol. 35v) (EV 31973)
Yf Busse bee Fetor, and Bess bee fetyt (fol. 71r) (EV 10657)
Yf Care inforce Complaint, why do I hide my woe (fol. 46v) (EV 10666)
Yf painfull nature bent with redy will (fol. 73r) (EV 11156)
Yf tales be trew, & Poets tell no Lyes (fol. 25v) (EV 11273)
Yf that the inward Grief, which festereth in my Hart (fol. 47v) (EV 11331)

Editing a Recent Mary Wroth Letter[1]

MARGARET J. ARNOLD

A PART FROM HER REMARKABLE LITERARY ACHIEVEMENTS, LADY MARY Wroth shared the experience of many contemporaries in negotiating her personal and financial needs. An uncatalogued holograph letter, MS Crawford 177, in the Department of Special Collections in the Kenneth Spencer Research Library at the University of Kansas, sheds light on Lady Mary's active participation in seeking the economic authority to act on her own behalf. Writing on 19 March 1613 to her father Robert Sidney, then Viscount de Lisle, Lady Mary requests documentation regarding her jointure as well as a report on the arrangements already in progress to build "waulks" at Loughton Hall, Essex, so that she can respond to enquiries from the "keepers" who approach her for advice.[2]

The Spencer Library letter supplements the ten holograph letters Josephine Roberts included in her pioneering edition of Lady Mary's poems. Only Wroth's petition to Queen Anne seconding Robert Wroth's request to the King for permission to lease Loughton Hall (n.d. but before 1612) precedes it.[3] The new letter is

---

[1] The present discussion expands a paper delivered in the "Editing Early Modern Women" session of the Thirty-Seventh Congress on Medieval Studies, Kalamazoo, MI, 2–5 May 2002. I wish to thank Margaret P. Hannay, who chaired the session, and Arthur Kinney, who responded to the papers, for their helpful comments and questions. A shorter version, introducing and duplicating the letter, appeared in *English Literary Renaissance* 35:3 (2005): 454–58.

[2] Reproduced by permission of the Department of Special Collections of the Kenneth Spencer Research Library at the University of Kansas, No. 177 of the recently catalogued Crawford Collection. I am especially grateful to Ann Hyde, retired Research Librarian, who catalogued the item and drew it to my attention.

[3] Josephine A. Roberts, ed., *The Poems of Lady Mary Wroth* (Baton Rouge, LA and London: Louisiana State Univ. Press, 1983), 234–35. Roberts' "Appendix: The Correspondence of Lady Mary Wroth," 233–45 assembles the extant material.

also the only additional message written during the period in which Wroth wrote as a *feme covert*, needing to negotiate her legal and economic future through her husband, the younger Robert Wroth, and her father. It is also the second extant message she writes as a daughter. Only her 1614 letter asking Robert Sidney to shelter her son James survives among the messages Roberts transcribes. The recent letter regarding her jointure deserves contextualization. After a discussion verifying her authorship, I advance some possible reasons for her choice and her subject. The letter is valuable because we have so few of her holograph works. Although many more women's letters are available now than in the past, their range and variety still falls short of the many collections devoted to men's correspondence.[4] Further, an additional letter by Mary Wroth not only helps us understand her colorful life and works but also shows her negotiating some of the problems faced by many other married women of her time. Her jointure (an agreement to hold money or property in common with her husband) is important to her economic survival, yet her security is not guaranteed.[5] The letter also contributes to her individual biography, providing further documentation of her seeking aid from the extended Sidney network. In addition, the document ties her more closely with the country setting of Loughton Hall, Essex, implying a mutual interest in owning this estate through her marriage with the younger Wroth. My paper falls into two sections. The first presents evidence that Mary Wroth is indeed the author. The second examines its significance in more detail, raising questions for further investigation.

I

MS Crawford 177 closely matches Lady Mary's formal italic hand. At this point a reader of editions and articles reproducing her distinctive signature will notice the similarity in the photographic reproduction. After observing some details and exploring its likely provenance, I draw some conclusions about its significance and hope to elicit comments for further investigation. I have spelled out abbreviations in the transcription.

---

[4] For additional discussion of women's letters, especially on the Continent, see *Writing the Female Voice: Essays in Epistolary Literature*, ed. Elizabeth C. Goldsmith (London: Pinter, 1989).

[5] The general definitions of legal terms are based on Amy Louise Erickson's *Women and Property in Early Modern England* (London and New York: Routledge, 1992), esp. p. 238. Some uncertainties noted by Lloyd Bonfield and Patricia Spring are discussed below.

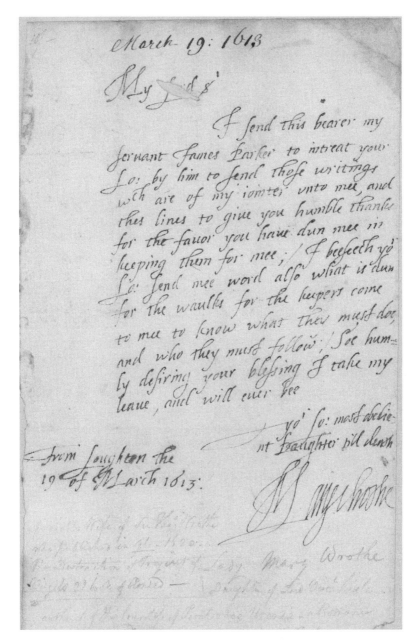

Figure 1. Letter of Lady Mary Wroth to her father Robert Sidney, Viscount de Lisle, 19 March 1613. Kenneth Spencer Research Library, University of Kansas, MS Crawford 177. Used by permission.

March 19, 1613
My Lord,
        I send this bearer my
servant James Parker to intreat your
Lo[rdship] by him to send those writings
w[hi]ch are of my iointer unto mee, and
thes lines to giue you humble thanks
for the fauor you have dun mee in
keeping them for mee; / I beseech yo[u]r
Lo[rdship] send mee word also what is dun
for the waulks for the keepers come
to mee to know what they must doe,
and who they must follow; / Soe hum -
ly desiring your blessing I take my
leaue, and will euer bee
                Yo[u]r Lo[rdship's] most obedie -
                nt Daughter till death
From Loughton the
19 of March 1613:   Mary wrothe

Some penciled notes identifying Wroth and her works do not show on the photocopy. A later hand, probably from the nineteenth century, identifies her as the daughter of Viscount de L'Isle and, erroneously, as the wife of "Sir Thomas Wrothe," the author of a translation in 1620 of a selection from Book Two of Virgil's *Aeneid*. Lady Mary's "The Countess of Pembroke's Urania, a romance published in 1621, Tragidy interspersed with Poetry" represents the anonymous annotator's information about Wroth and her work.

Although the Department of Special Collections at Spencer Library does not have a precise record of purchase for MS Crawford 177, its presence is consistent with Crawford family interests. It appears in a file of approximately two hundred heterogeneous items originally belonging to the Lindsay family, the Scottish Earls of Crawford, who built up an extensive library beginning as early as 1552.[6] The majority of the Crawford documents date from the nineteenth century. The collection, however, contains a number of entries related to the Sidney family, including a letter from Sir Henry Sidney to his son Philip, and a note observing the

---

[6] James Lindsay, ed., Bibliotheca Lindseiana: *Catalogue of the Printed Books Preserved at Haigh Hall, Wigan,* 5 vols. (Aberdeen: Aberdeen Univ. Press, 1910), Introduction to Vol. 1, vi. Lindsay mentions an ancestor's friendship with Drummond of Hawthornden, who certainly knew of Lady Mary's work.

existence of Joshua Sylvester's elegy on the death of Mary Wroth's brother William (Lindsay, Bibliotheca, 8307–9).

Comparing Mary Wroth's penmanship with reproductions of her hand in the editions and articles of Josephine Roberts and the editors of *The Second Part of the Countess of Montgomery's Urania*, I find her handwriting quite close to their reproduced samples of her formal italic hand.[7] The individual letters are somewhat less ornate than those of her more public message to George Villiers, Duke of Buckingham, written in response to complaints about her 1621 publication of part of the *Urania* and promising to withdraw it from circulation. Still, the salutation includes Lady Mary's crossed "s"; her capitals "I," "J," are looped back and crossed as in her formal letters, and her "L" is looped. Clubbed ascenders distinguish some of the "b" consonants (line 1) and "h" in "him" (3), "humble" (5), and "have" (6). The most obvious clubbed "d" begins "desiring" in the penultimate line of the text. She lifts her pen with nearly every letter except for the acceptable formal ligature of "ch" in the abbreviated "which" (4). The lines are inclined slightly and uniformly to the right, and no blots or strike-outs appear. Somewhat less formally, she joins "se" in "servant" (2) and the double "e" in "mee" (4, 6). As in her other manuscripts, Lady Mary uses the virgule (/) to indicate a new paragraph. These notes, suggestive but not exhaustive, certainly verify Lady Mary's authorship of the letter. The relative formality elevates the parent above the author, not only as a family authority deserving respect but as the recipient of a serious request.

II

Why is the letter important? Even within the well preserved family correspondence of Robert and Barbara Sidney, as Margaret Hannay has noted, Barbara's signature appears, but we lack her responses to Robert in her own hand. Granted, his letters are invaluable to our knowledge of Wroth so that "We . . . have more documentation for the early life of Lady Wroth than for almost any other early modern writer."[8] Within the letters, however, we learn that Wroth has written,

---

[7] The earliest and clearest discussion identifying Lady Mary's hands is still Roberts, "The Huntington Manuscript of Lady Mary Wroth's Play, *Loves Victorie*," *HLQ* 46 (1983): 146–74. Roberts also reproduces the letter to Buckingham in *Poems*, 77. Concerning the challenges of transcribing many of Wroth's pages, see Suzanne Gossett's "Lady Mary's Handwriting," Section 6 of *The Second Part of The Countess of Montgomery's Urania*, ed. Roberts and completed by Gossett and Janel Mueller (Tempe, Arizona: Renaissance English Text Society, 1999).

[8] Margaret P. Hannay, Noel J. Kinnamon, and Michael G. Brannan, eds., *Domestic Politics and Family Absence: The Correspondence (1588–1621) of Robert Sidney, First Earl of Leicester, and Barbara Gamage Sidney, Countess of Leicester*, The Early Modern Englishwoman

but the letters are not preserved. Another letter to Barbara comments that Robert Sidney has enclosed a written message from another daughter, Katherine Maunsell, yet the letter does not appear in the archive.[9] Even the only extant holograph letter from Mary Wroth to her father in 1614 was attributed to her servant H. Landsbrooke until this century (Roberts, *Poems*, 234).

Considering the Crawford letter in comparison with Wroth's 1614 request in her widowhood for support in raising the infant James Wroth provides a context for the close father-daughter relationship Lady Mary maintained with Robert Sidney during her marriage and after Robert Wroth's death. Both letters reveal Lady Mary's family allegiance, yet her rhetorical strategies differ. In both, her persuasive skill permits her to assert her dignity at the same time that she accords her father the respect that a daughter owes him.

In the newly discovered Crawford letter, she evokes the family relationship to act within the legal restrictions common to married women. The "writings" her father can supply provide evidence she needs in order to deal with workers on her husband's estate. Her message appears in a formal hand, a brief petition unmarred by insertions or words begun but written over. Both this letter and the published 1614 message support her strong family identification. When she writes the 1613 letter, she balances her family deference with her status as a married woman assisting in decisions related to her husband's grant of Loughton Hall. The appeal addressed to Robert Sidney uses the term "jointure," yet Lady Mary conveys the idea that her father's compliance grants her freedom to act in her own interests when her right to deal with workmen is questioned. She accords her father respect, clarifies the matter at issue, gives a reason for her request, and closes warmly. The relative formality elevates the addressee above the author, not only as a family authority deserving respect but as the recipient of a serious request. The placement of the closing words and signature at the extreme right are forms of deference.[10]

1500–1750, ed. Betty S. Travitsky, Anne Lake Prescott, and Patrick Cullen (Aldershot: Ashgate, 2003), 1.

[9] De L'Isle manuscript U1475, correspondence series 81, letter 223 (24 August 1611). Parts of the letter appear in *HMC*, De L'Isle and Dudley, IV, 283. I wish to thank the Viscount De L'Isle for permission to examine letters related to Wroth and other family members at the Centre for Kentish Studies and to refer to them in this context. An accurate published form now appears in the excellent edition of Robert and Barbara Sidney's correspondence edited by Hannay, Kinnamon, and Brennan cited in the preceding note.

[10] For an example of "utmost humility" in placing the signature at the bottom edge of the right margin, see Margaret P. Hannay, *Philip's Phoenix* (New York and Oxford: Oxford Univ. Press, 1990) in reference to a letter from Mary Sidney, Countess of Pembroke, to Elizabeth I, (164). Although Wroth is much less humble, she places her father in a position of superiority.

The new letter provides an opportunity to re-examine the manuscript of Wroth's 1614 plea for her father's help to safeguard Loughton for the infant James Wroth, an epistle Roberts presents ably in print. In the 1613 letter Lady Mary's rhetorical balance of agency with deference is particularly striking. At the same time that she "intreats" her father to send her the written material she requests and "humbly" desires his blessing, Wroth asserts her independence. The jointure documents belong to "mee," she writes, and thanks her father for serving as their steward in the meantime. With "I beseech you send mee word also what is dun for the waulks for the keepers come to mee . . . ," she supplies a reason for her request. Within a polite letter she has asserted her right to the papers, implied that she is supervising "keepers," and established herself as the person sought out for directions leading to the actual accomplishment of the work.

The 1614 letter, written when Lady Mary lacks funds, represents her as a widow asking her father to protect the legal rights of his grandson James Wroth. After working to improve Loughton Hall, she and her infant son find themselves in a conflict with Robert Wroth's brother in administering the estate. Her plea continues to indicate her autonomous action, but she makes at least one tentative statement. She has acted independently in writing to one of the Wroth brothers; nevertheless, she adds the more tentative, "I hope I have dun noe hurt in it butt good rather, for the profitts of the lande yo[u]r Lo[rdship] must stand upon them. . . ."[11] Her life circumstances have altered. In 1613 she could call for documents she held while her husband lived. Widowed, with her income threatened, she hopes that her father, her most powerful male relative, will stand between her and the Wroth uncles. Her concern with holding the land and earning support from it has not changed, but her rhetorical stance has. In this letter she appeals to her father's feelings of kinship: "as hee is yours in blood soe I hope hee shall one day live to deserve yo[u]r love to him," an effective balance of the grandfather's heritage and the child's future hope of fulfilling his part in it. She also anticipates negative arguments from the surviving Wroths who, if they have denied her account, "sayd amiss." Her words affirm her membership in her original family, even mentioning some news her mother wishes her to convey to Robert Sidney. The 1614 holograph manuscript contains a less formal hand with several insertions, placing "in blood" after "yours" (line 3) and inserting "profits of the lande" after words of concern for Wroth mismanagement (line 19). Several letters are written over, and the final sentences conclude in several lines along the left-hand margin.

---

[11] Mary Wroth to Robert Sidney, De Lisle correspondence, MS C 52, 17 October 1614. See Roberts, *Poems*, 234–35. My additional comments result from comparing the KU manuscript letter with the holograph document in the Centre for Kentish Studies.

The two letters together show Wroth striving for independence, adapting her language to the circumstances surrounding her: a childless wife in early 1613 and a young widow and mother by October of the following year. In 1613 Lady Mary needed to secure her social and financial future. At the time she penned the letter, she had not yet conceived an heir to assure any claim to income from land. The other Wroth family holdings were entailed and would pass to her husband's brothers if he died without a male heir. Robert Wroth's only son and heir, James Wroth, was born in February of 1614, a month before the death of Mary's husband on March 14, 1614, and eleven months following the date of her letter to Robert Sidney found in the Crawford Collection. In 1613 and early 1614 she could not foresee the ensuing struggle for safeguarding James's interests during his brief life. Nor in her 1614 letter could she foresee her child's death in 1616.

The newly discovered letter thus allows us an opportunity to see more than one dimension in Lady Mary's relationship with her father. In addition, the manuscript extends into the social history of the extended Sidney family and its relatively brief intersection with the Wroths.

Lady Mary was uniquely placed in a wide circle of family mentors and friends to support her request for her jointure documents and to develop the Loughton estate. The "writings" may date from either of two periods: the negotiations in which Barbara Sidney participated in arranging the original marriage portion in 1604 and the testamentary provisions Robert Wroth made during a serious illness of 1608.[12] Although Lady Mary did not bring a landed estate to the Wroths, unlike her own mother and her sister-in-law, the Sidneys and the Wroths, according to Robert's man of business, Thomas Nevitt, did agree on a dowry of 3000 pounds.[13] In the process of itemizing family expenses regarding Lady Mary's dowry, Nevitt refers to "500 [pounds] Sir Robert Wrath (sic) gaue to my Lady Mary which she calling for, it was taken vpp at interest and soe continued. . . " (Nevitt, fol. 8v). The conjunction of the new holograph letter with Nevitt's indication that Mary asked for and received some money held in trust for

---

[12] Hannay, Kinnamon, and Brennan note Barbara Gamage Sidney's part in negotiations with Hugh Sanford (*Correspondence*, 13). De L'Isle correspondence, Series 81, no 106 (*HMC* III.127, London: 14 July 1604) describes negotiations between Robert Sidney and Robert Wroth, Senior, alluding to the son's visit to Penshurst. A few days later, 16 July 1604 (Series 81, No. 112) he "wil bee here again tomorrow to make an end with Sir Ro: Wroth." The actual marriage took place on 17 September 1604.

[13] British Library Additional MS 12,066, Thomas Nevitt, "Income and Expenses of the First Earle of Leicester," London, 16 October 1626. An accurate transcription is available in Samuel Butler, ed. *Sidneiana* (London: William Nicol, 1837. See <http://www.english.cam.ac.uk/ceres/sidneiana/nevitt.htm>.

her suggests that her plea—if not the 1613 one, very likely another—received an affirmative response.

A second allusion to a written agreement appears during Robert Wroth's serious periods of illness in 1608. Robert Sidney writes home from London on 16 October 1608, that he has good hope for his son-in-law's recovery but that, "if God call him he deals exceeding kindly with his wife. For besides her first jointure and the lease, he gives her one hundred pound a year towards the building of Loughton, and all the plate and household stuff which he hath bought since his father's death. The 1,000 l. I should pay him he did indeed remit unto me and left it to me how I would dispose of it, but I have caused it to be put down in the will, that it shall be disposed of to my daughter's use."[14] The term "jointure" occurs both in Nevitt's records and in Robert's letter home. In the 1608 context "remit" can imply a financial exchange, or, more likely, an agreement to "forgive" part of the money still owed toward the marriage settlement. At the point of making the agreement, the younger Wroth had inherited his father's entailed estates. Even though he lived on to make the testamentary document Roberts cites, expressing good will toward Mary, the 1608 illness was sufficiently severe that making provisions in the event of his death seems reasonable. At the time, too, the younger Wroths could still hope to earn income from a well-maintained and well-developed Loughton rather than the debts with which he ended his life. Thus, the "writings" Lady Mary requests in MS Crawford 177 may well refer to Robert Sidney's comment about Robert Wroth's promises "put down in the will," as well as to the original jointure negotiations.

Another implication of the KU letter for Wroth's biography arises from her statement that the "keepers come to mee to know what they must doe." Although Robert Wroth had the legal right to take the initiative in directing improvements, he may have been ill. On the other hand, Mary's experience in negotiating practical matters related to work on an aristocratic estate may well have resulted in her responsibilities. In addition to the model of her aunt Mary Sidney Pembroke, who wrote to the Queen and chief ministers on behalf of her husband and sons, Mary Wroth grew up in a household in which her mother supervised workers who constructed walls and built stables.[15] Most likely, the "waulks" concern the

---

[14] Quoted in Hannay, Kinnamon, and Brennan, *Correspondence*, 140. De Lisle MS U1475, Series 81, No. 166 (London: 16 October 1608), *HMC* IV, 53.

[15] Naomi Miller's chapter, "Matriarch's Daughter: Ties that Bind," in *Changing the Subject: Mary Wroth and Figurations of Gender in Early Modern England* (Lexington, KY: Univ. of Kentucky Press, 1996), 64–108, pays important attention to extended duties outside of simple household supervision by women in Mary Wroth's family. See also Hannay's "'Your vertuous and Learned Aunt': The Countess of Pembroke as a Mentor to Lady Wroth," in Naomi Miller

development of Loughton, although the term at the time, along with the questions from "keepers," could have applied to Robert Wroth's more extensive responsibilities as a Forester. Formal "waulks" surrounded the developed gardens at Loughton. Yet another contemporary meaning of "waulk" was "a division of a forest placed in the charge of a forester, a ranger, *or keeper*" [emphasis mine] (*OED* "walk" n., 10a).

Her letter illustrates the determined effort of an exceptionally articulate married woman to use her skills, backed by the support of a closely-knit extended family, to perform tasks similar to those her aunt and mother accomplished. Since her jointure land depended on a royal grant from the King to her husband, she worked in cooperation with him, as Roberts indicates.[16] The context is important because of her father's standing and her own earlier favor from Queen Anne. After her own court appearances, her sister Philip gained royal favor and also attended the Queen. In addition to family members, Lady Mary could call upon Sidney friends, her petition being forwarded by Lady Southampton, whose husband served with Robert Sidney.[17]

In an era when women's legal rights were precarious, Mary Wroth thus used every venue legal scholars outline for married women and widows. She draws upon her family members' support, augmenting their good will and maintaining their outward dignity in her addresses to her father and more highly ranked members of the court, including Queen Anne herself. When she refers to jointure, she addresses a problem the legal scholar Lloyd Bonfield considers transitional in the period of the KU letter. He suggests that jointure agreements drawn up after marriage were less secure that those prepared at the outset.[18] Examining

---

and Gary Waller, eds., *Reading Mary Wroth: Representing Alternatives in Early Modern England* (Knoxville, TN: Univ. of Tennessee Press, 1991), 16–34.

[16] Roberts observes Lady Mary's wit in the letter to Queen Anne transcribed on pp. 233–34 of *Poems*. The letter refers specifically to Robert Wroth's willingness to designate the estate and its income for her jointure because the other Wroth holdings are entailed. His own letter to the King is recorded in Vol. XX of the Salisbury (Cecil) Papers, p. 315. Robert Wroth's message, like Lady Mary's, refers to the present decay of the estate which is "unfit to receive the King at his repair to the forest." Wroth also promised the payment of "four years fine" and vowed to spend 500 pounds on the house within six years. Wroth's generosity toward Mary in this document implies a hope of developing the estate, and promised Mary Wroth her jointure.

[17] See the note accompanying the summation of Lady Mary's letter to Queen Anne in *HMC* Salisbury, XXII, e. Robert Sidney mentions the company of Lord Southampton to Barbara Sidney, Series 81, letters 247 and 248, written from Spa and Aachen in July 1613: *HMS* De L'Isle and Dudley, V, 112–13.

[18] Lloyd Bonfield, *Marriage Settlements, 1601–1740* (Cambridge and New York: Cambridge Univ. Press, 1983), 49. Lady Mary's financial provisions, as noted, date from at least two points in her married life. Eileen Spring, *Law, Land, & Family: Aristocratic Inheritance in*

the settlements of aristocratic women, Eileen Spring stresses the precarious nature of property agreements at this social level. Her most telling illustration concerns Lady Anne Clifford, who married Lady Mary's cousin Philip Herbert after the death of Susan de Vere, to whom the *Urania* is dedicated. Lady Anne, as Josephine Roberts mentions, describes her positive memories of association with Wroth (Roberts, *Poems*, 27). Because Lady Clifford also wrote, she could add her own story to that of Lady Mary, allowing readers to see the financial balancing women needed to negotiate in periods of marriage and widowhood.

Would Robert Sidney have answered the letter from Mary asking for "writings"? If he could have assisted, he was likely to have done so, as Nevitt's comment indicates. Among his frequent positive allusions to Mary cited in the family correspondence, I mention only one that concerns her support after her marriage. A letter to Barbara in 1605 offers to repay any money she has given his "daughter Wroth" because he does not desire to see her in want.[19] After Robert Wroth's death, the senior Sidney's letters frequently bless James as well as his own daughter Barbara. Many letters indicate that Wroth is visiting Penshurst and sharing some of the family resources. As noted above, Mary Wroth certainly sought specific help in safeguarding the wardship of James Wroth. An independent confirmation of Sidney's effort appears in a letter from Sir Nicholas Throckmorton, with whom he served abroad, wishing him well in his dispute over the wardship of his grandson.[20] In personal correspondence, in good wishes from others, and in Thomas Nevitt's accounting, we find Sir Robert, while he faced the many business and military expenses related to his station, most favorably inclined to help a daughter in need.

MS Crawford 177, a formerly "lost" letter, thus increases our attention to Mary Wroth's personal and practical activities at an important point in her life. It opens new ways to look at her initiative and life choices through her letters in

---

England, 1300 to 1800 (Chapel Hill and London: Univ. of North Carolina Press, 1993), esp. 109, 119, and 180, provides some case histories for Mary Wroth's contemporaries, especially that of Lady Anne Clifford. Her illustration strengthens the argument that even generous provisions for women left their security precarious within the fundamentally patrilineal system preferred by aristocratic families.

[19] U 1474, Series 81, Letter 145. Sidney here states that he has seen a letter from Mary Wroth about her needs, yet no copy of such a request has appeared to date. It is another "lost" letter which should be sought. See also Hannay, Kinnamon, and Brennan, *Correspondence*, 124.

[20] U1475, C9, Letter 306, 17 March 1614, Flushing. Sir John Throckmorton to Viscount Lisle. Throckmorton expresses sympathy for the loss of "Sr Robert Wrothe. . . . it would be of great comforte of h[our] L[ordship] obtained your full desyer of the wardship of your grandchild." *HMC*, V, 164–65.

addition to her literary creations. In it she negotiates her independence at the same time that she pays rhetorical justice to her status as daughter, wife, and widow. Perhaps the reproduction of her distinctive hand will encourage other researchers to seek it in miscellaneous collections. In addition to Lady Wroth's personal and family contexts, every piece of information that illuminates the balance of dignity and independence required of women of all estates helps us understand what women practiced rather than what was prescribed for them.

UNIVERSITY OF KANSAS

Editing the Early Modern Miscellany: Modelling and Knowledge [Re]Presentation as a Context for the Contemporary Editor

RAYMOND G. SIEMENS
with Caroline Leitch[1]

IF ANYONE UNDERSTANDS THE REAL ISSUES RELATING TO REPRESENTATION of knowledge, it is the textual editor. Born in traditions associated with transcription, comparison, collation, and classification; working in varied media and across traditions and formats within and among those media; and holding high ideals, or at least striving for accuracy often difficult to achieve in pragmatic terms, the editor practices the science of knowledge conveyance, re-presenting and representing, modelling and then transmitting the contents of textual human artefacts from one form to another, pouring old wine (as has been said very many times) into new bottles . . . and, of late, doing so into containers quite unrecognisable to all but the most contemporary of authors. If we are to believe scholars such as Northrop Frye, humanists have always "lived in a far more efficient technological world than most of their contemporaries" (7–8); this technological advantage, Frye asserts, has historically been connected to the prestige of humanists. So, too, can this be said of the editor . . . perhaps especially so in a contemporary climate that pits page against electronic-hyperlinked-scroll, and print-codex against ephemeral internet and other forms of electronic data transmission.

---

[1] Originally presented at the RETS Josephine Roberts Panel, MLA December 2004 (Philadelphia) / RSA April 2005 (Cambridge, UK). The work presented here reflects also the involvement of Caroline Leitch, who has investigated collation tools for use on the *Devonshire MS*.

The rise of the electronic medium in the past two decades—especially the increase in efficiency and affordability of electronic methods to manage and disseminate textual and extra-textual materials—has allowed us to realise the ideals of one of the most important schools of contemporary thought surrounding archival representation, what is often referred to as social theories of editing, theories that expanded the notion of edited text to include what were often considered to be extra-textual elements.[2] Such thinking, combined with computing technology, has brought about significant change in our field, perhaps most noticeably in the role of the textual scholar working in the electronic medium over the past decade, who increasingly began to accumulate information rather than synthesise it[3]—an accumulation, made possible only by computing, also associated with the critical process of unediting, paying an increased attention to the full materiality of the texts that are, ultimately, the objects of our consideration.[4]

Like a number of us, across the past decade, I've had the pleasure of editing both for print—which people have said, for several years, is moving on the way out and, yet, it shows no real sign whatsoever of doing so—and the electronic medium, which, for a decade or longer, has been heralded almost as a saviour, of sorts, but has yet to manifest itself to us in any form nearly as "intuitive" or familiar as what can be captured and navigated in print form. I'm overstating, to be sure, but do so to the good end of drawing attention to the fact that, contrary to speculation some time ago, the book is not nearly dead, nor do we yet understand the electronic medium well enough for it to live up to its promise. The reason for this, I would urge, is largely because we have yet to articulate the salient features of the new electronic book—and, more specifically, the new scholarly edition in electronic form—in a way that suggests the place of the new electronic book in our personal and professional lives, in our ways of doing things when we work alone, and in our ways of doing things when we work and meet with others.

An example not drawn from the world of the book might bear this out more clearly. Anyone participating in what has often been termed an "electronic conference" will know that it is not like a conference at all; rather, if the e-mail listserv is the computing facilitator of interaction, it is like passing notes around in a darkened room, where you can read what people have to say but not hear them or see them. Aural and visual technologies are making this better, of course, but

---

[2] Such as visual presentation, incorporation of visual and aural material, &c.; the best foundational arguments for this are found throughout in McKenzie (*Bibliography*), and McGann (*Critique, Textual Condition*).

[3] See Schreibman ("Computer-Mediated Texts," 283 ff.).

[4] See McLeod ("Information," 240–245 ff., "UNEditing," 26 ff.), and Sutherland ("Revised Relations," 17 ff.).

there is no technologically-facilitated substitute, yet, for live contact and collegial interaction as one finds at a conference. Those who develop such technologies have not yet been able to model, accurately, and to represent, adeptly and conveniently, the processes and practices of the conference environment such that the virtual has something on the real.

So, too, perhaps, it is with the edition and the electronic edition—thus far at least. But I would suggest that we are closer in modelling the scholarly edition electronically than others have come in modelling the conference via electronic means—in large part because of groups such as that which drafted the MLA Guidelines for Electronic Scholarly Editions, and I would urge in larger part this is because the scholarly editing community has always lived with an awareness of the demands essential to the proper transmission of textual content from one object to another, from one form to another, and from one medium to another . . . ideas central both to modelling and to the re-presentation of knowledge.[5]

Miscellany Editing

Indeed, it is such a community awareness that I've enjoyed alongside the experience of editing by relatively traditional means the *Henry VIII MS* (BL Add. MS 31, 922), then carrying out revisions on that edition while in the early stages of preparing an electronic edition of the *Devonshire MS* (BL Add MS 17, 492), which I'm editing as part of a joint pilot project between MRTS and ITER.

These works are both miscellanies, both originating in English royal circles within fifteen years of one another. The *Henry VIII MS* is one of three early Tudor songbooks, and can be dated ca. 1520–1523, reflecting events and activities from before 1509 until mid-1522. It is most notable in that it is the primary evidence of Henry VIII's poetic and musical prowess; it allows us a glimpse into the way he chose to use these forms of expression to fashion himself, as a young

---

[5] For primers into these concepts in a humanities context, please see Unsworth and McCarty. As Unsworth notes, "[k]nowledge representation draws on the field of artificial intelligence and seeks to produce models of human understanding that are tractable to computation"; further, to paraphrase, he states: While fundamentally based on digital algorithms, knowledge representation privileges traditionally-held values associated with the liberal arts and humanities: general intelligence about human pursuits and the human social/societal environment; adaptable, creative, analytical thinking; critical reasoning, argument and logic; and the employment and conveyance of these, in and through human communicative processes and other processes native to humanities. McCarty's argument suggests that, in activities of the humanist using the computer, knowledge representation manifests itself directly in issues related to archival representation and textual editing, high-level interpretive theory and criticism, and protocols of knowledge transfer—all as modelled with computational techniques; we model our data, our intellectual processes, and beyond.

monarch championing the ideals of courtly love, in a court that all too often attempted to impose its fashions and those of his father upon him.

The *Devonshire MS* is best called, as Paul Remley has, "a courtly anthology"; it is of 1525–1559, with the period of its greatest activity being the mid-1530s. It has been a standard witness for Wyatt's poetical works for several centuries, but is today most notable because it presents the earliest sustained instance in the English tradition of a literary writing community comprising both men and women and, thus, a primary site of women's involvement in the poetic-political world captured by the early Tudor lyric.

Both editions aim to serve a similar audience, scholars interested in early Tudor poetry; therefore my treatment of each text has been in accordance with the school of documentary editing and conforming to well-accepted editorial standards. But there are differences: specifically in the areas of transcription and collation, which must be considered if we are to describe a model of the new scholarly edition in electronic form. I'd like especially to highlight those differences as they relate to the promise of modelling that new scholarly edition.

Transcription

As we know, simply put, transcription is the act of copying from one textual instance to another. When we transcribe an early modern work, we represent that work in our character set, with a set of accepted protocols to facilitate this, and an understood way of handling the expansion of early abbreviations, digraphs, non-modern characters, and so forth. These protocols we outline for the most part in a statement of editorial principles, especially so if our own practices represent a slight deviation from accepted practice. Figure 1 suggests to us some of those practices, as carried out on the text immediately underlaid the third musical voice, which comprises the first stanza of "Pastyme with good company."

> Pastime *with* good *com*pany
> I loue *and* schall do tyl I dye
> gruche who lust but none denye
> so god be plesyd *thus* leue wyll I
> for my pastance
> hu*n*t syng *and* dance
> my hart is sett
> all goodly sport
> for my *com*fort
> who schall me lett.

Figure 1: Image and Transcription, Henry VIII MS ("Pastyme with good company," third voice, ll. 1–10, 15r). Note variable spellings of "pastime."

While working on the Henry VIII MS, I transcribed as many did at that time in the Manuscript Students Room at the British Museum, from original manuscript, to paper, with pencil. This passage of information capture was one that would be quite familiar to most: I kept a list of character forms and abbreviations for each of the several hands of the manuscript, and attempted to represent graphically the yoghs, digraphs, abbreviations, and other forms that I knew, later, would have to be represented in some way via our standard character set when I ultimately re-transcribed this work into the computer. I checked readings against microfilm and, ultimately, again against the original. Further, as some do, I held

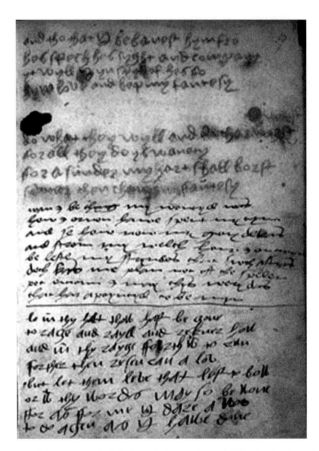

<div1 type="poem"rhyme= "16:4x4 abab8" id= "LDev087–TM1042"><head><bibl><title>my hart ys set not remoue</title>unattributed [Margaret Douglas]</bibl></head>

<lg n="3"><l n="9">and tho that I <sic corr="be banished">bebanest</sic> hym fro</l>
<l n="10">hes spech hes syght and company</l>
<l n="11">yt wyll I yn spyt of hes ffo</l>
<l n="12">hym love and kep my fantesy</l></lg>

<lg n= "4"><l n="13">do what they wyll and do ther warst <addrend="superscript">w<gap/>
st</add></l>
<l n="14">ffor all they do ys <sic resp="RGS" corr= "vanity">wanety</sic></l>
<l n="15">ffor a sunder my hart shall borst</l>
<ln="16">sow<gap/>er then change my ffantesy</l></lg></div1>

Figure 2: Image and Transcription, Devonshire MS ("My hart ys set not remoue," ll. 9–16, 59r).

off converting the yoghs, digraphs, and abbreviated forms until I'd done the collation and was prepared to make a commitment to consistent re-presentation of these forms. Happily, the hands were legible (because the scribes were professional), the texts were clear, and the only thing that caused me significant concern at this point was the fact that I was transcribing, for a literary audience, a text which was so very clearly aligned with the music. But the music of the manuscript had been thoroughly treated by the musicological community as much as the lyrics of the manuscript had been overlooked; so, there was justification to provide a proper edition and study of the lyrics alone, for a literary-studies audience.

                           ≈   ≈   ≈

Transcribing the Devonshire MS was a very different enterprise. The majority of its contents are lyrics, but they are captured solely in textual form by the manuscript's compilers. Hands were more difficult (because they are predominantly amateur), and texts were obscured at times, a function of this manuscript having very different characteristics and uses from the Henry VIII MS. Transcription was from microfilm and electronic facsimile (derived from microfilm), directly into a text editor on laptop computer. Here, I worked with two research assistants, and we independently duplicated each other's work—comparing results at set intervals using a collation program, with the understanding that this process would highlight areas that would require special attention when I checked our full transcription against the original in the British Library. Transcribing directly into the computer meant that we had to make immediate decisions about character sets to represent earlier forms, such as digraphs and abbreviations, and to accommodate this we adopted and augmented a list of standard earlier forms and semi-standard ASCII-text representations which has been published by the Renaissance Electronic Text series at the University of Toronto.

The biggest difference in transcribing the two manuscripts, however, was not in workflow, nor in the use of computing technology itself as part of the transcription process. Rather, the biggest difference was found in the demands that a computing approach to transcription made on our group once we had finished our initial transcription and verified it against the original. We had deliberately held off as long as possible on introducing an essential component of the transcription process in the electronic medium: the application of an appropriate document encoding system. So, at the stage we might well have been making ready for other tasks associated with creating the edition, we began preparing the transcribed text for the application of a system conforming with Text Encoding Initiative XML—at the same time as a subset of the TEI Consortium group was working toward establishing the protocols for describing the type of documents that were our focus. This involved modelling our textual data with a Document Type Definition that had as much parity as possible with the TEI—and looking further to projects such as the Digital Scriptorium at Berkeley and Kevin Kiernan's Edition Creation Tools at Kentucky for their own modelling practices. Once modelled, we applied the DTD to the text in several passes, initially with a focus on structural and surface-level elements;[6] that transcription and encoding is represented in Figure 2.

Time-consuming as this process was, it has added significant value to the work we will ultimately produce. As proponents of TEI and other encoding systems will say, modelling the data of an edition with a DTD forces editors to make explicit their understanding of the work being represented, in a constrained logical vocabulary that has application to other edited works as well. That DTD becomes the textual-critical vocabulary of the edition, a description of the edited text that can, by itself, facilitate study of the original artefact.

Collation

Collation, the second of the areas I'd like to highlight, makes for a different type of story. The collation associated with the Henry VIII MS was typical, initially involving a standard visual comparison of the base text against witnesses as I was able to encounter them. Since the works in the manuscript are polyphonic, in most cases I had "internal" witnesses to consider among the several lyrical voices of each piece. I'd transcribed all the witnesses and, in the end, I entered those transcriptions into the computer so that I could check my initial collation with the results provided by the best computing tools available at the time: early versions of the Donne Variorum Collation Program, PC-CASE, and UNITE. This was all to good end, as the use of these tools allowed for detailed comparison such that my initial work was augmented and, further, one of the tools assisted in the formatting of my textual apparatus, which is typical of the apparatus one would expect in a good print edition. The final results appear, roughly, as below:

> Texts Collated:
>   *H1,2,3* (14v–15r, ll. 1–10 *H2,3*), *LRit(1)1,2,3* (136v–137r, ll. 1–10), *LRit(2)1,2,3* (141v–142r) Emendations of the Copy Text (H1):
>   4   leue] loue *H1*, leue *H2,3*, lyf *LRit(1)1,3*, lyue *LRit(2)1*, lyfe *LRit(2)2,3*

---

    [6] I've discussed details of some of the more interesting problems we encountered in encoding the Devonshire MS in a forthcoming article, "The Devil is in the Details."

15   for] ffor *H1,2,3*, *LRit(1)1,2,3*, For *LRit(2)1,2,3*Collation (Substantive Variants):
2   vntyll] tyl *H2,3*, vnto *LRit(1)1*, vn to *LRit(1)2,3*, *LRit(2)1,3* I] I do *H3*
3   *substitute* for my pastaunce *LRit(1)2* who lust] so wylle *LRit(1)1,3*, so woll *LRit(2)1*, so wyll *LRit(2)2*, who wyll *LRit(2)3*
4   *substitute* honte syng *and* daunce *LRit(1) 2 thus*] so *LRit(1)1,3*, this *LRit(2)1*, *this LRit(2)2,3* leue] *H2,3*, loue *H1*
5   *substitute* my hert ys set *LRit(1)2* pastance] dystaunce. *LRit(2)1*, dystaunce. *LRit(2)2*, dystaunce *LRit(2)3*
6   *substitute* yn sport *LRit(1)2*

[Collation of the Henry VIII MS]

In working on the Devonshire MS, computer-assisted collation was a process that we used as part of our transcription of the original document, to ensure the accuracy of our work at that stage. But the way in which we will collate the Devonshire MS against its witnesses is still a bit of a mystery to us. Let me explain what I mean by this. Following typical practice, we've gathered all the witnesses necessary for our edition, and we are nearly done with the process of transcribing and encoding them to a standard similar to that of our copy text. But we realise that the ultimate form of the textual apparatus, and the collation process we will employ to create that form, will be largely dependent on how we envision people making use of the edition of the Devonshire MS—and, further, the limitations of publication. We are considering, for example, creating a standard apparatus, based on the print model, integrated perhaps via hypertext with the various forms and instances of the texts the apparatus takes into account. Another possibility is for us to rely on our TEI encoding to house the various variants relating to the works in the Devonshire MS and to present the encoded manuscript and witnesses with software that would allow the readers themselves to carry out the collation, constructing their own apparatus in the process. In trying to find a computational solution to the problem of how best to collate the Devonshire MS against its witnesses, we experimented with a number of collation tools, including the Versioning Machine (version 2.1), Collate, and Juxta. While each of the tools we have worked with satisfied some of our needs, we found that no one tool was able to do it all.

In some ways, the tool with which we have had the most success is the Versioning Machine. The Versioning Machine satisfies our demand for open-source, freely distributed software and runs in the reader's browser without requiring plug-ins, making it ideal for most users. It allows the user to select and display

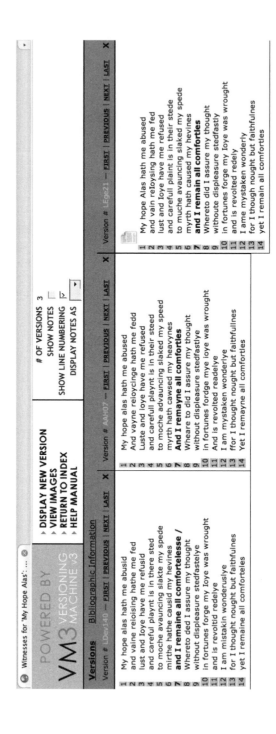

Figure 3: Collation results and formats of the Devonshire MS, Versioning Machine.

a number of witnesses in the same browser window, view images, and see textual and bibliographic information either inline or as pop-up notes. Most importantly, the Versioning Machine makes excellent use of the TEI's apparatus for comparing witnesses. By demanding well-formed TEI-conformant XML as its base, using the Versioning Machine encouraged us to pay close attention to our encoding standards, an important consideration if we are going to make the Devonshire MS and its witnesses available in their encoded form. As an added benefit, the Versioning Machine is a current project which means that the tool is not static. Rather, it is being updated and improved as we use it.

Although the Versioning Machine has satisfied our requirements in terms of displaying entire witnesses side-by-side, it was not the ideal solution to our problems of how to display variation on a word-by-word basis and how to regularize orthographic variations. For that capability, we turned to Peter Robinson's program Collate, a collation tool which first appeared as a Macintosh program in the 1990s. Robinson himself admits that Collate, along with his XML publishing tool Anastasia, which we also experimented with, is very difficult to use. Robinson notes, "as their creator I think I am uniquely qualified to note that [Collate and Anastasia] are not easy to use: if everyone who wanted to make digital editions was required to use these two tools, very few digital editions would ever be made." After using Collate for many months, we are inclined to agree. That is not to say that Collate does not have its advantages. Collate has a simple, and surprisingly intuitive, interface for regularizing variants. Our experimentation with Collate has provided us with a wealth of raw material in the form of collations that allow us to focus our attention on substantive differences between texts without getting bogged down by orthographic variations. However, we did encounter many of the problems Robinson warns of: Collate is unpredictable at times, both in its performance and its results; it requires an older version of the Macintosh OS, one which a decreasing number of editors use; Collate is an older program that is not currently being updated.

The third collation tool we used, with mixed results, was Juxta, created by Applied Research in Patacriticism. We were pleased with the elegant way in which Juxta displays visual information. The reader can easily see variation on the level of the whole text, line-by-line, and word-by-word. Juxta also allows users to view digital images of manuscripts and includes a histogram tool. Like the Versioning Machine, Juxta relies on encoded texts. The encoding required by Juxta, however, is much more simplified than that required by the Versioning Machine. This is both an advantage and a disadvantage. Encoding using the TEI's critical apparatus tagset, as required by the Versioning Machine, while time-consuming, may be a better long-term decision because it lends itself to a wider variety of applications.

Another of our concerns with Juxta is that its performance has, at times, been inconsistent across platforms. Now that the source code for Juxta has been made available, we are looking forward to looking under the hood, so to speak, to see if we can tailor Juxta to our specific needs.

```
                                            LDev140-TM1046_collated
<lg n="1"><l n="1">
LDev140-TM1046  My hope alas  hath me abusid
AAHO7                                    abused
LEge21                        Alas       abused
<lg n="1"><l n="2">
LDev140-TM1046  and vaine  reioising   hathe me fed
AAHO7               And vayne  reioycinge hath      fedd
LEge21              vain    reloysing  hath
<lg n="1"><l n="3">
LDev140-TM1046  lust   and loye have me refusid
AAHO7              Luste      ioye         refused
LEge21                                     refused
<lg n="1"><l n="4">
LDev140-TM1046  and careful  playnt is in there sted
AAHO7              carefull            their steed
LEge21             carefull plaint     their stede
<lg n="1"><l n="5">
LDev140-TM1046  to moche avauncing   slakte my spede
AAHO7                   advauncing slaked      speed
LEge21              muche              slaked
<lg n="1"><l n="6">
LDev140-TM1046  mirthe hathe causid   my hevines
AAHO7              myrth hath cawsed      heavynes
LEge21             myrth hath  caused
<lg n="1"><l n="7">
LDev140-TM1046  and I remaine all comfortelesse /
AAHO7              And remayne   comforties   []
LEge21             remain     comforties   []
<lg n="2"><l n="8">
LDev140-TM1046  Whereto  ded I assure my thought
AAHO7              Wheare to did
LEge21                        did
<lg n="2"><l n="9">
LDev140-TM1046  without  displeasure stedfastelye
AAHO7                               stedfastlye
LEge21             withoute          stedfastly
<lg n="2"><l n="10">
```

Figure 4: Collation results and formats of the Devonshire MS, Collate.

If we have learned one thing from our experience using a variety of current collation tools, it is that customization is in our future. There is no one collation tool that satisfies the needs of our particular project. In an ideal world, we would obtain a tool that combines the TEI-based encoding of the Versioning Machine, the regularization interface of Collate, and the user interface of Juxta. Until such a tool exists, we must rely on the greatest advantage of all three of these tools: their ability to teach us more about how collation software works and does not work.

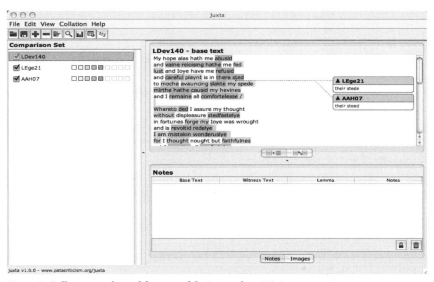

Figure 5: Collation results and formats of the Devonshire MS, Juxta.

Integration

In discussing my experience with transcription and collation with both of these projects, I don't think I've said anything that is startling or new. But these changes in the way things are done, and changes in the "end products" of each essential editing process, are new to us as we encounter them; and these ways and end-products in the electronic medium are changing with the introduction of new technologies and the research results of our colleagues. Furthermore, what the changes in each of these processes, and others, represent to the editing community is potentially something more significant than the sum of their parts. In the case of transcription, we find that the encoding now associated with transcription in the electronic medium provides an explicit model of those data, ultimately (in the best of circumstances) adding to the level of bibliographic description we give our texts and, in turn, the utility of those texts to those in our community and beyond. In the case of collation, we find that it is not the data but rather the process which is being modelled in the electronic medium—ultimately adding significant possibility to the way in which we represent the textual apparatus in our editions. Both have to do with strategies of the representation of knowledge, and both produce an electronic end-product whose utility is far greater than it would be if produced solely in print.

It is on this notion of greater utility that I should like to conclude. The promise of social theories of editing, and movements toward un-editing and what has been called material textuality, is a greater attention to the pertinent details of individual textual instances and the factors informing them. The promise of computation, in this context, is as facilitator for the processes involving the representation of those instances; here, transcription and collation have considerable importance, for the computer alters and enhances elements of each, both in process and in product. Further, there is also a larger context to consider here, one that involves the other actions pertinent to our discipline that are, ultimately, centred on the re-presented artefacts that our community produces; inherently connected to our representation of archival materials are the essential activities of critical inquiry and communication of results—and there are considerable gains to be realised here as well, gains the origins of which are found in these activities.

These are necessary steps toward a proper articulation of the salient features of the new scholarly edition in electronic form, a virtual object that, itself, will capture the best of our traditions at the same time as it explicitly integrates those traditions associated with archival representation with those relating to critical inquiry and the communication of results. Without doubt, the most interesting and profitable work in this regard is being done by members of our community. Returning to my earlier analogy of the electronic conference with reference to modelling practice, I'd like to point out, and happily so, that the way in which we are able to model the data of the transcription and the process of collation is well in advance of the passing-around-notes-in-the-dark model of the electronic conference.

UNIVERSITY OF VICTORIA

Bibliography

Digital Scriptorium. <http://www.scriptorium.columbia.edu/>.

Donne Variorum Collation Program. <http://donnevariorum.tamu.edu/down/downpage.html>.

Faulhaber, Charles B. "Textual Criticism in the 21st Century." *Romance Philology* 45 (1991): 123–48.

"Guidelines for Electronic Scholarly Editions." Modern Language Association Of America, Committee On Scholarly Editions. <http://www.mla.org/resources/documents/rep_scholarly/cse_guidelines>.

Frye, Northrop. "Literary and Mechanical Models." In Ian Lancashire, ed., *Research in Humanities Computing 1: Select Papers from the ALLC/ACH Conference, Toronto, June 1989*, 3–13. Oxford: Clarendon Press, 1991.

Kiernan, Kevin. *Edition Production and Presentation Technology.* <http://beowulf.engl.uky.edu/~eft/eppt-trial/EPPT-TrialProjects.htm>.

Marin, Francisco Marcos. *UNITE.*

McCarty, Willard. "Knowing true things by what their mockeries be." *Computing in the Humanities Working Papers* A.24 (2003). <http://www.chass.utoronto.ca/epc/chwp/CHC2003/McCarty2.htm>.

McGann, Jerome. *A Critique of Modern Textual Criticism.* Chicago: Univ. of Chicago Press, 1983.

———. *The Textual Condition.* Princeton: Princeton Univ. Press, 1991.

———, et al. *Juxta.* <http://www.patacriticism.org/juxta/>.

McKenzie, D. F. *Bibliography and the Sociology of the Text.* London: The British Library, 1986.

McLeod, Randall. [Random Clod]. "Information on Information." *Text* 5 (1991): 240–81.

———. "UNEditing Shak-speare." *Sub-stance* 33/4 (1982): 26–55.

PC-CASE.

Renaissance Electronic Texts. Ian Lancashire, general ed. University of Toronto <http://www.library.utoronto.ca/utel/ret/ret.html>.

Remley, Paul G. "Mary Shelton and Her Tudor Literary Milieu." In Peter C. Herman, ed., *Rethinking the Henrician Era: Essays on Early Tudor Texts and Contexts*, 40–77. Urbana: Univ. of Illinois Press, 1994.

Robinson, Peter. "Current issues in making digital editions of medieval texts – or, do electronic scholarly editions have a future?" *Digital Medievalist* 1.1 (2005) <http://www.digitalmedievalist.org/article.cfm?RecID=6>.

———. *Anastasia.* <http://www.sd-editions.com/anastasia/index.html >.

———. *Collate.*

Schreibman, Susan. "Computer-Mediated Texts and Textuality: Theory and Practice." 283--293. I in *A New Computer-Assisted Literary Criticism?*, ed. R.G. Siemens.

———, et al. *The Versioning Machine*. <http://v-machine.org/index.php>.

Siemens, Ray. "Textual Collation Software for the PC: A Review of *PC-CASE*, *UNITE*, and the *Donne Variorum Collation Program*." *Text Technology* 4.3 (1994): 209–22.

———. "The Devil is in the Details: An Electronic Edition of the Devonshire MS (British Library Additional MS 17,492), its Encoding and Prototyping." With Barbara Bond and Karin Armstrong, *New Technologies and Renaissance Studies*. Tempe: MRTS and ITER, in press.

Sutherland, Kathryn. "Revised Relations? Material Text, Immaterial Text, and the Electronic Environment." *TEXT* 11 (1998): 17–30.

Unsworth, John. "Knowledge Representation in Humanities Computing." Inaugural E-humanities Lecture at the *National Endowment for the Humanities* (April 3, 2001). <http://www.iath.virginia.edu/~jmu2m/KR/>.

Common Place, Common Space: Three Seventeenth-Century Verse Miscellanies as Examples of Material Culture

MICHAEL DENBO

T HE English Renaissance verse commonplace book holds a unique place in literary studies. Coming as it does during the advent of print technologies, the handwritten commonplace book appears to be a precursor *to* or a reaction *against* or at least a lesser example of the same. Indeed, according to the *OED*, the very word "manuscript" does not appear in English until 1597, when I. S. (?) printed a volume entitled *Certaine Worthe Manuscript Poems of Great Antiquitie*. Critically, these handwritten compilations, so common during their day, present us with vexing problems as to authorship and original text. John Donne, the seventeenth-century poet most famously aligned with this phenomenon, published very few poems in print during his lifetime, but is frequently found in commonplace books, including the three exemplars discussed in this paper. And, as we all know, no two handwritten copies of a Donne poem are identical, thus leaving scholars with the endless task of finding the *original* text of any one poem, or, equally daunting, deciding whether some poems attributed to Donne might not even have been written by him. These questions focus our attention on poets and their poems, ultimately prioritizing the poem as a nonmaterial abstraction which appears only when published in a

---

This paper was first presented at the 2004 MLA conference, Philadelphia, PA, at a panel entitled "The Josephine Roberts Forum: English Renaissance Manuscript Miscellanies," Steven W. May presiding.

particular physical construction or spoken out loud by a particular speaker. The model is elsewhere—perhaps called a copy text; however, whatever we read is a copy of what may actually have no surviving original. How ironic that our own critical practices tend to mythologize an original which to contemporary writers might have had little or no importance.

Equally complex, however, are the questions that emerge when we consider each commonplace book itself as both an object and an objectification of a cultural mind-set. Unlike a poem, a commonplace book *is* a physical construction, and although it is understood in a larger context, i.e., *commonplace book*, each book represents the discursive practices and social assumptions that led its compiler to create the book as a physical object. From this perspective, the texts of the individual poems do not lead us to a greater or lesser version of the original abstract phenomenon known as a poem. Instead, each book is its own object for interpretation, a place at which the circulation of individual poems both stops and is led forward by how a particular book was used. If the book is small—perhaps an octavo—it is a fair guess it was carried around in someone's pocket to record or share poems with friends. If the book is large—a folio—it stayed on someone's shelf and was used differently from the much smaller octavo, even though the poems themselves may be similar. Each book, then, found its own *common* place, and equally so, each poem also found its own common *place*—or those places—that allow us a glimpse of Renaissance discourse in a multidimensional framework. Ultimately at question, and it is much too complex even to begin to answer here, is how the creators of these books understood themselves, not just as social beings, but as intellectual beings, people who perceived the world in a specific manner and who, like us, needed to create objects that represented their own values and cultural mind-set. A set of paradoxical twins, *reading* and *writing,* are in question here: Why did these compilers go to such lengths, often over decades, to create these books, and what can the circumstances required to create them tell us about their creators?

For the purpose of this discussion, I focus on three early seventeenth-century commonplace books: the Holgate Miscellany, presently housed in the Morgan Library, New York City; and two manuscripts from the Yale University Osborn Collection, b 62, an anonymous Oxford manuscript and b 197, the Tobias Alston manuscript. Although the three manuscripts are unquestionably commonplace books, they are very different in scope and were used quite differently by their creators.

The Holgate Miscellany is a quarto gathered in fours comprising 182 poems and six prose entries.[1] It measures 7⅞ x 5⅝ inches. Its creator, William Holgate, was born in 1590 and died sometime after 1649, the terminus ad quem of the miscellany. Its paper was first found in 1619, making Holgate approximately twenty-nine years old when he started his miscellany. More than likely, most of the poems were transcribed during the 1620s, but for some reason Holgate added a few poems that date from the late 1640s. I can't account for the lack of use between the 1620s and 1640s.

From our perspective, the Holgate is a clear literary text. Among its identified contributors, either by names or initials, are William Holgate, the compiler, John Donne, James I, Richard Corbett, Ben Jonson, George Morley, Sir Walter Ralegh, Benjamin Stone, Barton Halliday, Sir Henry Wotton, Hugh Holland, Thomas Carew, Francis Beaumont, Christopher Brooke, and William Strode. The rare inclusion of Shakespeare's Sonnet 106 is anonymous. Seventy-one of the poems identify a poet, but as in any other verse miscellany, the attributions are frequently incorrect. More than likely, however, Holgate could identify many of the anonymous poems. For example, the Holgate includes fifteen poems by William Strode, all of which are grouped together between pages 198 and 211. However, only one of the poems specifically identifies Strode.

Perhaps the most important contributor, however, is William Holgate himself, who included six of his own poems, all funeral elegies, between pages 5 and 23. To this reader, his verse seems overtly and self-consciously poetic, his narrative stance being that of someone who is unsure of his own ability to interpret unfortunate events. His most serious poem is a funeral elegy on Dr. William Ashboold, rector of two neighboring churches in Cornhill, London. Since Ashboold died in 1622, I suspect that Holgate's interest in poetry led him to create this particular miscellany. Also included are funeral elegies on Ashboold's two daughters, both of whom died in 1621. I cannot explain Holgate's interest in this family. His name does not appear on either church register.

---

[1] See my dissertation, "The Holgate Miscellany (The Pierpont Morgan Library, MA 1057: A Diplomatic Edition)" (Ph.D. diss., City University of New York, 1997); and the forthcoming RETS edition; also idem, "Editing a Renaissance Commonplace Book: The Holgate Miscellany," in *New Ways of Looking at Old Texts, III: Papers of the Renaissance English Text Society, 1997–2001*, ed. W. Speed Hill (Tempe: Arizona Center for Medieval and Renaissance Studies in conjunction with Renaissance English Text Society, 2004), 65–73.

The miscellany itself demonstrates at least an attempt at general organization which ultimately breaks down because Holgate could not control which poems would come to him in what sequence. Holgate started his book by copying a few poems out of a printed book, Tofte's *Blazon of Iealousie*, which he transcribed with great care and precision. Also, in the last pages we find some prose works, including sections of John Earle's *Characters* and Robert Cecil's letter to his young son. Generally, the most canonical lyrics are found between pages 35 and 100, including several poems by Donne and the sonnet by Shakespeare. These are followed by a group of elegies on the death of Henry, Prince of Wales, who died in 1612, approximately ten years before the poems were entered into the miscellany. Toward the end of the collection there are several spiritual poems, including those already mentioned by Strode. There are some comic epigrams throughout the book, but when they appear they are grouped together. They are less sexually explicit than those we see in many miscellanies.

Of particular note concerning the Holgate is its attention to current events, especially poems about English soldiers fighting in Bohemia and the Lowlands, and also poems about the proposed Spanish Match, when James hoped that his son Charles would marry the Spanish Infanta, thus gaining himself power in what would later become known as the Thirty Years' War. In disguise as Tom and Jack Pan, Charles and Buckingham traveled to Spain in hopes of wooing the Spanish Princess. At stake, however, was whether England would survive as a non-Catholic nation, because if Charles married the Infanta, the nature of religion and English subjecthood might change.[2] The Holgate includes first-hand commentary on the Spanish Match, a satiric travel poem composed by a member of the English follow-up expedition, a group of ships meant to bring Charles and the Infanta home to England. Surprisingly, collation to British Library Add. Ms. 23229 demonstrates that Holgate personally knew at least one staff member to Edward, Viscount Conway, secretary of state to James, leading me to believe that the poem was transcribed by Holgate at or close to the time of the affair. To some modern readers, the poem is simply doggerel, but I doubt seventeenth-century readers would have taken such a negative view. As cultural satire, it is quite funny, and by itself, that quality would have lifted it above the ordinary. Commonplace books, as a rule, do not show us poetry on the vertical, and it is not surprising to find great poems, say by John Donne, next to poems about farting in church or on other scatological themes. The art of poetry (for its own sake) is

---

[2] For an extensive discussion of the Spanish Match, see Glyn Redworth, *The Prince and the Infanta* (New Haven and London: Yale Univ. Press, 2003; also Alexander Samson, ed., *The Spanish Match: Prince Charles's Journey to Madrid, 1623* (Aldershot: Ashgate, 2006).

only one aspect of the miscellany tradition, and if we are to understand this phenomenon, we will have to adjust our reading to other, less lofty questions.

A far different miscellany is Osborn b 62, an anonymous seventeenth-century miscellany described by Peter Beal as "compiled by an Oxford man."[3] Unlike the Holgate, it is a small book, only 3½ x 5½ inches, written in a frequently illegible, mixed hand. Presently, it is in very fragile condition, having, I suspect, suffered water damage at some point in its history. Its watermark is a pot, but I was unable to date the paper; but Beal dates the manuscript circa 1640. The one date found in the manuscript is May 29th, 1629, the birth and death of Charles's first son.

Organization is of little consequence here. Virtually the entire book comprises satiric elegies or epigrams, many of which are degrading to women. Of its 180 poems, only twenty-four have any attribution whatsoever, either correct or not. Among the poets identified are Richard Corbett, John Harington, "Dr. Dun," Thomas Carew, and King James. Among the political poems is an epitaph on John Felton, the presumed murderer of Buckingham. Poems about Felton are commonly found in these miscellanies. Like the Holgate, there are two poems about the Spanish Match, but unlike the Holgate, the two poems are not grouped in any organizational manner. Among the few poems of canonical importance to us would be Donne's sexually explicit Elegy 19, "Come Madam Come, all my powers defie," a poem which had been expurgated from the Holgate in the eighteenth century, and Donne's frequently transcribed epigram, "The Beggar." Harington's epigrams had been published in print at least a decade before they were transcribed into this miscellany. Of interest is a lyric from Ben Jonson's masque, "The Gypsies Metamorphosed." A longer section from the same masque can also be found in the Holgate. The masque itself was first performed three times before James in 1622, but it is noteworthy that a piece so openly teasing of James would find its way into several manuscripts. Since James also wrote manuscript poetry, it is clear that the tradition itself was not necessarily subversive, despite the fact that at least some manuscript poetry was aggressively unsympathetic to James and Charles.

It is reasonable to ask why someone would create such a miscellany. Surely it is not for its outstanding poetry. I think word games and male competition are important here. Poetic miscellanies at both the Inns of Court or the Universities have their own place in this tradition, and it is surely not difficult to imagine students sitting around together, drinking their way through competitive epigrams

---

[3] The manuscript is referenced several times in the index. For example, under the heading "William Strode," *Index of English Literary Manuscripts*, ed. Peter Beal (London: Mansell, 1980), Vol. 2, pt. 2, 407.

as to who could write (or rewrite) the most marginal lyric or how a previously published epigram could be adapted to suit the tastes of one or several friends. Collation demonstrates the wide variety of alternate readings for manuscript poetry, so varied in fact that it is not plausible to think that alternate readings come from lapses in memory or poor transcription techniques.

A third commonplace book demonstrates far different characteristics compared to what I have already discussed. The Tobias Alston manuscript, Osborne b 197, is a beautifully crafted manuscript, created with great care and printed in a highly legible and artistic hand.[4] No seventeenth-century manuscript that I have seen is any easier to read than this. Unfortunately, the book's original gatherings have been separated and are now maintained in individual envelopes, making it impossible to determine the overall design or organization of the original book. However, what is special is that many of its lyrics were obviously performed.

Tobias Alston, the compiler, of Sayham Hall, Newton Parish, near Sudbury, Suffolk, died in 1639, his approximate age being only nineteen. Since the date of the watermark is 1637, it is fair to assume the entire miscellany was created in the two or three years before Alston's death. The book measures 6⅜ x 4 inches. Of its 230 poems or lyrics, 61 include attribution. Among the best-known poets found in this manuscript are Ben Jonson, Francis Beaumont, Sir Walter Ralegh, Thomas Carew, George Herbert, Henry Wotton, and John Donne. Of particular note are twelve poems by Robert Herrick, several of which are found in the first envelope, therefore making it virtually impossible not to assume that Herrick's poetry, or at very least the type of elegant fantasy found in his writing, were the original instigation for this manuscript. There is no information that Herrick knew Alston, but according to papers found in the library, it is possible that Herrick knew Alston's brother. Several of the lyrics are clearly anti-Jesuit.

The clustering together of the Herrick poems seems typical of how Alston transcribed the poetry. Although there are not nearly as many epigrams or short epitaphs, when we see one, we are likely to see several, perhaps filling two pages in the middle of the text. The performance lyrics are also clustered together, perhaps because they were used as part of one particular performance. Although there are no musical annotations, tunes are frequently referenced, as on page 53 where we find the heading "A Proper new songe made of those y^t comenst the king being at Cambridge. December 1624. To ye Tune of Whoope doe me no harme." The song "Whoope doe me no harme" itself appears on page 110. A second lyric, "Is it not now a fortnight since," includes the instruction "rather to be sung then read to the tune of Bonny Nell." Surely to facilitate performance,

---

[4] Beal, *Index*, Vol. 1, pt. 2, 288.

stanzas are frequently numbered, and for one lyric even the lines are numbered. Also included are lyrics from two Ben Jonson masques, including the satire "The Gypsies Metamorphosed," which appears in all three miscellanies. Of particular interest is—in its entirety—"The Maske of Sr. John Crofts at the Kings being entertained there. Anno Domi," which contains stage directions and even the names of the performers, as on page 173, "Plumley to Dr. Randolph." A very different type of performance can be seen on page 227, "Epitaphium de vita et morte Iohannis Hilles," an elaborate transcription, among the most beautiful I have seen. Clearly the sense of space and physical hand were very important to Alston: the pages we see in the copy must have taken hours and demonstrate enormous patience and skill.

Speaking very broadly, then, I can say that although the three miscellanies are all part of the same tradition and their compilers drew on similar sources for their contents, each demonstrates a different aspect of culture and each transforms symbolic constructs into physical entities. The Holgate, with its inclusion of the compiler's own poetry and its structure built around literature, especially Donne, displays writing and reading; the portable and anonymous Osborne b 62, with its many jokes and demonstrations of wit, fosters friendship and laughter, and I suspect drinking; and as we have seen the Tobias Alston manuscript, with its many songs and intricate flourishes of letters and words, enacts artistic performance. These activities I take not merely as representations of culture, but manifestations, physical in every sense of the word, and real, if we accept the notion along with Foucault, that culture is more than just a tissue of cultural symbols.

But manuscript poetry, as material, is best understood when we focus on its transmission. Here it can be compared to mechanical print, which, though it must be produced or manufactured, tends to stop the development of a poem's text, the exact opposite to what happens in manuscript. Moreover, as we know, Londoners, in the early seventeenth century, reflecting and cultivating their own market economy, were actively engaged in material collections, books themselves being only one of those objects most popularly prized. Objects, of course, exist in time and space, but as Thomas Hobbes points out, objects exist as material culture when they are capable of being in motion.[5] That sense of movement— the fact that the poems could and did change—metamorphosed if you will— is what made them so attractive, and at least to me suggests why purists like Donne eschewed print in favor of manuscript. These poems were of great value, especially as exchange, and the care taken by these three compilers prove their

---

[5] David Harris Sacks, "London's Dominion," in *Material London, ca. 1600*, ed. Lena Cowen Orlin (Philadelphia: Univ. of Pennsylvania Press, 2000), 20–54, here 22.

inherent worth. Ironically, it is the anonymous epigram that best demonstrates this concept, which, because of its conciseness and frequent material crudity, tends to objectify its subject matter. No better example of this is Donne's own short, ever-changing masterpiece, "The Lame Beggar," found in the Alston manuscript, which marginalized the impoverished who so alarmed the shop owners and tradesmen in the expanding market culture.[6] In contrast, the poem itself, in its many transformations, accrues its own implicit value, as each individual compiler takes possession of whatever version he or she deems of particular value. It is not unlike the value we place on our own books, only here it is the poem itself that contributes to that particular value.

Equally important, however, is what happens when we examine the themes and genres that we commonly find in these texts. To an overwhelming degree, virtually all the poetry we find in the seventeenth-century commonplace book concerns three or four interlocking themes. They are about love and its failure, God and death, wit—i.e., how we can manipulate our sense of reality to make us laugh—or satire, mainly political, amorous, and/or religious. If we recognize that each of these themes or their attendant genres essentially mistrusts our sense of reality or attempts to explain reality as it pertains to us individually, then it is fair to ask if the political satire is about the political world itself, or is it instead about how each individual reader recreates or identifies him- or herself as a subject? For this, I will again return to the Spanish Match, which occurred in 1623 and is included in all three of these manuscripts. Surprisingly, the Tobias Alston man-uscript has eight poems on the affair, which occurred at least twelve years pri-or to Alston's transcription. One interpretation must be, then, that these poems were not so much ongoing contemporary satire as they were historic and criti-cal commentary on the then present king, Charles I, who so long before almost married the Spanish—and of course Catholic—Infanta. This reading can also be augmented by another common theme, the death of Henry, Prince of Wales, in 1612, also eulogized in all three manuscripts, who, had he lived, should have been king in the 1620s and '30s when these three commonplace books were cre-ated. Thus what the books are doing—through their ongoing textual instability and developing physical structures—is not so much recording what was going on in contemporary society, as instead creating and recreating the people who live in it, each of whom recognized his or her own being through the tried and true practices of reading and writing, speaking and laughing, singing or performing, and, yes, even transcribing. These activities we miss when we read these poems

---

[6] Patricia Fumberton, "Making Vagrancy (In)visible: The Economics of Disguise in Ear-ly Modern Rogue Pamphlets," in *Rogues and Early Modern English Culture*, ed. Craig Dionne and Steve Mentz (Ann Arbor: Univ. of Michigan Press, 2004), 193–210.

only as poems. They are much more (or less) than what they stand for. Although it is more than likely that the three compilers of these miscellanies did not know one another, they were actively tied together in a matrix of common practices and beliefs which allowed each to create himself in a manner recognized by the community.

Finally, manuscript poetry is much less about its writers than its readers, and the later shift to print technologies fosters the idealization—and ironically the objectification—of its writers by stabilizing discourse and de-emphasizing its material construction. As critics, we are frequently concerned with how one poet influences and changes another or how one period alters or affects what comes after, but we rarely consider the physical nature of reading, writing, and copying, nor the manner in which those activities create meaning and promote social identification.

BRONX COMMUNITY COLLEGE
CITY UNIVERSITY OF NEW YORK

Women's Verse Miscellany Manuscripts in the Perdita Project: Examples and Generalizations

VICTORIA E. BURKE

ENRY KING WROTE A POEM ENTITLED "UPON A TABLE-BOOK presented to a Lady" whose final lines are, "You have roome / Here both the Scribe and Authour to become."[1] Women during the early modern period took up that invitation, filling blank books, and writing on unbound gatherings, in larger numbers than scholars in this field thought likely twenty years ago. When we consider verse miscellany manuscripts in particular, numerous examples compiled by women survive, though not the scores that we see by men. I am going to discuss ten such manuscripts that were compiled mainly by women, manuscripts that are being catalogued for the Perdita Project, an online guide to early modern women's manuscript compilations from 1500–1700 in the British Isles <http://human.ntu.ac.uk/perdita>. I argue that though certain patterns in male-compiled miscellanies have been identified, the patterns are less obvious for women. We know that substantial circles of poetic production and transmission of verse took place in Oxford and Cambridge colleges and at the Inns of Court. Women less often had access to those centres, so the questions we must ask of their surviving manuscripts might have a slightly different emphasis. What kinds of poems did women transcribe in their manuscripts? Where did they get access to them? What relation do a woman's education, religion, political

---

This paper was first delivered at a joint annual meeting of the Renaissance Society of America and The Society for Renaissance Studies, United Kingdom (2005) in Cambridge, England, at a panel entitled "Manuscript Miscellanies of the English Renaissance," Steven W. May, Georgetown College, presiding.

[1] *The Poems of Henry King*, ed. Margaret Crum (Oxford: Clarendon Press, 1965), 154.

orientation, family situation, and geographical location have to how she produced her verse miscellany?

All of these are important questions, and without the kind of groundwork that involves searching for biographical information, social networks, and possible lines of transmission for individual poems (in print and manuscript) we could not possibly gain an accurate picture of any compiler's activities. But it is also crucial to look carefully at the structure of individual miscellanies, starting with their arrangement of items (which poem follows another and why? Were they acquired together as a batch of items? To what extent does every item in the volume indicate the compiler's personal choice?). We also need to consider the details of how the poems are inscribed into a manuscript (is there a title, an attribution?), and certain physical characteristics that might prove significant (were all items transcribed with the same ink, at one sitting? How many erasures are there? Was the miscellany written into a prebound book? Is its binding ornate?). In relation to the fourteenth-century manuscript miscellany British Library MS Harley 2253, Marilyn Corrie argues that it is important to compare texts with their sources and with other texts in the same genre, "but within the manuscript other associations and comparisons are suggested and invited, throwing into relief elements and aspects of the texts that may be disregarded if they are read in other contexts."[2] I thus intend in this paper both to give an overview of important external contexts in which women compiled verse miscellanies (for example, the family, religious circles, their access to certain printed books), and also to suggest that attending to the unique contexts of each manuscript can raise important questions.

A feature that one might notice about verse miscellanies is that often poems appear alongside shorter extracts and couplets, sometimes of a specifically moral nature, leading us to draw comparisons with the commonplace book. Ann Bowyer, writing early in the seventeenth century,[3] and Katherine Butler, writing late in the century,[4] are both drawn to proverbial wisdom, expressed succinctly by

---

[2] Marilyn Corrie, "Kings and Kingship in British Library MS Harley 2253," *Yearbook of English Studies* 33 (2003): 64–79, here 64.

[3] Oxford, Bodleian Library MS Ashmole 51: a miscellany containing sententious rhyming couplets, six poems, an inscription from a gravestone, notes on colours, and handwriting exercises. Ann Bowyer was one of two main hands that compiled the manuscript, c.1590s–1610. For discussion of this manuscript see Victoria E. Burke, "Ann Bowyer's Commonplace Book (Bodleian Library Ashmole MS 51): Reading and Writing Among the 'Middling Sort'," *Early Modern Literary Studies* 6 (2001): 1–28 <http://purl.oclc.org./emls/06/burkbowy.htm>.

[4] London, St. Paul's Cathedral Library MS 52 D.14: a miscellany in separate prose and verse sections containing entire poems and shorter extracts. It was compiled by Katherine Butler, 1696–c.1720, and then by later eighteenth-century hands.

their favoured poets (Drayton, Spenser, Chaucer, and the writers of *The Mirror for Magistrates* for Bowyer; Dryden, Katherine Philips, Denham, Cowley, Waller, and Thomas Creech for Butler). Bowyer lists attributions to works, sometimes erroneous, or highlights the person who is the subject of certain lines rather than their author (for example "Henry howard Earle of Surrey" [fol. 4r] does not refer to a poem by Surrey, but to a poem by Drayton in which Surrey is the speaker).[5] In contrast to focusing solely on authors (or speakers) and titles of works, Butler often distills extracts into topics, using marginal headings (e.g. "The Inconstancy of Desire" [fol. 177r], "Drydens Hind and Panther on Education" [fol. 177v], "S^r J: Denum on a good name" [fol. 178v]). In about half of the quotations Butler has also noted a page number, which corresponds to the page number of the edition she read (in the cases in which the edition has been determined).

Katherine Butler's apparent motive for compiling her miscellany is noted at the start of the poetic section of the manuscript in the following epigraph: "The reason why I wrote severall of these following Verses, was not that I thought them all good, but the subjects was—what, I had occasion to make vse of" (fol. 176v). Even on the rare occasion in which she transcribes entire poems, Butler highlights their moral message: her copy of Katherine Philips's poem "Against Pleasure, Set by Dr. Coleman" is headed "How Slight & trifling ye Pleasures of y^s world." This is followed by another poem on the same subject (which she indicates with "ibid"), John Norris's poem "Satiety" (fols. 181v–182r). Many of Butler's poetic extracts are dramatic in origin (by Dryden, Euripides, Waller, Roger Boyle, Samuel Tuke, John Webster, and William Walsh), and there is one attribution "Shakespear" (in the margin) "Says of Love" (as a heading, fol. 187v). But this is, in fact, four lines from Charles Gildon's *Measure for Measure, Or Beauty the Best Advocate . . . Written Originally by Mr. Shakespear: And now very much Alter'd* (printed in 1700). A good number of Butler's references are to classical sources. Horace, the most frequently cited classical source in her miscellany, was translated by John Oldham, Ben Jonson, Matthew Prior, Alexander Brome, Sir Richard Fanshawe, the Earl of Rochester, Abraham Cowley, and Dryden—all of whom are quoted in Butler's manuscript.

Another compiler drawn to proverbial wisdom often in couplet form is Elizabeth Lyttelton.[6] Her manuscript contains versified proverbs courtesy of

---

[5] "Henry Howard, Earle of Surrey, to the Lady Geraldine," one of Drayton's *Englands Historicall Epistles* (first printed in 1598). Bowyer has quoted six lines from this epistle (lines 89–92 and 87–88); *The Works of Michael Drayton*, ed. J. William Hebel, 5 vols. (Oxford: Shakespeare Head Press, 1961), 2:279 and 5:132.

[6] Cambridge University Library MS Add. 8460: a miscellany of religious and secular verse, Englished extracts from the classics, proverbial couplets, prose, and fragments from

a neighbour, Sir Philip Woodhouse, and couplets chosen from printed works. Perhaps the most important context for Lyttelton's miscellany is the family, and specifically her father, the writer Sir Thomas Browne. She took full advantage of the intellectual milieu he opened up for her. The source of several of Lyttelton's poems was her father himself, his library,[7] and his contacts, poets with whom he was known to have socialized such as Richard Corbett and Edward Reynolds. But Lyttelton shaped the material in her miscellany in a way that seems also to have reflected her own sensibility. She chose to write a number of hymns at the front of the volume[8] and some political material in the middle (namely, an extract from a speech of Sir William Scroggs urging against forgetting the example of King Charles I, who was "truly A DEFENDER of the FAITH" [p. 73 rev.], and a petition to Queen Anne which expresses the Commons's support of her prosecution of the radical preacher Dr. Henry Sacheverell [p. 71 rev.]).[9] Lyttelton completed the volume with a number of elegies (ten of the thirteen final items are elegies or epitaphs). It is therefore possible to see a rudimentary structure to this volume.

The family was similarly an enabling space for another compiler, Constance Fowler, who collected the verse of the tightly-knit circle of her Catholic family and friends.[10] A full thirty-six of the total sixty-five poems focus on Fowler's friends

---

Sir Thomas Browne's writing. It was compiled by Elizabeth Lyttelton, c.1665–1714. An earlier hand has written sermon notes from one end of the volume; Rebecca Rees has discovered that this is the hand of Elizabeth Lyttelton's mother, Dorothy Browne. For a discussion of this manuscript see Victoria E. Burke, "Contexts for Women's Manuscript Miscellanies: The Case of Elizabeth Lyttelton and Sir Thomas Browne," *Yearbook of English Studies* 33 (2003): 316–28.

[7] Lyttelton copied lines from volumes her father was known to have owned; see Jeremiah S. Finch, *A Catalogue of the Libraries of Sir Thomas Browne and Dr. Edward Browne, His Son: A Facsimile Reproduction* (Leiden: Leiden Univ. Press, 1986). Browne (or his son) owned Katherine Philips's *Poems* (1669: Finch, 46, no. 107), Charles Aleyn's *The Battailes of Crescey and Poictiers* (1633: Finch, 50, no. 67B), and Peter Heylyn's *Cosmographie in Four Books* (1670: Finch, 44, no. 10). Lines from each of these appear in Lyttelton's manuscript on pp. 70 rev., 69 rev., and 68 rev., respectively.

[8] "A Hymne to our Creator by D[r] Dillingham" (pp. 3, 4, 6), "An hymne to our Redeemer" subscribed "from Dr Evans" (pp. 6, 7, 8, 9, 18, 19), "An Euening Hymn" (p. 21), and "When our Emmanuell from his Throne came down" by Edward Reynolds, Bishop of Norwich (pp. 13, 15, 17), which has a repeated chorus. She has also included "An hymne to God the Father" by Donne slightly later in the volume (p. 62 rev.).

[9] The Scroggs speech does not appear to be extant; these lines do not appear in the speeches printed in 1676, 1678, and 1679. "The humble Addres of y[e] house of Com*m*ons to the Queen, March y[e] 7 1710" (a tilde appears above the "m" in "Comons").

[10] San Marino, California, Huntington Library MS HM 904: a miscellany of Roman Catholic and secular poetry compiled by Constance (Aston) Fowler, c.1630–1650s, another major hand, and two hands which have written one poem each. See the edition by Deborah Aldrich-Watson, *The Verse Miscellany of Constance Aston Fowler: A Diplomatic Edition,* MRTS 210 (Tempe, AZ: Arizona Center for Medieval and Renaissance Studies in conjunction with Renaissance English Text Society, 2000).

and family, sometimes immediate, sometimes extended (such as the scribe's brother Herbert Aston, his wife Katherine Thimelby, their friend Lady Dorothy Shirley, and their father's secretary Sir Richard Fanshawe). Many of the poems are secular, using pastoral names in their titles, such as "on Celestinæs goinge a Jorney in wett-weather" (fols. 27r–v) and "upon Castaries and her sitters [sisters] goinge Afoote in the snow" (fol. 28v), a number are elegies, and many celebrate love and related courtly topics (e.g. in "on black paches," fols. 145v–146r, the poet hopes his subject is not wearing black beauty marks for vanity but instead as marks of mourning for "harts forlorn"). A small number of poems in Fowler's hand are religious. All of the poems written in the second main hand (14) are religious, and specifically Roman Catholic (four are by Robert Southwell). This hand entered the verse in three separate sections, probably in pages left blank by Fowler (fols. 1r–5v, 53r–135v, 139v–143r, and 159v–182r were left blank and remain so). This second hand provides a clue as to how a later reader used the volume. It matches exactly with that of the scribe of Bodleian Library MS Eng. poet. b. 5, a collection of Catholic verse.[11] Cedric Brown has fascinatingly traced the recusant networks to which this volume attests, unearthing the Catholic families of the neighbourhood and county surrounding Wootton Wawen in Warwickshire, the likely hub of the manuscript's production.[12] That manuscript, written in the early 1650s, "seems to represent a collection of materials by a Jesuit missioner to suit his rural flock, whom he indoctrinates by this means in their gatherings," i.e. with the hymns and generalized stories of persecution of the faithful found in the manuscript. Brown has also tentatively suggested that the unusual shape of the Bodleian manuscript could suggest either an account book or a "holster book" that was carried on horseback, in both cases camouflaging the dangerous Catholic material within.[13]

Another intriguing possibility has been raised by Deborah Aldrich-Watson, who suggests that the second hand in HM 904, and the main hand in Eng. poet. b. 5, is that of Gertrude Thimelby, Constance's sister.[14] Thimelby's double identity

---

[11] See Aldrich-Watson, *Miscellany*, lx–lxii and Victoria Burke, "Women and Early Seventeenth-Century Manuscript Culture: Four Miscellanies," *The Seventeenth Century* 12 (1997): 135–50, here 138.

[12] Cedric C. Brown, "Recusant Community and Jesuit Mission in Parliament Days: Bodleian MS Eng. poet. b. 5," *Yearbook of English Studies* 33 (2003): 290–315. For another discussion of this manuscript see F. M. McKay, "A Seventeenth-Century Collection of Religious Poetry: Bodleian Manuscript Eng. poet. b. 5," *Bodleian Library Record* 8 (1970): 185–91.

[13] Brown, "Recusant Community," 307.

[14] Aldrich-Watson, *Miscellany*, xix, xxviii, xxxiii, and throughout the introduction. This identification was first suggested by Jenijoy La Belle in "The Huntington Aston Manuscript," *The Book Collector* 29 (1980): 542–67. La Belle writes, "This second hand is perhaps that of Constance's elder sister Gertrude, although it is quite similar to the handwriting of Winefrid Thimelby, the sister of Constance's close friend, Katherine Thimelby" (544). To my knowledge,

as both a participant in the courtly milieu of the Tixall circle and her later life as a nun make her a likely candidate for the scribe of the Catholic poetry that appears in both volumes.[15] Gerard Kilroy has argued eloquently for the role lay women played in safeguarding Roman Catholicism's written heritage during times of persecution, citing the cases of Gertrude Thimelby and Mary Brudenell.[16] If Thimelby is the main scribe of Eng. poet. b. 5, then the manuscript demonstrates "a woman acting in a strongly educational role: handing on the theological and ritual inheritance, perhaps in a community which only rarely saw a priest."[17] Huntington MS HM 904 attests to the intersection of two interconnected worlds with its very different types of poetry: elite, sometimes metaphysical verse, alongside less-fashionable Roman Catholic carols and poems, so essential to the preservation of a culture.

The issue of the use to which miscellanies could be put, in Fowler's case by specific religious communities, is also raised when looking at Mary Webber's collection of poetry and anthems from the late seventeenth century.[18] Webber has compiled the words to sixty-three verse anthems in two sections in her manuscript: from the front and from the back of the volume, reversed. She was not copying from a printed book of anthems. The layout of each anthem, however, comprising a title, words to the anthem, and then a composer's name at the bottom, is very similar to James Clifford's *The Divine Services and Anthems Usually Sung in his Majesties Chappell* of thirty years earlier (second edition, 1664). Nothing is known of Mary Webber, but her manuscript does tell us that the anthems

---

no known examples of Gertrude Thimelby's handwriting survive, unlike in the case of Constance Fowler for whom we have extant autograph letters in the Aston family correspondence, British Library MS Add. 36452. Arthur Clifford notes in *Tixall Poetry* (Edinburgh: Longman, Hurst, 1813) that he found "sixty or seventy very beautiful letters" in Gertrude's hand (xxv), but these do not seem to be extant.

[15] Gertrude was an active participant in the Tixall circle: at least four poems in the miscellany are addressed to or describe her (fols. 152v–153v, 155r–158r, 185v–186r, and 187r–v; Aldrich-Watson proposes that those poems addressed to "Castara" also refer to Gertrude; see *Miscellany*, lii–liv), and Arthur Clifford has argued that a substantial number of the poems in *Tixall Poetry* were written by her (85–106, 226, and 287–88; see also xi, xxiv–xxv, 357–64, and 397). Gertrude was to become a nun at St. Monica's convent in Louvain after the deaths of her husband and son, taking her vows in 1658 (Aldrich-Watson, *Miscellany,* xxviii). The dates work as well, since if the bulk of Eng. poet. b. 5's compilation took place in the early 1650s (Brown, "Recusant Community," 291), Gertrude was not yet on the continent.

[16] Gerard Kilroy, *Edmund Campion: Memory and Transcription* (Aldershot: Ashgate, 2005), 78–79, 24, and 144. Mary Brudenell transcribed 1,800 pages, fifty lines to a page, "as a record of Catholic beliefs and sufferings," now Bodleian Library MS Eng. th. b. 1–2 (24).

[17] Kilroy, *Campion,* 78.

[18] New Haven, Connecticut, Yale University, Beinecke Library MS Osborn Shelves b. 202: a collection of hymns and religious poetry compiled by Mary Webber, 1694–c.1700.

originated from Exeter Cathedral. This is because while many of the composers were popular (John Blow, Henry Purcell), a significant number have connections with Exeter. Matthew Locke and Henry Hall (and Edward Hooper from earlier in the century) are better-known composers who all spent time at Exeter Cathedral (as choristers or organists), but four less celebrated composers were all Exeter-based: Henry Travers, Robert Parsons, Tobias Langdon, and Peter Passmore.[19] It is thus likely that Webber compiled her collection of hymns from something like a manuscript part-book of anthems sung in the cathedral. This may have been the repertoire of the cathedral's choir at one point in their history, rather than one woman's choice of particularly meaningful hymns.

But a more personal element of choice seems to be apparent in the middle of the manuscript where five poems and one prose meditation have been transcribed.[20] This section contains something relatively rare (though admittedly more common in the later seventeenth century than earlier in the period): evidence of a woman reading another woman's poetry. The first two poems in this section are by Elizabeth Tipper, from her only published work, *The Pilgrim's Viaticum: Or, the Destitute, but not Forlorn. Being a Divine Poem, Digested from Meditations upon The Holy Scripture* (1698 and 1699). Webber has copied Tipper's autobiographical poem, "Some Experimental Passages of my Life," and a poem on the superiority of divine love over earthly love.[21] But Webber did not only transcribe up-to-the-minute verse like Tipper's, she also has copied items by George Herbert, Francis Quarles, Joshua Sylvester, and Henry More, apparently following late seventeenth-century taste in choosing to add these earlier religious poets. We do not know Webber's class or family situation, but we can surmise that she was affiliated with employees of Exeter Cathedral (vicars, organists, or choristers, perhaps). Her musical sources were probably from manuscript, but her poetic sources seem to have been from print, indicating that access to elite circles of manuscript circulation is not likely.

This contrasts with the milieu of Lady Margaret Wemyss, whose music book reveals a more courtly ethos, due perhaps to her elevated social status

---

[19] *Grove Music Online* <http://www.grovemusic.com>; Ian Spink, *Restoration Cathedral Music 1660–1714* (Oxford: Clarendon, 1995), 254–58; Watkins Shaw, *The Succession of Organists of the Chapel Royal and the Cathedrals of England and Wales from c.1538 Also of the Organists of the Collegiate Churches of Westminster and Windsor, Certain Academic Choral Foundations, and the Cathedrals of Armagh and Dublin* (Oxford: Clarendon Press, 1991), 106–14; *Oxford Dictionary of National Biography* <http://www.oxforddnb.com>.

[20] This section appears on pp. 91–98. Two more poems appear on pp. 101 and 103, respectively.

[21] Sigs. C1v–C3r and F3r–F4r.

as the daughter of an earl.[22] During the civil war period Margaret Wemyss
was learning to play solo lute and to sing with bass viol accompaniment, and
was reading poems in a variety of print and manuscript sources, presumably
provided by her music teacher. The miscellany section in Wemyss's manuscript
is in two parts of eight and nineteen poems, respectively, and this verse section
is almost without exception filled with poetry about love: the longing for it, the
happy achievement of it, or the mournful loss of it, by writers such as the Scottish
Alexander Montgomerie, Sir Robert Ayton, and James Graham, Marquis of
Montrose, but also Thomas Carew and Henry Howard, Earl of Surrey. In some
cases a pattern of arrangement seems evident: a poem in which the speaker
listens to the goddess Cynthia's lament for Titan is followed by a male-voiced
lament, similarly overheard.[23] Many of these poems (at least twelve of the twenty-
seven) have known musical settings, and several of them appear in manuscript
sources which attest to their availability to those who were well-connected like
Wemyss. For example, the Earl of Surrey's poem "If care do cause men cry"
(fol. 16r), first published in Tottel's *Miscellany*, was popular as a song setting in
seventeenth-century Scotland, though not printed as such until 1662.[24] Three
songs in Wemyss's miscellany also appeared in a manuscript connected with
the Maules of Panmure family.[25] Though Wemyss was in some sense isolated at
Wemyss Castle in Fife, and many of her chosen poems are decades old (suggesting
a retrospective or conservative cast to Scottish aristocratic literary culture), she
was also able to enjoy all that her class could offer her: education, access to French
lute music and printed songbooks, and songs known to have circulated amongst
noble families in Scotland.

Music features to a lesser extent in another manuscript miscellany, that of
Lucy Hutchinson.[26] This volume contains an interesting mixture of material: two
poems identified with song settings, and a ballad referring to the Parliamentary

---

[22] Edinburgh, National Library of Scotland Dep. 314/23: a music book containing songs
for voice and bass viol, poems, and solo lute music. The poetry was compiled primarily by
Margaret Wemyss, 1643–c.1649.

[23] "When Sinthia with sueet consent", fols. 71v rev.–70v rev., "When diafantes know",
fols. 69v rev.–68v rev. This last poem also appears in a longer version at fols. 65v rev.–61v rev.

[24] John Forbes, *Cantus, Songs and Fancies. To Thre, Foure, and Five Partes, Both Apt for
Voices and Viols* (Aberdeen, 1662), sigs. A1r–A2r.

[25] "Lyke as the heartt hurtt in the cheas" (fols. 59v rev.–58v rev.), "Com lowe [love] lets
walk into the spring" (fol. 66v rev.), and Sir Robert Montgomerie's "Whatt mighty motion" (fol.
58v rev.) all appear in the minister Robert Edward's manuscript (National Library of Scotland
MS 9450), though the variants between Wemyss's and Edward's versions are significant.

[26] Nottingham, Nottinghamshire Archives DD/Hu1: a miscellany containing poetry,
verse translations, psalms, a prose treatise, and a draft of a letter. It was compiled primarily by
Lucy Hutchinson, c.1650s–c.1660s.

Act of 1650 which outlawed adultery and fornication[27] at one end of the spectrum, and lengthy verse translations of the *Aeneid* by Sir John Denham and Sidney Godolphin at the other. The volume also includes a prose treatise on various emotions (pp. 147–191), and four songs on the topics of jealousy, feminine honour, the separation of lovers, and the incommunicability of love (pp. 231–235).[28] The thematic overlap between these two sections might suggest Hutchinson's recurring interest in these topics.

Hutchinson transcribed two poems by Edmund Waller, one of them his famous panegyric on the Lord Protector. It is the final item of the miscellany. Interestingly, she does not include her own critical response to this poem in this particular volume. That appears in British Library MS Add. 17018, fols. 214r–217v, endorsed "M^rs: Hutchinson's Answer to M^r: Waller's Panegirique to Cromwell."[29] Elizabeth Moyle was another compiler who included the panegyric by Waller in her manuscript.[30] But while this poem is allowed to stand unchallenged (and is prefaced by a copy of the title page from the 1655 edition, giving this poem alone a special weight in the volume), Moyle's miscellany opens with another poem by Waller on Cromwell's death (beginning "Wee must resign; heauen his great soule doth clame," fols. 1r–v) which is immediately satirically critiqued, point by point, by another writer (that poem begins, "Then take him Diuill, hell his soul doth claime," fol. 2r).[31]

Moyle's miscellany was bound with one volume of Waller's poetry printed in 1682; she also owned a 1690 edition, and one of Moyle's motivations in compiling it was to note ten other Waller poems that had not been printed in either volume (though she made one mistake). The first poems in the volume treat Cromwell's death, while the penultimate poem depicts Waller looking forward to his own death in "Of the last Verses in his Book wch are the diuine ones" (fol. 25v).

---

[27] "A Ballad vpon the lamentable death of Anne Greene & Gilbert Samson executed att Tyburne the second day of January for hauing beene taken in the act of adulterie To the tune of When I was a buxsome lasse" (pp. 239–241).

[28] These four poems were printed in Thomas Carew's *Poems* of 1640 (see Jill Seal Millman's catalogue entry for this manuscript on The Perdita Project <http://human.ntu.ac.uk/perdita>).

[29] David Norbrook, "Lucy Hutchinson versus Edmund Waller: An Unpublished Reply to Waller's *A Panegyrick to my Lord Protector*," *The Seventeenth Century* 11 (1996): 61–86, here 61.

[30] New Haven, Connecticut, Yale University, Beinecke Library Osborn pb 110 1: a miscellany of twenty-two poems, ten of them by Edmund Waller, bound with a 1682 edition of Waller's poetry. It was compiled by Elizabeth (Moyle) Gregor, 1684–1690s. The panegyric appears on fols. 4r–8v.

[31] Moyle claims its author as Sir William Godolphin, probably meaning Sidney Godolphin, but this is not the same poem that has been attributed to him in other manuscripts.

Moyle has grouped his two poems written in response to Anne Wharton's verse translations together (fols. 21r–22v), suggesting that Moyle transcribed them from Waller's *Divine Poems* of 1685. A few topical political poems appear (such as an attack on the Duke of Monmouth, elsewhere attributed to Rochester, fols. 16r–17r), contrasting with those more complimentary panegyrics by Waller. One such poem is entitled "one my Ld Cheif Justice Scrogs 1679" (fol. 15r), beginning, "Hear lyes a Judg will ly noe more." Unlike Elizabeth Lyttelton's citation from Scroggs's speech demonstrating his royalism, this abusive rhyme berates Scroggs for acquitting Sir George Wakeman for his alleged role in the Popish Plot.[32] Schwoerer notes that this incident caused widespread outrage and led to a campaign of harassment in the press: one particular piece *Satyr against Injustice, or, Sc--gs upon Sc--gs* consisted of abusive triplets that so upset Scroggs that its printer (Jane Curtis) was tried for publishing it. The poem in Moyle's miscellany is not the same as the printed broadsheet, but it follows the same format; evidently the version transcribed by Moyle enjoyed some circulation in manuscript, since Harold Love has found two extant versions of this lampoon.[33]

Another poem, an anti-Catholic or anti-Protestant satire, depending on how it is read, is found on folio 14v of Moyle's compilation. It was first printed in *Wits Recreations* of 1640 in two columns; if one reads the left column first the poem begins, "I hold as faith / What Rome's Church saith / Where th'King is head / The Flocks misled." But if one reads the first line of the left column followed by the first line of the right column the poem reads very differently, "I hold as faith / What England's Church allows / What Rome's Church saith / My conscience disavowes" (sig. F3r). Moyle's copy favours the Protestant position ("I hold as faith: what Englands Church allows") but the colons which appear after each half line hint at the original ambiguous structure of the poem. Sometimes attributed to William Strode, the poem became known as "The Jesuit's Double-faced Creed" and was printed in English, Latin and Greek in 1679.[34] The poem had a lively existence in manuscript.[35] Other well-known satirical pieces included by Moyle

---

[32] For a full discussion see Lois G. Schwoerer, "Scroggs, Sir William (c.1623–1683), judge," *Oxford Dictionary of National Biography* (Oxford: Oxford Univ. Press, 2004–2006) <http://www.oxforddnb.com>.

[33] Harold Love, *English Clandestine Satire 1660–1702* (Oxford: Oxford Univ. Press, 2004), 339 and 128–29. The poem appears in London, British Library MS Harl. 7317, fol. 57r and Oxford, All Souls College, Codrington Library MS 116, fol. 37v.

[34] August A. Imholtz, Jr., "The Jesuits' Double-Faced Creed: A Seventeenth-Century Cross Reading," *Notes and Queries* n.s. 24 (1977): 553–54. Imholtz notes that the three-language version was printed in Henry Care's *The Popish Courant* of 16 May 1679.

[35] In the William Strode section of his *Index to English Literary Manuscripts 1625–1700*, Peter Beal characterizes this poem as of uncertain authorship, listing thirty-one extant

also enjoyed a healthy circulation in manuscript; the poem on Monmouth, for example, beginning, "Disgracst undone forlorn," is extant in at least twenty-four manuscript versions.[36] The presence of poems such as these suggests that Moyle had access to certain channels of manuscript circulation in which satirical political poems were popular.

Both witty satire and political commentary figure in Folger MS V.b.198, a volume that its editor has wisely attributed to both Anne Southwell and her husband Henry Sibthorpe.[37] Her husband seems to have given the volume to Southwell on their marriage (as earlier memoranda by his relative suggest), and then to have organized it after her death, capping the volume with epitaphs, one of his own writing. Much could be said about this varied manuscript, which contains a great deal of Southwell's original and highly skilled poetry, as well as poems by writers such as Henry King and Sir Arthur Gorges, but I would like to note a few things about the choice of the placement of the items at the beginning of the volume. The first page of the miscellany announces itself as "The workes of the Lady Ann Sothwell / Decemb: 2° 1626." We know she wrote poetry before that

---

copies (vol. 2, part 2 [London: Mansell, 1993], 429–431; StW 1259–1289). At least one other manuscript copy exists, dated to c.1600: Washington D. C., Folger Shakespeare Library MS V.a.198, part 3, fol. 14r (as noted in Steven W. May and William A. Ringler, *Elizabethan Poetry: A Bibliography and First-Line Index of English Verse, 1559–1603*, 3 vols. [London: Thoemmes Continuum, 2004], 1:742; EV 9875). The poem was still popular into the eighteenth century, appearing in a commonplace book compiled from c.1746–c.1800 (Leeds University Library, Brotherton Collection MS Lt 106, fols. 89v–90r) and Melesinda Munbee's collection of poetry, 1749–1750 (Boston, Harvard Univ., Houghton Library MS Eng 768 [vol. 1], fol. 78v).

[36] Love, *Satire*, 327. Among what he has classified as manuscript anthologies of clandestine satire, Love has discovered eight copies of a poem on the Duchess of Portsmouth, attributed by Moyle to Rochester (beginning, "Who can on this picture look"), seven copies of Waller's elegy on Cromwell ("We must resign heaven his great soul does claim"), and four copies of Waller's panegyric on Cromwell ("While/Whilst with a strong and yet a gentle hand": 409, 398, and 408). The poems on Monmouth and the Duchess of Portsmouth are not listed in Beal, since they are not believed to have been written by Rochester, but Beal notes the wide circulation of the two Waller poems. Beal lists thirty-four copies of the elegy (which include the seven noted in Love) and twenty-five of the panegyric (to which we can add two more from Love's index; Beal, *Index*, vol. 2, part 2, 611–13 and 592–94). These four poems appear in Moyle's manuscript on fols 16r–17r, 14r, 1r–v, and 4r–8v, respectively. Thirteen manuscripts listed by Love contain two or three poems which also appear in Moyle's manuscript, suggesting that several of these poems typically circulated together.

[37] Washington, D. C., Folger Shakespeare Library MS V.b.198: a miscellany containing original poetry of Anne Southwell, transcribed poetry, letters, sermon notes, extracts from printed books, inventories, a catalogue of books, and memoranda. It was compiled by several hands including Southwell and her husband Henry Sibthorpe, c.1626–1636. It has been edited by Jean Klene as *The Southwell-Sibthorpe Commonplace Book: Folger MS. V.b.198*, MRTS 147 (Tempe, AZ: Medieval and Renaissance Texts and Studies, 1997).

date. Of the five poems that follow on that first page, at least three were printed in songbooks earlier in the century and so were not written by Southwell.[38] The next page similarly confuses, with a version of "The Lie," usually attributed to Sir Walter Ralegh, and our first sighting of Southwell's signature, beneath the poem (fol. 2r). The next item is a defence of poetry written in the form of a letter to a titled friend, Cicely, Lady Ridgway (fols. 3r–v). What follows this is a copy of a letter written by Southwell to Henry Cary, Lord Falkland, Lord Deputy of Ireland, pledging her own and her husband's support after his removal from office (fol. 4r). In the letter Southwell reminds Falkland, in a highly rhetorical manner, that he still has support. She begins the letter,

> Thrice honored Lord
> Will yow ~~yow~~ vouchsafe a pardon if I play the Critick wth this one word in yo[r] letter. Wherein yow say yow are depriued of all, Is the Sun bereft of his beames because a cloude interposeth betwixt him and o[r] watrye balls, Could a banis'ht Philosopher say vnto him selfe, *Omnia mea, mecum porto?* [I carry all my belongings with me] And can yow loose anythinge as longe as yow enioy yo[r]selfe, What, though yow hould not the sword & Scepter of a Kingdome still!

This is a miscellany that raises many questions in these early pages: is Sibthorpe trying to present his wife as a more prolific poet than she was with misattributions? Does he wish to showcase his wife's thoughts about poetry before revealing her own efforts? Does he wish to demonstrate his own and his wife's familiarity with courtly officials (never mind if those officials are now disgraced)?

A final manuscript I would like to briefly introduce is that written partially by Elizabeth Lenthall.[39] It is easy to see an organizing hand behind the material: she begins with an account of her husband's family history and then her own, later adding autobiographical verse (including, among others, poems upon meeting her husband, the deaths of her daughter and other relatives, and a Christmas feast, the last beginning with the memorable lines: "Cristmass is Come, Bring Up the Brawn and Capon / The braue Surloin and Noble Ham of Bacon / Plumb broath and Mince Pyes sett down in there Place / Wee may giue thanks with out a Very Long Grace", fols. 104v–105r). This inclusion of personal verse is true of

---

[38] The first song appears in Robert Jones, *Ultimum Vale* (1605) and Alfonso Ferrabosco, *Ayres* (1609), while the second and fourth songs were printed in Jones, *A Musicall Dreame* (1609).

[39] Perth, Scotland, Perth and Kinross Council Archive GB252/MS14/26: family history and original verse compiled by Elizabeth Lenthall, c.1705. It is prefaced by a selection of poems and verse satires in another hand, compiled 1686–c.1707.

male-authored miscellanies too (some university compilations have poems about particular students, colleges, or porters). The material in this volume has been carefully shaped by Lenthall, many years after it happened. In the margin beside one early poem written to her by her husband Lenthall has written, "Complement transsribed out of time Eaten Paper In Memorey of my dear Speranthis" (fol. 88r). Her motive in copying this poem was to preserve it, and to justify their relationship, which met with parental disapproval because they were so young. In this manuscript the poetry augments the picture Lenthall wishes to communicate about her life, one that name-drops about famous people known to her family (such as Sir Edward Dering and Sir Isaac Walton), but sometimes gets the facts wrong. For example, she writes a note that in June 1670 "the faithfull Lucinday Mrs Katherine Phillips," her relative and friend, died of the smallpox and is buried at Windsor (fol. 86r). If she means the poet, Katherine Philips did indeed die of the smallpox but in 1664 not 1670, she is buried in London not Windsor, and she was called the matchless Orinda not the faithful Lucinda. But perhaps factual accuracy was not the point: Lenthall gives two different birthdates for herself (1629 and 1631; fols 81v and 85r).

I anticipated that in the near future we will be able to generalize about these manuscripts once we have drawn a good number of them together. But I doubt I can neatly do that here. The miscellanies which perhaps best fit our preconceived notions of what a verse miscellany is are those of Margaret Wemyss and Elizabeth Moyle: collections of complete poems (songs of love in the case of the former, political poems by Waller and others in the latter, with both volumes showing evidence of the manuscript transmission of texts). Otherwise the surviving evidence thus far shows us the heterogeneity of these volumes: sometimes mixing prose with rhyming couplets, sometimes favouring musical or religious source material, sometimes seeming to have a clear political bent, other times not at all. We see varying levels of education in these volumes: Hutchinson translated from Ovid and from Casimir Sarbiewski's Latin epigrams (pp. 206–207), Lyttelton might have translated a Latin epitaph from Foxe's Book of Martyrs,[40] while Butler on the other hand transcribed English versions of the classics throughout her commonplace book. Religion is a significant factor in many of these compilations: perhaps since devotional writing was valued in women, these types of manuscripts survive in greater numbers: from Fowler's Catholic yet also courtly collection, to Lyttelton's Anglican hymns, to Southwell's original decalogue verse. The family context was important for several of these compilers: without the

---

[40] On p. 63, rev., Lyttelton wrote "The Epitaph upon that Blessed Martyr Walter Mill at St Andrews in Scotland" in Latin and English. Foxe prints only the Latin version of the epitaph, raising the possibility that Lyttelton translated it herself into English.

guidance of Lyttelton's father or the opportunity for handwriting exercises and reading given to Ann Bowyer and her siblings, these manuscripts would not have been produced. Class is an inevitable element to this inquiry: the highest-status woman, Lady Margaret Wemyss, had a manuscript which demonstrates perhaps the widest access to a range of print and manuscript sources. Most of the other women discussed here were of comfortable gentry standing, with opportunities for education, reading material, and contacts with differing social networks. But at least one (Bowyer)[41] and possibly also Webber and Butler were of more humble origins, since they rely on print texts and do not demonstrate an obvious link with centres of poetic production and dissemination. Then again, while Bowyer's slim notebook was bound together with two unrelated seventeenth-century works, the contemporary binding of Webber's volume is ornamented in gilt with elaborate floral and foliate borders around central panels and gilt corner pieces. Butler wrote her compilation at the end of an elaborate collection of sermons by John Donne and Joseph Hall from earlier in the century. Perhaps the physical details of these volumes can help us pinpoint the social status of their compilers, or suggest answers about how their texts were valued contemporaneously and by later readers.

Elizabeth Lenthall's control of her material shows us one end of the spectrum: a woman carefully organizing poetry to construct a narrative beneficial to herself. The other surviving miscellanies I have studied do not always so neatly demonstrate a woman's conscious control of her material, but perhaps all of them do have a tale to tell about how someone shaped a compilation, either a woman herself, a husband (Southwell's), or a community of which she was a part (Fowler's Catholic circle, Webber's Exeter Cathedral musicians). Some things of course could be outside of the compiler's control (binding, later additions in other hands, later excisions), but it is part of the story of a miscellany to try to uncover these elements. When considering female compilers we might need to be even more careful with the extant evidence than we need to be with male compilers since it is less easy to see wider patterns in their surviving volumes.

UNIVERSITY OF OTTAWA

---

[41] Bowyer was the daughter of a draper and later married a saddler. For biographical information on Bowyer see Burke, "Ann Bowyer's Commonplace Book."

Faire Phillis, The Marchants Wife, and the Tailers Wife: Representations of Women in a Woman's Early Modern Manuscript Commonplace Book

KATHRYN DEZUR

SOMETIME IN THE LATE SIXTEENTH CENTURY, A WOMAN NAMED ELIZABETH Clarke signed her name five times in a thin manuscript commonplace book, which now resides in the Folger Shakespeare Library's collection (x.d.177). Four of these signatures appear in the margins of the first folio (Figure 1), and the fifth appears on the verso side of the final eighth folio. She also likely transcribed or wrote a poem on the last folio—perhaps as part of her handwriting practice (Figure 2). What interests me so much about this small commonplace book is not only its status as evidence of one early modern woman's ability to read and write—a woman, unfortunately, about whom we know little—but also its capacity to tell us what sorts of texts some early modern women had access to, how those texts represented women, and how, in turn, a female reader might have understood herself in relationship to those representations. By examining the contents of the manuscript, we learn something about the potential processes of reader identification within a limited scope of possibilities.

Clarke's commonplace book contained content that would have horrified humanist educators—even the few in favor of female literacy; it contains both

---

This paper was first delivered at the 2007 meeting of the International Congress on Medieval Studies, Kalamazoo, MI, at a panel entitled "Early Modern Women's Manuscripts," Margaret P. Hannay, Siena College, presiding.

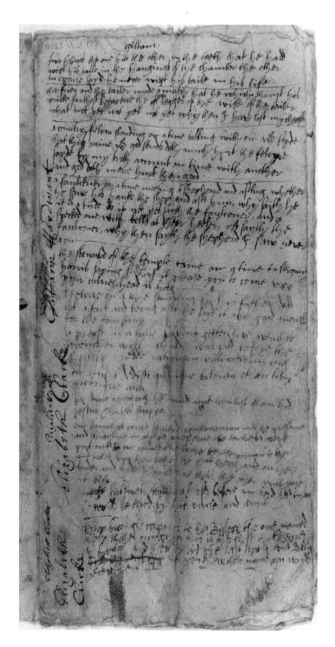

Figure 1. Commonplace book—jests and poems. 1595. Fol. 1r. Folger Shakespeare Library, x.d.177. Printed by permission of the Folger Shakespeare Library.

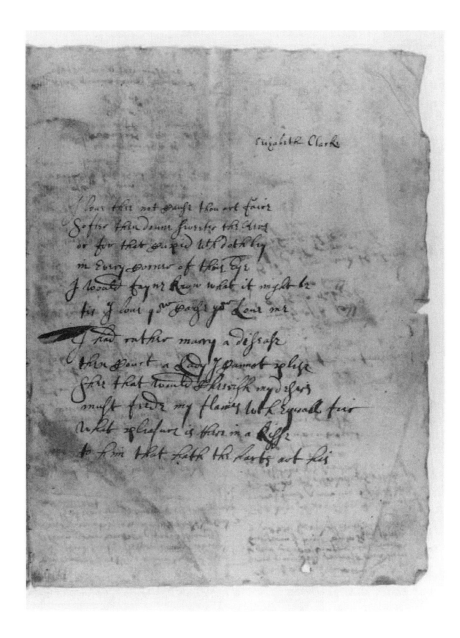

Figure 2. Commonplace book—jests and poems. 1595. Fol. 8v. Folger Shakespeare Library, x.d.177. Printed by permission of the Folger Shakespeare Library.

amorous verse and obscene jokes. Arthur Marotti states that "Since the manuscript transmission of verse was most frequently associated with all-male environments such as the universities and the Inns of Court, it is not surprising to find a large amount of bawdy and obscene verse in manuscript collections."[1] I suspect this commonplace book initially derived from such a context—it contains many different hands, as if each writer were given a chance to copy out his best jokes or poems and then passed it on to the next writer. Also, the manuscript's poems and jests contain some Latin. While it might seem surprising to find a woman with access to such a manuscript, both Ian Moulton and Patricia Allen Brown have described women's participation within erotic and/or pornographic discourses. Moulton points to both Clarke's and Margaret Bellasis's verse miscellanies, and Brown documents many instances of women's involvement as audiences or creators of jests.[2] Nonetheless, Clarke's access to this material would have transgressed the cultural ideal of confining women's reading to religious materials or to those texts devoted to her improvement as a wife, mother, or daughter.

While not all of the jokes and poems focus on women—for instance, several involve the perennially favorite topics of excrement, flatulence, and drunkenness[3]—many do, and the position the women occupy in them reveal varying levels of objectification.[4]

---

[1] Arthur F. Marotti, *Manuscript, Print, and the English Renaissance Lyric* (Ithaca: Cornell Univ. Press, 1995), 76.

[2] Ian Frederick Moulton, *Before Pornography: Erotic Writing in Early Modern England* (Oxford: Oxford Univ. Press, 2000), 54–64; Pamela Allen Brown, *Better a Shrew than a Sheep: Women, Drama, and the Culture of Jest in Early Modern England* (Ithaca: Cornell Univ. Press, 2003), 5.

[3] "Two felowes the one hitt the other in the teeth that he hadd / wipt his taile in the hangings of the chamber the other / in excuse sayd, he never wipt his taile in his life" (fol. 1r); "A felawe on a time staying by his father didd / let a fart and being ask he sayd it was good inough / for the company" (fol. 1r); "A drunkard in a dark night lying in the durti way / not being able to stand on his height one comes / by chaunce that way thinking it hadd been / theeues and bidd him stand why sayth the other / let [h]e stand that can for I cannot" (fol. 3v). One short comment even considers the reproduction and life-cycle of elephants (fol. 3v). Commonplace book—jests and poems. 1595. Folger Shakespeare Library, x.d.177.

[4] Ian Munroe has recently edited seven jestbooks that provide a wide range of examples demonstrating viewpoints about women in the early modern period: Ian Munroe, *"A womans answer is neuer to seke": Early Modern Jestbooks, 1526–1635*, Essential Works for the Study of Early Modern Women: Series III, Part Two, Vol. 8 (Aldershot and Burlington, VT: Ashgate Press, 2007).

Presumably the jests were written down because someone thought they were good, i.e. funny. Laughter, as Henri Bergson has observed, is a "social gesture."[5] It creates social bonds when shared, and at the same time defines an Other. To laugh requires critical distance from the object laughed at, and what we laugh at always has the status of an object, even when it is ourselves. In this manuscript, most of the women cause laughter not as agents, but as objects, and unsurprisingly, they are most often objectified in terms of their sexuality. For instance, the woman in the second jest on folio 1 has been completely relegated to the status of a sexual object of exchange: "The frier and the tailer made a match that he whiche thrust his / pricke farthest between the legges of the wife of the tailer / what not yet not yet not yet why then I have lost my cheese."[6] The tailor's wife has no agency in this circumstance; there is no sense that she would have the right to refuse involvement in the bet.

Whereas the tailor's wife is really only a means to a homosocial end, other jests target the women themselves. Bergson notes that humor often serves as social critique.[7] Humor, in its corrective function, also reveals whatever attendant anxiety provoked it in the first place, and in this case, that anxiety is fueled by fear of women's agency. Several of the jokes rebuke women who attempt to appropriate power for themselves through wit by relegating them to mere sexual objects. For instance, one reads, "a gentlewoman one a time seeing one want a knife she / sayd cut my finger he replyed you would say / finger my cut." Another, in the same hand, reads "a capitaines boy coming through cheape side with long / here a marchants wife sitting in her shopp calling / him sayd, yt he was bush naturall more here then / witt, he replyed [agin] to your cunt mistrese more here thou haveste."[8] The derision aimed at the women cuts across social statuses, targeting members both of the gentility and of the merchant class. Both women make the "mistake" of speaking provocatively or critically, and are reprimanded in return in such a way as to equate them with their sexuality.

In yet another jest, the humor stems not from a woman's transgressive agency but from her vulnerability to another's sexual desire: a gentlewoman is called

---

[5] Henri Bergson, "Laughter," in *Comedy*, ed. Wylie Sypher (Baltimore and London: Johns Hopkins Univ. Press, 1980), 73, 117.

[6] I am indebted to Heather Blatt's wonderful paper on cheese trenchers for my understanding of the last line of this jest—apparently cheese had symbolic resonances of sexual transgression both for men and for women throughout the early modern period, and cheese could indeed here stand in for ejaculation. Heather Blatt, "'My Cheeks resemble Famine painted on a clean Trencher': Dining and the Constitution of Self," presented at the Renaissance Society of America Conference, Miami, FL, 23 March 2007.

[7] Bergson, "Laughter," 63.

[8] Commonplace book—jests and poems, 1595, Folger Shakespeare Library, x.d.177, fol. 3v.

to court; while there, the lamps go out and she finds herself in darkness. "[C]omes one to the gentlewoman to her / and takes upp her clothes she put her hand on her / berde and sayde I will saue this the other will saue / it selfe."[9] The target of the jest is licentiousness at court—any blackout might be cause for sexual interludes. The gentlewoman does her best to protect herself from such improprieties: instead of turning her hand to relighting the lamps, she turns it to defense of her "beard" or genitals. In so doing, she asserts a kind of agency that seems to be approved of by the joke writer since she is maintaining the ever-important female quality of chastity, upon which a patriarchal and patrilineal system depends.

The poems within the commonplace book generally fall into the category of love lyrics. Diana E. Henderson has remarked that "if one dismisses the erotic plot and its lyric expressions, 'good' women in imaginative literature were, if not entirely erased, then most often reduced to ideologically proper silence and removed to religious pedestals far from the earthly realms of social power."[10] And this may be exactly why most educators did not want their pupils to have much of anything to do with such poems. Strangely enough, though, the male speakers (and likely the male authors) of these lyrics seem to share, if not educators' rejection of the genre, their desire to subjugate women and moderate women's social power. The poems do not attack or rebuke women in the same manner as the jests do because their primary tone is not humorous, but they do bemoan the agency of women who decide for themselves which lovers to accept or reject. One, on folio 8 recto, is written by a young man (23 years old he tells us) for his love Josphine Elizabethe, in which he begs both muses and nature to "bear witness y^t I am in loue." The verses balance classical allusions to Arethusa and Aganippe and a "prathing nymph turned to a stone" with floral references to primrose, cowslip, columbine, hyacinth, violets, roses, and Venus glove. The poem's lady is described with conventional imagery: "her lockes like yellow daffadils / her eyes like to the violets gray / more sweet then is the pimpernel / more fragrant then the flowers in may." This paragon of Petrarchan beauty, however, seems not to be responding to the speaker's lament, since every verse ends with the refrain that he needs someone or something to "bear witness" of his feelings to her; the sole exception to this repetition is in the third stanza, when the speaker ends with "oh y^t I might your senses moue."

Even more obstinate than Josphine Elizabethe as an object of desire is 'Faire Phillis,' who appears in a verse on folio 3:

---

[9] Ibid., fol. 1r.

[10] Diana E. Henderson, "Female Power and the Devaluation of Renaissance Love Lyrics," in *Dwelling in Possibility: Women Poets and Critics on Poetry*, ed. Yopie Prins and Maeera Shreiber (Ithaca: Cornell Univ. Press, 1997), 38–59, here 42.

> Sheapheard sawest thou not my faire phillis
> walking on this mountaine or in yonder plaine
> She is gone this way to dianas fountaine
> & hath left me wounded with her high disdaine
> Ay me she is ^faire & I must despaire
> Sorrowe come & shift[?] with me
> Thus my passions paine me for my loue hath chaine me
> Gentle sheapheard beare a part
> That the god of loue may from heaven aboue
> pearse my phillis flintie hart

This poem, of course, has all the earmarks of Renaissance lyric pastoral poetry: the speaker addresses a shepherd with his complaint about fair Phillis' unwillingness to entertain his amorous suit. She has maintained her chastity by retreating to Diana's fountain, and wounded the lover with her "high disdaine" and her "flintie hart." Phillis has imprisoned the lover, chaining his heart through his love for her, and has further punished him by making him a companion of Sorrow through her rejection of him. It seems as though fair Phillis has all the power in the relationship, a power that the speaker hopes will be subordinated to Cupid's arrow according to the poem's last line.

There is only one wholeheartedly positive portrayal of active female sexuality within the commonplace book—a small poem that appears on folio 8 recto: "sweet were the words / my mistresse sedd / put of thie clothes / and come to bedd." These four lines stand in distinct contrast both to the jests and to the lyric love poems that fill the manuscript; the poem's speaker is undeniably pleased at his mistress' forthright invitation that comes in the form of a direct order.

Another powerful and frustrating woman also appears in the manuscript's pages—Queen Elizabeth, though she does not occupy the status of beloved. A four-line poem entitled "Churchyards verses to the queen" reads:

> your grace didd promise on a time
> to giue me reason for my rime
> but from that time vnto this season
> I never heard of rime nor reason

Apparently the copyist was particularly fond of this poem, as he transcribed it twice—first on folio 3 recto where it appears amongst others of his transcriptions, including the faire Phillis poem and another entitled "verses upon mr. dunse," and then again on folio 8 recto. In the verse, the power the speaker resents is not

erotic, but rather economic. Churchyard castigates the queen for failing to provide the promised "reason" or patronage for his rhymes.

So, looking at the representations of women presented by both the jests and
the poems, we see a continuum which ranges from powerlessness to agency,
though of course that agency is—in all but the case of the sexually directive
mistress—highly resented by the presumably male speakers within the texts.
It is interesting, therefore, to see where Clarke may have chosen to identify on
this continuum. The last folio of the commonplace book contains, as mentioned
earlier, the fifth signature of Clarke. There also appear two stanzas of verse,
which I speculate Clarke herself transcribed. There are several reasons why I
propose this is true: first, the ink is the same as that of her signatures, and it is
distinct from the ink used by other scribes—the only other item that looks to be
in the same ink is the name of Nathann Hardinant, which also appears in the left
margin of the first folio.[11] Secondly, the first line of verse is of approximately the
same size as the signature, with the following lines becoming increasingly larger,
as might be expected of someone still practicing handwriting. Finally, several
letters—including the a, r, k, and e—have similar forms in both her signatures
and in the stanzas.

Several questions remain about the writing, including whether it is an
original composition or it transcribes an already existent text. Moreover, it is
unclear whether the stanzas comprise one poem or if they are two separate pieces.
Nonetheless, the verses, whether compositions or transcriptions, may provide us
with a sense of Clarke's preferences regarding the positioning of women within
literary texts. I must acknowledge, however, that this assertion rests upon a
potentially large assumption—that Clarke had some agency in choosing the text.
After all, it could have been written at the direction of a tutor, though the content
of the verses makes that unlikely, or at the direction of a male in her household
who wanted her to practice her handwriting—a father, a brother, a husband or
fiancé, perhaps Nathann Hardinant himself. Even if so, the text reproduced exists
in a new context—both in terms of where it was placed within the collection
and in terms of being literally "written" by a woman. As Susan Miller points
out in her study of early American commonplace books, "Positions in discourse
are always provisional, even when they are assumed through language that is

---

[11] As Anne E. B. Coldiron confirmed for me, Nathann Hardinant's name looks to be in
Clarke's own hand; perhaps Clarke wrote the name of her beloved as schoolgirls sometimes do
on textbooks, but this is purely speculation until some evidence can be found linking Clarke
and Hardinant.

rooted in tradition and directly copied in a new circumstance."[12] Clarke, whether she had an active choice in her material, provisionally "occupied" the rhetorical position of "speaker" of the poem(s).

That position acknowledges, at least in a limited fashion, women's power and agency. Yet this power remains insistently erotic, rather than economic, unlike in Churchyard's poem to the queen, and the male resentment of such agency is still clearly communicated. The two stanzas read:

> I loue thee not cause thou art faire
> Softer then down sweeter then Aire
> or for that cupid wch doth ly
> in every corner of thine eye
> I would fayne know what it might be
> tis y loue yow cause yow loue me
>
> I had rather marry a disease
> then court a Lady I[13] cannot plese
> Shee that would cheerish my desire
> must feede my flames wth equall fire
> what pleasure is there in a kisse
> to him that hath the harte not his.

Both stanzas secure some, if limited, agency for the implied female audience. The first stanza rejects the conventions of the Petrarchan tradition, which as we saw with the earlier poem to Josphine Elizabethe associates the lady with softness, delicacy, and shining eyes. Although the stanza could be read as less than complimentary (I couldn't find anyone better, and you love me, so I'll love you) or, conversely, very complimentary (in the same tradition as Shakespeare's "My mistress' eyes are nothing like the sun"),[14] the object of desire is also a subject of desire. The second stanza addresses a "Lady I cannot please," and the speaker's

---

[12] Susan Miller, *Assuming the Positions: Cultural Pedagogy and the Politics of Commonplace Writing* (Pittsburgh: Univ. of Pittsburgh Press, 1998), 3.

[13] I thank Helen Vincent of the National Library of Scotland for her correction of my transcription; this transcription supersedes the previous one contained in Kathryn DeZur, "'Vaine Books' and Early Modern Women Readers," in *Reading and Literacy in the Middle Ages and Renaissance*, ed. Ian Moulton, Arizona Studies in the Middle Ages and the Renaissance 8 (Turnhout: Brepols, 2004), 105–26.

[14] Henderson remarks that scholars have only recently linked English anti-Petrarchan satire "with male rebelliousness against female political authority (rather than [seeing it] as a reflection of the bluff and hardy English national character)": Henderson, "Female Power," 40.

rejection of her is a reaction to the lady's rejection of him—her "harts not his." The lady's rejection demonstrates the power of choice the addressed woman has exercised. This second verse embodies the notion that women's primary purpose for men is a sexual one—a view overwhelmingly propagated in the jests—but it also reveals a certain agency that women can exercise in choosing lovers, an agency completely denied, for instance, by the jest that assumes the tailor's wife will have no say in the competition between the tailor and the friar.

Clarke seems to occupy the strange, but perhaps quite common for early modern women, position of the transgendered speaker; the women represented in "her" text (both the verses she has transcribed and the commonplace book as a whole) possess some power—enough to create resentment, anxiety, humor, and some pretty mediocre love poetry. This combination leaves us with a number of questions: did she identify with the women represented, or with the male speakers she "voiced" and read? Did she experience a secret thrill at the implied power of the women, or anger at their transgressions of cultural norms, or fear that male reprisals such as those in the jests and poems might be directed toward her, deservedly or not? Such questions may not be answerable, at least as far as Elizabeth Clarke is concerned, but it is hoped that the emerging scholarship devoted to early modern women's reading and writing practices will provide us with a more complete understanding of the contexts in which such interactions and potential identifications took place.

STATE UNIVERSITY OF NEW YORK
COLLEGE OF TECHNOLOGY AT DELHI

Reading the Stage Rubrics
of Mary Wroth's Folger Manuscript of
Pamphilia to Amphilanthus

SUSAN LAUFFER O'HARA

W HEN EXAMINING LADY MARY WROTH'S FOLGER MANUSCRIPT OF
Pamphilia to Amphilanthus it is strikingly clear that Wroth intended
her collection of songs and sonnets to be read in separate groupings.[1]
What makes these groupings so dramatic are the blank pages that separate the
collection into three distinct groups that I will call Sections I, II, and III.[2] Perhaps
the most salient difference between the last two sections (Sections II, P56–P90
and III, P91–P103) and the first 55 songs and sonnets (Section I, P1–P55) is the

This paper was first delivered at the 42nd International Congress on Medieval Studies
(2007), Kalamazoo, MI, at a panel entitled "Early Modern Women's Manuscripts," Margaret P.
Hannay, Siena College, presiding.

[1] I wish to thank the staff at the Folger Shakespeare Library for their kind help and
knowledgeable assistance with the holograph copy of *Pamphilia to Amphilanthus* and the
printed version contained within *The Countess of Montgomery's Urania*. They were also very
helpful with Ben Jonson's somewhat frail holograph copy of *Christmas, his Show* contained
within *Dramatic and poetical miscellany*. I also wish to thank my research assistant, Aileen
Benitez, and Georgian Court University for their generous support in the form of a Faculty
Summer Research Grant, which funded this research project at the Folger.

[2] That Wroth used blank pages to separate the sonnet sections is not a new discovery.
Wroth critics have long noted this distinction. See Jeff Masten, "'Shall I turne blabb?': Circulation, Gender, and Subjectivity in Mary Wroth's Sonnets," in *Reading Mary Wroth: Representing Alternatives in Early Modern England*, ed. Naomi Miller and Gary Waller (Knoxville: Univ.
of Tennessee Press, 1991), 67–87.

grotesquerie which begins each of the last two sections.[3] The display of violence, sexual tension, and near-chaotic unrest exhibited through the use of mythological figures constitutes the grotesque in the beginning of Sections II and III. This grotesquerie is in dramatic contrast to the elegant formality of "A Crowne of Sonetts dedicated to Love" which ends Section II and the stately tribute to a monarch which comprises the ending of Section III. It is differences such as these that lead us to question Wroth's adherence to the decorum of sonnet-sequence conventions. I propose, therefore, that the last two sections (Sections II and III) of *Pamphilia to Amphilanthus* comprise two masques, in essence a double masque, with the grotesquerie of each section constituting antimasques.[4] I also want to point out that the Folger manuscript of *Pamphilia to Amphilanthus* represents what I believe to be a *preperformance* text and not a *postperformance* text that we find when reading the masques from Jonson's folio with all the production descriptions added.[5] These two masques with their beginning antimasques, then, adhere to masque conventions while still retaining sonnet-sequence form.[6] Wroth is in effect synthesizing two genre forms. She is moving away from a conventional concept of form while still retaining that form. In fact, Wroth adheres so closely

---

[3] Sonnet numbers in parentheses for these and subsequent sonnets refer to the numbering system Josephine Roberts developed in her edition of the sequence. See *The Poems of Lady Mary Wroth* (Baton Rouge: Louisiana State Univ. Press, 1983).

[4] For explanations of double masques see Enid Welsford, *The Court Masque: A Study in the Relationship Between Poetry and the Revels* (New York: Russell and Russell, 1962), 143, 180, 189, 191, 217, and 283. I use the term "double masque" loosely because Wroth mixes the genders of her antimasque figures, having male and female figures within the same antimasque. The two masques, however, are so similar in theme, subject matter, and structure that we could consider them a double masque. It should also be noted that the second masque works to resolve (as far as that is possible) the "problem" of the first masque.

[5] See Jerzy Limon, "The Literary Masque," in *The Masque of Stuart Culture* (Newark, DE: Univ. of Delaware Press, 1990), 17–52. In this chapter Limon discusses all the various "texts" which go into creating a final postperformance text like the one we see in Jonson's folio. Limon also notes that the Folger owns one of the few preperformance manuscripts that have survived. It is Jonson's manuscript for *Christmas, his Show* and Limon notes that it does not have the usual descriptions of stage design, entrances of particular characters are not marked at all, and the brief stage directions are in the imperative, as "singe."

[6] Ann Rosalind Jones, "Designing Women: The Self as Spectacle in Mary Wroth and Veronica Franco," in *Reading Mary Wroth: Representing Alternatives in Early Modern England*, ed. Miller and Waller, 135–53, here 150, notes the affinities between Jonson's *Masque of Beauty* and the "Crown of Sonetts." See also Ann Baynes Coiro, *Robert Herrick's Hesperides and the Epigram Book Tradition* (Baltimore: Johns Hopkins Univ. Press, 1988), 22–26. Coiro sees *Hesperides* as a poetic masque, but it is a masque turned upside down "with the antimasque voices of mockery, disorder, and warning raised very strongly at the end and never returned to their marginalized position" (24).

to masque conventions in Sections II and III of *Pamphilia to Amphilanthus* that I believe Wroth's masques could, indeed, be staged, and I will argue that her verse refers to stage directions which are conventional for masque poetry.

If we examine the preperformance text of Ben Jonson's holograph manuscript of *Christmas, his Show* (later published as *Christmas, his Masque*),[7] the process by which masques were written will be clarified. Figure 1 is a page from *Christmas* (1615), showing one of the few references to stage performance in the text. At the top of the first page of Figure 1, Jonson's stage rubric reads: "Drum & Fife sounds: and they march about once: at the second comming up, he proceeds in his song."[8] The only other indications of performance are the title and the word "singe." This grouping of songs and poems could easily be mistaken for a collection of poems, and it is surprising how "unmasque-like" it is. This holograph manuscript contains no other stage directions, no production descriptions, and no costume or choreographic descriptions that Jonson painstakingly wrote for his *postproduction* published masques. The manuscript, *Christmas, his Show*, is a striking reminder, as Jerzy Limon has argued regarding masque texts, that "We are actually dealing with three different texts, which belong not only to different genres but also to different systems" ("Literary Masque," 20). Limon goes on to say that the poetic or literary pre-text evolved into a "sum of texts" prepared by the poet, stage designer, stage engineer, composer of music, and choreographer.[9]

Figure 2 is from Jonson's masque *The Gypsies Metamorphosed*, published in the 1640 edition of *The Workes of Benjamin Jonson*.[10] Notice, in this published version, the stage rubrics indicating what characters recite the poetry and what characters sing or dance. In addition, within the text of Jackman's speech there are indications of stage actions, directing Jackman to call for his "Guittarra" and room to dance, as well as signaling the entrance of the "Chiefe," presumably the "Captaine" that soon enters. And, as anticipated in the Jackman speech, there is also a rubric directing the entrance of the Captaine with six attendants and an indication of when Jackman should begin singing. This published version of a masque, then, is very different from the sketchy, sparse rubrics we get in Jonson's holograph manuscript of *Christmas* discussed above. Indeed, the published version entitled *Christmas, his Masque* contains rubrics similar to those in *Gypsies*, indicating entrances and exits, descriptions of characters and costumes, and stage directions indicating singing and dancing. These rubrics are missing from

---

[7] The Folger Shakespeare Library, J.a.1.

[8] Limon overlooked this particular stage rubric in his examination of Jonson's *Christmas* at the Folger.

[9] Limon, "Literary Masque," 24.

[10] The Folger Shakespeare Library, *STC* 14754, vols. 2–3.

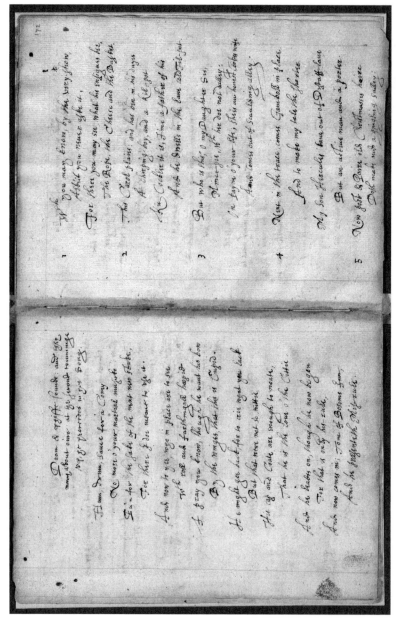

Figure 1. Holograph manuscript of *Christmas, his Show* from *Dramatic and poetical miscellany* (Folger J.a.1). Reproduced by permission of the Folger Shakespeare Library, Washington, D. C.

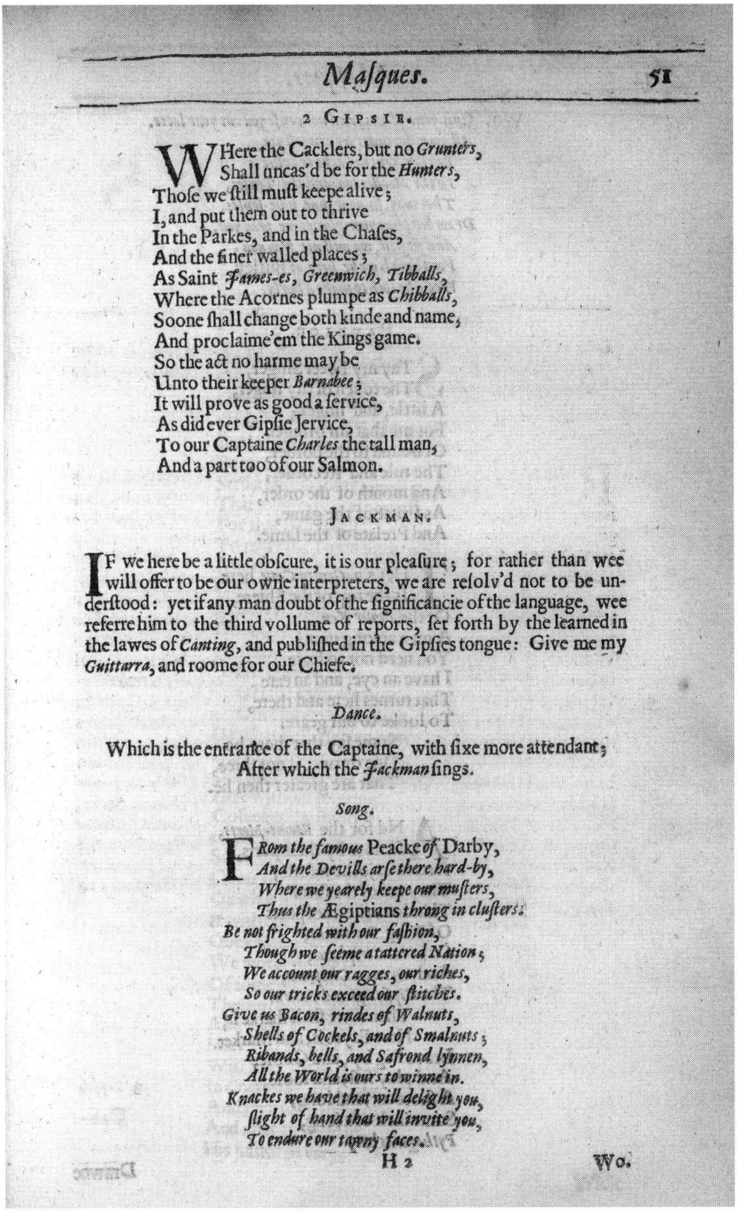

Masques. 51

2 GIPSIE.

WHere the Cacklers, but no *Grunters*,
Shall uncas'd be for the *Hunters*,
Those we still must keepe alive;
I, and put them out to thrive
In the Parkes, and in the Chases,
And the finer walled places;
As Saint *James-es*, *Greenwich*, *Tibballs*,
Where the Acornes plumpe as *Chibballs*,
Soone shall change both kinde and name,
And proclaime'em the Kings game.
So the act no harme may be
Unto their keeper *Barnabee*;
It will prove as good a service,
As did ever Gipsie Jervice,
To our Captaine *Charles* the tall man,
And a part too of our Salmon.

JACKMAN.

IF we here be a little obscure, it is our pleasure; for rather than wee
will offer to be our owne interpreters, we are resolv'd not to be understood: yet if any man doubt of the significancie of the language, wee
referre him to the third vollume of reports, set forth by the learned in
the lawes of *Canting*, and published in the Gipsies tongue: Give me my
Guittarra, and roome for our Chiefe.

Dance.

Which is the entrance of the Captaine, with fixe more attendant;
After which the *Jackman* sings.

Song.

FRom the famous Peacke of Darby,
And the Devills arse there hard-by,
Where we yearely keepe our musters,
Thus the Ægiptians throng in clusters.
Be not frighted with our fashion,
Though we seeme a tattered Nation;
We account our ragges, our riches,
So our tricks exceed our stitches.
Give us Bacon, rindes of Walnuts,
Shells of Cockels, and of Smalnuts;
Ribands, bells, and Safrond lynnen,
All the World is ours to winne in.
Knackes we have that will delight you,
Slight of hand that will invite you,
To endure our tawny faces.

H 2
Wo.

Figure 2. The Gypsies Metamorphosed, printed in the 1640 edition of *The Workes of Benjamin Jonson,* vol. 2–3 (Folger STC 14754). Reproduced by permission of the Folger Shakespeare Library, Washington, D. C.

the holograph copy of *Christmas, his Show* and were added later by Jonson for the published version.

The most important aspect of the Wroth text of Figure 3, taken from the 1621 printed version of *Pamphilia to Amphilanthus* contained within *The Countesse of Montgomery's Urania*,[11] is the fact that there should be a blank page after sonnet 14 (P90), according to the holograph manuscript of the sonnet sequence at the Folger. This printed version, however, joins the discrete groupings together, making the songs and sonnets appear as one complete sonnet sequence. It is at sonnet 14 that the first masque ends with Pamphilia trapped in the Labyrinth, and the second masque begins with the following song (P91), both of which should be separated with the blank page.

But how could what appears to be a sonnet sequence be performed on stage? We know that Wroth took part in Jonson's *The Masque of Blackness*, and there is a masque-like scene in the *Urania*. In addition, there are detailed descriptions of masques in *The Second Part of the Countesse of Montgomery's Urania*, and we can surmise that as an active member of the court Wroth had probably seen numerous court masques. We can thus assume that Wroth had a great deal of interest in masques and how they would be performed. Perhaps Wroth utilized sonnet-sequence form for her double masque to avoid the criticism heaped on Chapman for the long, incomprehensible speeches of his masques. Enid Welsford discusses Chapman's problem:

> The accusation against him [Chapman] seems to have been that his lengthy speeches and dialogues were not inserted for their interest and beauty, but from sheer necessity, because without them the meaning of the device . . . could not have been understood.[12]

Wroth's form, then, using a series of sonnets and songs, would be more easily comprehended by the audience, especially with Pamphilia as guide and narrator of the mumming, the pantomiming of each song and sonnet on stage.

To argue, therefore, that Wroth's sonnet sections are masques and anti-masques is not that great a leap in genre forms. Indeed, Elizabethan masques consisted, in part, of knights reciting Petrarchan sonnets to their ladies.[13] From medieval and early Tudor mummings and disguisings to Elizabethan masques there is rarely any dialogue spoken in these entertainments. Set speech follows set

---

[11]   The Folger Shakespeare Library, *STC* 26051.

[12]   Welsford, *Court Masque*, 257.

[13]   Stephen Orgel, *The Jonsonian Masque* (Cambridge, MA: Harvard Univ. Press, 1965), 35–36.

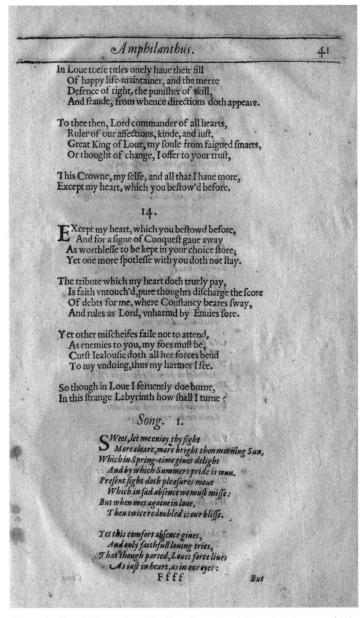

Figure 3. Pamphilia to Amphilanthus from the 1621 printed copy of *The Countesse of Mountgomeries Urania* (Folger STC 26051 Copy 1). Reproduced by permission of the Folger Shakespeare Library, Washington, D. C.

speech, with each speech constructed as an explanation of the pictures, the static visual stage tableaux. It is Wroth's utilization of these conventions that turns her sonnet sequence, her "speaking pictures," into a double masque. Indeed, even in a Jonsonian masque the courtly masquers rarely have speaking parts. Moreover, there is a tendency in the seventeenth century for antimasques to turn into pantomime. In addition, Wroth is incorporating medieval emblematic tradition into a finely-structured whole crafted around a central device creating a unified work of art that could, indeed, be staged. Therefore, the political and sexual nature of these songs and sonnets, the indications of stage rubrics and scenic devices, the grotesquery, the seventeenth century's adherence to medieval emblematic tradition, the blurring of boundaries between genres in this period, and Wroth's adherence to masque conventions all support a reading of these songs and sonnets as masques and antimasques.

It seems reasonable at this point to sketch out the central device and the structure of Wroth's two masques. The central device around which both masques revolve is Pamphilia's situation of tyranny imposed upon her by Amphilanthus and her own desires. In general terms, the display and the working out of this situation of tyranny comprise the action of both masques. Thus the first antimasque (P56–P76) of the first masque establishes Pamphilia's situation of tyranny by displaying a series of intimate revelations, setting up the problem for the formal masque that follows.[14] Pamphilia is grief-stricken at the impending departure of Amphilanthus for another woman, and appeals to Venus, goddess of desire, for help, but to no end. Then, in a pivotal song in the introduction to this antimasque Pamphilia establishes herself as a figure of Desire. Grieving for the loss of Amphilanthus and full of desire for him, Pamphilia begins to reveal the masochistic sexual pleasure she derives from the pain that she endures. The rest of the antimasque consists of a series of intimate revelations which further establishes Pamphilia's situation of tyranny since she has been caught in a web of sexual obsession, desire, jealousy, and fear of abandonment. In the unsettled, disordered world of this antimasque, these revelations are displayed through a parade of antimasque characters, manifestations of Pamphilia's inner turmoil

---

[14] For other readings of this group of songs and sonnets see the following: Elaine V. Beilin, "'The Onely Perfect Vertue': Constancy in Mary Wroth's *Pamphilia to Amphilanthus*," in *Spenser Studies: A Renaissance Poetry Annual II,* ed. Patrick Cullen and Thomas P. Roche (Pittsburgh: Univ. of Pittsburgh Press, 1981), 229–45, here 234–36. Barbara Kiefer Lewalski, *Writing Women in Jacobean England* (Cambridge, MA: Harvard Univ. Press, 1993), 259; Josephine A. Roberts, "The Biographical Problem of *Pamphilia to Amphilanthus*," *Tulsa Studies in Women's Literature* 1 (1983): 43–53.

and her situation of tyranny: Love as a juggler, Night, Suspicion, Love in chains, and Folly.

The problem of the masque has thus been established, and it is the formal masque (P77–P90) which now must resolve this situation of tyranny. The masque opens with Pamphilia trapped within the labyrinth of love, a symbol for her situation of tyranny. Once within the walls of the labyrinth of love, Pamphilia is transformed into a teacher of other lovers because of her arduous learning experience in the antimasque. The action of this formal masque, then, consists of a series of lessons on Pamphilia's conception of ideal love, a love based on equality, reason, trust, justice, and truth. But despite all of Pamphilia's lessons and antilessons on ideal love, she remains trapped within the labyrinth of love at the end of the masque.

The antimasque (P91–P98) of the second masque opens with Pamphilia still trapped within the labyrinth of love. The action of this antimasque consists of Pamphilia's encounters with antimasque figures that are manifestations of her fears. The action crystallizes midpoint in a debate between fear and desire. Pamphilia, of course, chooses desire and so remains trapped within the labyrinth of love. The action leads to the formal masque (P99–P103) and a conventional masque tribute to Amphilanthus, the "monarch" of Pamphilia's heart and the answer to all her desires.

Let us now look at two characters from the parade of antimasque figures in the first antimasque (P56–P76). These masque figures become projections of the turmoil of Pamphilia's inward state. In sonnet P64, Love (Cupid) enters as a juggler, a manifestation of the erratic nature of love. In addition, this sonnet also sets up the tyrannical nature of Pamphilia's situation:

> Love like a jugler, comes to play his prise,
>> And all minds draw his wonders to admire,
>> To see how cuningly hee, wanting eyes,
>> Can yett deseave the best sight of desire:
> The wanton child, how hee can faine his fire
>> So pretely, as none sees his disguise!
>> How finely doe his tricks, while wee fooles hire
>> The badge, and office of his tirannies,
> For in the end, such jugling hee doth make
>> As hee our harts, in stead of eyes doth take
>> For men can only by theyr slieghts abuse
> The sight with nimble, and delightfull skill;
>> Butt if hee play, his gaine is our lost will:
>> Yett childlike, wee can nott his sports refuse.

Love enters as a juggler, and the movement in "comes to play," "faine his fire," and "finely doe" suggests a performance, literally an antic dance conventional for an antimasque. There is a sense of audience viewing in "all minds draw his wonders to admire," in "none sees," and in "wee fooles hire." And there is a sense that this sonnet is all-inclusive, addressing all lovers. Yet the antimasque is progressing towards more specificity, for it is really Pamphilia's heart that Love has taken and it is really her "lost will" that is Love's gain. She is the fool that hires "The badge, and office of his tirannies" through her desires for Amphilanthus. The sonnet becomes an outward manifestation of Pamphilia's desires and her entrapment in those desires. It is a type of exhibitionism, for Pamphilia's most inward desires are manifested through the antic dance of Love. And, through implication, Amphilanthus is the tyrant, because he is the only one who can satisfy her desires.

There are a number of factors which suggest that sonnet P64 is literally an antic dance in an antimasque. First, the opening line seems to be a rubric signaling the entrance of Love as an antimasque figure: "Love like a jugler, comes to play his prise." Wroth's verse also suggests costume, for Love is "disguise[d]" like a "jugler" and is blindfolded. Love also seems to be juggling hearts and performing other feats of skill and perhaps playing games. All of these stage actions are conventional for an antimasque. An antic dance was often grotesque or acrobatic in nature.[15] And there is the tradition of game-playing, especially at dice, in the early mummings which carried over into masques.[16] As mentioned earlier, the antic dance in sonnet P64 is symbolic of the erratic nature of love, but it also signifies Pamphilia's entrapment in her situation of tyranny. She has hired "the badge, and office of his tyrannies," and Love's "gaine" is Pamphilia's "lost will." On a political level, however, Love could be symbolic of King James I, who "all minds draw his wonders to admire" while "wee fooles hire / The badge, and office

---

[15] Orgel, *The Jonsonian Masque*, 117. Compare Wroth's antic dance of Love the Juggler with Jonson's dance of virtues in the masque proper of *Love Restored*. Love is the power which orders virtue:

This motion was of love begot,
It was so ayrie, light, and good,
His wings into their feet he shot,
Or else himselfe into their bloud.
But aske not how. The end will prove,
That love's in them, or they'are in love.

See John C. Meagher, *Method and Meaning in Jonson's Masques* (Notre Dame: Univ. of Notre Dame Press, 1966), 90.

[16] Allegory eventually replaced playing at dice in the masques. But there were entertainments which were both masques and mumming and included games, especially dicing. See Welsford, *Court* Masque, 136; Glynne Wickham, *Early English Stages 1300–1660*, vol. 1 (New York: Columbia Univ. Press, 1980), 200.

of his tirannies." On the political level "wee fooles" become any courtier who plays the game of courtly favor. And the lure of this game is almost overpowering like sexual desire, for "cuningly hee, wanting eyes, / Can yett deseave the best sight of desire," and "childlike, wee can nott his sports refuse." The performance of this antic dance of Love is a display of sadomasochistic exhibitionism—that of Pamphilia and any courtier who seeks court favor. Wroth's verse has provided not only an entry into the inner workings of Pamphilia's sexual obsession, but also an entry into the machinations of the aspiring courtier whose ambition feeds upon itself in an eroticized dance of desire.

The next antimasque character, "Poore Love in chaines," again functions as an outward sign of Pamphilia's inward state. The fact that Pamphilia has learned the falsity of love in this antimasque is reinforced by the debate between Cupid and Diana that is played out in the following sonnet P70:

> Poore Love in chaines, and fetters like a thiefe
>   I mett led forthe, as chast Diana's gaine,
>   Vowing the untaught Lad should noe reliefe
>   From her receave, who glory'd in fond paine,
> She call'd him theife; with vowes hee did maintaine
>   Hee never stole; butt some sadd slight of griefe
>   Had given to those who did his powre disdaine,
>   In which reveng, his honor, was the chiefe:
> She say'd hee murder'd, and therfor must dy;
>   Hee, that hee caus'd butt love: did harmes deny
>   Butt, while she thus discoursing with him stood
> The Nimphs unty'd him, and his chaines tooke off
>   Thinking him safe; butt hee loose, made a scofe
>   Smiling, and scorning them, flew to the wood.

Pamphilia's education as to the falsity of love is demonstrated in this sonnet by her presence at and her viewing of the action. It is Pamphilia ("I mett") that meets "Poore Love in chaines." She is the onlooker; she is the narrator of events that we see through her eyes. Like the antimasque figure of Cupid as juggler, "Poore Love in chaines" has the antic disposition of a Jonsonian masque or a Spenserian masque of Cupid in the House of Busirane. As the spectacle of "Diana's gaine," Cupid is "fetter[ed] like a thiefe" and as such the debate ensues. Diana claims that Cupid will receive no relief from her since he "glory'd in fond paine." Cupid, for his part, states that he never stole, but admits to "some sadd slight of griefe." This slight grief was rendered to those who disdained his power, so it was an act of revenge to mollify his honor. Diana retorts that he is a murderer and must die, while Cupid claims that, "hee caus'd butt love: did harmes deny." The dispute is settled with the intervention of the "Nimphs" who unwittingly take off his chains "Thinking him safe." Cupid, realizing that he is free, scoffing, smiling, and scorning the nymphs, flies to the woods.[17] The undertones of these seemingly light-hearted quips convey a sense of malevolence—Love *will* falsify. And it is the unknowing, inexperienced nymphs that are taken in by the words of Cupid much the same way Pamphilia was taken in by the "flattery, and skill" of Amphilanthus. It seems, then, that the duping of Pamphilia is reenacted in the debate between Cupid and Diana and in the deception of the nymphs. The antimasque is thus built around two central debates, the internal debate between Pamphilia's heart and mind in sonnet P69 and the debate between Cupid and Diana in sonnet P70.[18] The resolution to both of these debates is that Love (Amphilanthus, Cupid) *will* falsify.

The first two lines of sonnet P70 are rubrics indicating the action that should take place on stage: "Poore Love in chaines, and fetters like a thiefe / I mett led forthe, as chast Diana's gaine." This sonnet could easily be mimed since the verse describes fully what should be enacted. Pamphilia meets Love being led forth by Diana. While the debate ensues, the Nymphs untie him and, scoffing, he flies to the wood. Besides action, costume is also indicated. Cupid would be fettered like a thief in chains. This sonnet might also contain an antic dance, since Cupid scoffs, smiles, and scorns the Nymphs before flying to the woods. All of these actions in an antic dance would be of wild gyrations, highly exaggerated facial and hand motions, and, of course, deft footwork—anything to heighten the grotesquery. Indeed, Cupid's flight to the woods could be interpreted literally, given the nature of stage machinery and scenic devices in this time period.

What, then, are the implications of Wroth's sonnets as antimasque? Certainly we have a display of female sexuality by a woman writer that is very rare for this time period. What we also have is a female narrator, an inversion of the male persona of the sonnet-sequence tradition. In addition, Petrarchan images and figures of speech that are standard sonnet-sequence form become something other, become something overtly political when used as a public performance in a genre that was traditionally politically charged. What Wroth is doing is providing a medium, and what is being played out is the courtier's desire

---

[17] See Lisle Cecil John, "The Alexandrian Conception in the Sonnet Sequence," in *The Elizabethan Sonnet Sequences: Studies in Conventional Conceits* (New York: Russell and Russell, 1964), 67–77.

[18] See Orgel, *Jonsonian Masque*, 46, 55, for a discussion on how the Jonsonian antimasque was structured around a debate.

for favor, for prestige, for wealth in very sexual terms. The songs and sonnets of this antimasque, then, are performance, an idiom within which jealousy, desire, sadomasochism, and voyeurism become conflated and enacted in a world of real lovers and real courtiers. When sonnets are no longer static, when they are presented as performance, the political significance is no longer metaphoric, but literal. Metaphor is transformed into a performative reenactment of life at court, the masochistic pleasure in the pain of the game.

Wroth, then, has successfully moved beyond sonnet sequence form, yet surprisingly still retains that form. Her sonnets read as masques and antimasques move from the intimate private sphere of sonnet sequence to that of public performance. By situating Wroth within the context of the evolution of the masque we may better understand how she achieves this synthesis of genres. More important, Wroth has provided us with an entry into the public, politically-charged, titillating milieu of the masque where private intrudes on public, where performance, performer, and audience meet in an axis around which revolves the social, cultural, and political world of the court.

GEORGIAN COURT UNIVERSITY

From *Margin to Milieu: The Authorship of* Le tombeau de Marguerite de Valois, Royne de Navarre

T HOUGH RECENT CRITICAL ATTENTION HAS ACKNOWLEDGED THE importance of the Seymour sisters' panegyric on Marguerite de Navarre, which was, as Brenda Hosington notes, "the only published composition in Latin by any Englishwoman before 1560,"[1] many facets of its creation and dissemination remain under-explored. My paper examines the provenance of this poetic miscellany to further uncover its importance to the canon of early modern women's writing. The original composition makes a provocative transition from private to public sphere, beginning as a manuscript of elegiac couplets composed in 1549 for their former tutor by the teenaged Seymour sisters Anne, Margaret, and Jane, ultimately circulating in two print versions within two years of its original composition. The lattermost volume was published in France in 1551, and contained contributions of prominent Pléiade members Pierre de Ronsard, Antoine de Baïf, and Joachim du Bellay. The volume's re-dedication to Marguerite, Duchesse de Berry, casts its dedicatee as the inheritor of a new generation

---

I would like to thank Margaret P. Hannay, Siena College, for guiding a thought-provoking session entitled "Early Modern Women's Manuscripts" at the 42nd International Congress on Medieval Studies (2007) at Kalamazoo, MI.

[1] Brenda Hosington, "England's First Female-Authored Encomium: The Seymour Sisters' *Hecatodistichon* (1550) to Marguerite de Navarre. Text, Translation, Notes, and Commentary," *Studies in Philology* 93 (1996): 117–63. The most substantial critical treatments of the Seymours' work to date are Hosington's and Patricia Demers, "The Seymour Sisters: Elegizing Female Attachment," *Sixteenth Century Journal* 30 (1999): 343–65, both of which offer translations of the *Hecatodistichon*.

of French intellectualism descending from Marguerite de Navarre, and reaches out to the French court by portraying its authors as English "princesses," implying a regal sisterhood as well as an intellectual sisterhood between the courts of England and France. In this way, I suggest, this later text seeks to re-locate its principal authors from the margins of the English court to its center by figuring a familial relationship with the court household of France.

The collection is important from several perspectives, primarily for its treatment of the court as a domestic sphere, and also as an artifact depicting courtly and domestic reciprocity. Yet the extension of these lines of exchange to academic culture in a context that crosses registers with devotional practice is especially intriguing in the volatile political and religious climate of England in the years following the death of Henry VIII. It is therefore important to give greater critical attention to the interrelation of its literary subject and its historical moment as mutually influencing factors. Indeed, the scholarly promise of *Le tombeau* inheres in the intersection of its rhetorical objectives, both literary and social, as a key example of what Margaret Ezell has described as "the intertwined nature of the private/public/social spheres" that marks discursive practice in early modern culture.[2] My primary focus in this essay, therefore, will be to elaborate upon the political context informing the text's evolution, examining a corresponding shift in the attribution of authorship and the volume's rhetorical and material design.

In 1547, Edward VI held the throne as a minor, and his poor health made the question of succession a concern. The controversy surrounding the legitimacy of Henry's daughters, Mary and Elizabeth, created the opportunity for frequent plays for the crown by highly-placed court families, such as the Seymours and several others. In 1550, Anne Seymour was married to John Dudley, Viscount Lisle. Lisle was the oldest son of the Earl of Warwick (future Duke of Northumberland), who had taken the political control of the Protectorship from Anne's father, Edward Seymour, Earl of Somerset, two years earlier. Warwick's attempt to place Lady Jane Grey and her husband Guildford, Warwick's third son, on the throne upon the death of Edward VI in 1553 is a much more famous exploit; yet John Dudley's marriage to Anne Seymour represents a similar manifestation of Warwick's political ambition. The sisters figure prominently in this network of relations, and the turning of this private encomium to a published declaration of a familial courtly coterie reflects the evolving political objectives within Anne's new household.

---

[2] Margaret J. M. Ezell, *Social Authorship and the Advent of Print* (Baltimore: Johns Hopkins Univ. Press, 1999), 39.

The original work, titled *Hecatodistichon*, can be viewed in company with other such projects, notably the teenaged Elizabeth's translation of Marguerite's *Le Miroir de l'âme pécheresse*.[3] Like Elizabeth's work, the Seymours' text is a scholarly exercise with an appropriate topic: it offers a collection of 104 elegiac couplets tracing the journey of Marguerite's soul through life and death, offering laudatory admiration of its subject in terms of piety, virtue, and chastity. Indeed, like Elizabeth's *Glass of the Sinful Soul*, which was made a gift to Catherine Parr, in whose household the young Elizabeth later resided, the Seymours' *Hecatodistichon* would have made an appropriate gift for a woman in a comparably powerful and hospitable role.[4] Instead, however, the project was sent to the Seymours' former tutor, Nicolas Denisot, an intellectual formerly connected with the French court. Why this choice? Denisot's time in England had been something of a political exile, and he had found a secure position in the powerful Protestant household of the Seymours.[5] Having returned to France under suspicion of spying, however, Denisot was seeking occasion to renew his status at court, and his preexisting friendships with prominent young intellectuals such as Ronsard provided this platform; the Seymours' manuscript provided opportunity. Yet if Denisot seems the first to exploit the manuscript's social potential, further motives are suggested in the text's subsequent incarnations.

In 1550, Denisot expands and prints the original work, adding twenty-two poems praising the sisters' learnedness and piety. Contributors include Pléiade up-and-comers such as Antoine de Baïf, and more-established figures such as Jean Dorat, though the sisters' work remains the focus of the volume. The title page reflects this design, preserving the *Hecatodistichon* title and featuring the sisters' names prominently: *Annae, Margaritae, Janae, sororum virginum hero-dium anglarum, in mortem Divae Margaritae Valesiae, Navarrorum Reginae, Hecatodistichon. Accessit Petri Mirarii ad easdem virgines, Epistola: una cum*

---

[3] I have found Marc Shell's collection of materials to be of particular value in understanding the textual and historical context of Elizabeth's work: *Elizabeth's Glass, with "The Glass of the Sinful Soul" (1544) by Elizabeth I and "Epistle Dedicatory" & "Conclusion" (1548) by John Bale* (Lincoln: Univ. of Nebraska Press, 1993).

[4] On gender and gift culture in Tudor England, see esp. Jane Donawerth, "Women's Poetry and the Tudor-Stuart System of Gift Exchange," in *Women, Writing, and the Reproduction of Culture in Tudor and Stuart Britain*, ed. Mary E. Burke, Jane Donawerth, Linda L. Love, and Karen Nelson (Syracuse: Syracuse Univ. Press, 2000), 3–18.

[5] See John N. King, "Patronage and Piety: The Influence of Catherine Parr," in *Silent But for the Word: Tudor Women as Patrons, Translators, and Writers of Religious Works*, ed. Margaret P. Hannay (Kent, OH: Kent State Univ. Press, 1985), 43–60; also idem, *English Reformation Literature: The Tudor Origins of the Protestant Tradition* (Princeton: Princeton Univ. Press, 1982).

doctorum aliquot virorum Carminibus. Parisiis, ex officina Reginaldi Calderii &
Claudii eius filii. Anno salutis 1550 [One hundred distichs on the death of Marguerite de Valois, Queen of Navarre, by the three distinguished young English
sisters, Anne, Margaret, and Jane. To which is added an Epistle to the young girls
by Pierre des Mireurs, together with several poems of learned men. Paris: 1550].[6]
The still-small collection, which also included poems by Denisot's cousin and by
his wife, traded on the Seymours' learnedness as its primary subject, a positive
reflection on Denisot's role in their accomplishment.

The second printed volume of the following year, however, expands the collection further, including over fifty additional poems, several in modern languages, including French and Italian; most of these engage in dialogue with one
another as much as with the Seymours' work. More celebrity intellectuals grace
its pages, including Ronsard, whose endorsement appears as much to commend
the volume itself as a monument to international intellectualism as to admire
the work of its young contributors. The 1551 text thus takes the shape of a true
miscellany on the topos of Marguerite's life, though many of the poems retain
praise of the sisters and the virtues evident in their work. The rhetoric of praise
offered throughout the new volume is set in the context of neo-platonic humanism, recalling the link between Marguerite and the development of early modern
intellectual culture in the academies of Italy and France, and the contributors to
the volume, as well as their contributions, articulate this connection. The elite
community framed in this public "private" coterie would have served Denisot's
ambitions well. As Anne Lake Prescott has observed, "This was the right crowd"
in 1551.[7] Yet while Denisot's motives are clearly traceable in these terms, the decision to alter—and publish—the revised collections, especially the 1551 volume,
is not likely to have been his alone. Thus the question, "What had the Seymours
to gain through such 'publicity'?" takes on crucial importance.

Certainly, exposure of this kind would be effective promotion for marriage-
able daughters of prominent social standing and intellectual accomplishment—

---

[6] The translation is that of Hosington in her introduction to the facsimile edition of the
1550 *Hecatodistichon* in *The Early Modern Englishwoman,* Series I: *Printed Writings, 1500–
1640: Part 2,* vol. 6, ed. Betty S. Travitsky and Patrick Cullen (Aldershot: Ashgate, 2000), x.
The *Hecatodistichon* facsimile is reproduced from the British Museum edition, from which the
passages I quote are taken; a copy held by the Bibliothèque nationale de France can be viewed
online: http://gallica.bnf.fr/ark:/12148/bpt6k71120j. The edition of *Le Tombeau* in the same
facsimile volume, from which I also quote, is likewise held by the British Museum, and I have
examined an identical copy in the Folger Shakespeare Library (DC 112.M2.U7 Cage).

[7] Anne Lake Prescott, "The Pearl of Valois and Elizabeth I: Marguerite de Navarre's
Miroir and Tudor England," in *Silent But for the Word,* 61–76, 75.

accomplishment cast in the context, as was customary, of virtue and chastity.[8] Yet the ambitions of Anne Seymour's new family in particular seem most salient, and the changes in the authorship attribution of the 1551 publication and in its dedication seem specifically directed to serve Warwick's political motives. In the 1550 text, the Seymour sisters are described as "*sororum virginum, herodium Anglarum*," laudatory hyperbole, but essentially descriptive: they are three "distinguished young English sisters, Anne, Margaret, and Jane."[9] This version preserves the Latin of the manuscript, as well as the rhetorical design of the original composition in which the girls alternate in contributing distichs, each identified by its author. The French title of the 1551 volume, however, recognizes the Seymours collectively rather than by individual name as "*les trois Soeurs Princesses en Angleterre*": "three Sisters, English Princesses." Its new dedication also draws a parallel among its authors, its subject, and its dedicatee, Marguerite, Duchesse de Berry, the niece of Marguerite de Navarre, and sister to the sitting French king. The diction is appropriately deferential: "C'est à vous se dedie et consacre . . . pour une Princesse de France, Princesse tres illustre, perle & miroir de scavoir [ce qui a voir] religiõ & piete entre toutes les Dames de son Siecle" [It is to you this book dedicates and consecrates itself . . . for a Princess of France, Princess most illustrious, pearl and mirror of knowledge, of religion and piety, among all the noble Ladies of her Age]. The homage it pays, however, transcends the typical status gap between author and dedicatee, stressing the familial link among *all* of the courtly sisters that take part in this exchange. It begins quite naturally by drawing an analogy between Marguerite de Berry, "Soeur unique du Roy," and Marguerite de Navarre, playing upon the recognition that the current Duchesse's title is one formerly held by the queen, extending the parallel in their names through the "pearl" reference, a well-known pun on "Marguerite." Ultimately, though, the dedication circumscribes the English sisters within the poetic sphere it defines. As nieces to Jane Seymour, the deceased English queen of the same generation as Marguerite de Navarre, the text claims a parallel lineage for the Seymour girls.[10] The volume's English authors are "princesses" who share in this

---

[8] See esp. Prescott's discussion in "The Pearl of Valois," 73–76, of these themes in Marguerite's work and of the Seymours' poem in this context.

[9] I again quote Hosington's translation from the introduction to the *Early Modern Englishwoman* series facsimile, x. Demers translates this phrase as "Maiden Sisters and English Heroines"; see "Seymour Sisters," 357. Though Demers is, judiciously, more literal throughout her translation, "heroines" (or its literary allusion, "demi-goddesses") seems a slightly heavy-handed appellation. The introduction stresses the sisters' precocity in a poetic context, playing upon the relation between learned accomplishment and social distinction.

[10] The third wife of Henry VIII, Jane Seymour was mother of the current English king, Edward VI.

sisterhood comprised in equal measure of virtuous learning and royal familial relation. The dedication suggests that the embodiment of Marguerite's memory in the *"vers dignes"* and *"vers diuins"* of this *tombeau* ensures that all members of the sisterhood will be collectively immortalized in this gesture of pious remembrance. The dedicatory verses that follow invoke similar language and imagery, and all refer to the Seymours as "princesses." The dedication page, moreover, works iconographically to position Marguerite de Berry and the Seymour sisters on mutual homage-paying ground by casting them both as viewers of Marguerite de Navarre's image, setting a literal image of the queen on the facing page, book in hand, overlooking the dedicatory text. The shared participation in this *tombeau* thus fashions within itself a familial space shared among the "princesses of England" and the parallel generation of French royalty.

While the elision made in the volume's dedication between Marguerite$_1$ and Marguerite$_2$ was a compliment to the young duchesse, and a potentially ingratiating move by Denisot, acceptance of its "princess premise" did still more for the Seymours' reputation, or rather the *repute* of their lineage. The chief focus of this strategy was likely the newly-married Anne, a possible reason for the omission of the girls' names from the title page and dedication of the later volume, which would naturally have suggested a stronger parallel with the middle daughter, who shared the name Marguerite. It was Anne whose lineage mattered to the political shifts transpiring in England from 1550–1551. At that time, the Seymours and the Dudleys were among the families closest to the English throne. Both wielded considerable political power due to Edward VI's minority, the Protectorship resting with Anne's father, Edward Seymour, from the beginning of Edward's reign in 1547 until late 1549, when Seymour was ousted by Dudley in a political coup. Anne's 1550 marriage to Dudley's oldest son was likely seen as a step toward mending this rift, but the new Protector's ambitions appear in retrospect to pursue a lineal claim to the throne. A potential alliance with the royal household of France took shape in his new daughter and in her text.

The familial connection between the Seymours and the royal household of England extended many generations back from Anne's, and the Seymour line moreover traced its origins (and name) from an eighth-century French village, Touraine, St. Maur-sur-Loire.[11] [See Figures 1 and 2.] The precise timing and circumstances of the family's transition from France to England remain unclear, but a record of a William St. Maur owning lands in the Monmouthshire region corroborates their presence in England from 1240. The ancestry of Anne's grandmother,

---

[11] See A. Audrey Locke, *The Seymour Family, History and Romance* (London: Constable, 1911), 2. Locke notes that the pair of wings in William St. Maur's coat of arms still appear in the Seymour coat of arms in the twentieth century.

SEYMOUR FAMILY

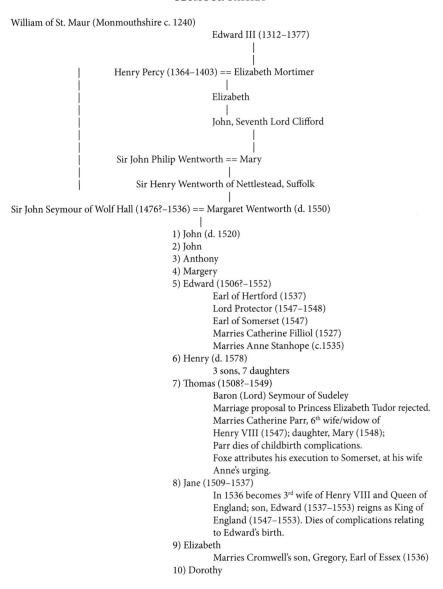

William of St. Maur (Monmouthshire c. 1240)

Edward III (1312–1377)

Henry Percy (1364–1403) == Elizabeth Mortimer

Elizabeth

John, Seventh Lord Clifford

Sir John Philip Wentworth == Mary

Sir Henry Wentworth of Nettlestead, Suffolk

Sir John Seymour of Wolf Hall (1476?–1536) == Margaret Wentworth (d. 1550)

1) John (d. 1520)
2) John
3) Anthony
4) Margery
5) Edward (1506?–1552)
     Earl of Hertford (1537)
     Lord Protector (1547–1548)
     Earl of Somerset (1547)
     Marries Catherine Filliol (1527)
     Marries Anne Stanhope (c.1535)
6) Henry (d. 1578)
     3 sons, 7 daughters
7) Thomas (1508?–1549)
     Baron (Lord) Seymour of Sudeley
     Marriage proposal to Princess Elizabeth Tudor rejected.
     Marries Catherine Parr, 6th wife/widow of
     Henry VIII (1547); daughter, Mary (1548);
     Parr dies of childbirth complications.
     Foxe attributes his execution to Somerset, at his wife
     Anne's urging.
8) Jane (1509–1537)
     In 1536 becomes 3rd wife of Henry VIII and Queen of
     England; son, Edward (1537–1553) reigns as King of
     England (1547–1553). Dies of complications relating
     to Edward's birth.
9) Elizabeth
     Marries Cromwell's son, Gregory, Earl of Essex (1536)
10) Dorothy

Figure 1. Genealogy of Seymour Family. Sources include: Locke, *The Seymour Family; Dictionary of National Biography*, ed. Sir Leslie Stephen and Sir Sidney Lee (Oxford: Oxford Univ. Press, 1921–22); *Oxford Dictionary of National Biography*, online library database, May 2007 update.

FAMILY OF EDWARD SEYMOUR, EARL OF SOMERSET

Edward Seymour, Protector Somerset (1506?–1552) ==

m. (1) (1527) Katherine Filliol   m. (2) (c.1535) Anne Stanhope (1510–1587)
                                                    Lady-in-Waiting to Katherine Howard,
                                                    privy chamber of Catherine Parr;
                                                    protested Parr's marriage to Thos. Seymour

    1) John (d. 1552)   1) Edward (1537–1539)
       imprisoned with his father in   2) Anne (1538–1587)
       Tower 1551, dies there 1552   Lady-in-waiting to Elizabeth I
    2) Edward (1529–1593)   Marries John Dudley, Viscount Lisle (1550)
       Knighted, Battle of Pinkie 1547   *Hecatodistichon* (1548) and (1550)
       Restored to blood 1553   *Le Tombeau de Marguerite de Valois* (1551)
       Contemporary descendants: Marries Sir Edward Unton (1555); children:
       Dukes of Somerset at   Anne, Cicely, Edward, Henry
       Berry Pomeroy   3) Edward (1539–1621)
                                                    Earl of Hertford
                                                    Secretly marries Katherine Grey (1560);
                                                    imprisoned by Elizabeth I; Katherine exiled;
                                                    sons: Edward (1561–1612), Thomas (1563–?)
                                                4) Margaret (1540–?)
                                                    Lady-in-waiting to Elizabeth I
                                                    Unmarried
                                                5) Henry (1540–?)
                                                    Admiral, Royal Navy
                                                6) Jane (1541–1561)
                                                    Lady-in-waiting to Elizabeth I
                                                    Unmarried
                                                    Assists brother's marriage to Katherine Grey
                                                7) Mary
                                                    Marriages: Andrew Rogers of Dorset
                                                                Sir Henry Peyton
                                                8) Catherine
                                                    Lady-in-waiting to Elizabeth I
                                                    Unmarried
                                                9) Edward (1548–1574)
                                                10) Elizabeth (1550–?)
                                                    Marries Sir Rich. Knightly, Northamptonshire

Figure 2. Family of Edward Seymour, Earl of Somerset. Sources include: Locke, *The Seymour Family*; *Dictionary of National Biography*; *Oxford Dictionary of National Biography*, online library database, May 2007 update.

however, is perhaps the more important in figuring Anne as a "princess" of England since the family of her father, Sir Henry Wentworth, traced its ancestry to
Edward III. Indeed, the connection seemed immediate enough for Elizabeth I to
perceive a threat in the marriage of Anne's brother Edward to Katherine Grey in
1560. That union threatened Elizabeth because a child from the marriage would
have had a strong claim to the throne, having royalty on both sides of its family: through the Seymours' descendance from Edward III and filial relation as
King Edward VI's cousin, combined with the Greys' more immediate descendance from Henry VIII's sister, Mary Tudor.[12] [See Figure 3.] Indeed, it is this
generation of Seymours and Dudleys, Anne's, Margaret's, and Jane's, contemporary with Elizabeth I, that is perhaps the most intriguing in terms of relations of
power gained and lost through familial connection. In particular, Anne's marriage to John Dudley brought with it a lineal claim to the political control of England that her father-in-law exercised as Protector, and likely coveted for his own
descendants.[13]

The union between the Seymours and Dudleys ended in 1554 with the death
of Anne's husband. He was not executed as his father and brother had been for
the treasonous plot to place Jane Grey, and thus the Dudley family, on the throne,
but was pardoned, only to die a few months later. In the following year, Anne remarried, to Sir Edward Unton. They had two daughters, Anne and Cicely, and
two sons, Edward and Henry, the latter of whom became a prominent courtier
and ambassador under Elizabeth. The portrait depicting Unton's life that now
hangs in the National Portrait Gallery in London contains a likeness of Anne,
wherein she is depicted as the mother holding the infant Henry. This portrait, of
cultural interest because of the many scenes in Unton's life it depicts, among them
an intricate wedding masque, appears in the *Riverside Shakespeare*, and is the
only historical image of any sort that remains of Anne; thus she is remembered

---

[12] In 1561, Elizabeth I had Edward and Katherine confined to the Tower after their secret
marriage, which had been facilitated by Jane, the youngest *Hecatodistichon* author.

[13] Ironically, the political ambition that included a rivalry with the Seymour family
would lead to Dudley's own demise. In arranging for the marriage of Lady Jane Grey to his
fourth son, Guildford, in 1553, Dudley—by then Duke of Northumberland—hoped to position the Dudleys as the royal family of England. This plan did not come to fruition, of course,
as Jane held the throne for only nine days before the governance of England passed to Mary
Tudor, and subsequently to Elizabeth. To further the irony in the subversion of Dudley's ambitions, it was under Elizabeth's reign that a royal marriage might have been possible for the
Dudley household since it was Dudley's sixth son, Robert, Earl of Leicester, who became the
favorite of the Queen. [See Figure 4.]

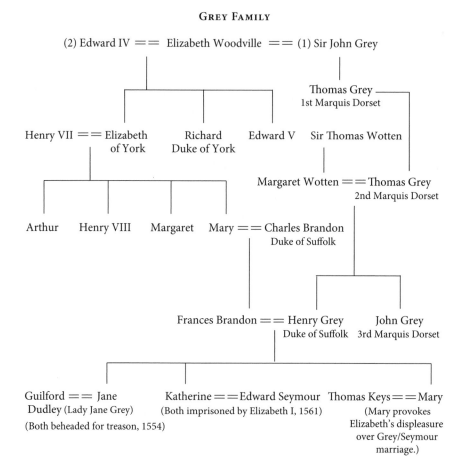

Figure 3. Genealogy of Grey family. Sources: *Dictionary of National Biography; Oxford Dictionary of National Biography,* online library database, May 2007 update.

DUDLEY FAMILY

Edmund Dudley (1462–1510)   ==   Elizabeth Grey (d. 1525)
   Privy counselor to Henry VII | Daughter of Edward Grey,
   ┌─────────────────────────────   Viscount of Lisle

John Dudley (1504–1553)   ==   Jane Guildford (c.1509–1534)
   Viscount of Lisle (1542) | Daughter of Sir Edward
   Earl of Warwick (1547)   Guildford
   Duke of Northumberland (1551)
   Lord Protector (1549–1553)
     Imprisoned in Tower for plotting
     to place his son on throne through
     marriage to Jane Grey
     Beheaded 1553

1)   John (1527?–1554)
        Viscount of Lisle (1547)
        Earl of Warwick (1551)
        Marries Anne Seymour (1550)
        Imprisoned in Tower 1553 for
        complicity in his father's plot re:
        marriage of Jane Grey to Guildford;
        pardoned 1554; died ten days later

2)   Ambrose (1528?–1590)
        Viscount of Lisle (1561)
        Earl of Warwick (1561)
        Imprisoned in tower 1553 for
        complicity in his father's plot Re:
        marriage of Jane Grey to Guildford;
        pardoned 1555

3)   Henry (1531?–1557)
        Killed in Battle of St. Quentin

4)   Mary (1531–1586)
        Marries Sir Henry Sidney;
        son, Sir Philip Sidney

5)   Guildford (1532?–1554)
        1553 married Lady Jane Grey under
        father's direction to facilitate Dudley
        succession to throne of England;
        imprisoned in Tower 1553;
        beheaded, with Jane Grey, for treason, 1554

6)   Robert (1533?–1588)
        Earl of Leicester (1564)
        Favorite of Elizabeth I

7)   Katherine (1535–1620)
        Marries Sir Henry Hastings, 3rd Earl of Hastings, whose
        father, Francis Hastings, had been imprisoned with
        Northumberland for the Lady Jane Grey plot

Figure 4. Genealogy of Dudley family. Sources: *Dictionary of National Biography*; *Oxford Dictionary of National Biography,* online library database, May 2007 update; Margaret Hannay, *Philip's Phoenix: Mary Sidney, Countess of Pembroke* (Oxford: Oxford Univ. Press, 1990).

in history through her role as mother to a prominent court figure.[14] In 1550, however, Anne's marriage to John Dudley represented a union of two powerful English families, at a crucial juncture in the transition of national leadership. The interest of Anne's new father-in-law in seeing her publicly figured as a member of a court household and royal family is consistent with his other plays for public power, and ultimately control of the English throne. The timing of *Le tombeau*'s publication coincides with this significant moment in the history of these families, whose unification is embodied in Anne's marriage. The attempt to assert the royalty of this family, to corroborate and enhance its prestige, is sought by forging a connection with the royal household of France through the image of regal sisterhood publicly figured in this text.

Perhaps the most striking element of its textual history is that none of the volumes are presented as a gift to a member of an older generation, as in the example of Elizabeth's *Miroir* translation. The *Hecatodistichon* manuscript is made a gift to Denisot, but this homage seems, in retrospect, a weak pretense for the volume's transmission. The dedication of the 1551 volume is a more overtly politic gesture, yet the homage *it* frames is idiosyncratic, as well. Marguerite de Berry and the Seymour sisters are contemporaries, and the dedication highlights this fact. Indeed, the dedication does not "gift" the collection to Marguerite as much as it includes her in its circle. The re-framing of the volume's structure as an occasional miscellany re-defines the boundaries of textual kinship within the collection, an act that alters the gift context further, revealing a fundamental link between the literary and the political communities it fashions within its pages. The volume as a whole represents the inclusion of equals; the voices of its new contributors, the blend of modern and classical languages it incorporates, and the spirit of inclusiveness shared among its participants make *Le tombeau* a Pléiade text. This new framework, however, does not so much suggest that the girls have joined the boys' club, but rather that this intellectual community centered around Marguerite de Navarre asserts parallel lines of royal and intellectual

---

[14] The inscription within the Unton portrait recalls the Seymour familial proximity to the throne: "This worthy and famous gentleman, Sir Henry Unton, was son unto Sir Edward Unton, Knight . . . and also his mother, the most virtuous Lady Anne Seymour, countess of Warwick, eldest daughter to the Lord Edward Seymour, duke of Somerset, uncle to King Edward and so protector of his person, and the realm. Her uncles were Thomas and Henry Seymour, which Thomas was Lord Admiral of England and married unto Catherine Parr, last wife of King Henry VIII. Her mother was duchess of Somerset; her aunt the Lady Jane Seymour, queen of England." The Unton portrait is part of the National Portrait Gallery collection (NPG 710, *Sir Henry Unton*, c. 1596); the detailed interactive image that documents the inscription text can be accessed online at: http://www.mape.org.uk/activities/unton/index.htm.

heritage cultivated in Marguerite's courtly household, a sphere that unites past and present, court and academy.

Thus, in its transition from private manuscript to published miscellany, *Le tombeau de Marguerite* inscribes a familial association within the textual boundaries it draws, literalizing textual kinship in a family circle that unites the court and royal households of England and France. As Hosington rightly notes, "this is a volume with an unusually strong feminine presence,"[15] reason enough, perhaps, to recommend continued attention to the Seymours' contribution to this work. Yet still further promise lies in taking deeper critical account of the volume's literary complexity in the context of its social complexity, reconciling the multiplicity of rhetorical objectives, textual and cultural, that emerge among its various incarnations. These features recommend not only its inclusion in the canon of important contributions by early modern women writers, but also the broadening of critical attention to both its artistic design and to the moment of cultural exchange its evolution represents.

PENNSYLVANIA STATE UNIVERSITY

---

[15] Hosington, "Encomium," 126.

Petrarchan Love and Huguenot Resignation in an Album Owned by Louise de Coligny (1555-1620)

JANE COUCHMAN

MANUSCRIPT 129 A 23 IN THE KONINKLIJKE BIBLIOTEEK OF THE Netherlands is described as: "French love poems collected by F. A. D. M. (= François Auzière de Montpellier) for Louise de Coligny . . . , last wife of William I of Orange-Nassau, at the time of her first marriage to Charles de Téligny. . . . With later additions."[1] Apart from an article by A.-G. van Hamel, published in 1903,[2] this manuscript has not been studied. It is an album containing love poetry, followed by lamentations on the Saint Bartholomew's Day Massacre, and a long poem recommending "Patience," creating a wonderful juxtaposition of Petrarchan eroticism and Huguenot resignation. The album is interesting because it offers a glimpse of the evolving taste and concerns of a woman who has been called "the great lady of the Reform." Daughter of the Huguenot leader Gaspard de Coligny, Louise de Coligny later became the fourth wife of William of Orange, Stadhouder of the Netherlands. She was connected to many of the most influential families in France and in the Netherlands as well as in

---

This paper was first delivered at the annual meeting of the Renaissance Society of America (2007), Miami, FL, at a panel entitled "Early Modern Women's Manuscripts I," Margaret Hannay, Siena College, presiding.

[1] "Franse minnedichten verzameld door F.A.D.M. [François Auzière de Montpellier] voor Louise de Coligny (1553–1620), latere echtgenote van Willem I van Oranje-Nassau, ter gelegenheid van haar eerste huwelijk met Charles de Téligy (–1572) in 1572 [sic: actually May 1571]. Met latere toevoegingen." See Appendix.

[2] A.-G. Van Hamel, "L'album de Louise de Coligny," *Revue d'histoire littéraire de la France* 10 (1903): 1–24.

England, among whom were her close friend and cousin Henri IV of France, her stepson Maurice of Nassau, the Earl of Leicester, and Sir Philip Sidney, the latter especially in the 1580s when they were in the Netherlands offering Elizabeth's support to the Protestant Netherlands in their struggle against the Spanish. From the time of her marriage to William in 1583 until her death in 1620, she played an important role as diplomat and negotiator in the relations among France, the Netherlands, and England. This manuscript album was begun at the time of her marriage to Charles de Téligny in 1571, continued after the deaths of her father Gaspard de Coligny and her husband in the Saint Bartholomew's Day Massacre in 1572, and taken up again after the assassination of her second husband, William of Orange, in 1584.

In addition to its connection with Louise de Coligny, the album is interesting because the choices of those who compiled it reflect shifts in taste for secular and religious poetry during the period from the early 1570s to the early 1600s. Of particular interest is the presence of poetry, including paraphrases of psalms, by both Catholic and Protestant poets, perhaps surprising in an album belonging to a convinced Huguenot, although, as we shall see, this mix was not as unusual in Henri IV's France as it might have been in England or in other parts of Europe.

The manuscript

The manuscript comprises 90 folios on rag paper, in an eighteenth-century binding.[3] Several distinct sections can be identified and dated, but only approximately (see Appendix I). The sections are marked by changes in handwriting, by pages left blank, and by changes in theme and style. An initial examination of the manuscript suggests that it was indeed a bound presentation album, with pages left blank for additions after the initial compilation.[4] But I have not yet studied the watermarks nor attempted to date the paper.

Louise de Coligny's relationship with the manuscript

The manuscript is dedicated to Louise de Coligny, as the "most illustrious and most virtuous lady, Madame de Telligny,"[5] apparently at the time of her first

---

[3] The pages have been slightly trimmed for the binding so that a few ends of phrases have been cut or obscured.

[4] Jacques Lavaud, *Philippe Desportes (1546–1606)* (Paris: Droz, 1936) writes, "L'album de Louise de Coligny . . . parait avoir été primitivement composé à l'occasion de son mariage avec Théligny; elle se servit, plus tard, des feuillets blancs à la fin du volume comme d'un album" (27).

[5] "A tresillustre et tresvertueuse dame, Madame de Telligny . . .", fol. 1v. The introductory sonnet is addressed to masculine plural readers/*lecteurs*; however, the writer refers to his reader

marriage. It was in her collection in the Hague at the time of her death. She seems to have carried it with her throughout her life, or at least retrieved it when she made significant moves. There are a few annotations, giving authors' names and in one case a title, in a hand that resembles Louise's writing in the holograph letters which I have examined, although I cannot identify the hand with certainty.[6] In a poem "On a Motto: Fire without Smoke,"[7] the verses are separated by Louise's monogramme.[8] Many of the poems could have been addressed to any "lady," but some contain references to Louise and her family. Authors can be identified for a few of the poems, but the authors and the dates of composition of most of the pieces are unknown. Louise does not seem to have composed or copied any of the poems herself. Did she choose any of them, perhaps from printed collections, or did any of the poets write in the album at her request?

Three major events in Louise de Coligny's life are marked in the manuscript: her marriage in May 1571 to Charles de Téligny; the Saint Bartholomew's Day Massacre in August 1572 when her father and her husband were killed; and the assassination of her second husband, William of Orange, in July 1584.

Celebrating a wedding: the first two sections of the manuscript

Born in 1555 to Gaspard de Coligny and his wife Charlotte de Laval, Louise grew up through the early years of the French Wars of Religion, moving from her family home at Châtillon-sur-Loing to Paris (when her father was in favour with the Queen Regent Catherine de Médicis), to Orléans (under siege during the First French Religious War in 1562–3) and to La Rochelle in August 1568 (where many Huguenot families, including Jeanne d'Albret and her son, the future Henri IV, took refuge). This is where Louise was married for the first time, and where the first two sections of the album appear to have been made, as a gift to the young bride.

The first section is made up of thirty-three folios containing a "tragic discourse," "terza rima," songs, "Stances," some twenty-four sonnets "On deaths,

---

more personally, as "you, who love the loving lesson, leaving the frown of the severe Cato" ("En quictant le sourcil du seuere Caton"). Since "the severe Cato" was one of the names admiringly attached to Louise's father (van Hamel, "L'album." 4), the phrase "leaving the frown of the severe Cato" could well refer to Louise's upcoming or recent marriage. Except where otherwise noted, translations are mine.

    [6] Van Hamel, " L'album," 1, is convinced that it is Louise de Coligny's handwriting.

    [7] "Sur une Devise Feu sans Fumée" (fols. 71r–73r)

    [8] Two interlaced lowercase Greek letters "lambda" framed by two fermesses, the Huguenot signs resembling "$".

pains, tears,"[9] and a "Complaint written at the hot springs of the Pyrenées." The poems have been transcribed with care and sometimes with ornamented initial letters, garlands, or appropriate images (e.g. "Sonnet contre le laurier" (fol. 27v), with a garland of laurel branches). Little is known about the copyist, François Auzière de Montpellier.[10] He had originally signed his name, but then glued a slip of paper over it and substituted his initials, F. A. D. M. We know this because, when studying the manuscript for his 1903 article, A.-G. Van Hamel reports: "I succeeded in ungluing the piece of paper which covered the signature. The signature had been carefully scratched out, and by dampening the scratch-marks with sulphuric acid, I was able to bring back the name Françoys Auzière de Montpellier, indistinct but clear enough to be read."[11] I can attest to the fact that the name can now be read, and also that, miraculously, the sulphuric acid has done no further damage to the manuscript.

François Auzière has initialed the introductory sonnet "To the readers," and he takes credit for a "line by line reply" to a poem "against women."[12] The sonnet "Reply of another poet In favour of the Laurel" bears his sign, a V overlapping with an inverted V.[13] In the introductory sonnet, "To the Readers, on the subject of this Book," the writer explains that he had originally believed that "all these fine speeches of unhappy lovers were nothing but fables," but that "Reading of the constant loves of this author," he had changed his mind. He urges his reader: "Read these fine writings . . . and you will see beneath the hope for life and for sweetness, that bitterness and death are found within love"—(a pun in French:

---

[9] "Des morts, des peines et des larmes," fols. 21r et seq.

[10] In Eugène et Émile Haag, *La France Protestante* (Paris: Sandoz & Fischbacker, 1877), T. I, col. 594, a short note describes him as follows: ". . . a merchant in Montpellier, he was one of the influential members of the Huguenot party in that city. He attended the Assemblé politique in Nîmes on December 1, 1569, and the Synod of Sauve in 1570, as well as the Synods of 1584 and 1594." In an account of the life of the Montpellier doctor, professor, and university chancellor Laurent Joubert, we read that "One of his daughters, Anne, married the doctor François Auzières." Whether there are one or two Françoys Auzières, he/they appear to have been active at a time and in a context which would have made it possible for him to have been at La Rochelle, and to have prepared this album for Louise de Coligny around the time of her marriage in 1571.

[11] Van Hamel, "L'album," 2: ". . . j'ai réussi, en décollant un morceau de papier qui couvrait une signature soigneusement grattée et en humectant le grattage d'une goutte d'acide sulphydrique, à faire revenir, vaguement mais assez distinctement pour être déchifré, le nom de Françoys Auzière de Montpellier." Van Hamel has thoughtfully re-attached the slip of paper bearing the initials next to the place where it was initially.

[12] "Response aux stances qui ont precedé: vers pour vers, faicte par Celuy qui a transcrit cest oeuvre" (fols. 19v–20v).

[13] "Response d'un autre autheur Pour le Laurier."

Que l'amer, et la mort dedans l'amour se treuve [*sic*]").[14] This poem is an *apologia* for the reading of love poetry, in a Huguenot setting which might be expected to be suspicious of such frivolity. It should be added, however, that Protestants from the French nobility were not as strict about such matters as was Calvin, and found ways to reconcile their customs as nobles with their Protestant faith.[15] We do not know the identity of the "author" whose "fine writings" François Auzière found worthy of being copied out for Louise de Coligny.

The love poems in this section do not refer to Louise nor to events in her life. They are marked by the violent and graphic imagery associated with baroque poetry in general, and with Agrippa d'Aubigné's early love sonnets. They express what Gisèle Mathieu-Castellani and Jacques Pineaux call "'black' neopetrarchism, which is its nocturnal version, a tragic exploration of a world experienced as in conflict with transcendence."[16] I wonder whether a young bride would have appreciated a poem which begins: "A miserable love, nourishing in his veins / The furnace of love, forger of his pains / Burning in the inferno of a hostile beauty / whose gentle ways mask her cruelty"?[17] Or: "Everything evil, stormy, tempestuous possessed / By the stars and the heavens was vomited upon my head / They used up their venom at my nativity"[18]? The sonnet in which François Auzière defends the Laurel is one of the few which deals with happy and faithful love: "I am not pleased with Spring nor its green hue, / But I love the unchanging hope of the Laurel /...Whose colour, use, and nature / Assure my hope of serving loyally."[19]

---

[14] "Aux Lecteurs, sur le subiect de ce liuvre"; "J'ay pensé maintesfois que tous ces beaux discours / Des malheureux amantz n'estoyent rien qu'une fable"; "Lisant de cest autheur les constantes amours"; "Lisez ces beaux escrits / . . . Vous verrez, soubs l'espoir de vie et de douceur, / Que l'amer, et la mort dedans l'amour se treuue" (fol. 2r).

[15] For example, the famous disagreement between the local clergy and Charlotte Du Plessis Mornay about whether she should be allowed to curl her hair and enhance it with false curls.

[16] ". . . le néo-pétrarquisme 'noir' qui en est la version nocturne, exploration tragique d'un rapport au monde vécu dans le conflit avec une transcendance. . . .": Gisèle Mathieu-Castellani et Jacques Pineaux, "La poésie," in Robert Aulotte, ed., *Précis de la Littérature française du XVIe siècle* (Paris: PUF, 1991), 211.

[17] "Un malheureux amant nourissant dedans ses veines / La fournaise d'amour forgeron de ses peines / Bruslant dans le brasier d'une ingrate beauté / Dont la douce façon couvroit la cruauté" (fol. 3r).

[18] ". . . Tout ce qu'avoient de mal d'orage et de tempeste / Les astres et les cieux fut vomy sur ma teste / finissant leur venin à ma nativité" (16v).

[19] "Je ne suis du printemps, ny de son verd content, / mais i'ayme du Laurier l'immuable esperance / . . . De qui et la couleur, l'usage, & la nature / Asseurent mon espoir de servir loyaulment" (fol. 29r).

A second section, from folio 34r to folio 54v, appears to date from about the same time. It too is made up of love poetry, but transcribed in several different hands. Perhaps the album was passed around at the time of the Coligny-Téligny wedding so that others could add their contributions? One "Sonnet" (35v), with "du Tasse" in the margin, is covered with blots and words scratched out, including a large blot just under the title, possibly covering the name of the author. In this section, the tone is happier: "To live and not to love is not to love to live."[20] A sonnet in this section, beginning "If the outrageous law of an unjust marriage / Takes from me your less perfect and less beautiful part" has been identified by Jacques Lavaud as being by the well-known court poet Philippe Desportes.[21] The poem reframes the topos that while the husband may possess the wife's body, the poet possesses her more perfect, more beautiful soul. This section is less "baroque" and more "mannerist" in its aesthetic. Robert Aulotte links Desportes with two other contributors to the album, Jacques Davy Du Perron and Jean Bertaut, as "the best representatives of literary mannerism."[22] Mathieu-Castellani and Pineau identify these same three poets with what they call "'white' petrarchism," elegant "poetry in which petrarchism has descended into gallantry."[23]

Several of the poems in this section refer directly to Louise. In the "Dialogue" of Volusian and Calliope (fols. 36r ff), Volusian exclaims: "What say you! Of Coligny she took her name, / Tiger of so many Mars, support of holy Parnassus." Calliope reports that at her birth, Minerva "Made a rich gift to her of all she possessed."[24] Other poems praise her beauty and virtue, and mourn her departure: "When your eye and your face / Are far from here / The court can say / Where is my luster and my grace / Where is the flower of princesses / Virtue, decency, / honour and chastity / And the riches of the springtime?"[25] At the beginning of another of the love poems, the hand that may well belong to Louise has

---

[20] "Car vivre et n'aymer pas, cest n'aymer pas a vivre" (fol. 34r).

[21] "Si l'outrageuse loy d'un injuste hyméné / De vous moste la part moins parfaitte et moins belle. . ." (fol. 46r). Cf. Lavaud, *Philippe Desportes*, 267. It is the final sonnet in Desportes' *Cléonice* and is an imitation of Bernardo Tasso, not Torquato. Lavaud speculates about how this poem made its way into Louise de Coligny's album, and whether other poems in *Cléonice* may have been written for her.

[22] Aulotte, *Précis de la Littérature française du XVIe siècle*, 202.

[23] Mathieu-Castellani and Pineau, "La poésie," 210–11: ". . . le néo-pétrarquisme 'blanc' des épigones de Desportes (Bertaut, Du Perron, . . .), . . . où le pétrarquisme se dégrade en galanterie. . . ."

[24] "Comment! De colligny son nom elle a donc pris / Tigre de tant de mars / L'appuy du saint parnasse," "De tout ce quelle avoit luy fit un riche don" (fol. 38r).

[25] "Quand vostre oeuil et vostre face / Seront esloignez dicy / La court pourra dire ainsy / Ou est mon lustre et ma grace / Ou est la fleur des princesses / La vertu lhonnesteté / Lhonneur et la chasteté / Et du printems les richesse. . ." (fol. 39r).

written the name, "Mayson fleur" (fol. 40r), identifying the author as the Huguenot poet best known for his *Cantiques spirituelles*.[26] The first letters of the lines
of another sonnet, "Love which has always known my will,"[27] spell out the words
"Louise de Collini." A sonnet near the end of this section confuses the chronology of the manuscript, by referring to Louise's father and to her husband in the
past tense, as if it were written after the Saint Bartholomew's Day Massacre. The
poem reads: "Daughter of an Admiral, of that great leader of the army / Who,
wise and courageous, was unsurpassed, / Wife of a Téligny, who, noble warrior /
Encircled the entire world with his renown."[28] The poem takes a more Calvinist
turn, concluding: "It is indeed within the power of heaven and of fate, / Not to obscure what is divine in you, / ... but to cut through your most happy plans, / For
the most worthy do not always have the favour of the heavens, / Taking eternity
as the goal for their victory."[29] Poems in this section celebrate love as an honorable passion, sent from God, and praise the perfections of a beloved lady, with
none of the torments expressed in the first set of poems.

After the Saint Bartholomew's Day Massacre

Louise and her family travelled to Paris in the spring of 1572 to prepare for the
wedding of Henri of Navarre to Marguerite of Valois, daughter of Catherine
de Médicis, a marriage that was understood as, and perhaps intended to bring
about, a reconciliation between the Protestant and Catholic factions in France.
Instead, shortly after the wedding, Louise's father was the principal target for
assassination, in what became the Saint Bartholomew's Day Massacre of August
1572. Louise's husband was also killed. She fled to Berne and then to Basel. In
1576, the Edict of Beaulieu offered limited tolerance for Huguenots, so that
Louise could return to France, where she lived on her late husband's isolated
property of Lierville.[30]

---

[26] "Le soleil qui fait son séjour / Dedans les hauts cieux n'a que faire / De se montrer sans
quil esclaire / vos yeux esclairent un beau jour" (fol. 40r).

[27] "L'Amour qui a cognneu tousjours ma volonté" (fol. 50v).

[28] "Fille d'un Amyral, de ce grand chef d'armee / Qui saige et courageux neut jamais son
premier / Femme dun Telligny qui genereux guerrier / Borna du monde entier lheur de sa re-
nommee" (fol. 53v). Cf. Van Hamel, "L'album," 14.

[29] "Il est bien au pouvoir du ciel et du destin / non d'obscurcir en vous ce qu'on voit de
divin / ... / Mais bien de traverser vos desseins plus heureux / Car touiours les meilleurs nont
la faveur des cieux / Prenans l'eternité pour but de leur victoire" (fol. 53v).

[30] There is something of a transition between the love poetry and the laments on the
Saint Bartholomew's Day Massacre, created by a "Pastorale" on the death of a relative of Lou-
ise, a certain "Odet." Van Hamel identifies the subject as Odet d'Andelot, younger brother of
Louise, who died suddenly in Nîmes in 1580 (Van Hamel, "L'album," 14). It is unlikely that the

The poems commemorating the Saint Bartholomew's Day Massacre must obviously have been added to the album after August 1572, most probably after Louise's return to France.[31] The Massacre, a turning point in French history, also marked a shift in literary taste. Before the Massacre, as Ulrich Langer has explained, poetry such as that of the Pléiade and Desportes was enjoyed "as an aesthetic *game*, . . ." which "combined and rearranged motifs and rhetorical devices culled from classical and Italian literature . . . little concerned with the relationship between its language and immediate reality." After the Massacre, "literature [was] directly determined by experience," and play and disengagement were no longer possible.[32]

This section begins with a poem on Coligny's death: "On the death of Monsieur the Admiral."[33] There are two paraphrases of psalms, both by Catholic writers, both suitable to the theme of this section. The hand which may be Louise de Coligny's has identified one of them as "Psalme 20 de Monsr du perron"(fol. 63r). It begins "May the King of Kings, in the day when the tempest with a thousand waves threatens your head, show care for your needs."[34] The author of a paraphrase of Psalm 148 (fol. 64r) is identified in the same hand as "Monsr bertaut." This section closes with the "Canticle made by Monsr de Maisonfleur after the Massacre in Paris," written by the Huguenot poet Étienne de Maisonfleur immediately after the event, and one of the most dramatic evocations of the Massacre.[35] "Of new cruelty / Your faithful Jerusalem / Is prey and booty . . . Pour, O

---

subject was Louise's uncle Odet de Coligny, patron of Ronsard. It could not be said that fate "had taken his life as soon as it was given" ("A reprise ta vie aussi tost que donnee," fol. 55v), since Louise's uncle lived well into maturity, although he had died in March 1571, two months before her marriage.

[31] A sonnet included in this section on the death of "This brave Chastilon" (fol. 62r) might offer a clue to the date when these poems were added to the album. It may refer to François de Chastillon, Louise's brother, who died in October 1591, or to his son Henri de Chastillon, who died in 1601 at the seige of Ostende (Van Hamel, "L'album," 17). The poem could have been copied in later; however, it comes on the same page as the first sonnet on the death of Gaspard de Coligny and appears to be in the same hand.

[32] Ullrich Langer, "In the St. Bartholomew's Day Massacre, Thousands of Protestants are Killed in Paris and Throughout France: Poetry and Action," in Denis Hollier, *A New History of French Literature* (Cambridge, MA and London: Harvard Univ. Press, 1989), 231–36, here 231–33, 235.

[33] "Sur la mort de Monsieur l'Admiral" (fols. 62r –78r).

[34] "Puisse le Roy des Roys au jour de la tempeste / De mille flots armés menassera ta teste / De tes veux auoir soin." This psalm (19 in the Catholic tradition) can be found in Du Perron's *Oeuvres* (1622, p. 15); cf. Van Hamel, "L'album," 20. It had already appeared in *Les Muses raliées* in 1599 and in an anthology compiled by Benfons (1598) with the initials C. D. P.

[35] "Cantique faict par Monsr de Maison fleur Apres le Massacre de Paris" (fols. 76r–78r).

God, to destroy them, / The phials of your ire . . . To avenge on them your glory / Give them blood to drink." [36] We should not be surprised to find both Catholic and Protestant poets represented in an album belonging to a convinced Huguenot, for this eclecticism marked the court of Henri IV, and Terence Cave has demonstrated that the collections of religious poetry of the day, among them the very popular *Cantiques* of Maisonfleur himself, include works by both Protestant and Catholic writers.[37]

It is more surprising to find love poetry in this section, including a sonnet "Imitation de Pétrarque," interspersed among the religious poetry. The poem called "Setances" (fol. 66r), also by Bertaut, praises virtuous love which brings out the best qualities in the lover, and a "Chanson" (fol. 67r) by the same author concludes "Those who cease to love, cease also to live / Or live without pleasure, thinking to live without pain."[38] Another sonnet takes Louise de Coligny herself as its muse. It begins "Race of Dukes of Gaul, Princess whose fame will be the holy enamel which will gild my verses."[39] The mixture of love poetry with Maisonfleur's heartfelt anguish on St. Bartholomew's Day and the meditational psalms of Du Perron and Bertaut suggests that perhaps the works in this section of the manuscript were added at different times; or perhaps by the time they were transcribed, the initial horror aroused by the massacre had passed, and normal life had to some extent been resumed.

---

[36] "D'une cruauté nouvelle / Ta Jerusalem nouvelle / est la proye et le butin . . . Verse o Dieu pour les destruire / Les phioles de ton ire . . . Pour venger sur eux ta gloire / donne leur du sang a boire. . ." (fols. 76v–77r). Marguerite Soulié, in *L'Inspiration biblique dans la poésie religieuse d'Agrippa d'Aubigné* (Paris: Klincksieck, 1977), 19, writes: "Le gémissement le plus émouvant, car le rhythme du vers rend le souffle court des victimes épuisées d'horreur et de tourment, et comme frappées de stupeur, s'exprime dans le Cantique sur le massacre de la Saint-Barthélémy par Etienne de Maisonfleur, gentilhomme huguenot, le 30e d'août 1572. . . . Le rhythme, constitué par ces courtes notations juxtaposées, parait inspiré par les lamentations de Jérémie. . . . C'est en effet le rythme de la qîna, complainte biblique au rhythme boiteux."

[37] Terence Cave, *Devotional Poetry in France, c.1570–1613* (Cambridge: Cambridge Univ. Press, 1969), 18–23, 286: "Anthologies of the new century often include the whole range of styles in religious poetry, which suggests that the reading public was far from intransigent in its literary preferences."

[38] "Ceux qui cessent d'aymer, cessent de vivre aussy / Ou vivent sans plaisir pensans vivre sans peine" (fol. 67v).

[39] "Race des ducs Gaulois, Princesse dont la gloire / Sera le saint Email qui dorera mes vers . . ." (73r). Van Hamel, "L'album," 23, attributes this poem to Michel Hurault de Belesbat, son of the Chancellor Michel de l'Hopital, who figures in at least one of Louise's letters: 26 April 1586, to Hotman, in Louise de Coligny, *Correspondance*, ed. Paul Marchegay et Léon Marlet (Genève: Slatkine, 1970; réimpression de l'édition de Paris, 1887), 31.

A second marriage, a second assassination

When the French king Henri III received a request for advice as to a marriage-partner from William of Orange, Stadhouder of the United Provinces of the Netherlands, whose third wife had just died, he suggested Louise de Coligny. The marriage took place in April 1583. Nothing in the album refers to this wedding. Less than two years later, in July 1584, William too was assassinated.[40] Louise must have brought the album with her when she came to the Netherlands to marry William, for its final pages (fols. 83r to 90v) are taken up with a poem dedicated to her after William's death: "La Pascience: A Madame Madame la princesse Dorange Comtesse de Nassau etc." The title most probably refers to the words Louise is recorded as crying out as her husband lay dying, and which became part of her legend: "My God, … grant me the gift of patience, and to suffer, according to Thy will, the death of my father and of my two husbands, all three assassinated before my eyes."[41] The poem has been attributed to Anne de Rohan, daughter of one of Louise de Coligny's dear friends Catherine de Parthenay, but the attribution has been questioned, especially because in the final "Envoi" the poet uses masculine forms of the past participles.[42] The poet, appropriately melancholy and half-dreaming, is visited by an allegorical figure wearing a white robe: "Daughter, I believe, of the great maker of the Skies / Solemn was her posture, and solemn her countenance / Her look was gentle and full of assurance / At once humble and full of majesty."[43] "Patience" introduces herself, and speaks in terms that would be familiar to any Calvinist. She explains how she helps mortals deal with the apparent vagaries of fortune and suffering. God is not limited by human understanding, and often appears to punish the just and forgive the unjust: "…who are you, O vermin, / To set yourself up as judge of

---

[40] Lisa Jardine, *The Awful End of William of Orange* (New York: Harper Collins, 2005).

[41] "Mon Dieu… accorde-moi le don de la patience et de souffrir, selon ta volonté, la mort de mon père et de mes deux maris, tous trois assassinés devant mes yeux": Lapise, *Histoire de la principauté d'Orange*, 546, cited by Jules Delaborde, *Louise de Coligny, Princesse d'Orange* (Genève: Slatkine Reprints, 1970; réimpression de l'édition de Paris), 1890, 133.

[42] In two articles, "'La Patience': Un poème inédit d'Anne de Rohan, publié d'après le manuscrit de la Bibliothèque royale de la Haye," *Bulletin du Protestantisme français* (15 janvier 1886): 3–19 and "Un poème inédit de Mademoiselle Anne de Rohan-Soubize," *Annuaire de la Société d'émulation de la Vendée* (1885): 1–16, Paul Marchegay and Jules Bonnet argue that the poet is Anne de Rohan. Van Hamel disagrees ("L'album," 1), but does not include this poem in his study of the Album.

[43] "Fille Comme je croi du grand ouvrier des Cieux / Grave estoit son mantien grave sa Contenance / Son regard estoit doux et tout plein dassurance / Il estoit humble ensemble & plein de majesté" (fol. 83r).

his divine greatness?"[44] "But the just person in his suffering arms himself with patience / He acknowledges his faults and suffers with constancy."[45] Suffering is given by God to the just not as punishment but to perfect them for salvation. After delivering her lengthy encomium, Patience excuses herself, for she must now visit "A princess, to whom I want to present / . . . this beautiful crown / Similar to the one that encircles my head."[46] Guessing that the princess is the widow of the great Prince of Orange and daughter of the great Coligny, the poet asks Patience to do him the honour of allowing him to present the crown to her himself. Patience agrees, and in the "envoi" the poet makes the presentation.

Thus ends the manuscript which began at such an auspicious time in Louise de Coligny's life, a time that also appeared to augur well for a reconciliation between Catholics and Protestants in France. As we've seen, the Album encompasses tormented, baroque neo-Petrarchan poetry, elegant, mannerist neo-Petrarchan poetry, poetry of action and revolt, and finally a call for patience in the face of God's inscrutability. A postscript: Louise lived for over thirty-five years after William's death, but none of her subsequent activities is reflected in the album.[47]

GLENDON COLLEGE

---

[44] Fol. 85v, ". . . qui es tu o vermine / qui testablis pour Juge a sa grandeur divine."

[45] Fol 86r, "Mais le juste en son mal s'arme de pascience / Il recongnoist sa faulte et soufre constamment."

[46] "Une princesse a qui je voudroi presenter / Au premier de Janvier cette belle couronne / Semblable a celle la qui mon Chef environne" (fol. 90r).

[47] She raised her son and four of the youngest of William's 12 children; made good marriages for her stepdaughters; supervised her son's education; served as liaison between her stepson Maurice of Nassau and Henri IV of France; negotiated with Leicester and Sidney for English support for the United Provinces; played a role in the acceptance of the Edict of Nantes; and facilitated negotiations between Henri IV and her son-in-law the Duke of Bouillon, whose capitulation crowned Henri's pacification of France. She died in November 1520 at the Chateau de Fontainebleau, the guest of the Queen mother, Marie de Médicis. See Delaborde, *Louise de Coligny*; Jane Couchman, "'. . . give birth quickly and then send us your good husband. . . .': Form, Persuasion and Informal Political Influence in the Letters of Louise de Coligny," in *Women's Letters across Europe 1400–1700 : Form and Persuasion*, ed. J. and A. Crabb (Burlington, VT, and Aldershot: Ashgate, 2005), 149–69; eadem, "Lettres de Louise de Coligny aux membres de sa famille aux Pays-bas et en France," dans *Lettres de femmes, XVIe–XVIIIe siècles*, éd. E. Goldsmith et C. Winn (Paris: Champion, 2005), 89–133; eadem., "La lecture et le lectorat dans la correspondance de Louise de Coligny," dans *Lectrices d'Ancien régime*, éd. Isabelle Brouard-Arends (Rennes: Presses universitaires, 2003), 399–408.

Appendix

*Manuscript 129 A 23, Koninklijk
Biblioteek, The Hague, Netherlands*   *My translation:*

Franse minnedichten verzameld door F.A.D.M. [François Auzière de Montpellier] voor Louise de Coligny (1553–1620), latere echtgenote van Willem I van Oranje-Nassau, ter gelegenheid van haar eerste huwelijk met Charles de Téligy (–1572) in 1572 [*sic*: actually May 1571]. Met latere toevoegingen.
Band uit de Derde stadhouderlijke binderij, ca. 1760–ca. 1766.

Voormbezit:
1) Louise de Coligny (1572); prinsen van Oranje-Nassau; stadhouderlijke bibliotheek in Den Haag (cat. 1686, f. 222r nr. 747)
2) Oranje-Nassau, prinsen van
3) auctie P. van Cleef en D. Monnier te Den Haag, 1 dec. e.v. 1749, cat Frederik Hendrik, p. 217 nr. 60)
4) Gekocht door J. Royer voor stadhouder Willem IV
5) stadhouder Willem V
6) in 1798 verworven, stadhouderlijke bibliotheek (cat. 1795, fo. 105, nr. 98).

French love poems collected by F.A.D.M. (= François Auzière de Montpellier) for Louise de Coligny (1553–1620), last wife of William I of Orange-Nassau, at the time of her first marriage to Charles de Téligny (d. 1572). With later additions.

Binding from the Stadhouder's bindery, ca. 1760–ca 1766.

Provenance:
1) Louise de Coligny (1572); the princes of Orange Nassau; the Stadhouder's Library in the Hague (cat. 1686, f. 222r nr. 747)
2) The Princes of Orange-Nassau
3) Auction, P. van Cleef and D. Monnier, The Hague, 1 Dec. 1749, cat. of Frederik Hendrik p. 217 nr. 60.
4) Purchased by J. Royer for Stadhouder William IV
5) Stadhouder William V
6) In 1798, deposited, Stadthouder's Library, The Hague (cat. 1795, f. 105, nr. 98)

Description of the Manuscript

90 folios on rag paper, in an 18th-century binding.

Pages slightly trimmed for the binding, a few ends of phrases cut or obscured.

Dedicated to the "most illustrious and most virtuous lady, Madame de Telligny." ("A tresillustre et tresvertueuse dame, Madame de Telligny . . .")

Contents

Ff. 1 to 33—Transcribed by François Auzières—La Rochelle?—ca. May 1571?
  1^v^ Dedicatory eight-line poem :
  2^r^ Sonnet "Aux Lecteurs sur le sujet de ce Livre."
  (*Love poetry, various forms: Discours tragique, Complaintes, Chansons, Stances, Odelettes, Sonnets "Des Morts, Des Peines, et des Larmes"*)

Ff. 34^r^ to 54^v^—Several hands—La Rochelle?—ca. May 1571?
  (*Love poetry, various forms: Stances, Dialogue de "Volusian et Callioppe," Chansons, Quatrains, Sonnets*)

Ff. 55^r^ to 59^r^—"Pastorale" elegy for "Odet."—Place?—Date?
  (*Possibly for Louise's younger brother Odet d'Andelot, who died suddenly in Nîmes in 1580?*)

Ff. 59^v^ through 61^v^
Blank

Ff. 62^r^ to 78^v^ —Several hands—Place?—after August 1572
"Sur la mort de Monsieur l'Admiral"
  (*Sonnets, one an "Imitation de Petrarque," two Psalm paraphrases, by Du Perron and by Bertaut, Setances by Bertaut, one Chanson, three-line Latin epithet, "Sur une devize / Feu, sans Fumée," "Cantique faict par Monsr de Maison fleur Apres le Massacre de Paris fait a la saint Bertelomy 1572"*)

Ff. 78^v^ to 82^v^
Blank

Ff. 83^r^ to 90^v^—"La Pascience"—The Hague?—after July 1584
"A Madame Madame la princesse Dorange Comtesse de Nassau etc."

"Heare Councill and Receiue Instruction": Situating the Mother's Legacy in Manuscript

SUSAN E. HRACH

MOST CRITICAL TREATMENTS OF MOTHERS' ADVICE BOOKS HAVE argued that the genre offered a socially acceptable means for women to write and to aspire to a public audience, specifically predicated upon the writer's impending death. Imminent personal demise through illness or childbirth, so the critics contend, offered the only sort of extreme circumstance that could serve to legitimate ordinary women's breaking into print.[1] The writers' rhetorical strategies for publicly acknowledging and yet circumventing the cultural restriction on women's speech are especially evident in the books' opening dedicatory epistles, which is where the bulk of critical attention has been focused. While the work of the last decade or so has offered some stimulating readings of these prefaces, the bodies of the advice books are due for closer inspection. The advice proffered in mothers' legacies demand both broader and deeper comparison in order to make useful distinctions among them, as well as to test the thesis that the subject matter itself facilitated these writers' bids for public authorship.[2]

This paper was first delivered at the 2007 Annual Meeting of the Renaissance Society of America, Miami, FL, for a panel entitled "Early Modern Women's Manuscripts I," Margaret P. Hannay, Siena College, presiding.

[1] See Kristen Poole, "'The fittest closet for all goodness': Authorial Strategies of Jacobean Mothers' Manuals," *Studies in English Literature* 35 (1995): 69–88; and Wendy Wall, *The Imprint of Gender: Authorship and Publication in the English Renaissance* (Ithaca: Cornell Univ. Press, 1993).

[2] Margaret J. M. Ezell has pointed out that "our current modes of analyzing authorship do not deal with [a] type of author who had no desire to publish or to 'go public,' except to form

One intractable problem with this subject has been the difficulty in defining the scope of the genre itself. Is a mother's advice book necessarily one which appeared in print, with the author's explicit or implied consent to publish? Should advice texts in manuscript deserve equal attention? Must the text be discrete, or can it exist as part of a commonplace book, or within a letter? How short can the text be? Would something in brief verse count? The majority of critical attention has focused on those texts which make some internal reference to their status as "legacies," which offers at least a provisional way of circumscribing the genre according to the stated purpose of the advice, i.e., as a bequest for children in the event of a mother's death. My proposal here is to suggest reading these texts with an eye to describing them within the prevailing legal notions of a legacy. Mothers' advice should be situated as pieces of writing that occupy positions both inside and outside available discourses of the period, whether in print or in manuscript.

The English institution of coverture plays a critical role in shaping our understanding of what a mother's legacy might entail. Archival research is revealing the gap between the officially sanctioned restriction on women's will-making and the regular practice of women's will-making in the absence of a living husband/father/brother/uncle to fulfill his normal function.[3] But this practical necessity did not seem to present a major challenge, at least in the early seventeenth century, to the ideological pervasiveness of coverture. Where women have no *normative* legal right to bequeath material possessions, and female activity is widely held to belong properly to the realm of the domestic or private devotion, the neat substitution of a spiritual bequest places the mother's legacy on safer grounds. Thomas Goad's Approbation to Elizabeth Joscelin's legacy describes her efforts quite openly as a spiritual will:

> Our lawes disable those, that are under covert-baron, from disposing by Will and Testament any temporall estate. But no law prohibiteth any

---

theories to explain the motivation behind what *we* see as authorial self-destruction": *Social Authorship and the Advent of Print* (Baltimore: Johns Hopkins Univ. Press, 1999), 43.

[3] See Susan Dwyer Amussen, *An Ordered Society: Gender and Class in Early Modern England* (Oxford and New York: Basil Blackwell, 1988); Lucinda M. Becker, *Death and the Early Modern Englishwoman* (Aldershot and Burlington, VT: Ashgate, 2003); Amy Louise Erickson, *Women and Property in Early Modern England* (London and New York: Routledge, 1995); Nesta Evans, "Inheritance, Women, Religion and Education in Early Modern Society as Revealed by Wills," in Philip Riden, ed., *Probate Records and the Local Community* (Gloucester: Alan Sutton Publishing, 1985), 53–70; and Mary Prior, "Wives and Wills, 1558–1700," in John Chartres and David Hey, eds., *English Rural Society, 1500–1800: Essays in Honour of Joan Thirsk* (Cambridge: Cambridge Univ. Press, 1990), 201–25.

possessor of morall and spiritual riches, to impart them unto others, either in life by communicating, or in death by bequeathing. The reason is, for that corruptible riches, even to those who have capacity of alienating them, bring only a civill propriety, but no moral & virtuous influence for the wel dispensing, or bestowing them: whereas virtue and grace have power beyond al empeachment of sex or other debility, to enable and instruct the possessor to employ the same unquestionably for the inward inriching of others.

Goad's description of Joscelin's efforts here compares her "virtuous" work favorably to the merely "civill propriety" of will-making. He goes beyond defending her writing to asserting its morally superior purposefulness: "the inward inriching of others." Joscelin herself does not shy away from the interpretation of her writing as will-making, comparing her "inheritance" to the acts of "men who purchase land, and store up treasure for their unborne babes," and naming her text, "this my little legacy, of which my Childe is Executor."

While Goad and Joscelin explicitly take up the matter of how to read this act of female will-making, other mother's-advice writers seem unwilling to name the activity in the same way. Elizabeth Grymeston deems her legacy a "Register of heavenly Meditations" and uses both metaphorical and literal language to position herself as an instrument, rather than a source, for conveying moral guidance. The title page of Grymeston's 1604 book includes, in fact, a motto in both Latin and English: "*Non est rectum, quod a Deo non est directum* / It cannot be good which God directs not." If God becomes the source of direction, it would seem to be His will being carried out by the writer, rather than an expressing of her own.

Recent treatments of women and wills in early modern England reveal that women frequently participated in legal transactions as executors of their male relations' (especially husbands') wills. The duty of an executrix was a conspicuously public one, requiring an oath-swearing at the time of probate to promise to fulfill the terms of the testator's directions, and obligating the executrix to render an account of her duties when they had been fulfilled.[4] The figurative space of the executrix, then, deserves equal consideration as a possible means of understanding women's discursive positions as legacy writers. As an executrix, the author of the legacy becomes a vessel for officially conveying moral guidance, a vehicle for

---

[4] During "Term Days" or "Sessions," the public gathered in large numbers to witness probate execution, among more sensational matters. I am grateful to Stephen Hyles for this understanding of historical English legal practice, as well as for his expertise in defining precisely the role of executors.

transmitting valuable, if intangible, property. The source of the spiritual riches remains with God and His Will as revealed in the Bible.

A discursive stance as an executrix is distinguished by the writer's choice to incorporate material from other sources, or wholly fashion her legacy with extracts from her commonplace book, for example, or from prayer books or classical sources or biblical scripture. Both the commonplace book and the inventory would serve as rhetorical models for the writer. Legacy-writing in the executrix mode represents an attempt to provide one's children with the spiritual apparatus one has found valuable, which not only supplies the labor with a moral justification, but also allows the writer to perform a suitably modest and socially legitimate function. A rhetorical stance as a will-maker, on the other hand, seems appropriate to texts in which the writer chooses to generate and compose original material, that is, to create the text's structures and sentences, a solitary activity that we more commonly associate with modern conceptions of authorship. A legacy could employ shifting rhetorical stances, as in the case of Elizabeth Richardson's prayer book legacy. Richardson dispenses, like an executrix, many prayers for various occasions and circumstances. Woven among these texts are brief reflections addressed directly to her daughters or other readers, clearly in Richardson's own will-maker voice, about how or when she herself would make good use of them.[5]

I'd like to focus for the moment on two Westmorland family texts in manuscript that I find interesting for several reasons, and which have not (to my knowledge) been included in critical conversations on mothers' legacies. The commonplace book of Sir Francis Fane, held at the Folger Shakespeare Library (V.a.180), and the Westmorland Book of Advices to the Children, held at the Northamptonshire Records Office [W(A)misc.vol.35] contain a common set of letters composed by several generations of parents, both fathers and mothers. The two texts are written in different hands, with several long letters copied into each, followed by a "signature" of the family member (often deceased) who had originally composed them. Advice letters to children and grandchildren are included from Sir Walter Mildmay (Chancellor of the Exchequer and Privy Counsellor to Elizabeth I), from his daughter-in-law, Lady Grace Mildmay, from Grace Mildmay's only daughter, Countess Mary Mildmay Fane, and from Francis Fane's mother, the Lady Mary DeSpencer. Mary DeSpencer's own mother, the Lady Frances Abergavenny, dedicated "The Praiers . . . committed at the houre of hir death" to her daughter in *The Monument of Matrons* (1582), which suggests

---

    [5] See Margaret P. Hannay's article on the mixed discursive styles employed by Richardson in a different text: "Elizabeth Ashburnham Richardson's Meditation on the Countess of Pembroke's *Discourse*," *English Manuscript Studies 1100–1700* 9 (2000): 114–28.

that the practice of legacy-writing in various forms was well-established on both the Mildmay and Fane sides of the family tree.

One of the letters included in both of these manuscripts is "signed" by Lady Grace Mildmay, and its transcribed text has been included in books by both Linda Pollock and Gerald Morton.[6] The lengthy letter is addressed in particular to Lady Mildmay's grandchild, Mildmay Fane, and is focused entirely on spiritual guidance for her grandson; Pollock supplies the text with the appropriate subtitle, "Virtuous Principles." Both of the recently published transcriptions of the text, however, have opted to include only the body of Lady Grace's letter and to exclude the copious marginal references to verses of biblical scripture tucked into the edges of both manuscript versions. This omission, while not affecting the clear and intended sense for modern readers of Lady Grace's piety, does considerably change how we might view her act of authorship. If we compare a transcription of the manuscript letter's body to a pasted-together text of the marginal Biblical verses (here I've used the text of the Geneva Bible, which seems to fit most appropriately for reasons of chronology as well as for Mildmay family religious leanings), we can see that the content of Lady Grace's advice is closely paralleled by the Bible verses listed alongside them (see Appendix).

The opening salutation, for example, "I your loving and old grandmother, exhort you in the name of the Lord, receive my words acceptably, even as you would be accepted of God and be blessed of him," is paired in the margin with Proverbs 19:20, which reads, "Hear counsel and receive instruction, that thou mayest be wise in thy latter end." While the wording differs, both Lady Grace's salutation and the Proverbs verse work toward the same purpose: they are admonitions to their reader/listener to pay attention, and they each precede a long series of various pieces of advice. Lady Grace's text continues in the same vein: "Heare the word of God attentively and diligently" is paired with Deuteronomy 5:1, "I propose to you this day, that yee may learne them, and take heede to observe them." "Attentively and diligently" would correspond rather closely with "learne and take heede" regarding the proper attitude toward God's word. The letter works like a condensed version of all of the Bible verses listed in its margins—while the exact wording is not often repeated, the sense of the passage is very closely followed.

Lady Grace's description of Holy Scripture as "opposite wholly unto all sinn and uncleannesse" is paired with a reminder from Romans 7:12 that "wee are

---

[6] Linda A. Pollock, *With Faith and Physic: The Life of a Tudor Gentlewoman, Lady Grace Mildmay, 1552–1620* (New York: St. Martin's Press, 1993, repr. 1995); Gerald W. Morton, *A Biography of Mildmay Fane, Second Earl of Westmorland, 1601–1666: The Unknown Cavalier* (Lewiston: E. Mellen Press, 1991).

debtors not to the flesh" in our relationship to God's law. She emphasizes the "onely truth" that God's word represents, "opposite against all heresy and lies," while providing a connection to the Psalmist's proclaimed fidelity to God in Psalm 89, verse 33, who promises, "neither will I falsify my truth." This passage is followed in Lady Grace's letter in both the Folger and the Northampton manuscripts with a biblical citation fully inserted into the body of the text: "I will not suffer my truth to fail," Romans 3:4, which essentially repeats the message from Psalms, but in a briefer and more condensed form. Here again, both of the recent scholarly transcriptions have omitted the short biblical passage. I must speculate as to the transcribers' intentions in choosing to omit this particular (admittedly anomalous) single sentence of the letter, but I imagine that as a guiding principle they were interested in representing the text as a coherent, readable, meaningful whole from which modern readers could draw a clear sense of Lady Grace's style and persona. For that significant purpose, the inclusion of marginal biblical references and short biblical passages in the main text would potentially only distract the reader. Nonetheless, the pairing of the letter with its referenced verses of scripture introduces the possibility that we are working too hard in general to give the text a coherent kind of personal voice that its original method of composition didn't much value.

How are we to read Lady Grace's act of writing? The letter isn't precisely a sort of cut-and-paste operation, because most of the passages of scripture are longer and less to the point than the sentences of the legacy letter to which they're attached. The Bible verses seem to comment or elaborate on the phrases of the letter, but in such close fashion at many points that the letter's own meaning becomes disconcertingly derivative. If the ideas, per se, are suddenly less than original—or at least exclusive in the modern sense of intellectual property—how are we to imagine such a text was composed? At the very least, the biblical citations seem an important demonstration of Lady Grace's impressive knowledge of the Bible. At her death in 1620, this kind of command of Christian scripture, both Old and New Testaments, must have been a relatively remarkable accomplishment. Her thinking was apparently intimately shaped by her study of the Bible, so that in this particular letter of advice, there is no sentence of her own unaccompanied by a scriptural reference. When she makes use of special figurative language, as in her repetition of Revelation 2:10 "crowne of life" as the "crowne of Glory," Lady Grace seems to call more than subtle attention to the source of her inspiration.

I submit that this fascinating intertextuality between an epistolary example of mother's advice and its own internal references to biblical scripture reveals Lady Grace Mildmay's rhetorical position as being like that of an executrix. The letter's existence in two separate, bound family manuscript collections and its direct address to "My deare child Mildmay Fane" makes a fairly strong case, I think, for its basic classification as a mother's legacy or mother's advice text. It was not printed, however, during the seventeenth century or even closely thereafter. It makes no acknowledgment of any present or future audience other than the grandchild it addresses. Its overt signals pointing to an outside source of authority mark it as a different kind of text from the spiritual will-making legacy of Elizabeth Joscelin, for example, in both style and form. The number of advice texts, both printed and in manuscript, offers strong evidence that constant, repeated exhortations to godliness constituted dutiful parenting for the post-Reformation English Christian; this readily apparent cultural emphasis on admonition helps to ground our understanding of the impetus behind legacy-writing. The sort of rhetorical framework I am suggesting as a way of differentiating among the various sorts of legacy texts, then, may help us to see each text on its own terms as well as reconsider the genre's cultural status on the whole. If mothers' legacies are commonly, conveniently, socially "fit for print," the existence of various manuscript versions as well as real differences in the writers' rhetorical postures would suggest that print may not have been their foremost point.

COLUMBUS STATE UNIVERSITY

Appendix

From Lady Grace Mildmay's manuscript legacy letter to her grandchild, Mildmay Fane

MS margin	MS body text	Geneva Bible text
Pro: 19:20	My deare child Mildmay Fane, I your loueing & old Grandmother, exhort you in the name of the Lord, receive my words acceptably, even as you would be accepted of God and be blessed of him.	Heare counsell and receiue instruction, that thou mayest be wise in thy latter ende
Deut: 5:1	That is to say Heare the word of God attentively and diligently, which word is onely.	I propose to you this day, that yee may learne them, and take heede to obserue them
Rom: 7:12	pure and opposite wholly vnto all sinn and vncleanesse.	Therefore brethren, wee are detters not to the flesh, to liue after the flesh:
Psa: 89:33: 34:35:37	Which word is the onely truth and opposite against all heresy & Lyes.	Yet my louing kindnesse will I not take from him, neither will I falsifie my trueth. My couenant wil I not breake, nor alter the thing that is gone out of my lips. I haue sworne once by mine holines, that I will not fayle Dauid, saying, His seede shall endure for euer, and his throne shalbe as the sunne before me. He shalbe established for euermore as the moone, and as a faythfull witnes in the heauen.
	I will not suffer my truth to faile Rom: 3: 4	
Psa: 119:9	Which word is the onely direction	Wherewith shall a yong man redresse his waie? in taking heede thereto according to thy woorde.

Deu: 11:1	Of a good & godly life & conversation with the vndoubted prom-ises of happy sucksesse in this world, and an	Therefore thou shalt loue the Lord thy God, and shalt keepe that, which he commandeth to be kept: that is, his ordinances, and his lawes, and his commandements alway.
:13:14		If yee shall hearken therefore vnto my commaundements, which I com-maund you this day, that yee loue the Lorde your God and serue him with all your heart, and with all your soule, I also wil giue raine vnto your land in due time, the first raine & the latter, that thou maist gather in thy wheat, and thy wine, & thine oyle.
15:19:20:21		Also I will send grasse in thy fieldes, for thy cattel, that thou maist eate, and haue inough. And ye shall teach them your chil-dren, speaking of them, whē thou sittest in thine house, and when thou walkest by the way, and when thou liest downe, and when thou risest vp. And thou shalt write them vpon the postes of thine house, and vpon thy gates, That your daies may be multiplied, and the daies of your children, in þe land which the Lorde sware vnto your fathers to giue them, as long as the heauens are aboue the earth.
Rev: 2:10	everlasting crowne of Glory in the life to come.	Feare none of those things, which thou shalt suffer: beholde, it shall come to passe, that the deuill shall cast some of you into prison, that ye may be tryed, and ye shall haue tribulation tenne dayes: be thou faithfull vnto the death, and I will giue thee the crowne of life.

From Folger Ms V.a.180 and Northamptonshire Records Office W(A) misc. vol. 35.

Missing, Marginal, Mutilated:
Reading the Remnant
of Women's Manuscripts

SHARON CADMAN SEELIG

R ATHER THAN FOCUSING ON A SINGLE MANUSCRIPT, THIS ESSAY COVERS
ground rather quickly, referring to a number of texts that may well be
familiar in order to raise some general questions about our approach
to manuscripts and editions of them. The good news is well known to all here:
Shakespeare, in Virginia Woolf's phrase, not only had a sister, he had aunts and
cousins and nieces—women of the early modern period who wrote plays, mothers' advice books, treatises on breast feeding, family histories, romances, diaries,
dream visions, defenses of women, lyric poetry, translations, autobiographies,
biographies, hymns, letters, commonplace books, and more. These writers were
not silent and obedient; they chose those avenues open to them and forged new
ones, sometimes with modest disclaimers, sometimes with bold and challenging
statements; sometimes they demurred, sometimes they attacked; sometimes they
simply recorded. But in this prized corpus there are frustrating gaps—missing
names, missing lines, missing or unreadable passages, missing years. Sometimes
the gaps are physical and obvious; sometimes they are simply ways in which these
texts lack material that would seem essential to the project in hand. Of the many

---

This paper was first presented at the 2007 Annual Meeting of the Renaissance Society of
America, Miami, Florida, at a panel entitled "Early Modern Women's Manuscripts II," Elizabeth H. Hageman, University of New Hampshire, presiding.

examples that might be found, I'll use instances I became aware of while working on my recent book, subtitled "Reading Women's Lives, 1600–1680."[1]

For six years, from 1599 to 1605, Lady Margaret Hoby (1570/1–1633) kept a diary of her daily activities—most notably her devotional and scriptural reading, prayer, and household tasks. But the diary is detailed precisely where we might expect it to be minimal, and minimal precisely where we might expect it to be detailed. Here, for example, is the entry for a fairly typical day, Friday, 25 July 1600:

> After priuat praier I brak my fast with Mr Hoby : after, I went to the church, then I came home and praied, dinner, and wrett in my testement : after, I was busie about diuers thinges, and, when I had walked abroad, I praied priuat and so went to supper: after supper I went to the lecture, and, when I had praied priuatly, I went to bed.[2]

This entry is like a blank schedule book, indicating how Hoby filled her time, but it is maddeningly short on detail: what were the "diuers things" she was "busie about"; what was the content of the lecture; what did she pray about; what did she read; what were her thoughts and concerns during the day? In short, precisely what we would expect a diary to do—give some indication of the thoughts, the feelings, even the specific activities of the writer—is precisely what this text does not do. Even with regard to the most dramatically disruptive event in the diary— a near riot in her own home, perpetrated by a drunken hunting party hostile to the Hobys' beliefs and practice—commentators have discerned only that her handwriting seems somewhat larger, while the account itself is taciturn in the extreme:[3]

> After I was readie I spake with Mr Ewrie, who was so drunke that I sone made an end of that I had no reasen to stay for : and, after, praied, brake my fast, praied, and then dined : after, I was busie about the house and then I went to priuat examination and praier : after, I went to supper, and, when I had praied, I went to bed[.] (27 Aug. 1600)

---

[1] Sharon Cadman Seelig, *Autobiography and Gender in Early Modern Literature: Reading Women's Lives, 1600–1680* (Cambridge: Cambridge Univ. Press, 2006).

[2] *The Private Life of an Elizabethan Lady: The Diary of Lady Margaret Hoby, 1599–1605*, ed. Joanna Moody (Stroud, Gloucestershire: Sutton, 1998), 101. All references to Hoby's diary are to this edition.

[3] Dorothy Meads, ed., *The Diary of Lady Margaret Hoby, 1599–1605* (London: Routledge, 1930), 272 n. 396. Meads, ed., *Diary*, 269–72, and Moody, ed., *Private Life*, Introduction, xlvi-li, give detailed accounts of the episode and its repercussions.

But if these entries seem insufficient to us, Margaret Hoby probably did not think she was omitting anything essential: the general lack of detail exemplifies the differences between her expectations and ours. She set out to keep an account of her devotional life—the hours of prayer, meditation, and instruction—though not of its content, and if we were to adopt Sara Mendelson's term "serial personal memoranda"[4] rather than diary, even spiritual diary, we might have a more accurate description of the nature of the text.

There are also physical lacunae: the manuscript is frayed and torn at the beginning and the end, so that the entries on the first and last pages are fragmentary. Because later entries are less regular and less complete than the earlier ones, certainly less detailed about spiritual observance, some readers have inferred a waning interest on Hoby's part in keeping a diary of this sort.[5] But it looks as if she began keeping this record on 9 August 1599, the third anniversary of her marriage to her third husband, Sir Thomas Posthumous Hoby, and, although the last entry is 21 July 1605, given the torn condition of the last sheet, it is quite possible—though not certain—that she continued until 8 August, completing the six-year cycle; and that intriguing fact—if it is a fact—may reflect a shaping of this text through time and selected moments of time.

Anne Clifford (1590–1676) is also remarkably taciturn in the diary she kept from 1616 to 1619, even though it is less restricted in the kinds of events and encounters recorded, and includes more details of her reading and secular activities. Although Clifford describes some of her emotional states, as in the entry from February 1616, "All the tyme I stay'd in the Country I was sometimes merry & sometimes sad, as I heard news from London,"[6] much goes unstated—for example, her reaction to the several days' visit of her husband's mistress and that lady's husband to Knole in August of 1619. And although this diary is often referred to as the 1616–19 diary,[7] the year 1618 is simply missing. While it seems likely that Anne Clifford kept a diary for much of her life, we have day books of this sort only for the years 1616, 1617, and 1619, and the three months of 1676

---

[4] Sara Heller Mendelson, "Stuart Women's Diaries and Occasional Memoirs," in *Women in English Society, 1500–1800*, ed. Mary Prior (London: Methuen, 1985), 181–201, here 181.

[5] E.g. Mary Ellen Lamb, "Margaret Hoby's Diary: Women's Reading Practices and the Gendering of the Reformation Subject," in *Pilgrimage for Love: Essays in . . . Honor of Josephine A. Roberts*, ed. Sigrid King, MRTS 213 (Tempe: Arizona Center for Medieval and Renaissance Studies, 1999), 63–94, here 71, 85; and Moody, ed., *Private Life*, xxxi.

[6] *The Diary of Lady Anne Clifford, 1616–1619*, ed. Katherine O. Acheson (New York: Garland, 1995), 40. All references to Clifford's diary are to this edition, except where otherwise noted.

[7] Or the Knole diary, Anne Clifford having been mainly resident at Knole, as Countess of Dorset, when she kept it.

immediately before her death. (There is evidence that Clifford's day books for the intervening years were used to compile the annual summaries, which still exist, and were then "laid aside.")[8] And what we have is not a holograph, but rather two copies, one from the eighteenth, the other from the nineteenth centuries.[9] Since the year 1618 is missing from both manuscripts, it seems likely that the loss of that year preceded the copying. But why is that year missing? Was Anne Clifford too frank about her relations with her husband to suit later generations? Was that section simply misplaced? And how do we read documents like this that seem inherently elliptical and restrained? Have we again mistaken the writer's purpose? Did Anne Clifford keep a diary not to record her feelings but to document her own uprightness (like the time she had "a paper drawne" to state that she would have gone down to London but that her husband had explicitly commanded the contrary (1 April 1616), or to record her vow "that [she] wou'd never part with Westmorland while [she] lived upon any Condition Whatsoever" (18 January 1617), and to report her triumphs, achieved with the help of Almighty God?

If the manuscript of Hoby's diary is frayed by time[10] and Clifford's diary missing a single year, suspiciously, but without clear evidence of the reason, in the cases of Lucy Hutchinson, Anne Halkett, and Ann Fanshawe, we have more dramatic loss. The lively autobiography of Anne Murray Halkett features two serious relationships, one with a younger man who threatens to go to France and become a Capuchin friar if she won't see him, and another with a Royalist courier and agent during the English civil wars who deceived her about being a widower—all this before she met the respectable man who became her husband.[11] Anne Halkett tells her story vividly, frankly, sometimes even melodramatically, but at two crucial points in the narrative, a whole leaf has been removed from the manuscript. In the first instance she has been commenting, not very charitably,

---

[8] As stated by Edward Rainbow, Bishop of Carlisle, *A Sermon Preached at the Funeral of the Right Honorable Anne, Countess of Pembroke, Dorset, and Montgomery* . . . (London: Printed for R. Royston and H. Broom, 1677), 51.

[9] For an account of these manuscripts, see Katherine O. Acheson, ed., *The Memoir of 1603 and The Diary of 1616–1619: Anne Clifford* (Peterborough, Ont.: Broadview, 2007), 7, 37–40.

[10] And the hand small and the ink penetrating the paper so that one is extremely grateful for the excellent transcriptions and editions of Meads and Moody.

[11] Colonel Joseph Bampfield has been considered a double agent by a number of historians, but the charge is rejected by John Loftis and Paul H. Hardacre in their edition, *Colonel Joseph Bampfield's Apology* . . . *1685,* and "Bampfield's Later Career: A Biographical Supplement" by John Loftis (Lewisburg: Bucknell Univ. Press, 1993), 13–14; 17–30, 140; 155–87; 238–52. See also Alan Marshall, "Bampfield, Joseph (1622–1685)," *Oxford Dictionary of National Biography* (Oxford: Oxford Univ. Press, 2004); http://www.oxforddnb.com/view/article/1259, accessed 18 Sept. 2007.

on the misfortunes of her first suitor, Thomas Howard (who had unwisely and unworthily married another woman). When the account resumes, she has already begun describing the second, more serious, relationship with Colonel Joseph Bampfield, who seemed to have remarkable difficulty ascertaining whether his first wife was dead (as he claimed) or alive, as she later proved to be. The second gap occurs just as Anne Murray learns that "undouptedly C.[olonel] B.[ampfield]'s wife was living and was now att London, where shee came cheefely to undeceave those who beleeved her dead," whereupon she recalls: "'Oh,' said I, with a sad sigh, 'is my misfortune so soone devulged?' . . ."; and there a leaf is missing.[12]

In short, precisely when we are eager to hear more, and just where the narrator herself, quite unlike Clifford or Hoby, seems to have gone into considerable detail, a leaf has been removed. In a narrative that is often dramatically self-presentational but that seems explicitly designed to demonstrate Lady Halkett's integrity and loyalty, it is likely that these pages were too frank for other members of her family. No obvious suspect has appeared: two possible candidates, Anne Halkett's son Robert and her husband's elder son, Sir Charles Halkett, were both living when she wrote the account of her life, but both predeceased her. There are other missing sections, but of a different kind: both the opening pages, devotional in nature, and the concluding pages, which break off with an account of Sir James Halkett under pressure in 1656 to become a Justice of the Peace under the commonwealth, are frayed. Since Sir James Halkett lived for fourteen more years and Anne Halkett wrote her memoir in 1677–78, a considerable amount of material may be missing; indeed, a 1701 biography draws on a more complete version of Halkett's life than is now extant.[13] But since there is no special drama at this point in the text, we are more likely to suspect the hand of time than the hand of man or woman.

The holograph of Lucy Hutchinson's brief autobiographical fragment no longer exists; we have only a transcription by the Rev. Julius Hutchinson, published in 1806, that notes the ways in which the manuscript was truncated. Lucy Apsley Hutchinson's account of her life begins on a grand scale, with the history of the British Isles and the providence of Almighty God, demonstrated also

---

[12] *The Memoirs of Anne, Lady Halkett, and Ann, Lady Fanshawe*, ed. John Loftis (Oxford: Clarendon Press, 1979), 72. All references to Halkett's autobiography are to this edition.

[13] *The Life of the Lady Halket*, by S.C. (Edinburgh, 1701), cited by Loftis and Hardacre. Subsequently identified as the Rev. Simon Couper, S. C. was the person to whom Halkett gave her manuscripts (Susan Wiseman, "'The Most Considerable of My Troubles': Anne Halkett and the Writing of Civil War Conspiracy," in *Women Writing, 1550–1750*, ed. Jo Wallwork and Paul Salzman [Bundoora, Australia: Meridian, 2001], 25–45, here 29). Recently Suzanne Trill, ed., *Lady Anne Halkett: Selected Self-Writings* (Aldershot: Ashgate, 2007), 52, has suggested Couper as the person most likely to have removed pages from Halkett's autobiography.

in her birth, before dawn on the 29th of January 1620, in the Tower of London; it continues with praise of her parents' virtue, wisdom, and child-rearing practices. Lucy's adolescence included attendance at sermons and rather priggish exhortation of her mother's maids, but she also "thought it no sin to learn or hear witty songs and amorous sonnets or poems."[14] Hutchinson describes herself as "the confidante in all the loves that were managed among my mother's young women;" and writes, "there was none of them but had many lovers, and some particular friends beloved above the rest. Among these I have . . ." (Keeble, ed., Memoirs, 15). And here Julius Hutchinson notes, "Many leaves were at this point torn from the ms."[15] The text continues, ". . . any one mentioned him to me, I told them that I had forgotten those extravagancies of my infancy, and knew now that he and I were not equal; but I could not for many years hear his name without several inward emotions. . . ." And here again there is a gap in the manuscript, accompanied by the editorial speculation that "this is a reference to 'some amour in which Mrs H. was disappointed'" (Keeble, ed., Memoirs, 345n). After one more sentence, Julius Hutchinson reports, "Here the story of herself abruptly ends."

The evidence certainly suggests that we have a sanitized version of these fascinating early lives: Lucy Hutchinson, the exemplary wife who composed a lengthy and admiring apologia, The Life of John Hutchinson of Owthorpe, seems to have described her interest in the affairs of her mother's maids, and an early amour of her own, one that left her with a lingering emotional attachment. In this case N. H. Keeble's speculation, ". . . that this autobiographical project was abandoned by LH in favour of the Life of her husband" (Memoirs, 345n), suggests a woman less concerned with recounting her own life than paying homage to her husband. But in fact, The Life of John Hutchinson presents Lucy in a quite prominent role, destined by Providence to be the spouse of this extraordinary man, so that modesty may not have been her motive for breaking off. Moreover, as David Norbrook argues, it's by no means clear that this manuscript fragment precedes her writing of the life of John Hutchinson.[16] In effect, the speculations about such

---

[14] "The Life of Mrs. Lucy Hutchinson," in Memoirs of the Life of Colonel Hutchinson, with a Fragment of Autobiography, ed. N. H. Keeble (London: J. M. Dent, 1995), 15. All references to Hutchinson are to this edition.

[15] Keeble, ed., Memoirs, 345 n., cites the conjecture of Julius Hutchinson.

[16] David Norbrook, "'But a Copie': Textual Authority and Gender in Editions of 'The Life of John Hutchinson'," in New Ways of Looking at Old Texts, III: Papers of the Renaissance English Text Society, 1997–2001, ed. W. Speed Hill (Tempe: Arizona Center for Medieval and Renaissance Studies in conjunction with Renaissance English Text Society, 2004), 109–30, at 126, first cites Sidonie Smith's view of the matter: "Hutchinson abandoned her autobiographical project after describing her parentage and early years, and turned instead to the biography of her husband . . . as if her own life story ended after adolescence when marriage subsumed

missing material may tell us more about the editor's thinking than about the actual circumstances of composition or transmission.

Happily, we do have a manuscript version of the memoirs of Lady Ann Fanshawe (1625–1680), not a holograph but a handsome copy to which she made corrections. It is safely in the British Library (Add. MS. 41161) and no leaves have been torn from it. But there are interesting deletions, or rather overscorings, that seem to have been Ann Fanshawe's own (and that suggest that she wanted to remove any passage with the least hint of impropriety). Fortunately, as her editor John Loftis notes, "the cancelled passages are supplied by recopyings, in handwriting much later than the seventeenth century, on blue slips of paper pasted into the volume after the folio leaves were bound."[17]

The first of the canceled passages I want to note is from a description of the hardships Sir Richard and Lady Ann Fanshawe endured early in 1650 while fleeing Ireland before the advancing Parliamentary forces. Of their accommodations in Galway, Fanshawe writes: "Our house was very clean; onely one maid in it besides the master. We had a very good supper provided and, being very weary, we went early to bed,"—and here is the section crossed out by Fanshawe:

> but we could not rest very well, fancying our legs bit.
>
> The next morning, as soon as my husband had put on his gown and begun to put on his stockings, he called me, saying, 'My heart, what great spots are these on my legs? Sure, this is the plague, but I am very well and feel nothing.' At which I ran out of the bed to him and saw my own legs in the same condition, and upon examining the cause we found that the sheets being short and the blanketts full of fleas, we had those spots made by them. (Loftis, ed., *Memoirs*, 126)

And in a second passage, taking her leave at court before she and her husband, the King's ambassador, left for Spain in January 1664, Ann Fanshawe visited the Duke (later James II) and Duchess of York, "who received me with more than ordinary kindness; who after an houre and a half discourse with me saluted me and gave me leave to depart." What follows has been crossed out: "Going along

---

her identity in her husband's." But Norbrook reaches a different conclusion: "In fact her reference to 'my house at Owthorpe' strongly suggests that she was writing [the autobiographical fragment] after her husband's death, when she was precisely not a *feme covert* but an estate-owner."

[17] *The Memoirs of . . . Ann, Lady Fanshawe,* ed. Loftis, 91–92. Loftis goes on to suggest, "Probably the readings of these passages were taken from some other manuscript of the Memoirs—perhaps the one from which the amanuensis employed by Lady Fanshawe copied in May 1676."

the matted gallery from His Highnes the Duke of York his lodgings, entering into His Majesty's withdrawing room, I found a twenty shillings piece of gold, which nobody owning that was by, I kept" (Loftis, ed., *Memoirs*, 152–53).

These two passages seem harmless enough, leaving one to wonder just why Fanshawe, having written them, then deleted them. Her account, particularly of her early life and adventures, is full of lively detail, but it may be that being flea-bitten seems a little low, or a little absurd, for the King's ambassador, and that perhaps finding (and keeping) a twenty-shilling piece seems beneath the character of the ambassador's wife. There are other examples as well, including one that depicts them at the mercy of circumstances in the midst of the Civil War, complaining "of the cruelty of the rebells that forced us to wander."[18] In these cases, the censorship is self-censorship, and fortunately we still have the evidence of what has been omitted. Loftis's exemplary edition carefully indicates passages that were crossed out; nevertheless, this information is given in the textual notes, where a reader of the explanatory notes might miss it. In other words, however convenient or excellent the edition, consulting the manuscript is indispensable, for it may raise points we had not even thought to wonder about.

In contemplating these several omissions and alterations, are there any general rules for dealing with such textual problems? The first two instances, the diaries of Hoby and Clifford, have to do both with material gaps in the text and with things omitted that—by our conception—should be included. The latter issue is more easily resolved: the fault is not in the diary, but in ourselves, that we are post-Romantic, that we expect something that these records were never intended to produce. We may also answer many questions about events and emotions by reading carefully, by noting repeated actions or patterns that allow us to understand the strong emotional currents of these texts. Even though Clifford and Hoby do not explicitly describe an emotional state, they record, often without comment, events that produce that reaction. For example, in February and March of 1617, Clifford makes several urgent requests to her husband Dorset to "take Knoll in his way as he goes to London," to "come & see me & the Childe as soon as he cou'd."[19] And in February 1619, Clifford writes, "my Lord shou'd have

---

[18] The passage as a whole reads as follows, with material obscured through the word 'wearynes': "We praised God; I wept, your father lifting then up his hands admired so great a salvation. Then we often kissed each other, as if yet we feared death, sithed, and complained of the cruelty of the rebels that forced us to wander. Then we again comforted ourselves in the submitting to God's will for his laws and our country, and remembered the lott and present suffering of our king. The much discourse and wearynes of our journey made us fall a sleep" (*The Memoirs of . . . Ann, Lady Fanshawe*, ed. Loftis, 131).

[19] 3 March 1617, and 20 March 1617; Clifford's language is emphatic: "I wrote a letter to my Lord to *beseech* him that he wou'd take Knoll in his way. . ." and "I wrote a letter to my Lord to *intreat* him that he wou'd come & see me. . ."; Acheson, ed., 73, 75.

gone to London the 24th of this month but I intreated him to stay here the 25th because on that day 10 years I was married, which I kept as a day of Jubile to me so my Lord went not up till the 27th" (Acheson, ed., *Memoir and Diary*, 100–1), clearly revealing how much more seriously she takes their wedding anniversary than he.

This strategy of close reading, of course, does not give us the missing year of Clifford's diary, 1618. But in other documents, for instance the family chronicles and the diary of the last months of her life, we find Clifford looking back, connecting the end of her life with the beginning in ways that shed light on the earlier period and establish patterns of emphasis and modes of understanding. In her last months she notes the anniversaries of a range of events: the birth of her son Thomas fifty-six years before (2 Feb. 1620) and Dorset's paternal visit two days later; a quarrel with her husband in January of 1624, and her last parting from him on 9 Feb. 1624, before his death in March of that year. She remembers, as she had in the diary of 1619, her wedding anniversary on 25 February, and even represents their journey northward together in February 1616 in a way that sounds far more harmonious than the initial diary account.[20]

In the cases of Hutchinson and Halkett, the pages and passages that have been forcibly removed will in all likelihood never be recovered, but the evidence of removal at least indicates that something significant has been lost, that these writers did not initially choose silence. Here too we may find supplemental evidence elsewhere, like that which suggests that Anne Halkett and Joseph Bampfield were married in the Netherlands,[21] or the 1701 biography based on a more complete version of Anne Halkett's life than we now have.[22] And the crossing out

---

[20] *The Diaries of Lady Anne Clifford*, ed. D. J. H. Clifford (Stroud, Gloucestershire: Sutton, 1990), 246, 242, 250, 257. On 18 January 1676, Clifford recalls her audience before King James fifty-nine years before, an event recorded in the earlier diary, but also a number of other occurrences for which we have no record: on 25 January, "how this day was 52 years [since] in the withdrawing chamber at Knowl house in Kent, as wee sate at dinner, had my first Lord and I a great falling out, when but the day before I came from London from being God-mother to his Brother's youngest Son" (242). Clifford also remembers learning of the death of her second husband, Philip Herbert, Earl of Pembroke and Montgomery, 23 January 1650, and recites details of the death of Pembroke's first wife, Susan Vere, 1 February 1629 (242, 245).

[21] John Loftis, "Bampfield's Later Career: A Biographical Supplement," in *Colonel Joseph Bampfield's Apology*, ed. Loftis and Hardacre, 248–52. See also Sheila Ottway, "They Only Lived Twice: Public and Private Selfhood in the Autobiographies of Anne, Lady Halkett and Colonel Joseph Bampfield," in *Betraying Our Selves: Forms of Self-Representation in Early Modern English Texts*, ed. Henk Dragstra, Sheila Ottway, and Helen Wilcox (New York: St. Martin's Press, 2000), 136–47, here 145–46.

[22] Recently Ellen Moody has used the Life by S. C. in a speculative construction of Halkett's untruncated memoir; Moody, "'Cast out from respectability a while': Anne Murray Halkett's Life in the Manuscripts," a paper delivered at an East Central/American Society for

of Ann Fanshawe's franker or livelier views, apparently in order to give us a more acceptable, more exemplary view of her life, allows us to return to the manuscript to see what her first thoughts were, and what her second, providing an even more nuanced sense of her self-presentation than in Loftis's excellent edition.

Having described things missing from manuscripts, I'd like to note briefly what may be missing from editions. I mentioned the two extant manuscripts of Anne Clifford's 1616–1619 diary (the Portland MS, an eighteenth-century copy by Margaret Bentinck, Duchess of Portland, and a nineteenth-century copy, probably by Elizabeth Sackville and her sister Mary).[23] There are also three useful modern editions, two of them by Katherine Acheson: the first, a critical edition, based on the Portland manuscript, is unfortunately out of print, but the very recent Broadview edition incorporates many of its features. Because the text is intended for classroom use, Acheson has (understandably, if regrettably) modernized spelling and punctuation. But in contrast to an earlier (1990) edition of the diary by D. J. H. Clifford,[24] Acheson preserves another significant aspect of the text, namely its organization on the page: she presents the text in two columns, with the daily entries on the right and Clifford's marginal notes on the left. This arrangement conveys the sense of margin and text in interaction, with the marginal material coming second in time but not in importance, serving variously as gloss, comment, guide, or counterpoint to the body of the text.

In his Everyman edition of the *Life of Colonel Hutchinson* (published 1995), N. H. Keeble makes a different compromise, in order, he says, "to present Lucy Hutchinson's complete text accurately and faithfully but in a form which is accessible to the modern reader" (Keeble, ed., *Memoirs,* xxxi). Among other points, he notes that

> Lucy Hutchinson's interlinings and marginalia have been silently incorporated into the text. . . . More sustained passages cancelled in the manuscript are included or omitted as indicated in the notes. . . . Lucy Hutchinson's paragraphs are very long and it is an idiosyncrasy of hers to use virtually no punctuation. . . . Her sentences neither begin with a capital letter nor end with a stop. In this edition, punctuation is always and paragraphing usually editorial, following modern practice so far as Lucy Hutchinson's fluid syntax allows. (Keeble, ed., *Memoirs,* xxxi)

Eighteenth Century Studies Conference, 27 October 2006, Gettysburg College; http://www.jimandellen.org/halkett/CastOut.html.

[23] See Acheson, ed., *The Memoir of 1603 and The Diary of 1616–1619,* 38.

[24] *The Diaries of Lady Anne Clifford,* ed. D. J. H. Clifford (above n. 20).

While Keeble has given us a very useful edition that in a number of ways improves on its predecessors, he also eliminates several aspects of the holograph that we might find especially interesting. It is not always clear which passages were initially canceled and now included, and since "interlinings and marginalia have been silently incorporated into the text," it's much harder to follow the process of Hutchinson's composition. We might wonder why some material was in the margin rather than in the text: is this material, as in the case of Anne Clifford, a later addition, in dialogue with the body of the text, or is it a guide to the reader? And might we react differently to the more fluid version of Lucy Hutchinson's prose than we do to the modernized, organized version? Might it give us a different sense of her as woman, wife, and author? Fortunately David Norbrook has indicated his intention to address—and to provide us with the means to address— just such questions as these, in his forthcoming edition of Hutchinson.[25]

The editions from which I've been quoting are enormously useful, the result of growing attention to early modern women's writing among students and scholars. But of course manuscripts, even fragmentary ones—or perhaps especially those—remain invaluable, since they contain material clues that even good editors may have considered unimportant: as Heather Wolfe says about her edition of Elizabeth Cary, rather than "smoothing over the peculiarities of the manuscript," she aims "to set forth the meanings in and of its imperfect state."[26] We can advocate for editions that make those peculiarities clear, like Acheson's of Clifford's 1616–1619 diary, even as we prize editions, like Joanna Moody's of Hoby's diary, that make a difficult manuscript accessible and legible. As for what is missing, there is always hope that the archives and attics will yield more material to fill in the gaps and broaden the context of our understanding. And we can continue to consider the life as a whole, as Margaret Ezell has in placing Anne Halkett's fragmentary autobiography in the context of her voluminous output—"twenty-one folio and quarto manuscript volumes composed between 1644 and the late 1690s."[27] Finally, I hope you will not be scandalized if I point to a pedagogical opportunity: we can suggest to students that they "discover" the lost pages of Anne Halkett's or Lucy Hutchinson's autobiography. While no

---

[25] Norbrook, "'But a Copie'."

[26] Heather Wolfe, "A Family Affair: The Life and Letters of Elizabeth Cary, Lady Falkland," in *New Ways of Looking at Old Texts, III*, ed. Hill, 97–108, here 104.

[27] Margaret J. M. Ezell, "Ann Halkett's Morning Devotions: Posthumous Publication and the Culture of Writing in Late Seventeenth-Century Britain," in *Print, Manuscript, and Performance*, ed. Arthur F. Marotti and Michael D. Bristol (Columbus: Ohio State Univ. Press, 2000), 215–34, here 217. Halkett's contemporary biographer testifies that there were also "about thirty stitched Books, some in Folio, some on 4to. most of them of 10 or 12 sheets, all containing occasional Meditations" (S. C., *Life of the Lady Halket*, 64; cited by Ezell, "Culture of Writing," 217).

substitute for the original, the attempt at filling in the blank pages can teach them a great deal about seventeenth-century mores, diction, and style.

SMITH COLLEGE

Petitioning Power:
The Rhetorical Fashioning
of Elizabethan Women's Letters

ERIN A. SADLACK

IN 1559, RICHARD MULCASTER DESCRIBED ELIZABETH'S ENTRY INTO London for her coronation, noting that if the people "moved to her any suit, she most gently, to the common rejoicing of all the lookers-on and private comfort of the party, stayed her chariot and heard their requests."[1] According to Mulcaster, Elizabeth's willingness to hear petitions "implanted a wonderful hope in them touching her worthy government." By involving her subjects in that theatre, Elizabeth invited both men and women to see themselves as active participants in the political drama she was producing. Archival records testify to the extent of their response: over fifty petitionary letters by women from the period 1570 to 1599 are preserved in the Public Records Office, while Privy Council registers refer to hundreds of other petitions no longer extant. The surviving petitions testify that women from all classes had the right to participate in government on this individual basis, indicating that the petition was one of women's first political rights.

My research on petitions was made possible through the gift of generous grants from the Cosmos Club Foundation's Grants-in-Aid to Young Scholars Program and the English Department at the University of Maryland. I also acknowledge with deep gratitude the feedback I received from Jane Donawerth, Theresa Coletti, Meg Pearson, Erin Kelly, and Laurie McMillan, whose careful readings enhanced the quality of this article. This paper was presented at the 2006 MLA Convention in Philadelphia, PA, as part of a panel entitled "Early Modern Women's Manuscripts," Margaret P. Hannay, Siena College, presiding.
    [1] *Elizabeth I: Collected Works*, ed. Leah Marcus, Janel Mueller, and Mary Beth Rose (Chicago and London: Univ. of Chicago Press, 2000), 53.

Proclamations from the period acknowledge without comment the existence
of petitioners (also called suitors) of both sexes. If a suitor should arrive at court,
notes one 1594 proclamation, "Porters ... shall direct *him or her* to the Chamber
of one of the Masters of Requests."[2] Neither Elizabeth nor her councilors made
any distinction between the rights of men and of women to ask for assistance.
Many petitions were made in writing, but even oral petitions needed a written
version that could be endorsed or passed to others for investigation.[3]

The number of people who took up the invitation to petition the Queen and
her Privy Council became a source of anxiety. In 1589, Elizabeth directed the
Lord Deputy of Ireland to seek justice for Agnes Chamberlain, but she ordered
that if he found Chamberlain had misrepresented her suit, then he was to punish
her. Elizabeth was concerned that too many suitors had "used the like pretences
to coller their repaire hither here to begge and live lewdelie beinge otherwise
hable to worke for their livings."[4] The Privy Council, desperate to stem the tide
of petitioners clogging the court, issued several orders encouraging such individuals to pursue their appeals in the Court of Requests.[5] And during outbreaks
of the plague in 1592 and 1593, Elizabeth issued proclamations ordering suitors
to stay away from court in order that she and her attendants might "be the better
preserved from the infection of sickenesse in this time."[6]

These orders reflect anxiety over the presence of bodies in the court and the
potential danger of petitioners waiting for direct access to the Queen. Yet the
1592 order allowed an exception: if the suitor only wanted to deliver a letter, she
might send it past the gates. And for women petitioners in particular, who faced
the added problem that petitioning was deemed public display, and so immodest,
a written letter would mitigate the problematic presence of the body.

Petitioners would thus have been aware of the vital need to fashion their letters carefully, taking into account both language and appearance to represent
themselves when they could not be physically present. The written petitions that
survive today are records of their writers' rhetorical choices. We ought to look at

---

[2] Emphasis mine. The proclamation, dated 20 August 1594, is titled, "A Commandment
that no suiters come to the Court for any private suite except their petitions be indorsed by the
Master of Requests": *A Book Containing All Such Proclamations As Were Published During the
Raigne of the late Queene Elizabeth, Collected Together by the industry of Humfrey Dyson* (London: Printed by Bonham, Norton, and John Bill, 1618), *STC* 7758.3, 327.

[3] G. R. Elton, *The Tudor Revolution in Government* (Cambridge: Cambridge Univ. Press,
1953), 278.

[4] PRO PC 2/16/266. 5 September 1589.

[5] *Acts of the Privy Council*, PRO PC 2/16/357, 8 October 1589 and PRO PC 2/18/363–4,
27 June 1591.

[6] *Proclamations Published during the Raigne of Elizabeth*, 312. 12 October 1592.

these letters in the original wherever possible and to convey as much of the manuscript condition as we can in our scholarship. Only by looking at these texts in manuscript can we obtain a more complete picture of women's rhetorical ability. Such evidence of the context in which these letters were created is crucial to understanding the extent of women's literary activity in the early modern period.

Anyone who has worked with archival materials can testify to the benefits of direct access to manuscripts, especially those that have been damaged. Scorched writing completely obscured on microfilm is often legible in person. Similarly, one can try to examine the revision process by peering beneath a writer's crossed-out lines and blots. These elements represent important benefits of archival work, but in this article I want to focus on what we can learn about petitions by studying three aspects of manuscripts: physical appearance, including scribal hands; enclosed supporting documents; and marginalia, then illustrate the value of manuscript study by finishing with a case study of one petition.

Highly cognizant of the impact created by a letter's appearance, writers paid close attention to script and layout. Jane Bolding's 1582 petition to Elizabeth decorates the descenders of letters with large swirls.[7] When Elizabeth, Lady Russell, and the other residents of the Blackfriars wanted the Council to stop Burbage's attempt to build a theater in their district, they wrote a petition using a beautiful italic hand for the opening salutation and the signatures, and laid out the names of the residents in two neat columns, with the rest of the petition in a secretary hand.[8] The contrast between the two scripts emphasizes the importance of the names, headed by Russell, Lord Burghley's sister-in-law, and Lord Hunsdon, the theatre company's patron.

Other aspects of layout suggest the petitioner's awareness of the document's legal status. Every line in Phelippe Zouche's 1590 petition to Elizabeth over a land dispute with Sir Matthew Arundel ends with a pen stroke or a series of x's that fill in the space, thus preventing anyone from adding anything to the letter that might change her words.[9] Most petitions penned by professional scribes were written across the page in landscape orientation, leaving a large white space at the bottom, which conforms to the pattern of legal documents. However, writing across the wider horizontal page also creates the illusion that the petition itself is shorter. Scribes may be subtly suggesting the humble stance of the petitioner or that her request is only a small one.

Awareness of such patterns is necessary if we are to recognize the significance of a petition's deviation from scribal conventions. For instance, Elizabeth

---

[7] PRO SP 12/157/70. 1582?

[8] PRO SP 12/260/116. November 1596.

[9] PRO SP 12/235/45. 1590.

Longstone's 12 October 1586 petition to William Davison, asking him to take her son Thomas into his service, is written in portrait orientation, with none of the usual headings or opening formulae. This failure to conform to professional scribal practices indicates that either Longstone or her personal secretary drafted the letter. Since the signature is the same hand as the body of the petition, Longstone probably wrote it herself. She also writes familiarly to Davison, suggesting that she is a member of the same class. Nevertheless, she takes the rhetorical position of the "poore suter unto yow" and flatters Davison's good will to "suche as are widowes and ffatherlesse," phrases that evoke the language of professional petitions.[10] Such similarities in phrasing suggest a common language of petitioning, regardless of class, a fact less obvious if the petition's layout did not deviate from the norm, distinguishing this petition from one penned by professionals.

Many petitioners employed such professional scribes, so that even if the petitioner herself could not write, she was still able to petition.[11] Scholars such as James Daybell have taught us the value of paying attention to the collaboration between a letter's scribe and its sender.[12] Studying the manuscripts directly helps yield insight into that relationship. For example, the petitions of Annies Actton and Thomas Appletree requesting pardons are written by the same scribe and both contain similar phrases. Appletree had accidentally discharged a gun on the Thames while the Queen was sailing, wounding one of her bargemen, resulting in his arrest and that of his friend Barnebe, Annies's son. Actton pleads, "with wepping teears and bowinge knees beseching your honors" to free her son, while Appletree's petition on his own behalf uses the exact phrase, "with weeppinge teears and bowinge knees."[13] Whether the scribe introduced the phrase to both petitioners or whether he incorporated good ideas from the first into the second is impossible to say, but it is clear that the scribe certainly helped shape the content

---

[10] PRO SP 12/194/36. 12 October 1586.

[11] People would generally have had easy access to scribes. Keith Thomas notes that "a literate person in a country village could always supplement his income by writing accounts, letters, and bills for neighbors": "The Meaning of Literacy in Early Modern England," in *The Written Word: Literacy in Transition,* ed. Gerd Baumann (Oxford: Clarendon Press, 1986), 97–131, here 106.

[12] James Daybell, "Women's Letters and Letter Writing in England, 1540–1603," *Shakespeare Studies* 27 (1999): 161–87.

[13] Actton's petition is PRO SP 12/131/50. July 1579. Appletree's letter is PRO SP 12/131/51. 7/?/1579. It is impossible to determine conclusively which petition came first, but I would argue for Actton's. She does not mention the Queen's pardon in her plea, while Appletree does so. A royal pardon would be a powerful supplement to her petition, so it seems logical that it had not yet occurred when Actton's petition was written.

of these petitions. What is fascinating is that the petitioner's gender does not affect the choice of expression.

Examining the hands of other petitions, however, confirms that petitioners did exert a strong control over the content of their letters. When assessed a fine as a recusant, Margaret Blackwell acted decisively, sending two sets of letters, one to the Privy Council on 19 November 1585, and one to Walsingham separately on 25 November.[14] Each letter explains that she goes to St. Andrew's Church, but her neighbors in the Blackfriars have reported her as a recusant because she refused to attend the parish church. Accompanying each letter is a formal certificate from the parson and church wardens at St. Andrew's testifying to her attendance. The Privy Council's set of letters is in an entirely different hand from those sent to Walsingham, but the phrasing is almost identical throughout. Written six days apart and by different people, the language confirms Blackwell's role in shaping the content of both petitions and certificates.

For Blackwell, including a separate certificate of attendance in each petition indicates how desperate she is to verify her conformity to Elizabeth's laws. Such measures are unsurprising; given the difficulty of ascertaining religious belief, the certificates proving attendance represent objective evidence of her truth. Clearly she saw these supporting documents as part of her overall argument, and as such they merit consideration. Blackwell's formal language and presentation of the marks of each warden and the signature of the parson signal her awareness of the difficulty of proving one's faith and her knowledge of what would constitute evidence in a legal setting. When the texts of petitions are printed at all, such documents are often summarized, not transcribed in detail.

In rare cases, a series of petitions and counter-petitions survive; viewing such manuscripts in their original states can greatly facilitate the interpretation of these letters. For example, in March of 1586, the wives of mariners from the ships the *Emmanuel* and the *Julian* petitioned the Queen and the Privy Council for help getting their husbands released from a Spanish prison and for financial assistance.[15] Unable to effect the mariners' release, the Council attempted to alleviate the wives' suffering by calling Wolfstan Dixie, the Lord Mayor of London,

---

[14] PRO SP 12/184/46. 26 November 1585. The four documents are catalogued together; 46I is Blackwell's petition to the Council; 46II is the Parson's certificate sent to the Council; 46III is Blackwell's petition to Walsingham; and 46IV is the certificate for Walsingham.

[15] The only surviving wives' petition is PRO SP 12/187/63. 27 March 1586. In it, they refer to a previous petition to Elizabeth, which is apparently the one that set all the Council's actions in motion. The mariners of the *Emmanuel* had been detained in 1584 because one of the crew neglected to remove his hat before a procession of the Blessed Sacrament and the *Julian*, or *Gillian*, had been detained in Spain during a 1585 embargo. See Cheryl Fury, *Tides in the Affairs of Men: The Social History of Elizabethan Seamen, 1580–1603* (Westport, CT and London:

to summon the ships' owners, John Byrd and John Watts, to ask them for dona-
tions. When they declined to help, Dixie forced the men to write a letter to the
Council explaining why.[16]

The wives' petition is clearly written by a professional scribe; it follows all
conventions of orientation and salutation. By comparison, the letters by Dixie,
Byrd, and Watts are all in their own respective hands, in a portrait orientation.
The material letters themselves thus testify to the depth of the class divide of
these writers, painting a powerful portrait of the parties involved. The wives'
petition is moving, eliciting a strong response from the Council and Dixie, who
writes on their behalf directly in his own hand. Dixie's letter conveys his disgust
at the owners. After noting that he "carefullye treated with them for some succor
and relefe to those poore women," and was refused, he "willed them to sett downe
theire aunswers herein under theire handes which I have thowght good to send
your Lordships herein inclosed."[17] In effect, he has punished the owners by forc-
ing them to attempt to justify themselves to the Council, to admit their meanness
in their own hands. Those letters need to be viewed side by side to get the full effect of both the wives' ability to influence those in power and the humiliation the
owners must have felt in being forced to expose their stinginess.

On the back of the owners' letter, there is a summary of the contents: "The
marchantes do refuse to contribute to the relief of the marriners wiefes whose
husbandes are staied in Spayne: alleaging the great losses wch them selfes haue
suffered by the arrest." Notice that the summary grants them no endorsement;
it's not that the owners are unable to pay, but that they refuse to pay. This note
leads me to my last general point about manuscript study: the importance of
marginalia and other annotations. Clerks typically summarized the contents of
the petitions in this fashion. Seeing what they emphasize in the summary enables us to gain a sense of audience reception. In rarer cases, marginalia convey
the disposition of a particular petition or the actions taken to date. Joan Dennys's
1583 petition about being cheated out of money includes the marginal note: "the
Plaintyf to be called wth all," to appear before the Council.[18] Margaret Shaw's
1578 petition about her husband's imprisonment in Spain includes a note that

---

Greenwood Press, 2002), 115. The mariners received no help; the men of the *Emmanuel* were
condemned to death and five of the *Julian*'s crew perished of starvation in prison (168).

[16] PRO SP 12/187/57. 24 March 1586. Byrd and Watts, who received letters of reprisal
against Spanish ships, presumably were able to recoup their fortunes, since both backed ships
again. Another letter, undated, by their fellow owners, Richard Wyseman and John Hawes, is
PRO SP 12/187/59. Wyseman and Hawes received no such letters of reprisal, and so, they argued, they were doubly unable to relieve the wives' poverty.

[17] PRO SP 12/187/57.

[18] PRO SP 12/163/34. October 1583.

"A letter was written in May last to the k[ing] from hir Majestie for his release."[19] Many times, such notes are the only indication of actions taken, especially since many of the women making these petitions are from the lower classes, and thus would not otherwise leave an archival trail.

Before I conclude, I would like to examine one petition in detail to explore its rhetorical complexity and demonstrate how considering a manuscript's layout, handwriting, and marginalia can help us to understand its context and reception. Jayne Gouldwyar's 1580 petition to Walsingham seeks her release from the Clink, where she has been a prisoner for twelve months.[20] Her petition, which is in landscape orientation and opens with a typical salutation, includes a signature in the lower right corner in the same hand as the rest of the letter. If the hand is Gouldwyar's, it signifies that she knew the conventions of petitionary letters; even if the letter is written by a scribe, it is clear that she desired to use the proper forms.

The content of Gouldwyar's petition is painstakingly crafted to convey the right message. She outlines no less than five separate roles for herself at the start:

> yor pore and daylie oraratrixe Jayne Gouldwyar, a pore afflyctted creator, and one that hayth lyvd presoner in the Clynke this twellmoneth for hir consiaunce hawynge ffyve small children dryven to seke ther harde adventure in this wycked ayge by reson of the trobles of me ther poure mothar Whoo is and Ewar wylbe a lovynge and dughtiffull subiect to her magiste.[21]

Her first four categories of self-identification—a daily petitioner, an afflicted creature, a prisoner, and a mother of five—demonstrate her attempts to appeal to Walsingham's pity; Gouldwyar evokes a terrible picture of a miserably worried mother locked in prison while her young children are left alone to shift for themselves for a year. That image underscores the rationality of her request that Walsingham release her for two months to settle her affairs, especially since she promises to pay "sufficiente bayll" and to return after the two months to the Marshalsea prison for as long as the Queen pleases.

The last of Gouldwyar's five categories, that of "lovynge and dughtifull subject," reassures him that she is no danger to the Queen. At the same time, her insistence that she has been imprisoned "for hir consiaunce" suggests that she

---

[19] PRO SP 12/126/38. 1578.
[20] PRO SP 12/146/132. 1580?
[21] PRO SP 12/146/132. 1580?

is suffering for religion's sake. Although Gouldwyar concedes that she will not commit any offence "by instructing any others of hir Majesties subjectes," she still holds whatever beliefs caused her incarceration. Immediately she undermines her proffered compromise by insisting that she "but desiar[s] to lyve according to my Contiance tell [till] shouch tyme as it maye plese god that I maye confarr with shouch as shall perswayd me that I stand in Error." The ambiguity of this statement, that she will change her mind as soon as someone persuades her that she is wrong, allows her to profess an open mind, while insisting on her intent to follow her conscience until that unspecified day of conversion. Thus, even as she apparently grants a concession, she preserves her right to dissent.

Gouldwyar's final prayer contains further possibilities for slippage. After professing her allegiance to the Queen and her willingness to return to prison for as long as Elizabeth wishes, Gouldwyar vows to "offar upe to god hir dayle prayers for the longe and prosperus estayt of hir Majestie with increse of vartue." Read one way, Gouldwyar makes the innocuous suggestion that she is praying for Elizabeth's benefit. A different, ironic reading of this prayer implies that Gouldwyar believes the Queen requires an increase of virtue. Her careful maneuvering throughout the petition creates sufficient leeway to enable the existence of such veiled critique.

Despite such potential criticism of Elizabeth and her ambiguous professions of belief, studying the marginalia reveals a note on the petition, perhaps in Walsingham's own hand, that Gouldwyar is "To be released." The ambiguous phrasing makes it unclear whether this note is a summary of her petition or a note on the disposition of her case, but if the latter, Gouldwyar's emotional appeals, her reasonable tone, and her professions of allegiance have persuaded Walsingham that she merits her liberty. Regardless, her petition is a striking example of a woman's ability to craft a delicate rhetorical position even if working with a scribe, and the marginalia suggests its power to persuade.

Unfortunately, all too often scholars must rely on the descriptions of manuscript contents in the *Calendar of State Papers*, a fact that becomes particularly problematic for women's texts, which often get short shrift in the catalogs. In Gouldwyar's case, the *Calendar* reads only: "Petition of Jane Gouldwyar, a 'pore afflycted creator' to Sir Fr. Walsyngham. Has been a prisoner in the Clink for 12 months for conscience sake. Having 5 small children destitute and wandering about, prays to be released." Reducing Gouldwyar's complex self-representation to "a poor afflicted creature," this sparse account fails to capture the effect of Gouldwyar's moving and sophisticated plea, still less the fact that it may have succeeded.

These petitionary letters were written to represent their authors, to travel across literal distances to allow them to appear at court and to bridge even the metaphorical distance of class. Knowing that they might never appear in person before their audiences, these writers worked carefully to create the best persuasive arguments possible. But perhaps what none of these women could have imagined is that the letters would cross the boundaries of 400 years to represent themselves before us today. Only by looking at the material text of the letter can we approach a more complete understanding of the author's self-fashioning and the context in which each document was written. The manuscript letter mattered then. It still matters now.

MARYWOOD UNIVERSITY

'Saturn (whose aspects soe sads my soul)': Lady Hester Pulter's Feminine Melancholic Genius

ALICE EARDLEY

ONE DAY TOWARDS THE END OF THE 1640S LADY HESTER PULTER (1605–1678), who was confined to her husband's manor house, Bradfield in Hertfordshire, sat down and poured years of sorrow and frustration into a lengthy poem (MS Lt q 32, fols. 79r–81r). Complaining bitterly about being "shut up in a Countrey Grange," she rails against an injustice which means that, although dangerous creatures are allowed to roam freely, she will "in this sad confinement living Die." She is, she says, "inslaved to solitude" and "buried thus alive," but by far the most troubling aspect of this situation is that solitude is "the cruelest Curb unto a Noble Mind." At one point, she demands to know:

> Why must I thus forever bee confin'd
> Against the noble Freedome of my Mind

But the poem provides no answers, and nearly four centuries later we are left to speculate about the reasons for her strong sense of physical and mental oppression. A possible explanation is provided by the periods of confinement associated with childbirth. Between 1624 and 1648 Pulter gave birth to a total of fifteen children, only two of whom survived her. This means that for a period of twenty-four years Pulter was caught in an almost continual cycle of pregnancy,

This paper was first presented at the 2006 MLA convention, Philadelphia, PA, as part of a panel entitled "Early Modern Women's Manuscripts," Margaret P. Hannay, Siena College, presiding.

childbirth, and mourning. At the same time, she was also engaged in the composition of an extensive collection of poetry, over one hundred poems in total,
which she would later compile, together with a lengthy prose romance, in a handsome presentation manuscript now in the Brotherton Library in Leeds.[1] This text
is one of the most substantial literary manuscripts we have by an early modern
Englishwoman, but it is only just beginning to receive the critical attention it
warrants. With this paper I intend to provide some sense both of Pulter's literary
persona and also of her specific poetical achievement.

Pulter's father was James Ley, who would eventually become the first Earl
of Marlborough and one of James I's privy councillors. So Pulter was brought up
in close connection to the court during a reign often considered antithetical to
women's learning. The king's statement on the matter is well known:

> it hath like operation to make women learned, as to make foxes tame, which
> teacheth them only to steal more cunningly, the possibility is not equal, for
> where it doth one good, it doth twenty harm.[2]

But Pulter's manuscript suggests that not only was she very well educated, she
was also keen to assert her intellectual status. She displays her learning through

---

[1] Leeds Brotherton MS Lt q 32. I would like to thank Dr. Elizabeth Clarke for introducing me to this manuscript.

For a detailed biography and account of the manuscript see Sarah Ross, "Women and Religious Verse in English Manuscript Culture, c. 1600–1668: Lady Anne Southwell, Lady Hester
Pulter and Katherine Austen" (D.Phil. diss., Oxford, 2000).

Pulter's own manuscript provides conflicting evidence about her date of birth, but in a
manuscript entitled "Ley: his pedigree" (W.R.O., 366/1) her father, James Ley, states that she
was born "neere Dublin, in the realme of Ireland, uppon Saturdaie beinge the viiith daie of
June in the yeare of the raigne of King James of England and Ireland the 3, and of Scotland the
xxxviiith Anno dmi. 1605."

Selections of Pulter's poetry are reproduced in: Jane Stevenson and Peter Davidson, eds.,
Early Modern Women Poets (Oxford: Oxford Univ. Press, 2001), 187–94; and Jill Seal-Millman
and Gillian Wright, eds., *Early Modern Women's Manuscript Poetry* (Manchester: Manchester
Univ. Press, 2005), 111–27. For further information about Pulter see Mark Robson, "Pulter,
Lady Hester (1595/6–1678)," *Oxford Dictionary of National Biography* (Oxford: Oxford Uni-
versity Press, 2004), 45:559. For discussions of Pulter's poetry see Jayne Archer, "A 'Perfect
Circle'? Alchemy in the Poetry of Hester Pulter"; Elizabeth Clarke, "Introducing Hester Pulter
and the Perdita Project"; Mark Robson, "Reading Hester Pulter Reading"; and Sarah Ross,
"Tears, Bezoars and Blazing Comets: Gender and Politics in Hester Pulter's Civil War Lyrics,"
all in *Blackwell Synergy: Literature Compass*, vol. 2, Issue 1 (2005).

[2] Reproduced in Thomas Bayly, *Witty apophthegms delivered at several times, and upon
several occasions by King James, King Charls, the Marquess of Worcester, Francis Lord Bacon,
and Sir Thomas Moor; collected and revised* (London: Matthew Smelt, 1669), 19.

the wealth of references that saturate her poetry and also through her evidently sophisticated knowledge of contemporary literary culture. She appropriates the literary tropes conventionally associated with poetry by men and uses them to explore specifically female experiences. A central theme of her poetry is her grief at the loss of so many children, and she flouts religious conventions dictating that the expression of excessive maternal grief was inappropriate. In many of her poems she engages in activities expressly forbidden in contemporary advice manuals, such as dwelling on her own personal loss and recalling the physical beauty of her dead children.[3] In order to legitimise the expression of her grief in this way, Pulter adopts the conventional persona of the "melancholy poet." This enables her to identify her poetry with a discourse which privileged grief, sorrow, and mourning as a sign of artistic and creative superiority. The sense of intellectual status and learning that Pulter is keen to display through her poetry is reinforced by the physical apparatus of the manuscript, including marginalia and binding, which are designed to foster a sense of literary professionalism and to locate both herself and her text within a broad intellectual community.

Pulter was well aware of the conventions of early seventeenth-century melancholy. In her prose romance, "The Unfortunate Florinda", her lovelorn hero appears in the guise of a "malecontented Lover walking (just like the picture in the frontispiece of Democritus junior with his hat over his eys)" (fol. 5r). So she was evidently familiar with Robert Burton's impressive study of the condition, *The Anatomy of Melancholy*. A key emblem of the condition was the planet Saturn, which, Burton writes, if it is "predominant in his nativity" will cause a man to be "very austere, sullen, churlish, black of colour, profound in his cogitations, full of cares, miseries, and discontents, sad and fearefull, alwaies silent, [and] solitary."[4] Pulter certainly associates her own melancholic nature with the planet which, she says, is her "assendent" (fol. 57r).[5] In another poem she complains

---

[3] Elizabeth Clarke, "'A Heart Terrifying Sorrow': The Deaths of Children in Seventeenth-Century Women's Manuscript Journals," in Gillian Avery, ed., *Representations of Childhood Death* (Basingstoke: Macmillan, 2000), 65–86.

[4] Robert Burton, *The Anatomy of Melancholy*, vol. 1, ed. Thomas C. Faulkner, Nicolas K. Kiessling, and Rhonda L. Blair, with an introduction by J. B. Bamborough (Oxford: Clarendon Press, 1989), 396. For an exploration of the relationship between Saturn and the melancholic character see Raymond Klibansky, Erwin Panofsky, and Fritz Saxl, *Saturn and Melancholy: Studies in the History of Natural Philosophy, Religion and Art* (London: Nelson, 1964).

[5] The fact that Pulter was born on a Saturday supports her claim to have been born under the planet Saturn. Her contemporary, Elizabeth Isham, notes in her autobiography that her mother says she has a melancholic character because she "was borne on a Saturday and that the planet after which the day was called, had dominion over me": Elizabeth Isham (1609–1654), "Autobiography" (ca. 1640), Princeton University Library, Robert H. Taylor Collection RTC01 no. 62, fol. 17v.

that "Saturns heavie eye, /Frowns on [her] with Malignancie" (fol. 57r) and it is Saturn "whose aspects soe sads [her] soul." She blames the planet's influence for inducing the black moods so evident throughout her poetry. Traditionally associated with grief and loss, melancholy was a negative and undesirable condition. Aristotle however had observed that all great men were melancholics, and in the fifteenth century Marsilio Ficino had turned melancholia into a positive virtue for men of letters by insisting that those who fell under the unlucky planet were particularly gifted. Instead of being marginalised or alienated the melancholic man was in fact exceptional and talented.[6] But, as these examples suggest, women were systematically excluded from discussions of the melancholy character. Juliana Schiesari has argued that the discourse of melancholy, associated with inspired artistry and genius, grants male suffering a privileged spiritual and creative status, but that female loss or grief, characterised as a debilitating physical condition, is expressed as inarticulate mourning. She quotes Burton who, describing female melancholics, states that "Many of them cannot tell how to express themselves in wordes" (*Anatomy,* 415). Despite her obvious grief, Pulter, as her manuscript attests, was anything but inarticulate. Adopting the traditionally male persona of the melancholic artist, she rewrites her own personal, and feminine, grief as the expression of a superior intellect.

A particularly distinctive element of Pulter's poetry is that while she adopts the conventions of poetry traditionally written by men she does not negate her own female body in the process. Her poems frequently allude to the experience of her own body, either directly after she has given birth or in the poignant awareness of her gradual physical decline into old age. It is from this explicitly gendered body that Pulter's own experiences of grief and sorrow emerge. This is particularly clear in a poem with the exhausting title:

> This was written 1648, when I Lay Inn, with my Son John, beeing my 15 Child, I beeing soe weak, that in Ten dayes and Nights I never moved my Head one jot from my Pillow, out of which great weaknes, my gracious God restored me, that I still live to magnifie his Mercie. 1665 (fols. 67r–68v).[7]

Pulter identifies her poem with the illness she experienced during the period of confinement following the birth of her son John. The poem makes it clear that her illness is causing emotional in addition to physical distress, and that this suffering is a direct consequence of the specifically gendered experience of postpartum confinement. Similarly, in another poem entitled "A Solitary discours" she

---

    [6] Julia Schiesari, *The Gendering of Melancholia: Feminism, Psychoanalysis and the Symbolics of Loss in Renaissance Literature* (Ithaca: Cornell Univ. Press, 1992), 6–7.
    [7] From now on this poem will be referred to as "This was written."

associates her depressive state with darkness and "Melancholy Night" attributing it to "sicknes age and Grief (of all the worst)" (fols. 64v–67r). This grief takes the form of "Cipres Buds," symbols of mourning, placed within the garlands of love adorning her marriage, where they provide a reminder of the deaths of several of her young children. In this instance Pulter's sorrow is tied up in her earthly love for her husband. She alludes to the sexual elements of their relationship but provides a poignant reminder of a darker side to the pleasures of the "Nuptial Bed." (Both poems are provided in the Appendix to this paper.)

In both poems, Pulter legitimises the expression of her feminine grief by refashioning it along the lines of scholarly melancholy. This is primarily apparent in her references to Saturn, a figure presiding over masculine melancholy but also encoded with meanings particularly appropriate for Pulter's own experience of the condition. In "This was written," Pulter's reference to Saturn "who so sads [her] soul" is embedded within a mental exploration of the planets. In this instance, Saturn, in keeping with convention, presides over a melancholy temperament associated with intellect and learning. In "A Solitary Discours," however, Pulter blames the fall of mankind for the planets' malignant influence. She states that if this had not occurred:

> Then unto them [the planets] I should bee Independent
> Nor need ~~nor~~ I fear though Saturn's my assendent
> But now I'me troubled ready still to cry
> Cause at my Birth some Planet look't awry

Through their influence on the humours, the planets have a direct effect on the human body and, through this, the mind. Pulter blames this influence, particularly the influence of Saturn, on original sin, which was ultimately responsible for women's eternal suffering and punishment through childbirth. As a mythological figure, Saturn encodes these particular meanings: he ate his own offspring immediately after they were born and was therefore connected with the death, particularly during birth, of young children. With its dual significance, the figure of Saturn provides a symbol combining a specifically female mode of grief and emotional torment with a superior degree of learning and intelligence. Pulter's reference to the fall also provides a sinister reminder that original sin was associated with a woman's bid for knowledge. She asserts the ultimate justification for associating female pain and suffering with the quest for knowledge and learning.

Pulter claims to have written both poems from a position of segregation and confinement; in the one, the title makes explicit that her poem is a "*Solitary* discours" (my italics) and the other is located within the isolation of her bed. For the scholarly, intellectual male a sense of isolation, lack of recognition, and the melancholy induced by excessive learning were integral to the melancholic condition. Burton states that among men, scholars are particularly prone to melancholy because "they live a sedentary, solitary life . . . free from bodily exercise" and because they indulge in "overmuch study" (*Anatomy*, 303). Among women, however, melancholy afflicts "nice gentlewomen, such as are solitary and idle, live at ease, lead a life out of action and imployment, that fare well in great houses" (416). Pulter, who was herself subject to enforced periods of isolation and who was certainly genteel, sets about rewriting her seclusion as a space of study and intellectual exploration. In "This was written" she bids her thoughts transcend their physical incarceration and instead "take their flieght / Above the Gloomey shades of Death and Night." What follows is a detailed and learned exploration of the planets, bearing testament to Pulter's interest in the latest scientific developments.[8] It is also a spiritual meditation in which she contemplates God's creation until "their [the planets'] vast Brightnes soe [her] Mind amazed / That [her] afrighted Fancie Downward Flew." During her imaginative exploration she comes close to apprehending divine truths denied her human mind.

Pulter's knowledgeable exploration of the planets concludes with the alleviation of her suffering when "the Howers Auroras Curtain Drew." Similarly, in "A Solitary discourse," it is Aurora, the goddess of dawn, who "Doth scorn and Trample Melancholy Night." Unfortunately for Pulter this provides only temporary respite and she complains:

> But yet (alas) what comfort's in this Light
> That is alternately pursued by Night
> Insted of bringing of my soul relief
> It doth successivly renew my griefe

She describes a condition identified by Burton as a type of melancholy experienced only by women, particularly those who "lie in child-bed" which causes "much solitarinesse, weeping, distraction, etc., from which they are sometimes suddenly delivered, because it comes and goes by fits" (*Anatomy*, 414–15). For Pulter, the relief brought to her physical suffering is an ambiguous one because although it alleviates her pain, it also curtails the intellectual and spiritual freedom which she associates with this specifically female type of melancholy. Pulter's treatment of melancholy in this way has a significant precedent: in 1645

---

[8] Sarah Hutton, "A New Star: Astronomy and Platonism in the Poetry of Hester Pulter (1596–1678)," presented at the EMPHASIS seminar, Institute of English Studies, London, 4 November 2006.

John Milton had published "L'Allegro" and "Il Penseroso" in which he explores the significance of the melancholic temperament for poetical creativity.[9] During the early years of the 1640s Pulter's sister Margaret had been a neighbour and good friend of the poet and he had addressed his tenth sonnet to her, in which he praised the "ingenious" Margaret for possessing the learning and eloquence of her father.[10] It seems possible that through this connection, Pulter was familiar with Milton's writing. In "L'Allegro," Milton identifies melancholy with hell and "blackest Midnight" which are dispelled by Euphrosyne. He describes Euphrosyne, or mirth, as the daughter of "Zephyr with Aurora playing." Aurora's daughter ushers in a pastoral world of communal creativity adorned with the plays of Jonson and Shakespeare. Similarly in Pulter's "Solitary Discours":

> . . . Aurora sprinkles Dew like Pearles
> On Ceres Corn gather'd by Rurall Girles
> To wash the freckles from their lovly face
> That in their lovers eys they may find Grace

Aurora brings light to a pastoral world associated with the heathen fecundity of Ceres, goddess of grain and women, and the simplicity of "Rurall Girles," concerned only with their lovers. In "This was written" Aurora returns Pulter to a world in which "Mayds [her] Window Curtains Drew / And as [her] Pain soe Comforts did renew." The alleviation of suffering is associated with her return to the domestic world of her bedchamber. In both poems Aurora is associated with an earthly, female existence far removed from the spiritual and intellectual transcendence afforded by a condition of melancholy. For Milton, in "Il Penseroso," Aurora and the daylight she brings with her curtail the creative darkness associated with Saturn's daughter Melancholy. Similarly, Pulter's mental flights of exploration occur during her periods of physical and emotional suffering and are curtailed once she is restored to light and comfort. For both poets melancholy is an ambiguous condition bringing suffering but also spiritual and creative elevation. For Pulter specifically this condition emerges from the experiences of an explicitly female body.

The creative and intellectual superiority to which Pulter lays claim in her poetry, specifically through the adoption of a melancholy persona, is reinforced by the physical characteristics of her manuscript. The text is a presentation copy

---

[9] All references to Milton's poetry are taken from John Carey, ed., *John Milton: The Complete Shorter Poems*, rev. 2nd ed. (Harlow: Pearson Longman, 2007).

[10] Edward Phillips, *The Early Lives of Milton*, ed. Helen Darbishire (London: Constable, 1932), 64.

beautifully penned by a professional scribe, bound in brown velvet and embossed with gold lettering. Pulter herself carefully checked through the transcription correcting mistakes and adding annotations. But there is no indication that the text was intended for circulation beyond the confines of her immediate family. The specific concerns afflicting the male melancholic scholar, including lack of recognition among the scholarly community, are an inescapable part of Pulter's gendered existence when the opportunities available to the female writer were greatly restricted. Pulter, however, seeks to transcend this isolation through a deliberate and knowledgeable interaction with contemporary literary culture. Her identification with the wider scholarly community is reinforced by the series of references inscribed in the margins of her emblem poems. In his recent study of early modern melancholy, Douglas Trevor has explored the role played by the material text, specifically marginalia, in the construction of a (male) scholarly persona.[11] Exploring texts including those by Burton and Milton, he argues that the means and frequency with which authors use citations or quotations reveals a great deal about their scholarly confidence or anxiety. Pulter's marginal comments, appearing in both her own and the scribal hand, suggest that she was engaging with a wide range of contemporary and classical authors, including Pliny, Plutarch, John Donne, Robert Sanderson, Francis Bacon, and Richard Verstegan. What they reveal is that Pulter used her text as a means of entering into intellectual exchange with a scholarly community from which she was physically excluded. While several of the references are used to provide supporting evidence for her material, many more provide examples of conflicting uses of analogous ideas or images. She is therefore engaging in debate with these texts and in doing so she is asserting her own intellectual prowess. Pulter's self-conscious construction of an intellectual persona comes across most clearly in those examples where she has lifted references directly from other texts; in one example she takes an incorrect page reference to an example in Plutarch from Simon Goulart's commentary on Du Bartas' *Divine Weeks* (1621).[12] In these instances she is deliberately fostering the impression of knowledge which she doesn't necessarily have. Pulter is therefore reinforcing her claims to melancholic genius with the ostentatious display of knowledge. A comparison of Pulter's reading with the handful of studies that we have on the reading habits of her contemporaries suggests that, for her

---

[11] Douglas Trevor, *The Poetics of Melancholy in Early Modern England* (Cambridge: Cambridge Univ. Press, 2004).

[12] Simon Goulart, *A Learned Summary Upon the Famous Poeme of William of Saluste, Lord of Bartas* (1621). The incorrect page reference refers to Pliny's account of the stork; in Pulter's manuscript it is included in the margin to fol. 97r.

class and gender, her choice of texts is not unusual.[13] What is unusual, however, is Pulter's very deliberate claim to an elevated intellectual status, which is both specifically feminine and also on a par with that of her male contemporaries.

WARWICK UNIVERSITY

---

[13] These studies include Heidi Brayman Hackel, "The Countess of Bridgewater's London Library," in Jennifer Andersen and Elizabeth Sauer, eds., *Books and Readers in Early Modern England: Material Studies* (Philadelphia: Univ. of Pennsylvania Press, 2002), 138–59; Richard T. Spence, *Lady Anne Clifford, Countess of Pembroke, Dorset and Montgomery (1590-1676)* (Phoenix Mill: Sutton, 1997); Sister Jean Carmel Cavanaugh, S. L., "The Library of Lady Southwell and Captain Sibthorpe," *Studies in Bibliography* 20 (1967): 243–54.

Appendix

[64v] A Solitary discoars:[14]

How canst thou heavie bee now shee apears
My Pencive soul that with her Luster cheers
All drooping spirits lift up thy sad eyes
Behold \how/ horrid Darkness from her Flyes
Doe thou but look how at the sight of Day
With sable Wings shee scowling flyes away
Look how Aurora with her Orient Light
Doth scorn and Trample Melancholy Night
Nay pale facet Cinthia with her Glittring train
Hide all away for fear of her disdain   10
But yet (alas) what comfort's in this Light
That is alternately pursued by Night
Insted of bringing of my soul relief
It doth successivly renew my griefe
There is noe cheerfull light below the skies
Nor can wee see it till wee loos our eyes
Did I not hope my souls of Heavenly Birth
Let mee bee nothing if I debreath on Earth
[65r] But on condition of Eternall Glory
I am contented with my lifs sad story   20
For shame my soul l\eve/ this base discontent[15]
And cheerly look up to the firmament
See how Aurora sprinkles Dew like Pearles
On Ceres Corn gather'd by Rurall Girles
To wash the freckles from their lovly face
That in their lovers eyes they may find Grace
Alas whats beuty with such Care up Nurst
When sicknes age and Grief (of all the worst)
Have acted all their parts then comes \pale/ Death
And closes up their eyes and stops their Breath   30
How empty and how vain is Carnall Love
Compard but with a Glimps of Joyes above

---

[14] "A solitary discoars" inserted in Pulter's hand. The text that follows is an uncorrected transcription of the scribal manuscript.
[15] 'eve' inserted in Pulter's hand.

I was in youth a Modest Virgin Bred
And brought with Honnour to my Nuptial Bed
To a most Lovly Youth and Noblely Born
Vertue and Beuty did his youth adorn
Our Musick then had sweet and Pleasant Closes
Crownd were our Heads with Mertle and with Roses
Which to this Howr are Flowry Fresh and Green
Thoug\h/ Cipres Buds were here and there between   40
[65v] Stuck in By \advers/ fate to cool our love
Or elce that wee should place our thoughts above
Where onely is ~~pure~~ \true/ love and lasting Peace[16]
That ~~love~~ love shall last when Faith and hope shall cease
From Heaven my soul (From Heaven) thy comfort springs
For Earth (alas) nought but afliction Brings
Look up once more hears that thy Heart will ease
Or surely nothing will thy Fancie Please
Mark how Apollo this salubrious Morning
With Dazling beams his splendent Face adorning   50
Came Glittring Forth in most refulgent grace
Joying to run his Occidendentall Race
Scorning his eyes should take a slumbring Nap
Untill hee layes in Wanton Thetis Lap
His Flagrant Head, then shee in love belaves
His Burning Tresses with her cooler Waves
And that sweet Dew on Flowers Redolent
Which Breaths to us an aromattick ~~F~~sent
Hee with his Heat exhales above our vew
Which doth Nocturnally descend in Dew   60
See how the solysequem thrusts her Head
Up through the Center from that common Bed
[66r] Into the Liquid Azure Sea above Her
To follow Phoebus her admired Lover
When hee in our Horizon gives his Race
Then in the Ayr shee shews her Lovly face
Soe when hee is our Zeneth at mid Day
Shee at full Lenght her Beuty doth display
But when the sun is Nadar to us here

---

[16] 'true' inserted in Pulter's hand.

Shee meets him in the other Hemesspheir   70
To see these Marvels and this shineing Lamp
Dazles mine eyes and doth my spirit damp
For when I doe his Orient splendour see
It more discovers my deformitie
If I but look upon his blazing beuty
Hee burns mee black for fayling soe in Duty
But if in Innocence I had stood upright
Nor Sun nor Moon should hurt mee Day nor Night
But I (ay mee) in Adam fell from Glory,
Which makes mee live a Life most trancetory   80
Then those Celestiall Orbs that shine soe bright
Should Fellows bee and further our delight
Happy should bee their influence and Dances
Both their ful eyed aspects and secret Glances
[66v] Then unto them I should bee Independent
Nor need nor I fear though Saturn's my assendent
But now I'me troubled ready still to cry
Cause at my Birth some Planet look't awry
Forgetting him that them and mee did make
Who of his Children constant care doth take   90
And those Celestiall Works of Wonder
Hee knowes their Names, Natures and Number
Their turning and their constant stations
And every influence of those constellation
In God my soul trust ever and depend
Soe shalt thou live a life that nere shall end
Nor bee thou hopeles when thy Body's Crumbled
And with all Creatures in this Mass is jumbled
But at thy Death sing cheerfully a requem
For thou with joy shall like the Solisequem   100
Meet thy Redeemer in a Horiscope
Brighter then this thy Flesh shall rest in hope
And thou shalt see thy saviour with these eyes
When that bright sun of Righteousness shall rise
With Healing Wings hee shall from my sad eyes
And from all Faces elce wipe of the tears
Soe from all Hearts hee will dispell all Fears
[67r] Oh then (till then) send Grace into my Heart

Which from my Throbing Bosome ne're shall part
But I'le improv't my few and evill Dayes   110
Untill it doth exhale in thanks and praise.

This was written 1648, when I Lay Inn, with my Son John Pulter, beeing my 15
Child, I beeing soe weak, that in Ten dayes and Nights I never moved my Head
one jot from my Pillow, out of which great weaknes, my gracious God restored
me, that I still Live to magnifie his Mercie. 16565.[17]

Sad, sick and Lame, as in my Bed I lay
Least Pain and Passion should bear all the sway
My thoughts beeing free I bid them take their flieght
Above the Gloomey shades of Death and Night
They overjoyed with such a Large Commission
Flew instantly without all intermission
Up to that spheir where Nights Pale Queen doth run
Round the Circumference of the Illustrious sun
Her Globious Body spacious was and Bright
That Half alone that from Sols Beams had Light   10
The other was imured in shades of Night
Nor did shee seem to mee as Poets fain
Guiding her Chariot with a silver Rein
Attir'd like som fair Nimph or virgin Queen
With naked Neck and arms and Robes of Green
[67v] Love sick Endimion oft hath thus her seen
But as my thoughts about her Orb was Hurld
I did perceive shee was another World
Thus beeing in my Fancie raisd soe fare
This World apear'd to mee another star   20
And as the Moon a shadow Casts and Light
Soe is our Earth the Empres of their Night
Next Venus Usher to the Night and Day
Her ful Faced Beuty to mee did Display
Some time shee Waned then again increase
Which in our humours caus or War or Peace
My fancie next to Mercury would Run
But craftily hee popt b'hind the sun
A wonder t'is the medium beeing soe Bright

---

[17] In the manuscript '1655' has been added to the end of this line in an unidentified hand.

His splendencie should bee obscur'd by Night   30
Nor could I Sols refulgent Orb discrie
His raidient Beames dazled my tender eye
And now my Wonder is again renewed
That hee enlightening all could not bee vewed
Yet to my Reason this apeard the Best
That hee the Center was of all the rest
The Planets all like Bowlls still trundling round
The vast Circumference of the Glorious Mound
[68r] Hee resting quickens all with Heat and Light
And by the earths motion makes our Day or Night   40
Next Jupiter that Mild auspicious starr
I did perceive about his Blazing Carr
Four bright attendents alwayes hurrid Round
Next Flagrant Mars where noe such Moons are found
Then Saturn (whose aspects soe sads my soul)
About whose Orb two sickly Cinthias rowl
Then on the Fixed stars I would have Gazed
But their vast Brightnes soe my Mind amazed
That my afrighted Fancie Downward Flew
Just as the Howers Auroras Curtain Drew   50
At which the Uglie Wife of Accharon
Bid drive and slashed her Drousey Monsters on
With Her there went her first born Brat old errour
And Fierce Eumenedes poor Mortals terrour
Who with their snakes, and whips, and Brands were hurld
To strike amazement to the Lower World
Beeing scard themselves at the approach of Light
To our antipodes they took their Flieght
Sins Cursed ofspring with their Dam did Trace
That most Prodigious incestious Race   60
Pale Gastly shudring Horrour, lost despair
And sobbing sorrow, tearing of her Hair
[68v] These of her sable Womb were born and Bred
And from the Light with her now frighted fled
And then my Mayds my Window Curtains Drew
And as my Pain soe Comforts did renew
Unto the God of truth, Light Life, and Love
Ile such Layes Here begin shall end above

Print Studies

Chronicling Elizabeth Tyrwhit's Morning and Evening Prayers: A Narrative of Devotional Reform

SUSAN M. FELCH

I N THE SMALL VILLAGE OF LEIGHTON BROMSWOLD, THE PARISH CHURCH sits at the end of a quiet paved road. Most pilgrims come to see the unusual twin wooden pulpits, part of the renovations overseen by George Herbert during his tenure as prebend at Lincoln Cathedral. Many overlook the rather shabby tomb of a knight and his lady pushed against the outside wall in the northern apse, their figures recumbent on a marble slab. The monument is remarkable, however, because the lady, Elizabeth Oxenbridge Tyrwhit (ca. 1510–1578), clasps a small book in her hands. Although its inscriptions are worn away, it is tempting to imagine that the book's cover once read *Morning and Evening Prayers with divers Psalmes, Himnes, and Meditations made by the Lady Elizabeth Tirwit* and that the stone volume memorializes Tyrwhit's own prayerbook, entered in the Stationers' Register in 1569, first printed in 1574 in a 32° edition, and later reprinted in Thomas Bentley's 1582 *The Monument of Matrones*. A copy of the prayerbook itself, according to the eighteenth-century antiquarian John Nichols, was presented to the Princess Elizabeth during her 1554 confinement in the Tower of London by her sister, Mary Tudor.[1] His information came by good authority of the Ashby family, who owned a tiny girdlebook copy of the prayerbook. According to family lore, the Queen gave this book to one

This paper was first presented at the annual meeting of the Renaissance Society of America (2002) in Scottsdale, AZ, at a panel entitled "Editing Early Modern Women's Writing," Margaret P. Hannay, Siena College, presiding.

[1] John Nichols, *The Progresses, and Public Processions, of Queen Elizabeth* (London: Society of Antiquaries, 1788), 1:xxvi–xxvii note.

of her "women of the Bed-chamber," from whence it passed from generation to generation, a beloved and venerated object.

1554—the presentation to Elizabeth; 1569—entry in the Stationers' Register; 1574—first printed edition; 1582—inclusion in *The Monument of Matrones*: these four moments in the chronicle of a sixteenth-century prayerbook are drenched with romance. But the anecdotes are misleading, and not only because the purported presentation to Elizabeth antedates the actual printing of the volume. More importantly, they deform Tyrwhit's prayerbook into a sentimental keepsake, obscure its origins in the court of Katherine Parr, fail to account for the changes it underwent in the course of its printing history, and underestimate its significance as a text. What they *do* get right is a sense of Elizabeth Tyrwhit's importance to the narrative of devotional reform in the sixteenth century.

Elizabeth Tyrwhit is probably best known as a lady of the Privy Chamber in Katherine Parr's court and later as governess to the Princess Elizabeth during the brief period when Kat Astley was confined to the Tower of London. John Foxe names her among the godly women who were placed in jeopardy when Henry VIII questioned Parr's orthodoxy and loyalty, noting that Tyrwhit was "in very great favour and credite" with the queen by reason of "her vertuous disposition."[2] After Henry's death, Tyrwhit and her husband Robert, a cousin by marriage to the dowager queen,[3] continued to serve Parr and her new husband, Thomas Seymour, and gave testimony to the Privy Counsel regarding Parr's death.[4] One anecdote from this period confirms that Tyrwhit was known not only for her virtue, but also for her learning. In the course of an evening's conversation with her, Thomas Seymour remarked to Robert Tyrwhit, "Master *Tyrwhyt* I ame talkynge

[2] John Foxe, *[T]he ecclesiasticall history contaynyng the actes and monumentes of thynges passed in euery kynges tyme in this realme* (London, 1570; *STC* 11223), 1423. The account of Parr's gospelling activities and subsequent confrontation with Henry VIII is first recorded in the second edition of *Actes and Monuments* (1570), pages 1422–25, and is repeated in the 1576 (pages 1212–14) and 1583 (pages 1242–44) editions. Quotations from Foxe are cited from John Foxe. *Acts and Monuments [. . .]. The Variorum Edition.* [online]. (hriOnline, Sheffield 2004). Available from: http://www.hrionline.ac.uk/foxe/. [Accessed: 09.30.2004.]

[3] Sir Robert Tyrwhit's aunt Agnes (Anne) Tyrwhit married Thomas, third Baron Borough; Edward Borough, their son, was the first husband of Katherine Parr (A. R. Maddison, ed., *Lincolnshire Pedigrees*, Publications of the Harleian Society 52 [London: Harleian Society, 1904], 1019). Charles Best Norcliffe gives Agnes's name as Anne and incorrectly identifies her husband as the first Lord Borough (*The Visitation of Yorkshire in the Years 1563 and 1564*, Publications of the Harleian Society 16 [London: Mitchell & Hughes, 1881], 65). Susan James incorrectly identifies Agnes as Sir Robert's sister rather than aunt (Susan E. James, *Kateryn Parr: The Making of a Queen* [Aldershot: Ashgate, 1999], 153).

[4] Samuel Haynes, *A Collection of State Papers . . . Left by William Cecill Lord Burghley* (London: William Bowyer, 1740), 1:103–4.

with my Lady your Wyffe in Devynnyte," to which Sir Robert replied that Elizabeth "was not seyne in Devynnete, but she was halff a Scrypture Woman."[5] Since "seyne" here means "read," as in having read for a degree in theology, Robert's explanation that Elizabeth was "halff a Scrypture Woman" probably referred to her immense knowledge of the Bible, despite her lack of a university education, such that half of her conversation was composed of Scripture.[6] In 1577, a year before her death, the Puritan author John Field commended her "forwardnes, fidelity and sinceritie in the religion of Christ Jesus" in a dedicatory preface to the translation of a French theological treatise.[7]

Tyrwhit's fidelity to the religion of Christ Jesus may have begun before she arrived at Court sometime in 1537,[8] but it was shaped into a Lutheran-inflected piety by her association with Katherine Parr, who took pains to instruct her retainers in reformation theology. The queen, Foxe recounts,

> was very much given to the readyng and study of the holy Scriptures: and . . . she for that purpose had retained divers well learned and godly persons, to instruct her thoroughly in the same, with whom as at all tymes convenient she used to have private conference touching spirituall matters: so also of ordinarie, but especially in Lent every day in the after noone, for the space of one houre, one of her said Chaplaines in her privie chamber made some collation to her and to her Ladyes and Gentlewomen of her privy chamber, or other that were disposed to heare: in whiche Sermons, they oftymes touched such abuses, as in the Churche, then were rife.[9]

---

[5] Haynes, *State Papers*, 1:104.

[6] Without hearing Robert's tone of voice, it is difficult to know whether this claim was made depreciatingly or with some pride, but given other evidence of his positive relationships to his wife and Protestantism, it may well have been the latter.

[7] Jean de L'Espine, *An excellent treatise of Christian righteousness* (London, 1577; STC 15512), A2r–A3v. Franklin Williams identifies the dedicatee as Elizabeth Tyrwhit's half-niece, also named Elizabeth Tyrwhit, but Patrick Collinson is probably correct that Field is honoring the older woman (Franklin B. Williams, Jr., *Index of Dedications and Commendatory Verses in English Books before 1641* [London: Bibliographical Society, 1962], 187; Patrick Collinson, "John Field and Elizabethan Puritanism," in idem, *Godly People: Essays on English Protestantism and Puritanism* [London: Hambledon Press, 1983], 335–70, here 350).

[8] Tyrwhit is listed as a recipient of court gifts in 1537 and as a member of the Privy Chamber in 1538 (*Letters and Papers, Foreign and Domestic, of the Reign of Henry VIII, 1509–1547*, ed. J. S. Brewer, James Gairdner, and R. H. Brodie, 21 vols. [London: Longman, Green, Longman & Roberts, 1862–1910], 12:973i; 15:21; 16:1389).

[9] Foxe, *Actes and Monuments* (1570), p. 1422.

That Tyrwhit took these collations or sermons to heart can be seen not only in her husband's description of her as "halff a Scrypture Woman," but also in the prayerbook she composed, probably during her time of service to Katherine Parr or shortly thereafter. The first "moment" in the chronicle of Elizabeth Tyrwhit's *Morning and Evening Prayers* must, therefore, be moved back from 1554 and the legendary presentation of her prayerbook to the Princess Elizabeth to the 1540s when it was largely composed.[10]

It would be a mistake, however, to suppose that Tyrwhit's interest in reform cut her off from traditional books of prayer, and indeed she is indebted in many ways to the medieval Books of Hours that established daily devotional prayers for laypeople. In the previous two centuries, literally thousands of manuscript Books of Hours had been copied by hand, and after 1475 printing presses in Paris, Rouen, Antwerp, and London churned out over 100 printed editions for the English public. These manuscript Books of Hours, or primers as the printed versions were known, drew from a set of traditional prayers at the center of which stood an abbreviated version for laypeople of the eight canonical hours originally designed for use in monastic communities. This Little Office of the Blessed Virgin Mary was a set of prayers, psalms, hymns, and responses that began each morning with these words: "O Lord, open thou my lips."[11]

Against this background of traditional daily prayer for laypeople, the English Reformation inaugurated two major revisions. First, following the trajectory established by late medieval practice, it condensed the eight canonical hours of prayer into two—morning and evening prayers—and, through the Book of Common Prayer, attempted to move these devotions away from homes and monastic communities into the public worship of the church. Second, and inadvertently, by replacing the Books of Hours with common *public* prayers, it opened the door to a proliferation of new, individuated, *private* prayerbooks designed for use in the home rather than the church. The first revision—imposing uniform public worship—was implemented with all the authority of the established church; the second—encouraging the production of private prayerbooks—occurred despite official attempts at censorship.

---

[10] Sources for those parts of the prayerbook that are not original can be traced to books printed in the 1530s and 1540s; for a detailed analysis of these sources, see the introduction to *Elizabeth Tyrwhit's Morning and Evening Prayers*, ed. Susan M. Felch (Brookfield, VT: Ashgate, 2008).

[11] For a history of the Divine Office, see Robert Taft, *The Liturgy of the Hours in East and West: The Origins of the Divine Office and its Meaning for Today*, 2nd rev. ed. (Collegeville, MN: Liturgical Press, 1993).

Daily prayer for laypeople immediately prior to the Reformation was a personal, although not individual, affair. Jean Quentin's popular fifteenth-century treatise "The Preface and Manner to Live Well" recommended that one say the morning office of Matins privately—to oneself or with a friend or servant—in the bedroom or even in church while watching the priest officiate at mass.[12] With the establishment of the Book of Common Prayer in 1549, however, parishioners were expected, at least in church, to eschew private meditation in order to join in the common, public recitation of morning and evening prayers. They were to join their hearts and their tongues in unified, uniform worship. It was also the devout hope of the Tudor rulers that such uniformity be extended to private devotions.

Henry VIII, for instance, authorized a primer in 1545 to replace "the dyversytie of primer bookes that are nowe abroade, wherof are almoost innumerable sortes whiche minister occasion of contentions and vaine disputations, rather then to edifye."[13] Eight years later, the license for William Seres's 1553 prayerbook, *A Prymmer or boke of private prayer*, noted that it was designed in accord with "the booke of common prayers establyshed by us in our highe courte of Parliament," and stipulated that "it is requysite to have some uniforme of dayly prayers fytte to be used privately as of children and divers other our subjectes . . . shall have from tyme to tyme occasion to occupie."[14] "Requisite," in this case, had the force of law, for all "parsons what so ever they be, [who] prynte, utter, or sel, or cause to be prynted, uttered or solde . . . any other sortes or impressions of Primers or dayly Prayers . . . shall forfaite to our use al such sortes of primers where so ever they be founde."

Despite this alarming language, there is no record of prayerbook bonfires either in 1545 or in 1553. Indeed, Seres's own authorized prayerbook was issued in

---

[12] See, for instance, Jean Quentin's "The Preface and Manner to Live Well, Devoutly, and Salutarily Every Day for all Persons of Mean Estate" translated by Robert Copland in *This prymer of Salysbury use is set out a long without ony serchyng* (Paris, 1529; *STC* 15961.3). For discussions of "The Manner to Live Well," see Helen C. White, *The Tudor Books of Private Devotion* (Madison: Univ. of Wisconsin Press, 1951), 150–53; W. A. Pantin, "Instructions for a Devout and Literate Layman," in *Medieval Learning and Literature: Essays Presented to Richard William Hunt*, ed. J. J. G. Alexander and M. T. Gibson (Oxford: Oxford Univ. Press, 1976), 398–422, here 411–12; Mary C. Erler, "The 'Maner to Lyue Well' and the Coming of English in François Regnault's Primers of the 1520s and 1530s," *The Library*, 6th series, 6 (1984): 229–43; and Susan M. Felch, "The Development of the English Prayer Book," in *Worship in Medieval and Early Modern Europe: Change and Continuity in Religious Practice*, ed. Karin Maag and John D. Witvliet (Notre Dame: Univ. of Notre Dame Press, 2004), 132–61.

[13] *The primer, set foorth by the kynges majestie and his clergie* (London, 1545; *STC* 16034), ***1v.

[14] *A primmer, or boke of priuate prayer nedefull to bee vsed of all faythful Christians* (London, 1553; *STC* 20374), A1v–A2v.

two editions in the first year of publication: a blatantly Protestant one published
before the king's death, and a moderately conservative one printed later in the
year that quietly returned Thomas Becket and other Catholic saints to the Calendar, reinstated the dirge, and included prayers for the prosperity of Queen Mary.[15]
If the king's edict could not prevent his own printer from adjusting the contents
of a private prayerbook, it had even less effect on other authors. Throughout the
sixteenth century, the production of distinctive, individual prayerbooks, which
often bore little resemblance to the Book of Common Prayer, continued unabat-
ed. The two major Reformation revisions to the prayerbook tradition, therefore,
proceeded in opposite directions: toward greater uniformity in public worship
but toward greater individuality—and indeed toward "contentions and disputations" (just as Henry had feared)—in private devotions. By 1595, Andrew Maunsell's catalogue of theological books included nearly one hundred prayerbook entries, among them Elizabeth Tyrwhit's *Morning and Evening Prayers*.[16]

As the title itself indicates, Tyrwhit's prayerbook recognizes only two "hours"
of prayers, rather than the canonical eight, and a significant portion of her
prayerbook derives from English translations or imitations of Lutheran sources.
A number of hymns and prayers are drawn from the first reformist primer printed in English, George Joye's *Ortulus*, or from the Godly Garden primers that followed it, all of which, in turn, were heavily indebted to Lutheran doctrines and
forms.[17]

---

[15] *A prymmer or boke of priuate prayer* (London, 1553; STC 20373) was the original Ed-
wardian Protestant prayerbook; *A primmer, or boke of priuate prayer* (STC 20374) was the second, more conservative version.

[16] Andrew Maunsell, *The first part of the catalogue of English printed bookes which con-
cerneth diuinitie* (London, 1595; STC 17669), G6r–H2r. On sixteenth-century printed prayerbooks, see William Maskell, *Monumenta Ritualia Ecclesiae Anglicanae*, vol. 2 (London: William Pickering, 1846); Edgar Hoskins, *Horae Beatae Mariae Virginis, or, Sarum and York
Primers with Kindred Books and Primers of the Reformed Roman Use* (London: Longmans,
Green, and Co., 1901); White, *The Tudor Books of Private Devotion*; and Charles C. Butter-
worth, *The English Primers (1529–1545): Their Publication and Connection with the English
Bible and the Reformation in England* (Philadelphia: Univ. of Pennsylvania Press, 1953).

[17] *Ortulus anime the garden of the soule* (Argentine [i.e., Antwerp], 1530; STC 13828.4).
The Godly Garden prayerbooks included Joye's *Ortulus*; primers printed by Marshall, Godfray, Gouge, and Toye; Tyrwhit's prayerbook; the *Devout Meditacions* of Edward Whitchurche;
the primers written by John Hilsey, Bishop of Rochester, who worked under the aegis of Thomas Cromwell; and two later prayerbooks printed by Henry Middleton. These Godly Garden
prayerbooks shared numerous elements, although each is unique in its selection and arrangement of materials. For Marshall, see *A prymer in Englyshe* (London, 1534; STC 15986) and *A
goodly prymer in Englysshe newely corrected* (London, 1538; STC 15998); for Godfray, see *A
primer in Englysshe, with dyuers prayers* (London, 1535?; STC 15988a); for Gouge, see [*The
prymer of Salysbery use, bothe in Englyshe and in Laten*] ([Antwerp], 1536; STC 15992); for

Surprisingly, however, the longest poem in Tyrwhit's prayerbook is a unique translation of the seven hymns from the Hours of the Cross, a set of prayers supplemental to The Little Office of the Blessed Virgin Mary often found in Books of Hours and in traditional primers. Tyrwhit, however, does not insert these traditional hymns into her prayerbook unchanged, for she is not merely a compiler but an author. The title page specifies not only her rank and name, the Lady Elizabeth Tyrwhit, but also that the book is *made* by her, with the connotations of composition, authorship, and authority that term suggests.[18] In the Hours of the Cross, she revises the traditional material to emphasize doctrines prominent in the reformation:[19] as second Adam, Jesus overcomes original sin ("To suffer pains for Adams gilt, so was his fathers will"); his death, not the mass, constitutes the sacrifice for sin ("Yet receive this sacrifice, and my spirit undefild"); and he dies for the elect ("Then he thirsted for his elect, which subject were to thrall"). She also adds a Trinitarian refrain, which is carried through the entire prayerbook, and omits the last two hymns that meditate on Christ's dead body, ending instead with this triumphant assertion: "Blood and water then sprang from this blessed lamb, / Then graves opened, the dead alive foorth came."[20] Similarly, her opening sentence for Morning Prayer elaborates on the traditional formula taken from Psalm 51, adding a paraphrase that moves the simple invocation from a contemplative to a more ethically active stance: "O Lord open thou my lips, that my mouth may *speake and* shew foorth *that which is to* thy *glorie and* praise. *And*

Whitchurche, see [*Devo]ut meditacions, [psal]mes and praiers [to] bee vsed aswell in the morning as eauentyde gathered out of the holy scriptures and other godly wryters* ([London], 1548; STC 2998.5); for Hilsey, see *The manual of prayers or the prymer in Englysh & Laten set out at length* (London, 1539; STC 16009) and his children's prayerbook, *The primer in English moste necessary for the educacyon of chyldren abstracted oute of the manuall of prayers or primer in Englishe* (London, 1539; STC 16016a). For Middleton, see *A godly garden out of which most comfortable hearbes may be gathered for the health of the wounded conscience of all penitent sinners* (London, 1574; STC 11555); and the slightly revised *A godlie garden out of which most comfortable hearbes may be gathered for the health of the wounded conscience of all penitent sinners* (London, 1581; STC 11557).

[18] For the importance of artifact to authorial agency, see Paul Eggert and Margaret Sankey, eds., *The Editorial Gaze: Mediating Texts and Literature and the Arts* (New York and London: Garland Publishing, 1998), 111.

[19] To compare an English version of the traditional Hours of the Cross, see [*Thys prymer of Salisbury vse*] (London: W. Rastell, 1532; STC 15976), C6r–v; D3v; D8r; E4r; E8r–v; G3r–v; G7v.

[20] Thomas Bentley, *The monument of matrones: conteining seuen seuerall lamps of virginitie, or distinct treatises; whereof the first fiue concerne praier and meditation: the two last, precepts and examples* (London, 1582; STC 1892), Second Lamp, N2v–N3r.

shut my mouth from speaking of anie thing whereby I should offend thy divine maj-
estie, or be hurtfull to my neighbor" (italics indicate Tyrwhit's additions).[21]

Paraphrase is one of the primary means by which Tyrwhit not only revises traditional material, but also presses the didactic concerns of the Reformation. In addition, paraphrases push her prayerbook away from the common pool of re-cited prayers and toward an individuated experience of worship that requires lit-eracy, the ability to read her expanded texts. The relatively homogenous Books of Hours encouraged recitation: as the prayers in a Book of Hours or a primer were read over and over again, it is likely that sheer force of habit would inscribe their words on the memory. But the newly composed prayerbooks, each with its own distinctive set of prayers, discouraged memorization and necessitated devotional *reading* rather than recitation.

Paraphrase was, of course, a popular genre for the humanists. Although Roger Ascham and later Thomas Wilson, following Melanchthon, were dubious about its virtues, Parr's circle appropriated Erasmus, who valued paraphrase for retaining the authority of a given text while simultaneously making it clearer to the reader.[22] Tyrwhit includes paraphrases of traditional liturgical texts, as noted in the examples above, and also paraphrased psalms, most of which are taken from Richard Taverner's translation of the psalm paraphrases written by Wolf-gang Capito, a Protestant pastor in Strasbourg known for seeking rapprochement among the various reformers.[23]

Tyrwhit also includes another humanist genre, collage psalms, in which a va-riety of scripture texts are sewn together to create a continuous narrative. Com-posed almost entirely of biblical sentences, scripture collage sounds impeccably orthodox and conservative since nearly every word is a biblical citation, but in ac-tuality it creates forceful new narratives through the skillful manipulation of top-ical verses. One of Tyrwhit's collage psalms is borrowed directly from the seventh of the so-called "King's Psalms," originally written in Latin by John Fisher and

---

[21] Bentley, *The monument of matrones*, Second Lamp, M7v.

[22] See, for instance, Erasmus's letter to Charles V, constituting the preface to the para-phrase on Matthew (*The Correspondence of Erasmus*, trans. R. A. B. Mynors; annotated by James M. Estes, *Collected Works of Erasmus*, vol. 9 [Toronto: Univ. of Toronto Press, 1989], 9; also see p. 243); Nicholas Udall, under Parr's direction, organized the translation and publi-cation of Erasmus's *New Testament Paraphrases* and orchestrated the Royal Injunction that required parish churches to purchase it. The parish register of Tyrwhit's childhood church at Brede, for instance, records the expenditure of five shillings and two pence "for a boke of Er-asmus" in 1549 (Lewes County Record Office, PAR 253/9/1, fol. 8d).

[23] Richard Taverner, *An epitome of the Psalmes, or briefe meditacions vpon the same, with diuerse other moste christian prayers* (London, 1539; *STC* 2748); translation of Wolfgang Cap-ito, *Precationes Christianae ad imitationem psalmorum compositae* (Strasbourg: Rihel, 1536).

possibly translated by Katherine Parr.[24] Although Fisher was executed by Henry VIII in 1535 for opposing the royal divorce and the Act of Supremacy, his psalm collages were embraced by Protestants as unimpeachable statements of genuine piety and went through at least twenty editions in the reign of Elizabeth.[25]

Another of Tyrwhit's collage psalms is particularly striking insofar as it demonstrates her own literary and compositional abilities. Drawing largely on five psalms from the Taverner-Capito Psalter (Psalms 77, 89–92), she skillfully rearranges and edits the paraphrases while incorporating an array of verses from other biblical passages as well.[26] For instance, she alludes to Psalm 91 early in her collage psalm ("under the shadowes of thy wings to defend me") but then quotes the Taverner-Capito paraphrase of that psalm at length after a modified citation from their version of Psalm 90. As befits a text that begins Evening Prayer, Tyrwhit adds references to darkness, night, and the Trinity, focusing on the security and extent of God's care and protection throughout the day and night. Her collage paraphrase psalm concludes with excerpts from the "Canticle of the Three Children" and with additional psalm verses.[27] The scope of this collage psalm and its imaginative weaving of citations directly from scripture and from scripture paraphrase demonstrate clearly the extent to which Tyrwhit might well lay claim to being "halff a Scrypture Woman," and they showcase her literacy, her easy familiarity with sources, and her ability to "make" her own collations.

Trywhit's original contributions to *Morning and Evening Prayers* are not, however, limited to this collage paraphrase.[28] She tries her hand at a metrical

---

[24] *Psalmi seu precationes ex variis scripturae locis collectae* (London, 1544; *STC* 2994); *Psalmes or prayers taken out of holye scripture* (London, 1544; *STC* 3001.7). Cecilia A. Hatt does not believe these prayers are the work of Fisher (*English Works of John Fisher, Bishop of Rochester [1469–1535]: Sermons and Other Writings, 1520–1535* [Oxford: Oxford Univ. Press, 2002], 429). Susan James makes a case for Katherine Parr as the translator of these psalms in *Kateryn Parr*, 201–10.

[25] Fisher's psalm collage technique is one that Parr herself modifies in her paraphrase of the *Imitation of Christ*, which was popularly known as "The Queen's Prayers" (Katherine Parr, *Prayers or meditacions wherin the mynde is styrred paciently to suffre all afflictions here, to sette at nought the vayne prosperitie of this worlde, and alway to longe for the euerlastyng felicitie* [London, 1545; *STC* 4818.5]).

[26] Bentley, *The monument of matrones*, Second Lamp, N7v–O1r.

[27] A canticle is a biblical song not found in the Psalter. The "Canticle of the Three Children" records the thanksgiving of Daniel's companions, Shadrach, Meshach, and Abednego, after they were delivered from the fiery furnace (Daniel 3). The song is not found in the original Hebrew and Aramaic text and is omitted, therefore, from Protestant Bibles, but it does occur in ancient Greek and Latin versions, as well as in the Vulgate (Daniel 3:52–88).

[28] Although these psalms, hymns, and prayers appear to be original, it may be that subsequent research will uncover sources for some of them.

psalm, a unique rendition of Psalm 134 to which is added an evening blessing and the trinitarian refrain from her version of the Hours of the Cross. She also includes four new hymns including "The beamie sun large light doth give," which rolls along in rhyming fourteeners and "Swéet Jesus of thy mercie, our pitifull praiers heare," which calls to mind traditional meditative prayers on the person of Christ. Seven penitential prayers, three short prayers of blessing, two contemplative prayers, and a collection of moral "sentences," modeled after Erasmus's adages, round out Tyrwhit's original contributions. In these selections, Tyrwhit demonstrates a cheerful ecumenicity, drawing on traditional materials and newer genres, such as the metrical paraphrase, while adjusting the tone and theological emphases to align with Katherine Parr's Lutheran and Erasmian sensibilities. In her contemplative prayer on the passion, for instance, she eschews a traditional sympathetic identification with or imitation of Christ's suffering, asserting rather his substitutionary triumph over sin that enables the elect to vanquish evil in their own lives. It is Christ's blood that provides "cleane remission of our offences," and he himself, not the Eucharist, is the "sufficient sacrifice" and the "blessed oblation" by which believers learn, in the words of Erasmus, their "heavenlie Philosophie."[29]

As an artifact of the Henrician reformation, Elizabeth Tyrwhit's *Morning and Evening Prayers* offers insight into the evolving devotional practices of sixteenth-century England. Unlike disputes over Word and Sacrament, the practices of prayer did not draw sharp lines of distinction among Christian believers but rather incorporated traditional ecclesiastical forms along with newer humanist genres, quietly modifying doctrinal points as necessary. Prayers from the Books of Hours and psalms from Roman Catholic martyrs were juxtaposed with metrical psalms, Lutheran hymns, and original paraphrases. Reform, not replacement, was the theological watchword. Prayerbooks thus used tactics of accumulation and alignment rather than controversy, and the ecumenicity of Tyrwhit's *Morning and Evening Prayers* is both exemplary and typical in this respect. To use a biblical metaphor from Matthew's Gospel that Tyrwhit herself might have appreciated, her prayerbook, along with many others from the sixteenth century, draws from the storehouse of Christian piety treasures both old and new.[30]

Although an analysis of the prayerbook itself clearly locates its composition within the orbit of Katherine Parr's court, it is possible that Tyrwhit may have presented a manuscript copy to the Princess Elizabeth during her sojourn in the Tower of London, and that this manuscript version may have been encased in the tiny gold and enameled girdlebook that now contains the only extant copy of

---

[29] Bentley, *The monument of matrones*, Second Lamp, N2r–N2v.
[30] Matthew 13:52.

the 1574 printed text, thus giving rise to the Ashby family legend. If so, it would not have been a sweet, sentimental gift, but rather a bracing reminder, in light of Mary Tudor's return to the Roman Catholic Church, of the reformist heritage the two Elizabeths shared with Katherine Parr. As such, despite its accommodation of traditional forms, it may well have been seen in 1554 as a subversive and possibly radical document.

In 1569, however, when Christopher Barker registered the manuscript with the Stationers' Company, it was probably valued as part of the "heritage movement," that included such books as John Day's encyclopedic *Christian Prayers and Meditations* and was intended to bolster the Elizabethan settlement.[31] Yet by the time it was printed in 1574, Tyrwhit's prayerbook, at least in the form it now took, had been pressed into a more radical agenda. Printed the same year that four nonconformist ministers died in prison following years of agitation against the Book of Common Prayer, Tyrwhit's prayerbook, with its traditional materials and evocations of the queen's own beloved stepmother, may have been seen as an appropriate gift to regain the Queen's approval for the reformist members of her church and court. The printer, Henry Middleton, added a "Briefe exhortation unto Prayer" written by one of his Puritan authors, Henry Bull, that condemned "outward ceremonies" (such as those enjoined by the Book of Common Prayer); eliminated a number of prayers and hymns (nearly a quarter of the material is removed); reorganized the remaining prayers; and relegated all the poetry to an appendix. This comprehensive reformulation of Tyrwhit's prayerbook suggests that it was being aligned with other progressive prayerbooks of the period. Significantly, such an alignment did not require the excision of traditional materials— the translation of the Hours of the Cross, for instance, remains intact—but rather a structural reordering. Unlike the prayerbooks of the 1530s and 1540s, which follow the Books of Hours and primers in conjoining poetry and prose within a single office or hour of prayer, the Elizabethan prayerbooks established a pattern of prose-only prayers. Poetry or hymns, even metrical psalms, were published separately, and this is the format followed in the Barker-Middleton revision of Tyrwhit's prayerbook.[32]

One copy of Tyrwhit's slimmed-down version of *Morning and Evening Prayers*, printed in a tiny 32° format (along with a complete copy of the Litany, a copy of Katherine Parr's *Prayers* with incomplete Litany, and an incomplete

---

[31] *Christian prayers and meditations in English, French, Italian, Spanish, Greeke, and Latine* (London, 1569; *STC* 6428); cf. White, *Tudor Books*, 187.

[32] A reverse example, with poems displayed prominently and prose prayers relegated to an appendix, may be seen in the Sternhold and Hopkins Psalter; see, for instance, *The Whole Book of Psalms* (London, 1562; *STC* 2430), Dd6r–Ee5v.

Kalendar) was fitted into a binding finished off with clasps and loops that allowed it to be hung as a pendant from a belt or girdle. Probably the work of Hans von Antwerpen, a Flemish goldsmith working in London around 1540, the two embossed and enameled gold panels of the binding depicted Moses and the brazen serpent on the front and the judgment of Solomon on the back.[33] This costly, jeweled girdlebook may have been presented or re-presented to Queen Elizabeth as part of a concerted effort to regain her favor for the emerging Puritan party by reminding her through her beloved stepmother and her former governess of her own religious roots.[34]

By the time Elizabeth Tyrwhit's *Morning and Evening Prayers* was reprinted in 1582 as part of Thomas Bentley's encyclopedic compendium *The Monument of Matrones*, however, it had assumed the status of a "classic" work of devotion, placed in the second section, or "lamp," immediately following selections from the royal Protestant trinity of Elizabeth Tudor, Katherine Parr, and Jane Grey Dudley. As a dedicated antiquarian devoted to preserving the heritage of the English reformation, Bentley made every effort to be accurate, as is evident by comparing his versions of texts, such as Parr's *Meditations*, with other editions. In this he consciously imitates the craft inaugurated by that other great "Monument" work of the sixteenth century, John Foxe's *Actes and Monuments*, not least in his intent to protect the legacy of godly women and men by paying close attention to his sources.[35] Bentley repeatedly refers to himself merely as a compiler, a collector, or "a poore gleaner" in the vineyards of others, stating that he desires

---

[33] The binding is described and analyzed in Hugh Tait, "The Girdle-Prayerbook or 'tablett': An Important Class of Renaissance Jewellery at the Court of Henry VIII," *Jewellery Studies* 2 (1985): 29–57. See also Hugh Tait, "Historiated Tudor Jewellery," *The Antiquaries Journal* 42 (1962): 226–46; *Princely Magnificence: Court Jewels of the Renaissance, 1500–1630* (London: Debrett's Peerage in association with the Victoria and Albert Museum, 1980), 48–50; and Alexandra Walsham, "Jewels for Gentlewomen: Religious Books as Artefacts in Late Medieval and Early Modern England," in *The Church and the Book*, ed. R. N. Swanson, Studies in Church History 38 (Woodbridge: Boydell Press for the Ecclesiastical History Society, 2004), 123–42.

[34] Other such gifts included the 1572 manuscript of Bartholo Sylva's *Giardino cosmografico coltivato*, prepared by the Cooke sisters, Edward Dering, and Dering's wife Anne Vaughan Lock for presentation to Robert Dudley, the earl of Leicester (CUL MS Ii.5.37). In 1574, Anne Lock's *Sermons of John Calvin*, with its dedication to another reformist patron, Katherine Willoughby Brandon Bertie, the dowager duchess of Suffolk, was reprinted, although the single surviving copy (*STC* 4451) was destroyed during World War II.

[35] For a discussion of prayers, letters, and other written documents as "monuments," see Susan Wabuda, "Henry Bull, Miles Coverdale, and the Making of Foxe's *Book of Martyrs*," in *Martyrs and Martyrologies*, ed. Diana Wood, Studies in Church History 30 (Oxford: Blackwell, 1993), 249–50.

"simplie first to plaie the part of a faithfull collector, by following my copies tru-
lie, and placing their works and praiers together as I found them referred by the
authors for private or publike use."[36] In the case of Tyrwhit's prayerbook, Bentley
apparently had access to the manuscript or an earlier printed version, rather than
to the truncated edition of 1574.[37]

The *Monument* version of Tyrwhit's prayerbook contains nearly a quarter
more material than the 1574 version and is organized quite differently. Whereas
the 1574 edition relegates the poems to an appendix, the 1582 edition incorporates all the poetry, psalms, and prayers into the structure of morning and evening prayers, following the pattern of the earlier Lutheran-inflected prayerbooks
rather than the later Elizabethan devotional books. The 1574 Barker-Middleton version also shows evidence of greater editorial intervention and error than
does Bentley's 1582 version, the most notable example being the addition of "A
briefe exhortation unto Prayer." But omissions in the 1574 versions are consistent
with the desire to reduce perceived redundancy (prayers preliminary to Evening
Prayer are deleted, for instance, as are several psalms and one of the hymns) and
there are a number of compositor's errors. It is fortunate that Bentley restored
the text of Tyrwhit's *Morning and Evening Prayers* and that he did so in 1582. For
it would have been more difficult to publish a compendium with such historical and theological breadth, stretching from the proto-Protestant meditations of
Marguerite of Navarre to the Lutheran-inflected devotions of Katherine Parr's
court and on through the Calvinist catechism of Dorcas Martin,[38] after the accession of John Whitgift as archbishop of Canterbury in 1583.

Tracing the chronicle of Elizabeth Tyrwhit's *Morning and Evening Prayers*
as it moves from its composition in the late 1540s to its 1582 reprinting in
The Monument of Matrones enables us better to understand the narrative of
devotional reform in sixteenth-century England. Her prayerbook demonstrates
the continuity that persisted in the practices of prayer, but also shows the ways
in which doctrinal differences were inscribed in devotional life and the means
by which prayerbooks participated in cultural shifts, such as the movement
from recitation to reading, the reformational preference for prose prayers, and
the use of devotional artifacts in a patronage economy. While we may need to
abandon the romantic legend of a gilded girdlebook passed down from governess

---

[36] Bentley, *The monument of matrones*, B3r.

[37] For a detailed argument of the priority of the 1582 text over the 1574 text, see the introduction to *Elizabeth Tyrwhit's Morning and Evening Prayers*, ed. Felch.

[38] For a discussion of Dorcas Martin's catechism, see Micheline White, "A Biographical Sketch of Dorcas Martin: Elizabethan Translator, Stationer, and Godly Matron," *Sixteenth
Century Journal* 30 (1999): 775–92.

to princess to queen to lady-in-waiting as we chronicle Elizabeth Tyrwhit's *Morning and Evening Prayers*, what we recover is the no less intriguing history of one woman and her book that traversed and helped transform the experience of prayer in the sixteenth century.

CALVIN COLLEGE

"To take in hand the practise of phisick": Early Modern Women's Signatures in Print Medical Texts

REBECCA LAROCHE

T HE STATISTICAL, ARCHIVAL, ANTHROPOLOGICAL, AND SOCIOLOGICAL work undertaken by a score of medical, social, and cultural historians, including Doreen Evenden Nagy, Lynette Hunter, and Margaret Pelling, among others, has identified the names of over one hundred separate English-women undertaking some form of medical practice—whether as midwives, gentlewomen, housewives, herbwomen, wisewomen, witches, or empirics—in the sixteenth and seventeenth centuries.[1] The evidence these historians have cited

---

This paper was first presented at the 2006 MLA convention in Philadelphia, PA, at a panel entitled "Early Modern Women's Manuscripts," Margaret P. Hannay, Siena College, presiding.

[1] Doreen Evenden Nagy, *Popular Medicine in Seventeenth-century England* (Bowling Green, OH: Bowling Green State Univ. Popular Press, 1988); Lynette Hunter, "Women and Domestic Medicine: Lady Experimenters, 1570–1620," in Lynette Hunter and Sarah Hutton, eds., *Women, Science and Medicine 1500–1700: Mothers and Sisters of the Royal Society* (Stroud, Gloucestershire: Sutton Publishing, 1997), 89–107; Margaret Pelling, *Medical Conflicts in Early Modern London: Patronage, Physicians, and Irregular Practitioners, 1550–1640* (Oxford: Clarendon Press, 2003); Lucinda MacCray Beier, *Sufferers and Healers: The Experience of Illness in Seventeenth-century England* (London: Routledge & Kegan Paul, 1987); Elizabeth Lane Furdell, *Publishing and Medicine in Early Modern England* (Rochester, NY: Univ. of Rochester Press, 2002); Elaine Hobby, *Virtue of Necessity: English Women's Writing, 1649–89* (Ann Arbor: Univ. of Michigan Press, 1989); Kate Campbell Hurd-Mead, *A History of Women in Medicine, From the Earliest Times to the Beginning of the Nineteenth Century* (Haddam, CT: The Haddam Press, 1938); Roy Porter, *Health for Sale: Quakery in England, 1660–1850* (Manchester: Manchester Univ. Press, 1989); Andrew Wear, *Knowledge and Practice in English Medicine, 1550–1680* (Cambridge: Cambridge Univ. Press, 2000); and Charles Webster (with

comes from diaries, memoirs, manuscript and print receipt books, print manuals, inscriptions, memorials, wills, and historical records. In this paper, I will be considering one form of evidence in particular, that of early modern women's inscriptions in print medical texts. I will do so alongside other fragments from these women and in these considerations hope to uncover a nuanced understanding of the literary implications of this historical evidence.

We begin with an uncataloged signature in a 1578 herbal at the Yale Medical Historical Library.[2] The name "Elizabeth: Bagot" appears on this particular title page of Henry Lyte's translation of Rembert Dodoens's *Crüijdeboeck, A niewe herball, or, Historie of plantes*. The herbal contains knowledge about the physical and medicinal properties of herbs from antiquity to the present compiled by the Flemish physician. This translation and Dodoens's Latin treatise are significant sources for subsequent herbals in English, such as the better-known volume completed by John Gerard.

Elizabeth Bagot's signature—not confident, as the hand has crossed out one "B" and replaced it with one better executed—is most definitely that of Elizabeth Cave Bagot (d. 1638), child of Roger and Elizabeth Cecil Cave. Through her mother, she is also the niece of the royal minister Lord Burghley, William Cecil (1520/21–1598).[3] William Cecil is most recognizable as close advisor to Elizabeth I, but it is also important to note for our purposes that Cecil was famous for his gardens, and his gardener, John Gerard, in 1597 dedicated his often-reproduced herbal to him. This familial connection to Gerard's *Herball* suggests—as anyone of the Cecil clan would likely prefer to own a text with such ties—that Lyte's translation was purchased before the publication of the later text and that the signature was written in the herbal before 1597.

This date is entirely possible because Elizabeth Cave was married to Walter Bagot (c. 1557–1623) of Staffordshire in 1586.[4] We know much about Walter Bagot and his extended family because of the correspondence and private papers in the Bagot collection kept at the Folger Shakespeare Library. It is through the correspondence found there that we can identify with certainty the Elizabeth

---

Margaret Pelling), "Medical Practitioners," in *Health, Medicine and Mortality in the Sixteenth Century* (Cambridge: Cambridge Univ. Press, 1979), 165–236.

    [2] Much of the following information has been presented in Rebecca Laroche, "Elizabeth Bagot's Herbal," *Yale University Library Gazette* 81.1–2 (2007): 21–26.

    [3] M. W. Greenslade, "Bagot Family," *Oxford Dictionary of National Biography* (Oxford: Oxford Univ. Press, 2004–2006), 3: 236–38.

    [4] Greenslade, "Bagot Family."

Bagot in Yale's *Niewe Herball* as the wife of Walter, because this collection holds one letter with a signature nearly identical to the one penned in that book.[5]

The letter is an appealing example of familiar correspondence. Dated the 7th of July, 1614, Elizabeth's letter accompanies documents that Walter has requested be sent to him while he is away attending to business in London. The letter's body is written in a hand that does not seem to be Elizabeth's, being most likely that of a household secretary. Indeed only the hand of the signature bears resemblance to that of the Yale inscription. The letter tells us that she has been searching for items in her husband's study:

> My good Watt; I haue receiued yo[r] l[ett]re, and giue god thankes for your good health; and safety in yo[r] iorney. you wrytt to me to send you a blacke boxe of wryghtinges, which I haue sent you by this bearer hauinge in it these p[ar]cells, 2 ffynes, one Feoffm[en]t and one examplificac[i]on, w[ch] I founde at Blythfeild myself in your studie this day, and by chaunce knew them without any helpe.

The letter is compelling for our purposes in the way in which Walter Bagot's absence creates an occasion for his wife to venture into his study, which she seems to express some pride in negotiating successfully. We may thus read her signature on the folio herbal in a similar manner. Although the herbal is framed as a text embodying male study and experiment from antiquity to the present, her signature on it says that she has successfully negotiated its pages.

The existence of Bagot's letter allows us to give a background and history—however brief—to what would otherwise be just a signature. May we also ask what the inscription in and of itself tells us? In writing her signature, Elizabeth Bagot claimed her ownership of an expensive volume and the knowledge that it held. The book likely was an aid to her role as household healer. It stood in for the doctor she may have otherwise consulted in unusual cases. It gave her alternatives when one remedy proved ineffectual. The book was a guide, not the practitioner. Elizabeth Bagot was the healer, and with her signature, she claimed this role.

Women have claimed ownership to folio herbals either through inscriptions within the texts themselves or items in household inventories or at the end of their lives, in wills. My research has uncovered ownership by at least twenty early modern women—including the well-known examples of Margaret Hoby, Grace

---

[5] Folger Manuscript L.a.48. For a reproduction and transcription of the letter, see Rebecca Laroche, "Gendering Hands, Gendering Business: A Letter from Elizabeth Bagot," http://www.folger.edu/html/folger_institute/mm/EssayRL.html, June 2006. My thanks to Heather Wolfe and Steven May for their help in transcribing this letter.

Mildmay, and Anne Clifford—of the folio herbals published between 1550 and 1650 by William Turner, Dodoens, Gerard, and John Parkinson.[6] These comprehensive volumes earmark as their primary audience members of the male medi-

---

[6] My claims here are neither totalizing nor comprehensive. Resources and other constraints have made it possible to engage United States library collections only, and I realize that this fact may affect my results. Nine of the decidedly early modern examples come from evidence other than signatures in books. Through orthographic, paleographic, and biographic study, I have been able to confirm that ten of the signatures I have found are from the late sixteenth or seventeenth centuries (with some leeway into the early eighteenth). Four other examples remain to be confirmed. The examples I have found are as follows:

1) Margaret Hoby's diary entries from 1599 and 1600 mention three times "the arball," which, given the dates, as Joanna Moody notes, her husband's connections, and the authority which she gives it,"the arball," is likely to be Gerard's: Joanna Moody, ed., *The Private Life of an Elizabethan Lady* (Stroud, Gloucestershire: Sutton Publishing Limited, 1998), 18 n. 46; references to the herbal are on pages 18, 29, and 58.

2) Grace Mildmay's autobiography twice refers to reading an herbal, in childhood Turner's and as an adult "the herbal" that is not named: Linda Pollock, *With Faith and Physic: The Life of a Tudor Gentlewoman, Lady Grace Mildmay, 1552–1620* (New York: St. Martin's Press, 1993), 26, 35.

3) The left panel of "The Great Picture" commissioned by Anne Clifford Herbert, Countess of Pembroke, in 1646, depicts *The Epitome of Gerards Herball*, a volume that implies the presence of Gerard in the household.

4) Anne Southwell's miscellany contains a reference to books belonging to Anne and a list compiled by her husband, an item of which is "Gerard's Herball in folio": Anne Southwell, *The Southwell-Sibthorpe Commonplace Book: Folger MS. V.b. 198*, ed. Jean Klene, MRTS 147 (Tempe, AZ: Medieval & Renaissance Texts & Studies, 1997), 99, cited in Heidi Brayman Hackel, *Reading Material in Early Modern England* (Cambridge: Cambridge Univ. Press, 2005), 216.

5) Elizabeth Freke, whose manuscript at the British Library, Add. MS. 45718, contains "remedies abstracted from John Gerard's herbal": Raymond A. Anselment, *The Remembrances of Elizabeth Freke, 1671–1714* (Cambridge: Cambridge Univ. Press, 2001).

6) Similarly, Elizabeth Bulckley's "A booke of hearbes and receipts" (1627) contains herbal entries distilled from Gerard's *Herball*: Sara Pennell, ed., *Women and Medicine: Remedy Books, 1533–1865, from the Wellcome Library for the Understanding and History of Medicine* (Reading: Primary Source Microfilm, Thomas Gale, 2004), Reel 1.

7) Doreen Even Nagy cites Sara Gater's 1654 will as containing "Gerrards Herball": *Popular Medicine in Seventeenth-century England*, 66.

8) Similarity in wording between a 1641 letter by Brilliana Harley and the relevant entries in the herbals make it likely that she consulted either Dodoens or Gerard (the latter having as a source the former) in her prescription of angelica for preventing the plague: Brilliana Harley, *Letters of the Lady Brilliana Harley, Wife of Sir Robert Harley, of Brampton Bryan, Knight of Bath*, ed. Thomas Taylor Lewis, A.M., vicar of Bridstow, Herefordshire (London: Camden Society, 1854), 129. The list of autographs begins with the two references in this paper.

9) Elizabeth Bagot's 1578 Dodoens at the Yale Medical Historical Library.

cal triumvirate—physicians, surgeons, and apothecaries, but within various entries they acknowledge—or even overtly address—the gentlewoman reader. As a late example, Parkinson's *Theatrum Botanicum* (1640) articulates the gentlewoman's role in his description of a salve made of bugle, useful for "any good Gentlewoman in the land, that would do good either to her owne family, or other

---

10) Anne Purefoy's 1629 *Paradisus Terrestris* (I included this volume though questionable in its genre because of the ways in which Parkinson refers to it as the first volume in a two-volume project).

11) Jack Eckert, the Reference Librarian from the Countway Library of Medicine in Boston, Massachusetts, has provided me with the following information and a copy of the relevant page from that library's copy of Parkinson's *Theatrum Botanicum*: "The Parkinson . . . has the ownership inscription [crossed out] of Ann Stoughton and, below that, one of Margret Massingberd." Ann Stoughton's hand appears to be from the seventeenth century.

12) "Ann Loggin Her Boock," Library of Congress, *Theatrum Botanicum*, copy 3.

13) The wife of a John F. who died in 1672, according to his inscription on the blank page after the front matter, Library of Congress, *Theatrum Botanicum*, copy 2.

14) Signature of "Ann Parso[n]s" found in the New York Public Library's 1619 Dodoens, 3E3v, "Table of the Nature, Vertues, and Dangers," accompanied an inscription by of Richard Parsons from the second flyleaf recto dated 1628.

15) "Katherine Shirley her booke"on flyleaf of the Arizona State Univ. Patten collection's *Paradisus Terrestris* accompanied by the Shirley coat of arms. I have surmised from various evidence that this is Katherine Okeover Shirley (d. 1672), mother of Robert Shirley, first Earl Ferrers.

16) "Anne Whithall 1642," from the University of Pennsylvania's 1578 Dodoens.

17) "Jane Baker 1660," in a *Theatrum Botanicum* at the Academy of Natural Sciences, Philadelphia (I would also like to note here the lovely inscription, "Rachel Bolton her book A^o: D^i: 1767" also at the ANS in their 1636 Gerard).

18) The inscription "Mary Ellys's booke bought of Sister Stacy" from a 1633 Gerard at the Moody Library at the University of Texas Medical Branch implies two female owners (counted here only as one entry). The remaining signatures that remain to be seen or are more difficult to prove early modern:

19) "Jane Wilcocks" at the Philadelphia Horticultural Society, 1597 Gerard;

20) "Elizabeth Turner" in the 1578 Dodoens at the Huntington;

21) "Sarah Rodway her book March ye 16," William Turner's *A New Herbal* (1551) at the Folger Shakespeare Library;

22) "Elizabeth Hamond," 1578 Dodoens, Houghton Library.

At the time of this presentation, I had considered just over one hundred examples of these volumes, making the occurrence of women's autographs just under one in ten at the time. Of course, this number fluctuates with each library visited and has recently approached one in twelve. Along with the librarians and archivists from NYPL, Philadelphia Horticultural Society, and UPenn collections listed above, I would like to thank Karen Kukil at Smith College, Eric Pomeroy at Bryn Mawr, Jill Gage at the Newberry, and Stacey Peeples at Pennsylvania Hospital, who looked at their collections for me.

her poore neighbors."[7] It is important to note that in writing their names these women claimed *all* the knowledge within the herbal's pages, not just the entries addressed to gentlewomen. My general question about these signatures is, where is medical authority located in them? That is, is it located in the book or is the signature locating it in the woman who owns the book? Our next example pushes this question even further.

Whereas the authoritative herbal may seek to locate herbal authority within one volume, one woman's hand in different books shows how various texts held by one person locate the authority elsewhere. Recalling Heidi Brayman Hackel's discussion of women's marginalia and ownership of books, we can make much of a woman's pattern of inscription.[8] We currently know of three volumes with an inscription by Catherine (née Cromwell) Tollemache (1564–1621), wife of Lionel (1562–1613/4).[9] Two of these volumes are "books of secrets," collections of medical and other household instructions. Taking either book in isolation, one could make certain assumptions about Tollemache's relationship to the gendering of medical authority in the period. The assumptions we would make, however, would be contradictory to each other. One volume, an early Tudor manuscript now known as *The Tollemache Book of Secrets*, has no gender signifiers; the author and its readership remain anonymous and the manuscript contains all sorts of information, in both English and Latin, from the proper care of falcons to ingenious patterns for herb gardens. The volume contains a concise Latin herbal and several remedies. Catherine Tollemache's signature is the only indicator of readership, though we cannot be sure, as Nicholas Baker writes in the foreword to the facsimile edition, "whether she brought the book with her . . . or whether she found it at Helmingham [the Tollemache estate] already."[10] Whenever she acquired the book, her second inscription shows that her acquisitions were not simply left to happenstance.

---

[7] John Parkinson, *Theatrum Botanicum Theater of Plants* (London, 1640), 525.

[8] Heidi Brayman Hackel, *Reading Material in Early Modern England: Print, Gender, and Literacy* (Cambridge: Cambridge Univ. Press, 2005), 204–5.

[9] Rebecca Laroche, "Catherine Tollemache's Library," *Notes and Queries* 251 (2006): 157–58. For a discussion of the third book, a devotional work by Amandus Polanus, see Edward Wilson, "The Book-stamps of the Tollemache Family of Helmingham and Ham," *The Book Collector* 16 (1967): 178–85; quoted by Jeremy Griffiths, "Introduction," *The Tollemache Book of Secrets* (London: The Roxburghe Club, 2001), 1 n. 2. My thanks to John Blatchly, the Helmingham Honorary Librarian, for his correspondence. He adds to these insights, "The 12mo next to it has a similar case and may have been her book also. It is *STC* 23031: *A Clowd of Witnesses and They the Holy Genealogies of the sacred scriptures.* John Speed 1616. The final blanks have been mutilated and, had she inscribed this book in the same place as the Amandus Polanus, it would now be missing" (14 October 2006).

[10] Nicholas Baker, "Foreword," in *The Tollemache Book of Secrets*, xviii.

The other "book of secrets" at the Folger has an almost identical inscription, "Catheren Tallemache oweth [sic] this boock," in the left-side margin of signature E1 verso and was a popular household manual in the early modern period as discussed at length by Wendy Wall in *Staging Domesticity*.[11] The volume written by John Partridge has the extended title *The Treasurie of hidden secrets. Commonlie called, The Good-huswiues Closet of prouision, for the health of her Houshold. Gathered out of sundry experiments, lately practiced by men of great knowledge* (1600). Not only does this title designate its intended audience, "Good-huswiues," the title page also contains the directive "Not impertinent for euery good Huswife to vse in her house, amongst her owne family." Partridge seems intent on gendering the recipients of the knowledge within its pages as female, and once that readership has that knowledge, he looks to contain the practice it describes "amongst her owne family." At the same time, he locates the expertise in "men of great knowledge."

In line with what Wall has noted across several household manuals,[12] Partridge's framing of his project works toward defining the housewife's role. The Tollemache case, however, certainly shows us that the author's intended uses for his/her writing are simply that—intentions. Catherine Tollemache's possession of two volumes with similar but different information would seem to indicate that she was a collector of such books, preceding the concerted and much more varied acquisitions of her grandson Lionel (d. 1669) in the late seventeenth century. What is more, when we find through Jeremy Griffiths's discussion of her memorial that she was a woman "known for her skill in medicine," particularly in surgery,[13] the pattern of her textual holdings seems to indicate a purpose. A woman "known for her skill in medicine" certainly was practicing outside "her house" and family, and her inscriptions are a testimony to the knowledge she meant to put into practice. Thus a woman practicing medicine could refer to several different kinds of texts, or to no text at all. Just because medical authority is being gendered in certain texts, women did not necessarily read those texts or capitulate to the limitations within their pages. In discussions of women's reading, we need to consider that women may have owned texts for the knowledge they gained through them, not for the limits they defined.

Just as one woman's signature within two texts suggests that authority exists between texts, another inscription within a volume that is part herbal, part

---

[11] Wendy Wall first drew our attention to the existence of a signature in the Folger *Treasurie* in her influential study, *Staging Domesticity: Household Work and English Identity in Early Modern Drama* (Cambridge: Cambridge Univ. Press, 2002), 232 n. 54.

[12] Wall, *Staging Domesticity*, 166.

[13] Griffiths, "Introduction," *The Tollemache Book of Secrets*, 3 n. 5.

gardening manual, part picture-book, challenges our assumptions about the use of medical texts at the same time as it raises questions about the knowledge shared between women of different status. A volume of Parkinson's *Paradisi in Sole Paradisus Terrestris* (1629) at the Folger has the following inscription on its title page: "Anne Purefey her booke / giuen her by her deare sister / the Lady ffranklyn / June 22th 1643."[14] While Jane Donawerth may see in this an example of the gift exchange of herbal remedies between women, Linda Levy Peck finds evidence in it for her analysis of the leisured origins of luxury. Parkinson's text itself distinguishes between "the knowledge . . . [of] what Herbes and Fruits were fit, eyther for Meate or Medicine, for Vse or for Delight," but many plants he describes have both "use" and "delight" aspects to them.[15] In the end, we have to ask ourselves, is this a text indicative of women's work or women's pleasure?

The pages of the book, as Peck points out, show the dalliance of occasional painting of illustrations, which are large and undetailed. Are we to assume that this painting was done by the female hand, presumably Purefoy's? In describing as it does the "ordering of the Garden of Pleasure" and the "delights" to be found in flowers, the text itself would seem to invite such embellishment, especially in the winter months when an actual garden would not be available for the passing of pleasurable hours. Presented into "the hands" of Queen Henrietta Maria, Parkinson writes in his dedication to her that "this speaking Garden . . . may informe you in all the particulars of your store, as well as wants, when you cannot see them fresh vpon the ground" (**2r). In light of the author's prefatory materials, the woman's hand in the Folger volume would seem to be one of dalliance and to subscribe to the women's role as painted in its opening pages.

A central tension in the *Paradisus* comes from the ways in which this text specifically, but the print herbal tradition in general,[16] facilitates the practice of medicine by women at the same time as it increasingly circumscribes it with a

---

[14] I am grateful to Linda Levy Peck for drawing my attention to this inscription.

[15] John Parkinson, *Paradisi in Sole Paradisus Terrestris* (London, 1629), sig. **3r; subsequent citations included in text. Jane Donawerth, "Women's Poetry and the Tudor-Stuart System of Gift Exchange," in *Women, Writing, and the Reproduction of Culture in Tudor and Stuart Britain,* ed. Mary E. Burke, Jane Donawerth, Linda L. Dove, and Karen Nelson (Syracuse, NY: Syracuse Univ. Press, 2000), 3–18, here 14, and Linda Levy Peck, *Consuming Splendor: Society and Culture in Seventeenth-Century England* (Cambridge: Cambridge Univ. Press, 2005), 226.

[16] Eleanour Sinclair Rohde places this volume in the herbal print tradition while admitting it is "strictly not a herbal, but a gardening book": *The Old English Herbals* (New York: Dover Publications, Inc., 1971 [1922]), 142. I address the fluid genre of this volume at length in Chapter One of my forthcoming book, *Medical Authority and Englishwomen's Herbal Texts, 1550–1650.*

concept of "feminine" endeavors. As the most feminized (through the prefatory materials) of the volumes in the early tradition, the *Paradisus* includes various medicinal benefits of plants, though giving equal time to decorative foliage and often highlighting herbal values in cosmetics. Because of the publicly recognized cultural practice of gentlewomen taking care of the health of their household and their poor neighbors, however, Parkinson includes basic medicinal information; for example, "All the kindes of Cranes bils are accounted great wound herbes, and effectuall to stay bleedings" (230). Parkinson himself even provides cross-references to his earlier volume in the much more heavily medicinal *Theatrum Botanicum* of 1640. If we were to read this text as existing purely for one's leisure, then we would need to account for the inclusion of medicinal aspects of the plants.

The handwritten inscription in the volume may provide a means of furthering our analysis, as it indicates two relationships to its pages: one that relates to it as a female head of household, another as a yet unmarried girl. We need to consider the possibility that perhaps the two sisters saw the volume differently. Elizabeth Franklin, wife of a member of Parliament and mother of seventeen children by the time of his death in 1647, may have valued the volume for its medical knowledge.[17] Indeed, with her husband's position in Parliament, it is likely that Lady Franklin had many duties to oversee, not the least of which was the maintenance of the health of the household.

Anne Purefoy, still in her father George Purefoy's household in Berkshire at the time of the gift, certainly not in charge of any caregiving, perhaps saw a source for embroidery patterns and practice for painting. Then again, who is to say that her purposes for the book did not change over time? While a girl, Anne may have viewed the volume as a source of diversion; she may, however, have also seen the *Paradisus* as essential reading in her girlhood education and a resource in her future household work.

If we read Anne Purefoy's hand in a volume as only dabbling in the herbal tradition, we see her thus replicating the "dainty delight" prescribed for her in its pages; however, if we recognize the presence of her sister, a female head of a large household, we may read other ways in which the volume functioned, and the medicinal information in that volume, relatively limited as it may be, gains importance. Then again, perhaps the book's attractiveness as a gift was its variety

---

[17] We know this from a memorial in Middlesex to Sir John Francklyn that seems to have been written by her, found in Daniel Lysons, *The Environs of London: being an historical account of the towns, villages, and hamlets, within twelve miles of that capital*, Vol. III (London, 1795), 618. My thanks to Jason Powell for his help in finding this epitaph.

of functions. In the end, we can only take these prescriptive volumes for the information they give and cannot presume to know how they were used.

I hope these three examples of women's manuscript writing at its most basic level—the writing of one's name—have introduced the complex engagement of early modern women with medical texts. Marital status, economic means, number of children, family associations, geographic location, all become factors in such engagement. When we consider such factors, medical authority does not become one thing, a fixed male body of knowledge.

My intent is not to stop with the signature, however, but to consider how medical content within women's writing may be similarly various in its engagement with medical authority, how writings by Anne Wheathill, Isabella Whitney, Brilliana Harley, Anne Southwell, Margaret Hoby, Grace Mildmay, and Anne Clifford, among others, may similarly negotiate male textual authority, or not do so, as they extend female domestic practice through writing. I want to ask and have asked how factors such as marital and economic status, geographic location, and family background may differently inform how medicinal tropes function within various writings. And in literary terms, I want to know how writing in various genres—diaries, letters, poetry, and devotionals—and in different modes of production—manuscript and print—may determine the rhetorical purposes and strategies of such medical content. In such considerations, the historical practice of early modern women's medicine becomes not a monolith to be mapped onto various texts uniformly but rather a perceived source of dynamic textual potential.

UNIVERSITY OF COLORADO
COLORADO SPRINGS

Typographic Nostalgia:
Popularity and the Meanings
of Black Letter

ZACHARY LESSER

B LACK LETTER TYPE HAS LONG ENJOYED A PRIVILEGED POSITION AMONG scholars because it seems to provide a material key to readership, in particular to "popular" readership. Since the beginnings of modern bibliography in the early twentieth century, scholars have asked the black-letter typography of "cheap print" (broadside ballads, chapbooks, romances) to serve as a "social discriminant" in differentiating "high" from "low" readers.[1] But popular reading seems never to answer our demands to reveal itself, and our quest for it is thoroughly nostalgic. Nostalgia, according to Susan Stewart, involves the search for "re-union" or authenticity in the past, but such a "narrative utopia" works "only by virtue of its partiality," its tendentious and incomplete representation of history making any such re-union impossible. Nostalgia thus functions to reproduce itself endlessly, as it does not supply some present lack with the fullness

---

A longer version of this essay previously appeared as "Typographic Nostalgia: Play-Reading, Popularity, and the Meanings of Black Letter," in *The Book of the Play: Playwrights, Stationers, and Readers in Early Modern England*, ed. Marta Straznicky (Amherst: Univ. of Massachusetts Press, 2006), 99–126. This paper was presented at the 2005 MLA Convention in Washington, DC, as part of a panel entitled "Legal, Paratextual, and Typographic Concerns in Early Modern English Texts," Thomas Leland Berger, Saint Lawrence University, presiding.

[1] I refer to the titles of a few of the most influential studies dealing with black letter, all of which I discuss below: Tessa Watt, *Cheap Print and Popular Piety, 1550–1640* (Cambridge: Cambridge Univ. Press, 1991); Hyder E. Rollins, "The Black-Letter Broadside Ballad," *PMLA* 34 (1919): 258–339; Charles C. Mish, "Black Letter as a Social Discriminant in the Seventeenth Century," *PMLA* 68 (1953): 627–31.

of the past, but rather reproduces the desire for fullness itself: "nostalgia is the desire for desire."[2]

We can see a similar process at work in critical interpretations of black letter and "popular culture." Typographic nostalgia imagines the popular as a unified and distinct culture, locating in some (always shifting) past the moment of a split between high and low, elite and popular. But, as Scott Shershow writes, "rival social groups never really 'have' their 'own' separate and autonomous cultures but are, instead, participants in intricately interrelated fields of cultural production."[3] And as Roger Chartier argues, the search for popular culture relies on the flawed assumption "that the category of 'the people' or 'the popular' has sufficient coherence and stability to define a distinct social identity that can be used to organize cultural differences."[4] Because these assumptions nostalgically posit a unity and authenticity to popular culture that dissolves on closer inspection, in discussions of black-letter printing the "people" supposedly signaled as readers of this typeface slide up and down the social scale, and the moment when they became separated from "high" culture (or when elites "withdrew" from popular culture) slides back and forth in time. But the search continues: the study of popular culture is the desire for popular culture.

A brief review of the work on black letter reveals that this desire springs from a fundamental misunderstanding of the "systems of linguistic and bibliographical codings" that make up books.[5] Jerome McGann and D. F. McKenzie have stressed that the material aspects of books—typeface, layout, format—are semiotic codings and therefore must be interpreted just as much as language.[6] Almost all studies of black letter, however, see the typeface merely as a direct *index* to readership, one that has seemed all the more appealing, I suspect, because of the apparently empirical quality of bibliography as compared to literary criticism.[7]

---

[2] Susan Stewart, *On Longing: Narratives of the Miniature, the Gigantic, the Souvenir, the Collection* (Durham, NC: Duke Univ. Press, 1993), 23.

[3] Scott Cutler Shershow, "New Life: Cultural Studies and the Problem of the 'Popular'," *Textual Practice* 12 (1998): 23–47, here 24.

[4] Roger Chartier, *The Cultural Uses of Print in Early Modern France*, trans. Lydia G. Cochrane (Princeton: Princeton Univ. Press, 1987), 3.

[5] Jerome McGann, *The Textual Condition* (Princeton: Princeton Univ. Press, 1991), 15.

[6] McGann, *The Textual Condition*; D. F. McKenzie, "Typography and Meaning: The Case of William Congreve," in *Making Meaning: "Printers of the Mind" and Other Essays*, ed. Peter D. McDonald and Michael F. Suarez (Amherst: Univ. of Massachusetts Press, 2002), 198–236.

[7] The dichotomy, however, has been refused repeatedly by recent bibliographers, although the New Bibliographers, with their emphasis on scientific method, helped to establish it. See G. Thomas Tanselle, *A Rationale of Textual Criticism* (Philadelphia: Univ. of Pennsylvania Press,

Already in R. B. McKerrow's 1927 *Introduction to Bibliography for Literary Students*, black letter was seen as a marker of popular reading and used to distinguish "high" from "low" forms of literature.[8] But it was Charles Mish's 1953 essay on "Black Letter as a Social Discriminant in the Seventeenth Century" that most entrenched the notion that the typeface could serve as an index to popular culture. In his study of romance, Mish concluded that "there must have been two distinct groups of readers in early Stuart times, each with its own provender": black-letter chivalric romances for the middle class, and roman heroic romances for the upper class. As roman became the standard for English books around 1590, black letter became "a cultural retardation," indicating "the conservatism of the middle-class reading public."[9] Mish's argument has been accepted rather uncritically, and his notion that popular reading is a residue of formerly elite taste that has "sunk" to lower social ground has persisted in recent work. Paul Salzman writes that prose fictions printed in "unfashionable" and "conservative" black letter "were read by a less sophisticated public than the newly fashionable, more expensive heroic romances, printed in roman type."[10] Bernard Capp claims that John Taylor's readers "were the 'better sort,' respectable tradesmen with a sound schooling" because "his pamphlets were generally printed in roman type,

---

1989), 33–35; D. F. McKenzie, *Bibliography and the Sociology of Texts* (London: British Library, 1986), 14; Jerome McGann, "The Monks and the Giants: Textual and Bibliographical Studies and the Interpretation of Literary Works," in *Textual Criticism and Literary Interpretation*, ed. idem (Chicago: Univ. of Chicago Press, 1985), 180–99.

[8] Ronald B. McKerrow, *An Introduction to Bibliography for Literary Students* (Oxford: Clarendon Press, 1927), 297: "by about 1580 the use of black letter in plays *and the higher kinds of English verse*, as well as in Latin books, had almost ceased," while *"popular prose* and ballads, however, continued to be printed in black letter until well on in the seventeenth century" (emphasis added).

[9] Mish, "Black Letter," 628–29. The frequent, nearly ubiquitous, claim that black letter disappeared as the standard typeface for English books in the late sixteenth century deserves further investigation and some qualification. Given that black letter was used throughout the period for some of the books printed in the largest runs and most frequently reprinted—ballads, many of the translations of the Bible, catechisms, some of the most popular devotional books, even law books (which required frequent updates and new editions)—I suspect early modern readers were exposed to far more black letter during the seventeenth century than most scholars believe. The "disappearance" of black letter is skewed both by scholars' overreliance on first editions, rather than the total book trade, and by the lower survival rate of cheap, short books that would have been used to destruction.

[10] Paul Salzman, *English Prose Fiction 1558–1700: A Critical History* (Oxford: Clarendon Press, 1985), 265–67.

not the black letter still widely used for the most popular fare."[11] Examples could be multiplied.[12]

As I have argued elsewhere, however, while the material features of books testify to the readership imagined by publishers, the readings they expected from customers, and the marketing strategies designed to reach them, these features tell us less about the actual readers of books. Examining presentational choices like typeface, format, or the use of illustrations helps us to understand the position of a particular book within the marketplace of print, and books may indeed be positioned as "low" or "high" in this market, just as they may be positioned along a host of other ideological ranges. Books positioned as "low" did not automatically or exclusively have a "low" readership, merely a readership interested, for whatever variety of reasons, in a "low" book.[13] We owe the very survival of many seventeenth-century ballads to the collecting efforts of such elites as John Selden and Samuel Pepys, interested precisely in their power to capture what Selden called "the Complexion of the times."[14]

Much of the "conservatism" that Mish and his followers identify in fact resides not in readers' taste but in publishers' and printers' work habits. Typography was an extremely conservative medium in early modern England, and books rarely changed typeface from one edition to the next.[15] The fact that black letter was "still" used in later editions of books first printed in that typeface is not surprising, nor does it indicate an unchanging or static *reading of* these texts. And the mere fact that roman came to dominate many classes of books does not mean

---

[11] Bernard Capp, *The World of John Taylor the Water-Poet, 1578–1653* (Oxford: Clarendon Press, 1994), 67.

[12] See, for example, John Barnard, "Introduction," in *The Cambridge History of the Book in Britain, Volume IV, 1557–1695*, ed. idem and D. F. McKenzie, with assistance by Maureen Bell (Cambridge: Cambridge Univ. Press, 2002), 4–5; D. R. Woolf, "Genre into Artifact: The Decline of the English Chronicle in the Sixteenth Century," *Sixteenth Century Journal* 19 (1988): 321–54, here 328; Barry Reay, *Popular Cultures in England, 1550–1750* (New York: Longman, 1998), 56–57; David Cressy, "Literacy in Context: Meaning and Measurement in Early Modern England," in *Consumption and the World of Goods*, ed. John Brewer and Roy Porter (New York: Routledge, 1993), 305–19, here 312.

[13] See Zachary Lesser, *Renaissance Drama and the Politics of Publication: Readings in the English Book Trade* (Cambridge: Cambridge Univ. Press, 2004); Alan B. Farmer and Zachary Lesser, "Vile Arts: The Marketing of English Printed Drama, 1512–1660," *Research Opportunities in Renaissance Drama* 39 (2000): 77–165.

[14] "Libells," in *Table Talk of John Selden*, ed. Frederick Pollock (London: Quaritch, 1927), 72.

[15] See Mark Bland, "The Appearance of the Text in Early Modern England," *TEXT* 11 (1998): 91–154, here 95. John Wright, the publisher whom I will discuss below, changed the typography of a book from its previous edition only three times from 1605 to 1631, twice from black letter to roman, and once from roman to black letter.

that black letter is a residual "cultural retardation." As Tim Harris astutely notes, since culture is always changing, whenever one seeks to "identify what 'popular culture' was like" before some putative "long-term cultural change . . . it is inevitable that this traditional culture is always going to appear to be shrinking."[16] The Mish tradition similarly identifies black letter with "traditional" culture, then notes its shrinking use after about 1590, and concludes therefore that books printed in black letter after that date form the residual culture of the "people."

But who exactly were these "people"? For Mish, they are merchants and tradesmen, since the "lower class can hardly be said to constitute a segment of the reading public."[17] For Capp, the "people" are instead those Mish defines as the "lower class," since Taylor's roman works were read by the same "respectable tradesmen" whom Mish sees as the readers of black letter. For Hyder Rollins, black-letter ballads were "written down to the level of the least intelligent reader."[18] While black letter appears to be the material index to a class of readers, this class formation is never stable. What this instability reveals is that black letter is not an *index* but a sliding *signifier* of the "low" that depends on how the critic defines the total spectrum of readers.

A second highly influential strand of scholarship derives from Keith Thomas's groundbreaking article, "The Meaning of Literacy in Early Modern England."[19] Thomas accepts Mish's argument but adds another component by claiming that black letter was literally easier to read than roman: "black-letter literacy . . . was a more basic skill than roman-type literacy; and it did not follow that the reader fluent in one was equally at home in the other."[20] Thomas's argument too has been picked up somewhat hastily by scholars to indicate that, in the words of D. R. Woolf, "readers at the lower end of literate society" were "unable

---

[16] Tim Harris, "Problematising Popular Culture," in *Popular Culture in England, c. 1500–1850*, ed. idem (New York: St. Martin's Press, 1995), 1–27, here 23.

[17] Mish, "Black Letter," 27 n. 1.

[18] Rollins, "Black-Letter," 331. Rollins's view of the readers of ballads is a bit confused. He argues that it would be a "serious error to suppose that only the lower classes read ballads" ("Black-Letter," 332), but he then distinguishes between the news ballads read by the lower classes and the "more cultivated readers" for lyrical ballads, a distinction that simply relocates the divide to the aesthetic rather than the typographical realm. Elsewhere, he notes that ballads "have always interested educated men" but also claims that they were "produced solely for the common people. . . ." Hyder E. Rollins, *A Pepysian Garland: Black-Letter Broadside Ballads of the Years 1595–1639* (Cambridge: Cambridge Univ. Press, 1922), xi–xii. Ultimately, it seems Rollins adheres to the basic view of black letter as a key to popular readership, but qualifies this view in order better to make his polemical case that the ballads are "worthy" of study.

[19] Keith Thomas, "The Meaning of Literacy in Early Modern England," in *The Written Word: Literacy in Transition*, ed. Gerd Baumann (Oxford: Clarendon Press, 1986), 97–131.

[20] Thomas, "Meaning of Literacy," 99.

to read in Roman type works they had mastered in Gothic."[21] But Thomas in fact provides no evidence for his claim apart from the fact that books often used for learning to read (primers, catechisms, hornbooks) were usually printed in black letter. And the claim that some readers found roman type impossible or extremely difficult to read seems rather unlikely. For what it's worth, twentieth-century studies of typography by cognitive psychologists have generally concluded that all typefaces in wide circulation at a given time are equally legible.[22] More importantly, from the late sixteenth century on, almost no books were printed entirely in black letter: virtually all black-letter books contained a roman (and italic) title page.[23] Given that the title page was the most important marketing tool at the publisher's disposal, it seems odd to suggest that black-letter books were targeted at "early" readers, when the first part of the book these readers would see—and the part designed to attract their attention and their money—was printed in a typeface supposedly difficult for them to read. Similarly, black-letter broadsides like ballads and proclamations were almost always printed with roman headers, including the title.

Further, while stationers evidently did feel that these early reading books required black letter, they felt exactly the same way about a category of books obviously intended not for the common reader but for a highly specialized, elite reader: almost all lawbooks were printed in black letter. Notably, the various scholarly explanations for black-letter lawbook printing—that the type "confer[red] a kind of antiquarian dignity," or that it carried state authority (being also used for official proclamations)—all assert a *semiotic* not an indexical explanation.[24] But lawbooks—and large chronicle histories priced beyond the

---

[21] Woolf, "Genre into Artifact," 328 n. 22. See similar claims by Reay, *Popular Cultures*, 45; Cressy, "Literacy in Context," 312; Paul J. Voss, *Elizabethan News Pamphlets: Shakespeare, Spenser, Marlowe and the Birth of Journalism* (Pittsburgh: Duquesne Univ. Press, 2001), 80. Others make the same point without citing Thomas: Peter Blayney, "The Publication of Playbooks," in *A New History of Early English Drama*, ed. John D. Cox and David Scott Kastan (New York: Columbia Univ. Press, 1997), 383–422, here 414; Ian Green, *Print and Protestantism in Early Modern England* (Oxford: Oxford Univ. Press, 2000), 61, 65; Ian Green, *The Christian's ABC: Catechisms and Catechizing in England c. 1530–1740* (Oxford: Clarendon Press, 1996), 255. Andrew Murphy follows Blayney to argue that "works aimed at those who were less educated . . . were printed in blackletter": *Shakespeare in Print: A History and Chronology of Shakespeare Publishing* (Cambridge: Cambridge Univ. Press, 2003), 30.

[22] See Miles A. Tinker, *Legibility of Print* (Ames: Iowa State Univ. Press, 1963), 46–54.

[23] John Wright published sixty-six black-letter editions (non-broadsides) between 1605 and 1631; not a single one was printed with a black-letter title page. Ian Green offers a similar caveat, but seems to accept nonetheless that black letter was targeted at "early" readers (*Print*, 65).

[24] Blayney, "Publication of Playbooks," 414; Mish, "Black Letter," 630 n. 4; Bland, "Appearance of the Text," 93. Bland, it should be noted, does *not* fall into either of the two schol-

means of the "common people"—are almost always considered exceptions to the rule of the "popularity" of black letter, and thus contradictory evidence is simply excluded from consideration. Faced with the totality of evidence, however, we might conclude not that lawbooks and chronicles are the semiotic exceptions to an indexical rule, but rather that primers and catechisms were likewise thought to require black letter because the typeface carried meaning.

Black letter, after all, was also known as "English letter," because it was the dominant type for *vernacular* books for the first century of printing in England. Given this strong association, and the conservatism of typography, perhaps we should not be surprised that books designed to teach the reading of the English language were printed in English letter. We should not, however, conclude with Peter Blayney that more educated readers eventually graduated to roman type, leaving black letter behind; Blayney's claim that "the basic Latin school text, Lily's *Grammar*, was therefore printed in roman" needs to be qualified.[25] Most editions of William Lily's *Short Introduction of Grammar* were bilingual (with the latter half entirely in Latin and the first half in Latin and English), and throughout the early modern period, in fact, these editions used roman (or italic) type for their Latin and black letter for their English translations and instructions (Figure 1).[26] The typography of Lily's textbook, then, does not signal a split in the book trade between black-letter printing for less-educated and roman printing for more-educated readers. Rather, the typographic distinction between the two languages in the *Grammar* shows that more educated readers were still reading plenty of black letter, and it points us towards the semiotics of black letter in the hornbooks and primers that had earlier taught them their "English letter(s)." Similarly, as late as 1659, William Somner's trilingual dictionary used roman for its Latin and black letter for its English translations of Anglo-Saxon words (Figure 2). Printed at Oxford for scholars, with a Latin title page, the large folio dictionary was obviously not meant for the beginning reader. Most catechisms as well (*pace* Thomas) employed various typefaces, and they too illustrate the use of black letter as a signifier of basic English knowledge, for catechisms generally use roman for the questions and black letter for the responses demonstrating

---

arly traditions I am outlining here; his article is a rare exception that *reads* typefaces—black letter, roman, and italic—as bearers of semiotic meaning. For two other exceptions, see Lori Humphrey Newcomb's brief but trenchant critique of Mish in *Reading Popular Romance in Early Modern England* (New York: Columbia Univ. Press, 2002), 140; and Sabrina Alcorn Baron's fine article "Red Ink and Black Letter: Reading Early Modern Authority," in *The Reader Revealed*, ed. eadem, Elizabeth Walsh, and Susan Scola (Washington, DC: Folger Shakespeare Library, 2001), 19–30.

[25] Blayney, "Publication of Playbooks," 414.

[26] See Bland, "Appearance of the Text," 93.

the catechumen's knowledge and acceptance of the fundamental tenets of the English church.[27]

Much of the meaning of black letter may not have been fully conscious to stationers; its use may be another example of what I have elsewhere called "typographic inevitability."[28] But in charged political moments, the semiotics of black letter could become not only conscious but polemical: when Archbishop Laud tried to impose a new prayer book on the Scottish church in 1637, he had the commanding folio book printed in black letter, as virtually all folio Books of (English) Common Prayer had been printed. Part of the resentment aroused by Laud's effort, part of what sparked the rioting that ultimately led to war, was the typography of the book.[29] Laud's choice of black letter was designed to extend his drive for uniformity of religious practice ("common prayer") to the Kirk, which had long been printing its own Book of Common Order in roman, the typeface of the godly Geneva Bible.[30] Black letter here emphasized not only the antiquity and authority of black-letter chronicles and state proclamations but also something of the semiotics of primers and catechisms: the "Englishness" of the typeface and of the episcopacy was the central issue in many Scottish minds.

Black letter thus carried many meanings: state authority, antiquity, the English language, the established English church, even the foreign quality of the "stage Dutch" spoken by characters in some printed plays. And, of course, the use of black letter was also partially determined by the more mundane requirements of printers: the amount and kinds of type they stocked, the type used in other books they were simultaneously printing. We must resist the reductionism that would see only a single meaning to the typeface, or that would see no meaning at all in it, only an index to "popular culture." But one of the dominant meanings of black letter in this period, I am suggesting, was the powerful combination of Englishness (the "English letter") and past-ness (the "antiquated" appearance of black letter by the seventeenth century) that I call typographic nostalgia. It is this

---

[27] Green, *Christian's ABC*, 256.

[28] Zachary Lesser, "Walter Burre's *The Knight of the Burning Pestle*," *English Literary Renaissance* 29 (1999): 22–43, here 31.

[29] See Jonquil Bevan, "Scotland," in Barnard et al., eds., *Cambridge History of the Book*, 687–700, here 694. More than 80% of all English Books of Common Prayer printed in folio or quarto during the early Stuart period were black-letter books. For sizes of octavo or smaller, printers in the early Stuart period favored roman by almost the same margin, perhaps because black letter becomes increasingly difficult to read as the page gets smaller (and hence the proportion of black to white increases, far more so than with roman type), or perhaps because printers no longer stocked fonts of black letter in smaller sizes. The pattern is similar with Bibles, as Blayney ("Publication of Playbooks," 422 n. 66) and Green (*Print*, 60–66) both note.

[30] On the connotations of biblical typeface, see Bland, "Appearance of the Text," 94.

THE CONSTRVCTION OF THE

But when their commeth a Nominatiue case betweene the Relatiue and the Uerbe, the Relatiue shall be such case as the Uerbe will haue after him: as Fœlix quem faciunt aliena pericula cautum, Happie is he, whom other mens harmes do make to beware,

As the Relatiue may be the Nominatiue case to the Uerbe, so it may bee the Substantiue to the Adiectiue that is ioyned with him, or that commeth after him: as Diuitias amare noli, quod omnium est sordidissimum, Loue not thou riches, which to doe, is the most beggerly thing in the world.

Nounes Interrogatiues and Indefinites, follow the rule of the Relatiue: as Quis, uter, qualis, quantus, quotus, &c. which euermore come before the Uerbe like as the Relatiue doth: as Hei mihi, qualis erat? talis erat, qualem numquam vidi.

Yet heere is to bee vnderstood and noted, that the Relatiue is not alwayes gouerned of the Uerbe that it commeth before, but sometime of the Infinitiue mood that commeth after the verbe: as Quibus voluisti me gratias agere, egi: whom persons thou willedst me to thanke, I haue thanked.

Sometime of a Participle: as Quibus rebus adductus fecisti? with what things moued didst thou it?

Sometime of the Gerund: as Que nunc non est narrandi locus, which thing at this present is no time to tell.

Sometime of the Prepofition set before him: as Quem in locu deducta res sit vides: Unto what state the matter is now brought, thou seest.

Sometime of the Substantiue that he doth accord with as Senties qui vir sim, thou shalt perceiue what a fellow I am. Albeit in this manner speaking, Qui, is an indefinite, and not a Relatiue.
Sometime

EIGHT PARTS OF SPEECH.

Sometime of a Noune Partitiue or Distributiue: as, Quarum rerum vtram minùs velim, non facilè possum existimare, Of the which two things whether I would with lesse will haue I cannot easily esteeme.

Sometime it is put in the Genitiue case by reason of a Substantiue comming next after him: as, Ego illum non novi, cuius causa hoc incipis, I know him not for whose cause thou beginnest this matter.

Sometime it is otherwise gouerned of a Noune Substantiue: as, Omnia tibi dabuntur, quibus opus habes, All things shall be giuen thee, which thou hast neede of.

Sometime of an Aduerbe: as, Cui vtram obviam procedam, nondum statui, whom whether I will go to meet with, I haue not yet determined.

Sometime it is put in the ablatiue case with this figure than, & is gouerned of the comparatiue degree comming after him: as, Vtere virtute, quâ nihil est melius, Vse vertue, than the which nothing is better.

Sometime it is not gouerned at all but is put in the Ablatiue case absolute: as, Quantus erat Iulius Cæsar, quo Imperatore, Romani primùm Brittanniam ingressi sunt: How worthy a man was Iulius Cæsar, vnder whose conduct the Romans first entred into Brittaine.

Also when it signifieth an instrument wherwith a thing is to be done, it is put in the Ablatiue case: as, Ferrum habuit quo se occiderit, He had a knife wherwith he would haue slaine himselfe.

When a Relatiue commeth betweene two Substantiues of diuers genders, it may indifferently accord with either of them: as, Avis, quæ passer appellatur; or Avis, qui passer appellatur: The bird which

Figure 1. William Lily, *A Short Introdvction of Grammar, generally to be vsed* (London: 1633), D5v–D6r, showing the use of roman typeface for Latin and black letter for English. By permission of the Folger Shakespeare Library.

combination that allows black letter to evoke the traditional English community, and a large part of what scholars are discovering when they see "popular culture" in black letter is the construction of this nostalgia in the very texts they are reading.[31]

Certainly, many black-letter texts were among the cheapest and hence most widely available and read in the period; in this sense, we can speak of the part

---

[31] I am influenced here by, and paraphrasing, Shershow's incisive comment that "what scholars are really discovering when they piece together the scattered evidence of cultural reception and shifting aesthetic taste is a relentless effort to *construct* hierarchies which literally did not and do not exist except as they are proclaimed and deployed" ("New Life," 43).

Figure 2. William Somner, *Dictionarium Saxonico-Latino-Anglicum* (London: 1659), 2C1r; the dictionary uses Anglo-Saxon, roman, and black letter typefaces to denote linguistic difference. By permission of the Folger Shakespeare Library.

they played in the "common" culture of England. On the other hand, we should not assume that all people consumed these texts in the same way: a laborer who reads a printed ballad on a tavern wall is not quite reading the "same" text as a nobleman who transcribes it into his commonplace book, or as Selden and Pepys who collected them.[32] Focusing our analysis on the ways in which black letter could be *read*, the meanings it carried in the full context of both the book trade and English social hierarchy, offers the best cure for typographic nostalgia.

I want to suggest how such an analysis might proceed by looking briefly at the career of one important publisher of black-letter texts in the seventeenth century, John Wright. Very schematically, we can say that Wright was a "popular" publisher according to three specific, but not necessarily interrelated, meanings of that term: most simply, his books sold well and were often reprinted; second, he employed a business strategy that emphasized the "tried and true"; and, third, the books in which he specialized have traditionally (but, as I have been arguing, erroneously) been seen by critics as "for the common people." He brought out some of the period's bestsellers, but he generally did not publish all or even the majority of their editions. Wright employed a business strategy that might itself be described as "popular publishing," as he sought to acquire the rights to books that had already gone through a substantial number of editions for other publishers. Wright's edition of John Dod and Robert Cleaver's *Exposition of the Ten Commandments* claims to be the eighteenth overall, and the anonymous *Shepherd's Kalendar* had already gone through seventeen extant editions before Wright became involved; his first edition of William Perkins's *Death's Knell* claims to be the eleventh overall, and he began publishing Philip Stubbes's *Life and Death of Katherine Stubbes* with the eighteenth extant edition.

Since critics have generally expected that bestsellers, because of their very popularity, can "tell us about the values, tastes, and expectations of their mass audience," Wright will thus look like a publisher targeting the common people, the "little tradition," or the broadly consensual mainstream.[33] But he will look so *only as a side effect or epiphenomenon* of what seems to be an underlying business decision to invest in acquiring rights to profitable books, rather than searching for new copy in the hopes of correctly gauging the market himself. Even apart

---

[32] See Watt, *Cheap Print*, 17, on commonplace books, although she does not develop the point. For the theoretical argument, see Chartier (*Cultural Uses of Print*, 6–11), although he sometimes seems to replace the traditional dichotomy of high and low texts or cultural objects with a dichotomy of reading methods or ways of appropriating culture, almost equally static and reified.

[33] Bob Scribner discusses the problems with such an approach in "Is a History of Popular Culture Possible?" *History of European Ideas* 10 (1989): 175–91, here 176.

from the problems inherent in taking numerical popularity as a guide to popular culture, then, Wright's commercial strategy does not seem aimed at a specific
group of consumers so much as at a specific kind of book (the proven seller), and
without direct evidence (always hard to come by) we cannot be sure who the actual readers of these books were. As Tessa Watt has detailed, Wright helped to
develop the trade in "penny merries" and "penny godlies" that formed the core
of what has been seen as the popular print culture of later periods.[34] There can
be no doubt that Wright was specializing in "cheap print," but what is *not* clear is
exactly what "cheap print" tells us about "popular culture." As Watt herself concluded after her analysis, the idea that cheap books "were aimed at and consumed
by a definable social group may be a myth."[35]

While Wright might be considered a "popular" publisher in these specific
senses, and while black letter was clearly an important part of his specialty, his use
of the typeface cannot be easily or immediately taken to mean he was targeting
"common" readers. Rather, Wright often seems to have used it for the meaning it
carried. Like all ballads, his were printed in black letter, but he also brought out a
very similar category of book—which we might call "broadside news verses"—in
roman type. Like ballads, these broadside news verses were single- or half-sheet
folios with a woodcut illustration (Figure 3). Both categories must have been
among the cheapest books on the market, and, like ballads, the news verses dealt
with subjects accessible to people of all sorts and degrees, including the death of
King James and the return of Prince Charles from Spain, a mourning and a celebration respectively in which virtually all Londoners participated.

The comparison with broadside news verses should lead us towards a
semiotic—rather than an economic or indexical—rationale for the typographic
inevitability of the black-letter ballad. Typographic nostalgia, with its evocation
of the traditional English community, must be a part of this rationale. While
the broadside news verses were explicitly topical, clearly rooted in the historical
moment of their creation, ballads seemed to originate from communal and
timeless memory, imagined less as the product of an authorizing pen than of their
communal and repeated singing in tavern, village, and fair.[36] Fewer than one in
five of Wright's ballads contain an author attribution, while more than half of his
non-ballad books, and two of his three broadside news verses, do. Overall, the
titles that Wright published in roman were far more likely to attribute an author

---

    [34] See Watt, *Cheap Print*, esp. chap. 7; Watt is building on—and providing the prehistory
to—Margaret Spufford, *Small Books and Pleasant Histories: Popular Fiction and Its Readership
in Seventeenth-Century England* (Athens: Univ. of Georgia Press, 1982).
    [35] Watt, *Cheap Print*, 3.
    [36] Watt, *Cheap Print*, 81.

than his black-letter titles. Exactly this timeless, "common" quality of black letter creates the sense of unity and tradition so important to those books, like the Book of Common Prayer, that sought to *create* this unity.

Ballads epitomize cheap print, but another of Wright's black-letter books— and an early modern bestseller—must have been one of his most expensive. *The Shepherd's Kalendar*, which Wright published in 1631 even as he was building his catalogue of "penny" books, ran to fifty sheets folio and was his second-largest book during this period. What this massive folio shares with the broadside ballad, however, is a nostalgic idea of the English village community. As Natalie Zemon Davis has written, these calendars "appear a cross between a folklorist's recording and a pastoral, a shaped vision of the peasant world [enabling] country gentlemen and city people . . . to identify themselves with [its] simple wisdom."[37] Addressed to the "gentle Reader," Wright's edition offers this timeless country wisdom in the form of homely proverbs, religious catechisms, and numerous ballads sung by the shepherds. With its combination of the ancient, the pastoral, and the proverbial, the anonymous *Kalendar,* like the ballads, seems almost to emanate from the land itself. But its large format and length, and the Latin passages scattered throughout, indicate that its likely audience was socially far above the shepherds represented in the book itself.[38] Black letter here functions as the typographic analogue to the nostalgic process that Raymond Williams sees at work in some versions of Renaissance pastoral: "living tensions are excised, until there is nothing countervailing, and selected images stand as themselves: not in a living but in an enamelled world."[39]

A large part of the meaning of "popular culture" in scholarship since the late eighteenth century has been precisely this vision of the idealized "organic community" combined with the very *spectacle of* the "low" or the "common" by those

---

[37] N. Z. Davis, "Printing and the People," in *Rethinking Popular Culture: Contemporary Perspectives in Cultural Studies*, ed. Chandra Mukerji and Michael Schudson (Berkeley: Univ. of California Press, 1991), 65–96, here 68.

[38] *The shepherds kalender* (London: [Eliot's Court Press] for John Wright, 1631), A2r; for examples of Latin verses, see D5v–D6v.

[39] Raymond Williams, *The Country and the City* (New York: Oxford Univ. Press, 1973), 18. This is not to say that pastoral could never encode an oppositional or emergent ideology; for examples, see Lesser, *Renaissance Drama*, chap. 5. For a view of pastoral and especially the country-house poem that is consonant with but also qualifies Williams, see Don E. Wayne, *Penshurst: The Semiotics of Place and the Poetics of History* (Madison: Univ. of Wisconsin Press, 1984). Wayne emphasizes the "rhetorical and narrative strategies [of Jonson's country-house poetry] which, while often aimed at the resolution or containment of social contradictions, have the effect of revealing them in a new light" (130), and this revelation yields critique simultaneously with ideology.

Figure 3. William Hockham, *Prince Charles His Welcome to the Court* (London: 1623), one of John Wright's "broadside news verses," printed largely in roman typeface. By permission of the Society of Antiquaries, London.

occupying higher social positions.[40] Black letter embodies *both* a nostalgia for a time or place devoid of contemporary conflict *and* the packaging and commodifying of "low domains" as what Peter Stallybrass and Allon White call "the object of nostalgia, longing and fascination."[41] No wonder, then, that scholars have tended to find popular culture in black-letter texts, since part of the function of black letter was to create this (imagined) popular culture and make it available for consumption.

UNIVERSITY OF PENNSYLVANIA

---

[40] For the early history of the academic study of popular culture, see Peter Burke, *Popular Culture in Early Modern Europe* (New York: Harper, 1978), 3–10.

[41] Peter Stallybrass and Allon White, *The Politics and Poetics of Transgression* (Ithaca: Cornell Univ. Press, 1986), 191.

Paternal Paratexts:
Fathering Books in the Age
of Mechanical Reproduction

DOUGLAS A. BROOKS

> One of the major difficulties of the social history of philosophy, art or lit-
> erature is that it has to reconstruct these spaces of original possibles which,
> because they were part of the self-evident givens of the situation, remained
> unremarked and are therefore unlikely to be mentioned in contemporary
> accounts, chronicles and memoirs.
>
> Pierre Bourdieu, *The Field of Cultural Production*[1]

I WANT TO BEGIN AT THE END, OR AT LEAST NEAR THE END, A NARRATIVE
temporality which, it seems to me, is not wholly inappropriate to the topic of
paratexts. In fact, such textual *alongsides* or *outsides*, having come into being with the advent of the codex near the beginning of the Christian Era, almost
always appear at the beginnings and ends of books. Moreover, my interest in beginning near the end is linked to my concern here with what might be considered the end of beginnings, or, more specifically, the end of a reliance on a certain
metaphorics of beginnings to represent the ends of the process by which a given
early modern printed book made its way into the world.

This paper was first presented at the 2005 MLA convention, Washington, DC, at a panel entitled "Legal, Paratextual, and Typographic Concerns in Early Modern English Texts,"
Thomas Leland Berger, Saint Lawrence University, presiding.

[1] Pierre Bourdieu, *The Field of Cultural Production* (New York: Columbia Univ. Press,
1993), 31.

But before going on, I feel obligated to offer up something of a paratext of my own for the text that will constitute the body of this brief essay. In writing my beginning here I have rather shamelessly exploited—perhaps parodied, is more accurate—recent meta-textual scholarship by Jeffrey Masten that is mainly concerned with ends.[2] Whereas Masten focuses on the sodomitical relations that were encoded in early modern rhetorics of collaborative authorship, my concern here is with a later stage of book production, specifically what might be thought of as the end of a given text's journey that began in the mind or minds of its author or authors, its marketing. Indeed, while Masten is primarily interested in ends, by which I mean to recall his intellectual interest in the preposterous and the anus, my own interest is with beginnings, by which I mean the largely heterosexual discourse of procreation and childbirth that was so often plundered by the writers of paratexts when attempting to depict the complex circumstances in which the materiality of a book—rather than the ideality of its contents—came into existence. Certainly the early modern authorial mind was frequently thought of as a womb, its products a kind of offspring.[3] But what seems far more interesting to me than the mind-as-womb trope that can be traced back to Plato and beyond is the ways in which what we might identify as a metaphorics of ink and kin, of printing and parenting, came to dominate the discourse of textual production after the invention of the printing press.

When we examine a range of paratexts (dedications, prefaces, notes to readers, and errata pages, for example) to texts published in England between 1476 and the mid-seventeenth century, we find an increasing reliance on tropes of paternity and human reproduction to express a number of emergent notions about the material status of a given text in the marketplace, specifically as regards that text as a legitimate and saleable commodity. Indeed, within the London book trade efforts to lend printed texts some sort of credibility and authenticity were frequently sanctioned by the discourse of human reproduction. There were other metaphorics available, and one can find examples of them,[4] but by far the most popular forms of paratextual commentary on textual production link publishing to childbirth. But that's a beginning, and I promised to begin near the end.

---

[2] Jeffrey Masten, *Textual Intercourse* (Cambridge: Cambridge Univ. Press, 1997).

[3] See Katherine Eisaman Maus, "A Womb of His Own: Male Renaissance Poets in the Female Body," in Douglas A. Brooks, ed., *Printing and Parenting in Early Modern England* (Aldershot: Ashgate, 2005), 81–99.

[4] For a discussion of the range of reproductive metaphorics available to early modern writers, see Margreta de Grazia, "Imprints: Shakespeare, Gutenberg, and Descartes," in Brooks, ed., *Printing and Parenting*, 26–52.

The end I have in mind is very different from the one that preoccupies Masten's work on textual intercourse. To bring that end into view I want to begin again with the printed text of a play that is itself thematically concerned with the links between books and procreation. First published in 1640, some two years before the end of the first era of the popular stage in England, Richard Brome's play *The Antipodes* chiefly chronicles the fate of a character named Peregrine, whose obsession with books and reading threatens to undermine his ability to be a father.[5] Already married for three years at the beginning of the play, Peregrine has yet to have conjugal relations with his wife, Martha, who is compelled to ask another woman,

> How came you by your babes? I cannot think
> Your husband got them you.
> For were I now to die, I cannot guess
> What a man does in child-getting.[6]

The problem, Brome makes clear, is that Peregrine prefers textual intercourse to marital relations with his wife. The appearance of a play that dramatizes the preference for books over bodies, reading over sex, nearly two centuries after literacy had been radically expanded by the invention of the printing press is noteworthy, especially in light of the fact that the prevailing register for depicting the products of that invention had taken its semantic and notional cues chiefly from the discourse of procreation. More significantly, however, Brome's play appears at a moment in the history of the material book when that register, I want to suggest, is on the verge of becoming obsolete—soon to be replaced by an emergent discourse of biology.

Referring to the emergence of the early modern author function, Robert Weimann observes, "[t]he ties between product and producer had become so close and personal that the process of appropriation was often sanctioned by metaphors of procreation . . . the political economy of the product (the text in the marketplace, the book as a unit of exchange-value) could be almost obliterated in the biological metaphor of procreation, which suggested the process of

---

[5] For a fuller treatment of this play in the context of paternity and print, see my essay, "Inky Kin: Reading in the Age of Gutenberg Paternity," in Marta Straznicky, ed., *The 'Booke' of the Play: Stationers, Censors, and 'Curteous' Readers* (Amherst: Univ. of Massachusetts Press, 2006), 203–28.

[6] Richard Brome, *The Antipodes*, Globe Quartos Edition, David Scott Kastan and Richard Proudfoot, eds. (New York: Theater Arts Books/Routledge, 2000), 9.

'bringing forth one's own.'"[7] If authorship, as Weimann intimates, could be represented so successfully within proto-biologistic narratives of reproduction, it is partly because such narratives of fathers and children, of blood and kinsmen, are central in narratives of ancestor worship and life after death, the conceptual foundations of fetishism, in general. That the modern author emerged concurrently with the advent of print publication can be traced at least in part to the fact that the author—especially the author as father of his textual offspring—was integral to the nascent kinds of commodity fetishism that enabled printed books to begin to have credibility, legitimacy, and value for an existing market of readers accustomed to buying and valuing books copied by scribes. Like fetishes themselves, originally useless stones or crude figurines magically endowed with the presence of an absent ancestor, printed books came to be endowed with credibility and value by the authors/fathers—often dead—who had brought them to life. Furthermore, representing the relationship between producer and product as that of father and son—with likeness between the author's intention and the resulting material text increasingly essential to the latter's value, a likeness that was primarily in the hands of the midwife/printer who delivered the text into the world—in a marketplace of books utterly transformed by movable type may have been thought to reassure a rapidly expanding market of new readers that printed books were valuable commodities deserving of purchase. As Arthur F. Marotti and Michael D. Bristol observe, print "democratically opened up texts to potentially broad and heterogeneous readerships . . . knowledge was liberated from the control of a social (and academic) literate elite for an increasingly literate general populace whose access to texts entailed politically charged rights of interpretation and use."[8] For such readers, the rhetoric of procreation and paternity must have offered them a way of relating something new—the purchase of books—to something that was profoundly integral to their lives.

When one is confronted with something radically unfamiliar, some element of the familiar can be comforting, and the prototype of the fetishistic approach to the commodification of books that emphasized the procreative element of textual reproduction was not uncommon during the long reign of the parchment codex. Indeed, the paternal link between author and text had been a staple of scribal publication that rhetorically relied on a mating ritual of sorts involving the scribe, his pen, and his parchment. This reproductive aspect of scribal

---

[7] R. Weimann, *Authority and Representation in Early Modern Discourse*, ed. David Hillman (Baltimore: The Johns Hopkins Univ. Press, 1996), 180.

[8] Arthur F. Marotti and Michael D. Bristol, eds., *Print, Manuscript, Performance: The Changing Relations of the Media in Early Modern England* (Columbus: Ohio State Univ. Press, 2000), 5.

publication was acknowledged by Richard de Bury (1285–1345) when he wrote in *Philobiblon* (1345):

> For as the bodies of books [*librorum corpora*]... undergo a continual disso-
> lution of their structure . . . a remedy should be found, by means of which
> the sacred book paying the debt of nature may obtain a natural heir and
> may raise up like seed to its dead brother, and thus may be verified that say-
> ing of Ecclesiasticus: His father is dead, and he is as if he were not dead; for
> he hath left one behind him that is like himself.[9]

Writing before the putative birth of the modern author figure postulated by Foucault and so many others, de Bury is primarily concerned here with the paternal
relation between a decaying text and a subsequent scribal copy. With the introduction of the printing press, an introduction that had a devastating impact on
the intimacy that had once been central to the relationship among author, scribe,
and reader, the concern necessarily shifted from the preservation of an existing
text by means of a faithful scribal reproduction to the legitimacy of new texts
wantonly produced in a printing house by a number of workers and a machine.

Like fetishes, within the London book trade printed texts—lifeless bodies
with no inherent powers of their own—often appeared in the world as textual
children poised to take the places of the authors/fathers who brought them into
the world with the help of midwives/stationers. As Margreta de Grazia observes,
"[i]n the English Renaissance, comparisons of mechanical and sexual reproduction, imprints and children seem to multiply. . . . The textual imprint as child
recurs in preliminaries to early modern books, putting into play the semantics
shared by biological and textual reproduction."[10] Moreover, the links between
sexual and textual reproduction are endlessly rehearsed in the literary production of the period, often suggesting that the two discourses came to be inextrica-
bly linked. Shakespeare, for example, spends the first ten sonnets of his sequence
as it has come down to us extolling the physical beauty of a certain young man
and instructing him to procreate so that said beauty will not be lost to death. But
in the very next sonnet we see the introduction of a metaphorics that, I would
argue, shapes the thematic concerns of the remainder of the sequence. There the
"I" of the poem advises the young man, "Thou shouldst print more, not let that

---

[9] Quoted in Jan-Dirk Müller, "The Body of the Book: The Media Transition from Manuscript to Print," in *Materialities of Communication*, ed. Hans Ulrich Gumbrecht and K. Lud-
wig Pfeiffer, trans. William Whobrey (Stanford: Stanford Univ. Press, 1994), 32–44, here 39.

[10] De Grazia, "Imprints," 31.

copy die."[11] Shakespeare frequently relied on words and phrases pertaining to the
early modern publishing industry throughout his career when it came to matters of sexual reproduction;[12] especially in the later romances, wherein he turned
increasingly to "the proprietorial rights and productive relations" of the London
book trade to express his character's concerns about procreation, the legitimacy
of sons, and patriarchal authority.[13]

The frequency of conceptual/lexical conflations of parenting and printing—
and there are hundreds of them—in Shakespeare's work suggests just how readily
metaphors of textual reproduction could be appropriated for the discourse of human reproduction. Indeed, for Shakespeare, who wrote almost nothing about authorship or publication, books and print provided him with a ready set of terms
with which to represent the facts of life. For Ben Jonson, on the other hand, who
wrote often and in depth about authorship and publication, the facts of life provided him with a ready set of terms with which to characterize the material being in the world of his (and other authors') works. Jonson, like Shakespeare, did,
of course, write of children, but textual reproduction metaphors are conspicuous
in their absence. Even in his epigram "On My First Son," which meditates on fa-
therhood and loss, Jonson famously calls the dead son "his best piece of poetry,"
but makes no mention of the poem-child's textuality or its material coming into
being. In other words, a playwright closely affiliated with the stage sees children
in terms of print; a playwright closely affiliated with the page sees print in terms
of children.

In the paratexts of Brome's 1640 play, however, such tropes of textual/sexual
reproduction are conspicuous in their absence. Why should this be? Why is it
that the paratexts of a play that thematizes the relationship between textual and
sexual reproduction would be so curiously silent on the matter of printing and
parenting? The answer, I think, can be glimpsed in a kind of intercourse that gets
staged between the paratexts of the play and the text of the play itself.

The paratexts of Brome's play work hard to market the book of the play
according to what Marx in the first volume of *Capital* notoriously termed "the
whole mystery of commodities,"[14] resurrecting the dead—printed drama's earliest and most vocal proponent, Ben Jonson—in the first of its two commendatory

[11] Sonnet 11: *The Arden Shakespeare: Shakespeare's Sonnets*, ed. Katherine Duncan-Jones
(London: Thomas Nelson and Sons, Ltd., 1998), 133.

[12] See, for example, Ann Thompson and John Thompson, "Meaning, 'Seeing', and Printing," in Brooks, ed., *Printing and Parenting in Early Modern England*, 50–77.

[13] Richard Wilson, *Will Power: Essays on Shakespearean Authority* (Detroit: Wayne State
Univ. Press, 1993), 165.

[14] Karl Marx, *Capital: A Critique of Political Economy*, Vol. 1, trans. Ben Fowkes (New
York: Vintage Books, 1977), 169.

verses and privileging the printed text over the performed play in Brome's concluding address to the reader. But there is no procreation lurking here. No texts as babies cry out to be taken home with a prospective buyer; no author apologizes here for the premature birth of a text untimely exposed to the world by a greedy printer/midwife. In fact, as I have already suggested, the play itself makes the disjunction of books and babies, of reading and reproducing, one of its principal themes, even as it privileges the power of the stage over the power of the page.

I think we can begin to understand the absence of such paratextual concerns only if we approach it from the perspectives of both sexual and textual reproduction, the two sides of the same metaphorical coin that constitute the central rhetorical strategy for the marketing of texts after the invention of printing. In the case of sexual reproduction, I would argue that Brome's play is responding to an important moment in the history of patriarchal culture when the reign of what I want to call Gutenberg Paternity, nearly two hundred years on the throne, has finally consolidated its authority. If, as Friedrich A. Kittler observes, the paternal contribution to reproduction was once chiefly articulated in terms of "an omnipresent metaphor [that] equated women with the white sheet of nature or virginity onto which a very male stylus could then inscribe the glory of its authorship,"[15] it is also true that the invention of the printing press rather quickly rendered obsolete the primal scribal scene in terms of the proto-biological effort to understand and put into words those reproductive functions that remained largely invisible and unknowable till the nineteenth century when advances in biological knowledge began to give paternity a certain conceptual and factual stronghold it had previously lacked. And although scribal publication continued to be a vibrant medium well into the eighteenth century, the early modern father—compelled to await the certitude of scientific evidence that blood "types" and DNA testing would someday offer him—had pretty much completed the conceptual, semantic, and metaphorical transition from scribal technology to print technology by the middle of the seventeenth century. As such, the Gutenberg Father, armed with upgraded technological notions of paternity, may well have had a vested interest in covering his epistemological tracks. To not do so, in some sense, would have called attention to the fundamental absence at the core of paternity and paternal authority, as well as many of the cultural structures relied upon to maintain them in their privileged position. Thus, although Brome's play intimates links between fathers and books, literacy and legitimacy, ink and kin—links that are concisely expressed in Shakespeare's sonnets, in plays like *Cymbeline* or *The Winter's Tale*, and in the paratexts of thousands of early modern

---

[15] *Gramophone, Film, Typewriter*, trans. Geoffrey Winthrop-Young and Michael White (Stanford: Stanford Univ. Press, 1999), 186.

printed books—it nevertheless thematizes their disjunction and mutual exclusion by making them the before and after of Peregrine's inability to consummate his marriage and become a father.

In the case of textual reproduction, I would argue that the various embodiments that enabled the fetishistic commodification of printed books in the emergent book trade have been deployed so often by the time *The Antipodes* was published that they have lost a bit of their marketing magic. In fact, by 1640 these two inter-related discursive systems, these *mentalités* (Foucault might have called them), seem to have outlived their usefulness.

Paratexts obviously constitute one of the earlier forms of advertising. They stand at the margins of a book and invite the reader in. The invitation that has interested me here often relied on the image of a baby, a classic topos for inspiring caritas.[16] If in the end I have begun to suggest that such babies were eventually abandoned by those who sought to market printed texts in early modern England, I am not intimating that prospective book buyers stopped loving books. In fact, the seventeenth century can be seen as a period of tremendous bibliophilia and the first great age of book collecting. Rather, it seems to me that, two centuries into the age of mechanical production, texts had finally grown up, as it were. No longer objects of pity or concern, no longer requiring someone to justify or apologize for their existence, printed texts were finally ready to stand up for themselves as commodities in the age of capitalism.

TEXAS A&M UNIVERSITY, COLLEGE STATION

---

[16] For a detailed discussion of the role of paternity tropes in efforts by early modern printers/bookseller to advertise their wares, see Michael Saenger, "The Birth of Advertising," in Brooks, ed., *Printing and Parenting,* 180–200.

Thomas Heywood and
the Chronicling of Devotion

CHLOE WHEATLEY

THOMAS HEYWOOD (C. 1573-1641) HAS ALWAYS BEEN KNOWN AS THE great early modern popularizer of history. Throughout his career, he experimented with new methods by which to modify historical texts for a broadly conceived audience and reading public, shaping and reshaping accounts of the past into various dramatic, poetic, and prose forms.[1] Many of Heywood's historical adaptations are explicitly advertised as summaries, abridgements, or epitomes, and promise the reader a shortcut through more lengthy histories. For example, in *Troia Britannica* (1609), a narrative poem rehearsing the history of the world from creation to the accession of James I, Heywood defends his work by saying that "if you understandingly consider this project, you shall find included herein a briefe memory or Epitome of Chronicle, even from the first man, unto us" (A4r–A4v).[2] Heywood claims that in creating this history (which runs over 400 pages) he actually has "taskt [him]selfe to . . . succinctnesse and

---

This paper was first presented at the 2000 MLA convention in Washington, DC, at a panel entitled "Forms and Formats of Renaissance Historiography: The Josephine A. Roberts Memorial Forum," David Scott Kastan, Columbia University, presiding.

[1] For a succinct overview of his literary career and output see C. W. Sutton and A. S. Crosby, "Heywood, Thomas," in *Oxford Dictionary of National Biography* (Oxford and New York: Oxford Univ. Press, 2004), 26:982–86. For a fuller account, see Arthur Melville Clark, *Thomas Heywood: Playwright and Miscellanist* (Oxford: Basil Blackwell, 1931). The strongest defender of Heywood's taste for historical adaptation remains Louis B. Wright, particularly in "Heywood and the Popularizing of History," *Modern Language Notes* 43 (1928): 287–93.

[2] Throughout, I have made certain silent emendations to spelling: short "s" replaces long "s" and u/v and i/j usage have been modernized. *Troia Britannica* (London, 1609). *Early English Books Online*. Trinity College Library. 14 February 2008. http://gateway.proquest.com/openurl?ctx_ver=Z39.88-2003&res_id=xri:eebo&rft_id=xri:eebo:image:20398.

brevity"(A4v). Likewise, Heywood begins in *The Life of Merlin* (1641) by defending his work's value as a "short Abbreviary":

> For in the steed of a large study book, and huge voluminous Tractate, able to
> take up a whole yeare in reading, and to load and tyre a Porter in carrying,
> thou hast here a small Manuell, containing all the pith and marrow of the
> greater, made portable for thee (if thou so please) to beare in thy pocket, so
> that thou mayst say, that in this small compendium or abstract, thou hast
> *Holinshed, Polychronicon, Fabian, Speed*, or any of the rest, of more giant-
> like bulke or binding. (¶4v)[3]

What did Heywood believe were the specific rhetorical benefits to so explicitly
drawing attention to the abridged and some might say parasitic nature of his
texts? I hope to provide one set of answers to this question through closer consideration of one of Heywood's most interesting redactions, a duodecimo volume
entitled *Englands Elizabeth* (1631) that summarizes English history from 1501 to
1558. As this text's rhetoric, content, and format reveal, the assertion of a history's status as an epitome could serve as a means not only of historical transfer but
also historiographic transformation.

It is with great care that Heywood positions *Englands Elizabeth* as an epitome of an already published chronicle of Elizabethan history. He begins by pointing out that "the prosperous and successfull Reigne of this Royall Queene and
Virgin [Elizabeth I] hath been largely delivered in the Latine Tongue whereby all
forraigne Nations have beene made partakers of her admirable vertues and religious Government" (A11v).[4] This seems to be a reference to the recent publication of William Camden's *Annales*.[5] However, Heywood continues, "but for that

---

    [3] *The Life of Merlin* (London, 1641). *Early English Books Online*. Trinity College Li-
brary. 14 February 2008. http://gateway.proquest.com/openurl?ctx_ver=Z39.88-2003&res_
id=xri:eebo&rft_id=xri:eebo:imagie:57258.
    [4] *Englands Elizabeth* (London, 1631). *Early English Books Online*. Trinity College Library.
14 February 2008. http://http://eebo.chadwyck.com/search/fulltext?source=configpr.cfg&AC
TION=ByID&ID=D00000998397960000&FILE=../session/1226535558_28183&DISPLAY=d
efault. Philip R. Rider has edited a modern edition of *Englands Elizabeth* as Number 8 of the
Garland English Texts series (New York: Garland, 1982). There also exists a reprint of the 1631
Englands Elizabeth published in photo-facsimile as Number 528 of The English Experience Series (New York: da Capo, 1973). It should be noted that this photo-facsimile is a reproduction
of the Bodleian copy (in an uncorrected state) which incorporates selected signatures from the
British Library copies G.1509 and 610.a.30 (Rider, ed., xxxiii).
    [5] The *Annales* was first published in Latin in 1615; an English edition was published in
1625. Camden was not named author until the folio edition (in English) of 1630. As D. R. Woolf
has observed, Camden's was an official account of Elizabeth's reign explicitly commissioned

part of [Elizabeth's] Life, during her tender and sappy Age, all our domesticke re-membrancers have been sparing to speake. As they have shewed you a Queene, I expose to your view a Princesse; they in her Majestie, I in her Minority; they the passages of her incomparable Life from the Scepter to the Sepulchre, as shee was a Soveraigne; I the processe of her time from the Cradle to the Crowne, as she was a sad and sorrowfull Subject" (A12r). On one hand, this is a claim that sets *Englands Elizabeth* in a supplemental relationship to Camden's *Annales*; Heywood seems to promise, quite simply, to add to the record those details of which "our domesticke remembrancers have been sparing to speak." However, his decision to "expose to our view" a "princess" and its difference from Camden's choice to enumerate the political doings of a "queen" evokes more fundamentally the conceit expressed in other literature of the period that the child epitomizes the adult. In other words, in much the same way that in *Coriolanus* Volumnia imagines Marcius as a "poor epitome" who only needs the "interpretation of time" (5.3.32–34) to become a replica of his father, Heywood suggests that his Princess stands in synecdochal relation to Camden's Queen.[6]

---

by James. See D. R. Woolf, *The Idea of History in Early Stuart England* (Toronto: Univ. of Toronto Press, 1990), 180.

[6] In commenting on this passage, Michael Dobson and Nicola J. Watson in *England's Elizabeth: An Afterlife in Fame and Fantasy* (Oxford and New York: Oxford Univ. Press, 2002) focus on how "the antidote to hostile comments about the old Queen Jacobeans could remember was the deliberate idealization of the young princess whom they couldn't" (54). They are interested, in particular, in how this preface "renews" the Queen's fame in terms of how her Protestantism makes her "a representative of the English people" (54). *England's Elizabeth: An Afterlife* also tells the story of how representation of a "pastoralized Princess Elizabeth" later gets updated to make her a "victimized eighteenth-century sentimental heroine" (86). Other accounts of how Elizabeth's history has continued to be told and retold include Julia M. Walker, "Reading the Tombs of Elizabeth I," *English Literary Renaissance* 26(1996): 510–30; eadem, "Bones of Contention: Posthumous Images of Elizabeth and Stuart Politics," in eadem, ed., *Dissing Elizabeth: Negative Representations of Gloriana* (Durham, NC: Duke Univ. Press, 1998) 252–76; John N. King, "Queen Elizabeth I: Representations of the Virgin Queen," *Renaissance Quarterly* 43 (1990): 30–74; Curtis Perry, "The Citizen Politics of Nostalgia: Queen Elizabeth in Early Jacobean London," *Journal of Medieval and Renaissance Studies* 23 (1993): 89–111; Susan Doran and Thomas S. Freeman, eds., *The Myth of Elizabeth* (Basingstoke: Palgrave Macmillan, 2003). Studies concerned in particular with Heywood's representation of Elizabeth include Georgianna Ziegler, "England's Savior: Elizabeth I in the Writings of Thomas Heywood," *Renaissance Papers* (1980): 29–37; Kathleen McLuskie, *Dekker and Heywood, Professional Dramatists* (New York: St. Martin's Press, 1994); F. S. Boas, *Queen Elizabeth in Drama and Related Studies* (London: George Allen & Unwin, Ltd. 1950). Of particular interest is Sandra Logan's claim in "Making History: The Rhetorical and Historical Occasion of Elizabeth Tudor's Coronation Entry," *Journal of Medieval and Early Modern Studies* 31 (2001): 251–82, that Heywood's "primary interest is not in rendering accessible the information less easily obtained from other sources, but in appropriating the accounts of the

Heywood's choice to position his history in relation to Camden's is particularly worthy of note because *Englands Elizabeth* is most directly not an adaptation
of Camden but in the most closely textual sense a prose adaptation of Heywood's
earlier play, *If You Know Not Me You Know Nobody, or The troubles of Queene
Elizabeth* (c.1604–5; first printed 1605–6)—which itself was written as a dramatic
retelling of John Foxe's account, in *The Actes and Monuments*, of Elizabeth's role
in the English Reformation. Heywood's choice to position *Englands Elizabeth* in
relation not to his most direct sources but to an elite annalistic tradition marks
with particular clarity an innovative shift in the early modern deployment of the
epitome form's relational capacities. Identifying his text as an epitome of Camden provides Heywood with the means to assert a qualitative connection between two very different texts. Heywood thereby provides his pious handbook
with a bit of a competitive charge. We need only to read the account of Elizabeth's
"Minoritie," it seems, to discover the seeds of virtue that constitute the essence of
her subsequent prosperity and success as Queen of England.

There are certainly instances in seventeenth-century literature—in the poetry of Donne, for instance—where claims about the synecdochic capacity of the
partial account get called into question. For example, in "Eclogue. 1613. December 26" the speaker Idios claims that the private realm can carry the qualitative
essence of public experience, and thus renders that public or courtly domain superfluous. Invariably in Donne's poetry such claims are placed under considerable skeptical pressure.[7] But in *Englands Elizabeth,* instead of a critique of the
logic of synecdoche, we get a veritable how-to manual, a guide for the reader who
is interested in gaining access to broad areas of historical knowledge through
the contemplation of a carefully selected part of the past. I want to focus here on
how *Englands Elizabeth*, on the level of both content and visual format, draws on
well-established strategies of devotional practice in order to secure its status as an
effective—and affective—point of entry into the larger domain of Tudor history.

Heywood evokes early modern devotional practice, most obviously, by including the prayers of various Protestant figures within *Englands Elizabeth*.
Upon the eve of her execution, Anne Boleyn appeals both to the "Lords" who
are about to execute her and to the Lord Jesus whom she hopes will continue to
"blesse and save" her "Soveraigne & Master the King" (C3r). Heywood also transcribes a prayer that he claims Edward VI recited upon his death "thinking none
to have heard him" (D9r–v). Included as well are prayers made by Elizabeth dur-

---

early months of Elizabeth's reign for the purpose of representing the accession of Elizabeth as
part of God's master plan for the triumph of Protestantism" (268–69).

[7] *The Variorum Edition of the Poetry of John Donne,* ed. Gary A. Stringer, vol. 8 (Bloom-
ington and Indianapolis: Indiana Univ. Press, 1995), 133–35.

ing her time of imprisonment, such as "Q. Elizabeth's prayer coming out of the tower," in which she give thanks to "Lord Almighty and ever-living God" (L5r) for delivering her "as thou didst with thy true and faithful Servant, *Daniel* thy Prophet, whom thou deliverd'st out of the Lyons Denne, from the crueltie of the greedy and raging Lyons" (L5v). By including such prayers, Heywood participates in the early modern trend towards reproducing prayers with historical significance (see Figure 1).

Englands Elizabeth also participates in the visual convention of depicting Elizabeth reading or holding a devotional text (Figures 2, 3), and even talks explicitly about how Elizabeth engaged in the act of extemporal meditation, a practice that Joseph Hall (1574–1656) defines in *The Arte of Divine Meditation* (1606) as the use of any occasion or object presented by circumstance as a starting point for religious contemplation (B1r). "Our conceits herein varie according to the infinite multitude of objects, and their divers manner of profering themselves to the mind," Hall writes (B3r). A marginal note in *Englands Elizabeth* indicates one place in the text where the reader can find one of Elizabeth's extemporal meditations "as she walked in the Garden" (H10v). Heywood describes, more specifically, how Elizabeth "was alwayes employed in Devotion, taken up with one meditation or another" (H10v). Well-versed in the practice, "not the least pile of grasse shee trod on but afforded instruction" (H10v). Elizabeth likens herself to "grasse or grasshopper" (H10v), while she considers the "tall and stately Oakes" the nobility who oppress "the under-woods and lesser Plants, not so much as admitting any Sunbeame to reflect upon their Boughes" (H10v). Then, however, she comforts herself by noting that while her condition is humble, "the tempests that shake the mighty and blow over the meane . . . whilst those which are upon the ground march more securely" (H11r–v). This is a prime example of how an extemporal observation could lead to meditation and hence function as a directed mental exercise.

Most importantly for the purposes of this argument, *Englands Elizabeth* includes an example of how the events of Elizabeth's life could provide the reader with an occasion to practice similar meditational exercises and thereby gain not only heightened religious experience but also a powerfully totalized sense of historical understanding. Heywood guides the reader most directly towards historical-meditational practice in his revised account of the fire that threatened Elizabeth's life as she was imprisoned at Woodstock. Foxe in *The Actes and Monuments* briefly mentions this near-catastrophe, in which, before she was removed from house arrest in Woodstock, a fire "began to kindle between the boards and ceiling under the chamber where [Elizabeth] lay, whether by a spark of fire gotten

Figure I. Thomas Soroculd. *Supplications of Saints,* 1623, pp. 276, 277, 278, 279. Reproduced by permission of the Huntington Library, San Marino, California.

Figure 2. Richard Day. *A Booke of Christian Prayers*, 1578, frontispiece. Reproduced by permission of the Huntington Library, San Marino, California.

Figure 3. Thomas Heywood. *Englands Elizabeth: her life and troubles . . .* , 1631. STC 13313 copy 1, frontispiece and title page opening. By permission of the Folger Shakespeare Library.

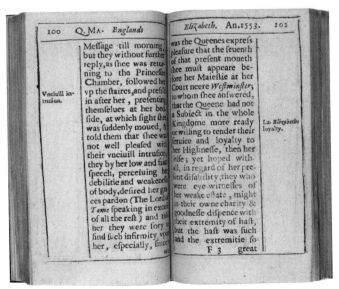

Figure 4. Thomas Heywood. *Englands Elizabeth: her life and troubles . . .* , 1631. STC 13313 copy 1, pp. 100-101. By permission of the Folger Shakespeare Library.

into a cranny, or whether of purpose by some that meant her no good, the Lord doth know."[8]

Heywood has amplified Foxe's brief mention of the fire at Woodstock in a variety of ways, specifically by deploying some of the meditational steps put forward by Hall whereby a chosen theme or "matter" (G2r) is amplified through the use of a variety of contemplative strategies. First, Heywood relates the event: "Shee had very neere been burned in her bed one night" (H11v). He continues, "She was in *medio ignis*, in the midst of a fire kindled, as it is reported, on set purpose to have consumed her" (H11v). In keeping with Hall's suggestion that the meditation can explore similitudes whereby a subject "may be most fitly set forth" (G2r), Heywood then makes a comparison between the fire in Elizabeth's chambers to "what may nearest resemble it" (Hall, G2r), the burning of English Protestants under Mary, and in this way "give[s] not small light to the understanding nor less force to the affection" (Hall, G2r).

"She was in *medio ignis*, in the midst," Heywood continues, repeating his conceit, "of that fiery triall" (H12r).[9] A "fire kindled" in a bedchamber becomes a figure for a much larger historical event: "The whole kingdom was then enflamed with the Bone-fires of Gods Saints." Heywood continues, "There was Fire in the Center, Fire all about the Circumference, Fire at home, Fire abroad, Fire in her private Chamber, Fire all over the whole Kingdom" (H12r). The reader is invited to move from consideration of center to circumference, home to abroad, private chamber to kingdom; Heywood thereby reinforces the synecdochic or qualitative connection between small and large, part and whole.

Most evidently, the reader of this passage is expected to take away—as does Elizabeth—an understanding of Elizabeth's fate as resting in the hands of Providence. Equally significant, however, is Heywood's choice to associate the fire in Elizabeth's room with the "Bone-Fires" of English Protestants, an association that works not only to amplify our understanding of Elizabeth's divine preservation but also to create a point of interpretive access for the reader who moves from reading about a single incident, a fire in a chamber, to an amplified understanding of a more broadly conceived historical crisis. Through an affective connection to the figure of Elizabeth, the reader comes to a broader understanding of the "truth" about Mary's reign. Heywood tells the story of a sorrowful subject,

---

[8] John Foxe, *The Acts and Monuments of John Foxe: A New and Complete Edition*. ed. Stephen Reed Cattley (London: Seeley & Burnside, 1837), vol. 8: 618.

[9] For commentary upon how fire imagery provides *Englands Elizabeth* with "a climactic intensity which its context does not support" and on how this imagery reappears in Heywood's representation of Gardiner's final illness, see Rider, ed., xiv–xx.

but it is also a story designed to provoke a specific image of the "spirit" or "temper" of a given historical moment.

Thus we can see how Heywood borrows extensively from meditational practice and its methods in order to create an affective connection of essential part to given whole. *Englands Elizabeth* contains material evidence, as well, that Heywood (or at the very least his printer, John Beale) understood the potential for the conventions of devotion to grant the partial history an epitomizing function. The words of *Englands Elizabeth* are framed, in this duodecimo text, by a hybrid layout that combines the visual conventions of both chronicle and devotional (Figure 4). Each page of *Englands Elizabeth* is also framed by rule lines that delineate an ample margin, a format convention that commonly was used for religious treatises, catechisms and prayerbooks.[10] This choice creates visual parallels between *Englands Elizabeth* and texts like Hall's *Arte of Divine Meditation* and Donne's *Devotions Upon Emergent Occasions*. The running titles of the verso page include the names of Tudor rulers in chronological succession, from "HEN. 8" to "Q.Ma." Dates are included on the recto page, running from 1501 to 1558. In this way, the text evokes the dynastic chronicle and its ordering logic, in which the passing of time is associated with the succession of kings. It quickly becomes clear, however—not least through the punctuation of the running title's dynastic and chronological emphasis with the book's title, "*Englands* [verso] *Elizabeth* [recto]"—that these successive Tudor reigns are valued only insofar as they reveal Elizabeth as a subject moving through them, preserving her own brand of Protestant integrity.

I began by noting how Heywood intimates that Elizabeth's tenure as Protestant Princess forecasts her success as English Queen, and have also pointed to how Elizabeth's experience as "sad and sorrowful subject" gets scripted as a point of intuitive access to the truth about the Tudor period, which begins to be conceptualized as a whole the character of which is reflected in its most faithfully Protestant manifestation. On a political register these adaptive strategies seem fairly conservative, as Heywood asserts above all the obedience even Elizabeth owes to a monarch hostile to her private religious convictions. However, in terms of historiographic form *Englands Elizabeth* is actually quite innovative: Heywood has drawn creatively upon the conventions of devotional practice and

---

[10] Rider describes the page layout in this way: "each page, including those of the dedication and the address 'To the Reader,' is outlined by a ruled box 123.5 x 66 mm (sig. D2r), encompassing both the headline and the direction line. There is another horizontal rule beneath the headline and another vertical rule approximately one-third of the way in from the outer edge of the frame, leaving a text 'box' of 115 x 45mm and a space of 115 x 21mm for the marginalia" (xxiv).

format in order to shape his vision of Elizabeth as epitome of her age. Elizabeth carries a representational charge, specifically, as a royal figure who gets separated out of a dynastic frame of reference in certain crucial ways. Heywood's humble history played its part, however innocently, in habituating early modern readers to think of the English commonweal as an entity with an intrinsic integrity not limited to the orderly succession of its kings. It is not very far at all from Heywood's representation of a princess as a most representative Tudor subject to the polemical assertion of some writers of the 1650s that the history and power of English kings must be abridged in order to preserve "the honour, welfare and security of this Nation."[11]

TRINITY COLLEGE, HARTFORD, CT

---

[11] Sir Anthony Weldon [?], *A Cat May Look Upon a King* (London, 1652), 97. *Early English Books Online*. Trinity College Library. 23 May 2008. http://gateway.proquest.com/openurl?ctx_ver=Z39.88-2003&res_id=xri:eebo&rft_id=xri:eebo:image:169924.

Editing the Renaissance Text

Cousins in Love

NANCY TAYLOR

. . . Cousin I think it will not be the safest way to inclose your letters in my uncles least thay be opened for me. +though+ he does not seem to be displeased nor to take the least notis of any thing. [He] only askes me what newes my cousin writes <~~me~~>; what his thoughts are I know not but if he saw more letteres I am afraid I should know to soon. . . .

>
> your constant and faithfull
>
> Ly[dia]: DuGard.

I N 1968 THE FOLGER SHAKESPEARE LIBRARY PURCHASED THIRTY-TWO personal letters written between 1665 and 1672 by Lydia DuGard, a young English woman, to her first cousin Samuel at Oxford. This purchase coincided with a growing interest in women's history and in the study of documents written by and about women. Of particular interest recently has been locating and analyzing letters by women. When I began searching for early seventeenth-century women's letters in the 1970s, I was told by a number of historians that very few (outside of those that had already been published) existed. I quickly found that not to be true. Hundreds of women's letters can be found embedded

This paper was first delivered at the 2003 MLA convention in San Diego, CA at a panel entitled "Remarks on the Publishing of Lydia DuGard's Letters and Other Documents," Arthur F. Kinney, Massachusetts Center for Renaissance Studies, presiding. The paper describes my edition of *Cousins in Love: the Letters of Lydia DuGard, 1665–1672*: with a new edition of *The Marriages of Cousin Germans by Samuel DuGard*, ed. Nancy Taylor, MRTS 268 (Tempe, AZ: Arizona Center for Medieval and Renaissance Studies in conjunction with the Renaissance English Text Society, 2003).

in family papers in record offices and libraries all over England. James Daybell estimates that some 10,000 items of women's correspondence are extant just from the period 1559 to 1642. Women's letters are unexpectedly easy to separate from men's letters, for women after about 1600 were taught the easier italic hand. The letters stand out immediately. Over time, the style and use of the letters change from formal, pragmatic, business, and functional letters to more informal, personal, intimate, and open letters. James Daybell's *Early Modern Women's Letter Writing, 1450–1700* documents "the emergence of [this] more personal epistolary form and the increasing range of private, introspective and flexible uses for which letters were employed."[1] But Lydia's letters are extraordinary even within this trend. They are reflective, almost literary, in tone. They tell a sustained personal story of love in an informal natural style; in fact, they document a courtship orchestrated by the very people involved, a highly unusual practice.

Lydia's thirty-two letters are in surprisingly good condition; only in a few places is the ink faded or the paper torn, and they are easy to read. Unfortunately none of Samuel's letters to Lydia have surfaced.

The sources for Lydia's story include not only the letters themselves but also tracts and writings of Samuel; the wills of her father, her uncle, her husband, and her daughter; parish registers from London, Warwickshire, Oxfordshire, Worcestershire, Staffordshire, and Shropshire, and documents from Oxford college libraries. The letters and the will of Lydia's daughter are now available in the 2003 volume along with a treatise written by Samuel DuGard himself, which can be read as a kind of response to Lydia's letters.

Here is, then, the story the letters and these documents tell. Lydia DuGard loved her cousin Samuel with all her heart. In 1665, at the age of fifteen, she began a correspondence with him which lasted until they got married in 1672. Her letters tell of her blossoming love and of her life in a small English village in Warwickshire. Her courtship with Samuel was complicated by their being first cousins. On the other hand, being first cousins may have provided the cover for her being able to carry on the courtship at all. Samuel's response, clearly based on his own love for Lydia and his determination to marry her, was to write a treatise in support of first cousin, or cousin german, marriages. This treatise is entitled *The Marriages of Cousin Germans, Vindicated from the Censures of Unlawfullnesse, and Inexpediency* (Oxford, 1673; Wing D 2459).

The letters are even more unusual because of Lydia's social position. She belonged to the self-described "middling sort" of people. These people, defined in part by their occupations, were made up of clergy, schoolmasters, farmers,

---

[1] James Daybell, ed., *Early Modern Women's Letter Writing, 1450–1700* (New York: Palgrave, 2001), 2.

tradesmen, and minor gentry who were elevated to gentle status by virtue of their education, their lifestyles, their civic responsibility, and their access to positions of authority.[2] In fact, Lydia came from a family of clergymen and schoolmasters, the intellectual fringe of the "middling sort," people with significant education and responsibility, but without significant wealth or land.[3] This singles her letters out since they allow a glimpse into the lives of women from a group not widely known. The letters tell an endearing story in a woman's own voice, a story about secret courtship and love and about the daily life and thoughts of a young English woman.

The sheer quantity of Lydia's personal writings furthers the possibility of studying how a woman constructs a self within the context of that society. Primary to that construction is her relationship with Samuel. Lydia presents herself as the person she wants Samuel to know; her letters are meant for him alone. Because the act of writing necessarily involves selecting and interpreting, the content of the letters cannot be seen as a transparent account of Lydia's experiences. However, as Clifford Geertz has said, the self is constructed within a network of social values and relationships. Reading Lydia's story involves uncovering at least three codes in this network: the codes of accepted women's behavior, of family and kin relationships, and of romantic love. Within these codes, and despite the way she foregrounds her relationship with Samuel, Lydia tells herself a story about herself.[4]

Because Lydia was the child of a professional teacher and printer, a surprising amount of her early history can be retrieved. Lydia was born to William and Lydia DuGard in London in 1650;[5] she lived with her family in the city until 1661.

---

[2] Keith Wrightson, "Estates, Degrees and Sorts: Changing Perceptions of Society in Tudor and Stuart England," in *Language, History, and Class,* ed. Penelope J. Corfield (Cambridge, MA: Basil Blackwell, 1991), 30–52, here 41.

[3] Margaret R. Hunt, *The Middling Sort: Commerce, Gender, and the Family in England 1680–1780* (Berkeley: Univ. of California Press, 1996), 20.

[4] Clifford Geertz, "Deep Play: Notes on the Balinese Cockfight," in idem, *The Interpretation of Cultures* (New York: Basic Books, 1973), 412–53, here 448.

[5] William DuGard married Lydia Tyler 22 March 1642 at All Hallows Stayning in London (*Allegations for Marriage Licences Issued by the Bishop of London,* extracted by Joseph Chester and edited by G. J. Armytage, 2 vols., Harleian Society 26 [London: Harleian Society, 1887], 2:264). This was the second marriage for both husband and wife. William's first wife, Elizabeth Adams, died in 1641 leaving behind two sons, Richard and Thomas; Lydia's first husband, John Tyler, goldsmith, died in 1641 leaving behind one daughter, Elizabeth. Lydia was baptized 30 September 1650 (St. Laurence Pountney Parish Register Guildhall Library, London, MS 7670).

Her father, William DuGard,[6] was headmaster of the Merchant Taylors' School and a member of the Stationers' Company. DuGard was an active printer who got into trouble with the authorities for printing a royalist tract condemning the execution of Charles I;[7] he was dismissed from the school and his family put out of its housing. He spent a month in Newgate Prison just before Lydia was born.

Lydia's mother was totally occupied by the bearing of and caring for her children. In her first marriage she had given birth to a daughter, Elizabeth,[8] who was just one year old when her mother remarried. Lydia and William had five sons between 1643 and 1649; three of these sons died before Lydia was born and two in 1650, the very year of her birth.[9] When Lydia's mother died in 1661,[10] William moved to nearby Sion College in London, a society established in 1623 especially

---

[6] William DuGard (1606–1662), B. A. (1626), M.A. (1630), Sidney Sussex College, Cambridge. (*DNB*, s.v. "Dugard, William;" Harry R. Plomer, *A Dictionary of the Booksellers and Printers Who Were at Work in England, Scotland, and Ireland from 1641–1667* [London: Oxford Univ. Press, 1907], 67–68; Anthony a Wood, *Athenae Oxonienses, To which are added, the Fasti or Annals of the said university,* ed. P. Bliss, 4 vols. [London: F. C. and J. Rivington, 1813–1820], 3:366, 491.)

[7] Plomer (1907), 67–68; Claudius Salmasius, *Defensio Regis Pro Carolo Primo* (London, 1650; Wing S737). In 1651, DuGard printed John Milton's *Pro Populo Anglicano Defensio* (Wing M2167), a rebuttal to Salmasius.

[8] Elizabeth Tyler, daughter of Lydia and John Tyler, was baptized in London 16 September 1641 just two days after her father's death (All Hallows Lombard Street Parish Register, Guildhall MS 17613). She must have been born a year earlier for she is mentioned in her father's will dated 6 November 1640 (Will of John Tyler, proved 14 September 1641, PRO, PROB 11/187 quire 99). She lived in the DuGard household until she married John Mitchell, 1 January 1658, and moved to Coventry (SLPPR, Guildhall MS 7670). Lydia lived with Elizabeth in Coventry after her father died (Folger MS X.d.477/2.) This is the Folger Shakespeare Library reference in full. All future references to Lydia DuGard's letters are indicated simply by their letter number in boldface within the text.

[9] They were William, born 1643, died 1643; John, born 1644, died 1647; Joseph, born 1645, died 1648; Benjamin, born 1648, died 1650; and Philanax, born 1649, died 1650 (St. Olave, Hart Street Parish Register, Guildhall MS 28868; SLPPR, Guildhall MS 7670). The death rate for children at this time was one in five before age ten; the highest death rate was in the first year. Clearly the DuGard family suffered extraordinarily. See Roger Schofield and E. A. Wrigley, "Infant and Child Mortality in England in the Late Tudor and Early Stuart Period," in *Health, Medicine and Mortality in the Sixteenth Century,* ed. Charles Webster (Cambridge: Cambridge Univ. Press, 1979), 61–95. Also, Patricia Crawford and Laura Gowing, eds., *Women's World in Seventeenth-Century England* (London: Routledge, 2000), 187.

[10] On 27 August 1661, William DuGard paid 0/13/4 to have his wife, Lydia DuGard, buried in St. Laurence Pountney Parish Church (Churchwarden's Accounts, Guildhall MS 7670).

for the clergy.[11] Apparently Lydia was sent off to Coventry to live with her now married half-sister, Elizabeth Tyler Mitchell. Just one year later, William himself died.[12] Out of the total of William's seventeen children, Lydia, the last born, was the only surviving child.[13] She was named sole heir of her father's estate and was entrusted to the care of a guardian, her father's good friend Edward Waterhouse, the heraldic and legal writer, who also resided at Sion College in London.[14]

Lydia, then, grew up in London, in the midst of a well-established school run by her father, who defied authority and participated actively in public affairs, and in the midst of extraordinary family suffering. It is impossible to determine how she was educated. Because no girls were enrolled at the Merchant Taylors' School, either she was tutored by her father or mother, or else she attended a London dame school or one of the increasingly popular girls' boarding schools.[15] She would have learned to read first and then to write, and since her writing is really very proficient, her schooling must have been extensive, whether at home or not.

Sometime between 1662 and 1665 Lydia moved from her sister's house in Coventry to Barford, a small Warwickshire village of some twenty households, to live with her father's brother and his family in the old rectory. Thomas DuGard, who had been headmaster of Warwick Grammar School for fifteen years, had become rector of St. Peter's in 1648. His first wife died in 1655 leaving Thomas with

---

[11] Sion College was founded in 1623 under the will of Dr. Thomas White as a "college for . . . ministers, parsons, vicars, lectures and curates within London and also for a convenient almshouse for twenty persons, ten men and ten women." It was built in 1629 and a library was added in 1630. The building was on the south side of London Wall, west and south of St. Alphege Church: William Reading, *History of Sion College* (London, 1724), 8–15.

[12] "3 December 1662 Mr. Will DuGard, a schoolmaster" (SLPPR, Guildhall MS 7670).

[13] In a poem written on the occasion of William DuGard's death, Samuel DuGard, his nephew, explicitly states that sixteen sons and daughters had preceded their father in death (Bodl., Rawl. Poet. fols. 32–32v, 33–33v).

[14] Lydia's cousin, Henry DuGard, was named beneficiary in the event that Lydia died before she was of age and able to inherit. Edward Waterhouse served as Lydia's guardian until his death on 30 May 1670. Will of William DuGard, in *Prerogative Court of Canterbury Wills (1661–1670)*, ed. J. H. Morrison (London: Morrison, 1935), 77–78 [1662/153 Admon. 1668, fol. 135; PRO, Will of William DuGard, proved 24 December 1662 PROB 11/309, quire 135].

[15] For a comprehensive description of education for girls in the seventeenth century see Dorothy Gardiner, *English Girlhood at School* (London: Oxford Univ. Press, 1929). Also see Hunt, *The Middling Sort*, 73–100; Anthony Fletcher, *Gender, Sex & Subordination in England 1500–1800* (New Haven: Yale Univ. Press, 1995), 364–75; Margaret J. M. Ezell, *The Patriarch's Wife* (Chapel Hill: Univ. of North Carolina Press, 1987), 9–16.

three children: Samuel, Henry, and Anna.[16] He remarried in 1660.[17] It was this second wife, Mary, who welcomed Lydia into her new home, and who provided her with motherly advice and help in her adolescent years. Mary died in October 1669, and sometime in 1670 Thomas married his third wife, Anne.[18] As seen in the letters, both stepmothers, Mary and Anne, played an important role as confidants to Lydia. Cousin Anna, only four years older than Lydia, lived with her in the rectory as a sister and provided continual companionship for her. Henry, the younger of the two brothers, lived in the household until 1664, when he left for Oxford to join his brother. Samuel had gone off to Trinity College, Oxford in 1661, so clearly she never lived with him growing up, but she must have gotten to know him over school holidays, and somehow they found time to fall in love.

Although the writing in the early letters is typically clear but labored, as is common among young women's writing, Lydia, by age 16, already displays a keen sense of what she wants and the resolve to get it. Her character quickly emerges as one of determination and certainty. These letters are private; they do not show someone involved in political intrigue like Brilliana Harley, or writing letters with an eye for publication like Dorothy Osborne.[19] Instead Lydia's letters portray a dutiful young woman of strong feelings, writing ardent, intimate letters to the one she loves:

> for me to excuse my self were but to agravate the faughlt: and you would
> question the truth of it if I should say I wanted time to write to you: no

---

[16] Samuel, Henry, and Anna were all born in St. Mary's parish in Warwick while Thomas was headmaster of Warwick School. However, exact birth dates cannot be ascertained since there is a gap in the parish register at the very time their births would have occurred. Letters written by Hannah DuGard to the Wyllys family in Connecticut indicated that Anna was born in May of 1646. See Hannah DuGard in the Biographical Appendix and *The Wyllys Papers, 1590–1796*, in *Collections of the Connecticut Historical Society* 21, ed. A. C. Bates (Hartford: Connecticut Historical Society, 1924), 90–91, 106–8. Samuel was most likely born in 1643 and Henry in 1645. Thomas DuGard recorded his wife's death in his parish register on 4 December 1655: "Death of Mrs. Hannah DuGard, the most vertuous and accomplish'd wife of Mr. Thomas DuGard, Rector" (Bradford Parish Register, DR48/3).

[17] Thomas DuGard and Mary Huggeford were married 26 April 1660 (Warwickshire County Record Office, Solihull Parish Register, DRB64/1).

[18] Mary DuGard died 4 October 1669 (BPR, DR48/3). Thomas DuGard married Anne Muston of Tibbols, Kinsbury, in Warwickshire sometime in 1670.

[19] *Letters of the Lady Brilliana Harley, wife of Sir Robert Harley of Brampton Bryan*, ed. Thomas Taylor Lewis, Camden Society, o. s. 58 (1854; repr. New York: AMS Press, 1968). Lydia and Dorothy Osborne do share in common their strong feelings about love. Both argue persuasively that they could love only one man, that they would rather remain single than compromise this love: *Dorothy Osborne: Letters to Sir William Temple*, ed. Kenneth Parker (London: Penguin, 1987), 161–62.

Cousen I know no employment would be more pleasing if my heade (which you know was never to pregnant) were as ready as my hand (2).

These are Lydia's first words sent to Samuel at Trinity College. Lydia is not an advocate for change or someone protesting oppression, but she knows what she wants. She does not define herself in terms of the tasks she performs, or as a member of a family with obligations, although she accepts her role as a woman and "husswife" and welcomes her membership in a family (27). Instead, at least in these letters, she sees herself as the one in love with Samuel DuGard, and this provides the center of her identity. Every action she takes, every word she utters is made with Samuel's views in mind (2, 6, 21, 29). In her eyes her future depends totally upon him.

However, Lydia lives in a gendered world, whether she states it explicitly or not, and the letters are permeated with signs of the authority of men over women.[20] She submits unhappily to her uncle's dictating whether and when she can travel and the routes she has to take (14, 17). She fears Thomas DuGard's criticism for spending too much money while living in Worcester, even though this money is her own (21). In her relationship with Samuel she actually asks him to tell her what to do, refusing to make decisions for herself. She cannot even have a good time with her young relatives in Worcester without having second thoughts, saying that she would rather be alone than have fun when he is absent (24). "I think I had more mirth in ten dayes there, then I have had in twice ten weeks before. but I am glad I am at home again: for I had as like be in my Chamber alone as in any company where you are not." In her mind Samuel gives her everything she wants: love, recognition, approval, support, praise, attention, advice, and security. Or so she tells the story. And she is happy to defer to him. Anything that gets in the way of her relationship with Samuel makes her unhappy, but it is in these situations that she shows her remarkable strength. For example, when her guardian attempts to match her with a gentleman from London, she scorns the attempt and persuades her uncle not to invite the young man to Barford (9). Yet outside the relationship with Samuel, Lydia fits a pattern typical of a seventeenth-century woman. She is loyal, sympathetic, protective, and motherly; she is sure of her feelings and unsure of her intellectual abilities. She wants to please, to be loved, to say and do the right things. She reflects the very common female traits of melancholy and self-doubt; she is fearful of authority and of what people think of her. Still, she is far from timid, and she is certainly capable of asserting herself

---

[20] See Keith Wrightson, *English Society 1580–1680* (London: Hutchinson, 1982), 90–92; Fletcher, *Gender, Sex & Subordination,* 376–400.

in writing. When she needs to act to protect herself from losing Samuel, she is perfectly capable of doing so.

What kind of a person was Samuel? In the absence of his letters to Lydia, there are two sources for his character: what Lydia reports him as saying in his letters to her and what he says in his own more official and public writings. Certainly Samuel had known Lydia as a child, for he was invited to visit his uncle, Lydia's father, in 1662, when she was twelve, and he wrote a poem on the occasion of William DuGard's death.[21] Judging by Lydia's responses to Samuel's letters, it appears that Samuel had as much affection for her as she did for him. Lydia indicates that he regularly sends letters to her expressing his love, including verses that Lydia does not show his father (17), and he sends little courtship presents. He worries about her if he does not receive a letter; he says he dreams of her and has her constantly in his thoughts (3). This loving attention begins very early in the correspondence and never wanes. He praises Lydia for her writing skill and for her intelligence, and states over and over again his respect for her (28). Exhibiting a strain of insecurity, he fears that Lydia would prefer staying in London or marrying a man with a greater fortune (22). He also goes through a period of melancholy, feeling confined in his fellowship at Oxford, fearing that he will not be able to provide well enough for Lydia and that she would be better off with someone else. Samuel does not want Lydia to suffer inconveniences and hardships on his account and asks her to try to be patient with him. He is turned down by several parishes and, at this point, he begins to show signs of bitterness, believing that men less qualified are getting positions that he deserves (27). In terms of his relationships with his family, he clearly honors and loves his father, but is intimidated by him. There are many references to his ability to win people over by his generosity, to comfort them, to treat them kindly, whether they are relatives, pupils, or neighbors. So the picture that emerges is of a kind, sincere, conservative, and gentle man, constant in his views and concerned about Lydia and about his family. However, as the letters show, he also accepts, without questioning, the dominant role he is expected to play in his relationship to Lydia, and he acts accordingly.

Through Samuel's own more official and public documents comes a slightly different picture.[22] In these writings he emphasizes not his personal relationship

---

[21] William DuGard wrote to Samuel at Trinity College inviting him to come to London for a visit, 8 July 1662. On 16 July, William wrote again saying that he approved of Samuel's declining to visit London without having first obtained permission from his father (Bodl., Tanner MS 48, fols. 16, 22). Samuel's letter to his uncle is not extant.

[22] In addition to *The Marriages of Cousin Germans Vindicated from the Censures of Unlawfullnesse and Inexpediency* (Oxford, 1673; Wing D2459), Samuel DuGard published

with Lydia, but his public identity at Oxford, within the church, and within the neighborhood. He constructs a self that is comfortable in the world of men, one of strong patriarchal values, of scholarship, and of religious conviction. However, even through his public statements written during his courtship, his love for Lydia is evident. As the author of *The Marriages of Cousin Germans*, he shows himself to be dutiful to his father, fearful about what he and Lydia might be getting into, and intellectually more systematic than original. He earnestly wants to justify his actions and he wants Lydia to feel confident in her marriage decision. In this public tract, Samuel alleges he was not a person involved in a cousin german marriage, but this is transparently false.[23] Here he is a bit disingenuous. He is desperately in love with Lydia and equally desperate to gain his father's approval. He aims his words particularly at these two: "But, if I may make a wish more than Ordinary for this Paper, I would Choose one place peculiarly for its good acceptance, and that upon the account of two Persons, whose Credit and Interest is no less dear to me then mine own. . . ."[24] He is writing these words at the very same time Lydia speaks of their growing love and his efforts to find a living, so that he can leave his fellowship and get married (**28**). And by the time his treatise is published he is indeed married, and he and Lydia have a young son.

The letters show Lydia and Samuel becoming more and more attracted to each other. Indications of the blossoming courtship are evident in the exchange of gifts,[25] the time spent alone together, the rejection of other matches, and, finally, their pledges of love. Lydia keeps telling him she cannot love him any more than she already does, because she loves him as much as is possible. She tries to control her expressions of love, for fear she might make a fool of herself, but she admits that "I can't keep my heart lockd and it will not be hid from him that has it"(**13**). When her guardian, Mr. Waterhouse, attempted to match her with a London gentleman in November 1667, when she was just seventeen, she indicates her firm commitment to Samuel and reveals her growing self-confidence: "thus Cousin I have accquainted you with his [Waterhouse's] intent that you may see how I can scorn and despise all others with one thought of you and how firm and unshaken my afection is". (**9**). The first mention of marriage comes in January

---

Polupaidia, or A Discourse Concerning the Having Many Children (London, 1695; Wing D2460) and *The True Nature of Divine Law* (London, 1687; Wing D2461).

[23] See *Marriages of Cousin Germans* in *Cousins in Love*, ed. Taylor, 151.

[24] See "The Epistle to the Reader," in *Cousins in Love*, 151.

[25] The receiving and acceptance of gifts was seen as evidence of intentions in court cases, underscoring the significance of sending gifts. See Laura Gowing, *Domestic Dangers: Women, Words and Sex in Early Modern London* (Oxford: Clarendon Press, 1996), 159–64.

1668; from then on the two are in charge of their own destiny.[26] Lydia's joking about sending her ring in a copy of *The Mother's Blessing*,[27] "I could find never another book I could so well spare," suggests their increased, but innocent, intimacy (**29**). The feeling is apparently mutual, for Samuel says if he cannot have her, he will marry no one. Lydia herself goes so far as to say that she has mean thoughts about men, but that Samuel is different: she would rather "venture leading Apes in hell" than marry anyone else (**23**). Samuel must have been proud of Lydia and pleased by his relationship with her, since he showed her letter to the president of his college (**28**). Lydia, though, shows herself to be much more idealistic about the marriage than Samuel. She has a positive frame of mind. He, on the other hand, is hesitant, not knowing how to act and wanting support at each step. He is certainly under much more external pressure. Yet when he does act, he does so impulsively. Once he decides to do what he wants—that is, to marry Lydia—he does so in short order. As late as 25 March 1672, Samuel had not made a decision, although he surely was talking about it. Just three weeks later, the two married—Lydia in her "old Cloaths, and with an empty purss" (**30**).

Clearly Lydia lived among educated women as well as men. In the course of her letters, she mentions nine women, relatives and neighbors: all of these women were literate. Her aunt, her sister, her cousins, in London, Coventry, Worcester, and Barford, her neighborhood friends, both young and old, all wrote letters routinely. It is widely accepted that people learned to write after learning to read, so these women were almost certainly readers, too.[28] Was the widespread literacy among these women unusual? Or was literacy a common feature of the wives and daughters of schoolmasters and clergy, the group to which most of these women belonged? Limited educational records suggest that daughters of the clergy were often sent off to school along with the daughters of the gentry, which might account for this situation, since so many of Lydia's relatives were members

---

[26] But they must wait until Lydia is twenty-one or else have the permission of her guardian, Edward Waterhouse. "The church canons of 1604 insisted that those marrying under the age of twenty-one should have their parents' or guardian's consent": Ralph A. Houlbrooke, *The English Family 1450–1700* (London: Longman, 1984), 166–67.

[27] Dorothy Leigh, *The Mother's Blessing* (London, 1616; STC 154020). By 1670 there had been fourteen editions of this book. See Elaine Beilin, *Redeeming Eve* (Princeton: Princeton Univ. Press, 1987), 275–80. It is available in full in *Women's Writing in Stuart England*, ed. Sylvia Brown (Stroud, Gloucestershire: Sutton Publishing, 1999), 3–87.

[28] Keith Thomas, "The Meaning of Literacy in Early Modern England," in *The Written Word: Literacy in Transition*, ed. Gerd Baumann (Oxford: Clarendon Press, 1986), 97–131, here 99.

of the clergy.[29] Literacy rates for women in the seventeenth century are difficult to ascertain. Scholars today assume the literacy rate of women to be quite low, especially in the provinces and outside the gentry.[30] However, Lydia's letters give anecdotal evidence for a more widespread literacy even in the provinces. In the DuGard family in the 1660s, all the women regarded letter writing as a normal, expected skill. To judge from Lydia's own letters, women's letters were not simply painfully chiseled notes but could rise to wit and eloquence.

Lydia wrote in the modified italic hand typical of women of her day. While she did not crowd the words on the page, she did write along the margins, so that the paper is often completely filled with words. The handwriting gets more and more fluent as the years go by. It is impossible to state for certain that these letters are the ones actually sent to Samuel. There is a great deal of talk in the letters themselves about copying letters and sending letters written to other people to each other for perusal. She asks Samuel, ". . . will you doe so much as send me this letter again tis call'd for, and so I cant have time to transcribe it" (22). Typically Lydia made copies of her own letters, but most of the Folger letters are most likely the ones actually sent. There are large gaps in the correspondence. Lydia talked about expecting a letter every week from Samuel while she was living in Worcester, so clearly not all the letters that Lydia wrote to Samuel over the five years were preserved.

Numerous handbooks, published during Lydia's lifetime, were aimed especially at women, instructing them on how to construct letters and address people

---

[29] In a letter dated 1 April 1647, Stanley Gower, vicar, wrote to his son about taking in his granddaughter to learn reading, writing, and cookery, and possibly sewing and starching, saying they are great assets in marriage (Folger X.d.428/199). Ralph Josselin, vicar in Earls Colne, Essex, sent his daughters off to various boarding schools in Bury St. Edmunds, Colchester, and Hackney, London, from the time they were ten to fourteen to learn to read and write (Alan Macfarlane, *The Family Life of Ralph Josselin,* [London: Cambridge Univ. Press, 1970], 49, 93, 112). Martha Mayhew, niece and adopted daughter of Reverend Giles Moore, a Sussex parson, was sent in 1667 "to school to learne to write of Mr John Breukes of Rotherfield," then in 1669 and 1670 she was sent to Mrs. Chaloner's school in London (*The Journal of Giles Moore,* ed. Ruth Bird [Lewes: Sussex Record Society, 1971], 72–74, 76).

[30] David Cressy puts literacy rates for women at 11 percent in general, but at 22 percent in London in the 1670s, while J. Paul Hunter surmises that they are greater than that, possibly 30 percent. See David Cressy, *Literacy and Social Order: Reading and Writing in Tudor and Stuart England* (Cambridge: Cambridge Univ. Press, 1980), 147; J. Paul Hunter, *Before Novels: The Cultural Contexts of Eighteenth-Century English Fiction* (New York: W. W. Norton, 1990), 73. For general discussions of literacy see Cressy, *Literacy and Social Order;* Liza Picard, *Restoration London* (London: Weidenfeld & Nicolson, 1997), 184–90; Peter Earle, "The Female Labour Market," *Economic History Review* 42 (1989): 328–53.

of various ranks.[31] Historians have assumed that these manuals, such as Henry Care's *The Female Secretary*, were necessary because education levels were so low that model letters were needed. This may be true, but Lydia's letters point in the opposite direction. She at least felt free to express herself in her own voice. Her spelling, punctuation, and use of upper- and lower-case letters might be idiosyncratic, but that reflected emerging conventions rather than lack of knowledge. Her later letters are as sophisticated and flow as smoothly as letters written by men of the same social station. Her self-confidence and individuality are evident in the way she differed from the models in the handbooks. She did not need them any more than did the "Ladies of Noble Birth" whom Henry Care addressed.[32]

Lydia did, of course, follow some standard conventions. She always addressed her letters "Dear Cousin" or "Dearest Cousin," and signs most of her letters "your faithfull" or "your afectionate and faithfull." She adhered to the convention of making the ending "seem naturally emergent from the precedent matter."[33] Henry Care had a great deal of fun with his letters. Although there is no evidence that Lydia read Care's handbook, its utility for her would in any case have been slight. She chose her own words, expressing herself naturally by making the "style match the substance and suit the audience."[34] Lydia wrote a great deal; in fact she stated that expressing herself in writing came easier than in spoken words (**28**). Writing for Lydia was a passion, not an ordeal. And clearly she used her own writing to think through what she believed and who she was.

Clearly family was central to Lydia's life. There has been considerable discussion among social historians about relations among kin in seventeenth-century England.[35] In family, Lydia included her substitute nuclear family, where her primary loyalty lay, but also her extended family, composed of aunts and

---

[31] Henry Care, *The Female Secretary* (London, 1671; Wing C519); Hannah Woolley, *The Gentlewoman's Companion* (London, 1675; Wing W3277); John Hill, *The Young Secretary's Guide* (London, 1687; Wing H1992).

[32] Jean Robertson, *The Art of Letter Writing: An Essay on the Handbooks Published in England During the Sixteenth and Seventeenth Centuries* (London: Univ. Press of Liverpool, 1943), 60.

[33] Care, *Female Secretary*, 146.

[34] For examples of Care's style see *Female Secretary*, 15–16.

[35] Macfarlane, *Family Life of Ralph Josselin*, 127–39, 154–58; Wrightson, *English Society*, 44–51; Lawrence Stone, "Family History in the 1980s: Past Achievements and Future Trends," *Journal of Interdisciplinary History* 12 (1980): 51–87, and idem, *Family, Sex and Marriage in England, 1500–1800* (New York: Harper and Row, 1977), 123–32; Rosemary O'Day, *Family and Family Relationships 1500–1900* (Basingstoke: Macmillan, 1994); Houlbrooke, *English Family*, 39–58; David Cressy, "Kinship and Kin Interaction in Early Modern England," *Past and Present* 113 (1986): 38–69; Miranda Chaytor, "Household and Kinship: Ryton in the Late 16th and Early 17th Centuries," *History Workshop Journal* 10 (1980): 25–60.

uncles, cousins, and more distant kin. From her letters (and from other contemporary letters written by women)[36] it is easy to see that women played an essential role in "kinkeeping."[37] That is, very often the duty and obligation of maintaining kin contact fell to women. They did this not only out of obligation, but also because they were the most likely ones to benefit from keeping up such ties. For women, social contacts were much more restricted than for men. Their friends were drawn from neighbors and kin almost exclusively, while men's circles of friends more often came from their schooling, their profession, their travel, and their much wider business associations. Lydia exemplified this restricted social life, although she was probably more adventuresome than most since she had the wherewithal to travel and relocate as she pleased. She saw kin as providing a wonderful advantage, not a restriction, for they gave hospitality when she traveled, housing when she was in need or wanted to go somewhere to study, companionship, entertainment, emotional support, and security. In fact, most of the people with whom she interacted were relatives. They felt obligations for one another. Her uncle came to her rescue when her parents died; other more distant relatives such as the Pettifers and the Kimberleys were interested in her welfare as well. She made continual efforts to maintain kinship ties with her DuGard relatives in London and elsewhere through letters and visits (2, 6, 8, 14, 17, 24). Ironically, Lydia's close ties with family gave her freedom. As a young orphaned woman she was able to move from relative to relative, withdrawing from under the pressure of her uncle's household in Barford when necessary, but still feeling family loyalty and security. She was even able to move to Worcester to follow her passion for music because her relatives, the Ashbys, were willing to house her (19–25). And her Kimberley relatives from Whitford, near Bromsgrove in Worcestershire, provided her great joy and companionship (8, 17, 24, 32, 35) during the sad time when her Aunt Mary died. Certainly for Lydia no other people were as important to her well-being as kin.

---

[36] For example, see Margaret Verney in Frances Parthenope Verney, ed., *The Memoirs of the Verney Family*, 4 vols. (New York: Barnes & Noble, 1970); *The Oxinden Letters 1607–1642*, ed. Dorothy Gardiner (London: Constable & Co., 1933); D'Ewes Correspondence, BL MSS. Harl. 382.69e; 384; Harley Correspondence, BL, Add. MS 70233 and *Tixall Letters,* ed. Arthur Clifford, 2 vols. (London: Longman & Co., 1815). There are many collections of unpublished women's letters in county record offices that illustrate this point. For example, see Surrey Record Office, Guildford Muniment Room, Loseley MSS, Correspondence/1083; Cumbria Record Office, Lonsdale Collection, D/Lons/L1.

[37] David Cressy confirmed that women were often the main "kinkeepers" through their letters; that is, they had a central role in maintaining contact among relations: Cressy, "Kinship and Kin Interaction in Early Modern England.".

But Samuel shared his friends with Lydia as well, so she wasn't totally limited in her exposure to society. She specifically mentions four Trinity College colleagues who came to Barford to visit and whose company she enjoyed very much. John Cudworth, Thomas Twithy, Thomas Jekyll, and John Willes all joked with Lydia and knew about her relationship with Samuel (9, 13, 23, 27, 29, 31, 32). She wrote to them and was included in college life through their friendship.

In the midst of Lydia's words of love and support are comments about what she did each day. One of her greatest enjoyments was music. Both Samuel and Lydia were fond of playing the viol and singing. Lydia mentioned learning to sing and to play the viol early in the letters (2). She also attended concerts, for she mentioned one musician, Peter Young, and recommended that Samuel travel to London to hear him play at court (25). Girls of her background going to boarding school learned to sing and to play various instruments as a regular part of their curriculum. She might have had this experience.[38] She deliberately went to Worcester to live with her relatives, the Ashbys, so that she could take viol lessons from Mr. Wright, a music master. She practiced conscientiously; in fact, keeping up her lessons was one of her main reasons for staying in Worcester. She hoped that by the time she returned to Barford, in about nine months, she would be able to play well enough to please Samuel (21). She found great comfort in playing music that Samuel himself played:

> I sit as contentedly in my chamber as can be: and have as good company as in your absence I can wish for, tis your letters and my viol, whilst I read the former I fancy you present, and talking to mee. and when I play upon the latter I fancy, (especialy and I play some of your things,) that I hear you play (22).

But she made a point of saying that she could not play nearly so well as he. Apparently she was playing divisions, for Samuel asked for his division book to be sent to him at Oxford (33). Playing divisions was a particularly popular discipline in the mid-seventeenth century. It is not easy, requiring the performer to be skilled at improvising. Lydia took her viol playing seriously and got great pleasure from it.

---

[38] Music was an important part of the curriculum in all the girls' boarding schools in London and in the provincial towns, and even girls who were tutored at home often had music masters come to their houses. John Evelyn records when his daughter Mary began to learn music (*Diary of John Evelyn*, ed. E. S. DeBeer, 6 vols. [Oxford: Clarendon Press, 1955], 4:271). Susanna Perwich taught music at her mother's school (John Batchilier, *The Virgin's Pattern* [London, 1661; Wing B1076], 2). The five daughters of Anthony Walker, rector, had a singing master teach them in their house at fit seasons (Anthony Walker, *The Holy Life of Mrs. Elizabeth Walker* [London, 1690; Wing W305], 18).

Inquiring after and reporting on the illnesses[39] and deaths of relatives and friends is a regular feature of personal letters, then and now. Women and men in the seventeenth century did this with an almost formulaic frequency. For Lydia to ask about and be worried about health matters is expected. But her dwelling on Samuel's conditions and her agonizing over his illnesses is best explained by her close identification with him. Lydia's attitude is made even clearer by Roy Porter's comment that "Conditions of the body, registering the ups and downs of health and sickness, meshed with wider ideas of identity and destiny, or social, moral and spiritual well-being."[40] Talk of health was one of the many ways that Lydia expressed her love: ". . . if I have not had perfect health of late twas to simpathise with you for I heard you were ile. now you are well I shall be better," and "you need not ask how I doe you may know by your self sinc I am as you are. if you are sick I cant be well if you are in health I am so too" (**10**). She made the same kind of comment again when Samuel suffered from a cough, which she feared would turn into consumption: "I cant be well if you are not. and if I have health at any time I could wilingly [forsake] it if it would contribute to yours" (**13**). Lydia was troubled by Samuel's scurvy and wanted to send him Goody Hawkes's water, since it had helped her in the spring (**16**). She was aware of her exaggerated concern, though, for she said in February 1669 that she knew she feared the worst when others thought there were few grounds for fear, but she knew that Samuel would understand her over concern for his welfare (**17**). Lydia chastised Samuel for not reporting immediately to her on his health as country folk normally did, and for her having to get the news from others that he was not well. Other than this mention of Goody Hawkes's remedy and a reference to a nurse for Mrs. Dodds, Lydia mentioned no medical practitioners, confirming the notion that people depended upon neighbors, friends, and relatives, oftentimes women, more than on professionals to help them deal with their maladies. Her attitude toward health and medicine exemplifies a way of thinking described by Roy Porter: "Illness was seen as a life event, integral to the sufferer's whole being. Sickness meant that the body was out of balance rather than the modern notion of the body being attacked by external bugs (i.e. flu) or broken (i.e. heart failure). Sickness was seen as personal and internal. Treatment consisted of restoring lost

---

[39] A detailed description of illness and people's experience of it can be found in Lucinda McCray Beier, *Sufferers & Healers: The Experience of Illness in Seventeenth-Century England* (London: Routledge & Kegan Paul, 1987).

[40] Roy Porter, *Disease, Medicine and Society in England, 1550–1860* (Basingstoke: Macmillan Education, 1987), 24.

equilibrium. Health then was a personal responsibility, not a doctor's."[41] In Lydia's case Samuel's health was her responsibility as well as his.

Their words and actions toward each other, whether they be about music or health, daily activities or travel, all demonstrate that the notion of romantic love was for them a familiar one, and that individual initiative was an accepted factor in determining marriage partners. Marriage based on personal choice was not new in the late seventeenth century.[42] In fact, once men and women came of age,[43] the only essential ingredient to a legal marriage was the individual consent of the two people involved. Still, all kinds of factors could keep couples from exercising their legal rights to marry: financial arrangements, respect for family wishes, personal situations, prospects for employment, and the need to abide by church regulations. The normal pattern was to adhere to the wishes and suggestions of family and friends in making such an important decision. Samuel and Lydia, both quite dutiful by nature, want their family's blessings, so they carry out their courtship with sensitivity. Ironically, their being first cousins allowed them the cover to carry on a correspondence which might not have been acceptable between an unrelated man and woman. They were fortunate in having a sympathetic family, who gradually came to accept their love. Moreover, they also had an advantage over other couples, for neither one was financially dependent on family money alone. Samuel would surely have acquired a living eventually, and once Lydia reached the age of twenty-one she was legally entitled to her portion.

Other couples handled situations involving parental unease or displeasure differently. Dorothy Osborne and William Temple waited until their parents died before marrying, in order not to go against their wishes.[44] In another less well-known case, Brilliana Mitchell married the man she loved, Richard Smith, in spite of family objections, both religious and social. Mr. Smith was Roman Catholic and a glover, a station beneath the Harley family. Edward Harley, Brilliana's guardian, made every effort to annul her marriage, but he could not

---

[41] Porter, *Disease*, 24.

[42] Alan Macfarlane, *Marriage and Love in England 1300–1840* (Oxford: Basil Blackwell, 1986), 124.

[43] The Civil law and the Common law state that females come of age at twelve and males at fourteen. However, as indicated above, church courts stated both men and women were supposed to have permission from parents or guardian to marry if they were under twenty-one. "Children under the age of 21 were forbidden to marry without the consent of their parents or guardians, while marriage by license required proof of parental consent irrespective of the age of the parties; but marriages made in contravention of these regulations were not declared invalid": Martin Ingram, *Church Courts, Sex and Marriage, 1570–1640* (Cambridge: Cambridge Univ. Press, 1987), 135–36.

[44] *Dorothy Osborne: Letters*, 4–6.

interfere in this personal choice to marry.[45] He did, however, make Brilliana suffer financially for acting without his approval, and she was only able to gain her portion by court order one year after her marriage and after a long, painful ordeal with her relatives.

In Samuel and Lydia's case, the objection was never very strong and appeared limited to Thomas DuGard, who was won over before the wedding took place, even though he refused to marry them himself (**29**). Something about the personality of the two can be seen, however, from their patience and concern not to offend their family and not to draw attention to themselves; the letters never even hint of an open confrontation.

However, there were three impediments to Lydia and Samuel's marriage, all alluded to in the letters: the sensitivity over the controversy surrounding the marriage of first cousins; the need for Samuel to obtain a living, so that he could provide for Lydia and himself; and the settling of Lydia's portion. When Lydia mentions the "matter" or the "business," she is always referring to her hopes for marriage.

There was never any question about the legality of a marriage between Samuel and Lydia as cousins german. Such marriages had been legal in England since 1563. Still, some memory of the old prohibition must have lingered, and even in the 1670s people remained concerned about kinship marriages despite their evident legality.[46] Thomas DuGard was hesitant about giving Samuel and Lydia his unconditional approval (**11**), and there are frequent hints in the letters that friends and neighbors looked upon the relationship disapprovingly. Thus both Lydia and Samuel felt cautious about announcing their desire to marry and tried to keep their plans secret (**4**).

Samuel's preoccupation with this issue of the marriage of first cousins is clear from *The Marriages of Cousin Germans*, which he wrote in 1672 and eventually had published in 1673. Obviously, Samuel felt hostility from his own countrymen. As can be seen in the treatise, the people he wanted most to convince

---

[45] Brilliana Mitchell married Richard Smith, glover of York, on 26 September 1685. She had been apprenticed in the Royal Exchange from 1682 and had two more years remaining when she married secretly. Edward Harley, her guardian, was in the midst of arranging a match for her at the time. She was under the age of twenty-one, which meant that in the eyes of the church she could not marry without her guardian's permission. Nevertheless, the marriage was legal since both partners had consented. Settling Brilliana's portion involved complicated legal maneuvers and endless agony for the Harleys. She was finally paid her portion by court order in 1686. The whole story can be found in BL, Add. MS 70233, fols. 183–84, 267.

[46] Sir John Bramston expressed great nervousness when his daughter married her first cousin: *The Autobiography of Sir John Bramston*, ed. Lord Braybrooke, Camden Society, o. s. 32 (London: John Bowyer Nichols and Sons, 1845), 105, 348.

were his friends, his neighbors, and especially his father, for he referred to them directly, not to the academic or clerical community in Oxford. He ended his treatise "Sir, if you will please to think well of this *Paper,* and will give me that share in your *Love,* which I have had hitherto beyond my Deserts it shall the less matter what others think of it, or me."[47] Lydia's letters are more understandable if read with this very sensitive issue in mind.

The second impediment to the marriage was Samuel's inability to contribute his share to the marriage contract. He had become a fellow of Trinity College in June of 1667 (7). Soon after, he had received his M.A. and was ordained.[48] Under the college's rules he would lose this fellowship (22) if he married, so he needed to obtain a living in order to provide for his future wife and family.[49] There are numerous references in the letters to his attempts to secure a position, but by 1672 he had not yet been successful (20, 22, 27). He was considered for a preferment in October 1670 in Baginton, near Coventry; however, the salary was very low—sixty pounds a year—and even though Sir William Bromley, patron of the living, was a friend of the family, Samuel decided against the position (20).[50] He was also hoping to become the rector of St. Nicholas, Warwick, but lost to Samuel Jemmatt in 1672;[51] he had asked Walter Blandford, the bishop of Worcester, to write a letter supporting his candidacy for this position. After he was rejected, Samuel wrote to Blandford again, complaining that he had lost to a less qualified man and asking for aid in securing another position.[52] At this time he was obviously upset about his situation and Lydia tried to cheer him up, assuring

---

[47] See *Marriages of Cousin Germans* in *Cousins in Love,* ed. Taylor, 190.

[48] H. E. D. Blakiston, *Trinity College* (London: F. E. Robinson, 1898), 59.

[49] The statutes of Trinity College held that fellows would lose their fellowship claims in the case of "marriage, heresy, misconduct, absenteeism, or a benefice or an inheritance worth a hundred shillings a year": C. E. Mallet, *A History of the University of Oxford,* 3 vols. (1924–1927; repr. New York: Barnes and Noble, Inc., 1968), 2:158.

[50] Ralph Josselin was paid eighty pounds a year from 1641–1683 for his living in Earls Colne, Essex: Macfarlane, *The Family Life of Ralph Josselin,* 17.

[51] There is no clear indication that the man appointed was less qualified than Samuel. Samuel Jemmatt, son of the puritan divine William Jemmatt, became vicar of St. Nicholas, Warwick, 8 February 1672, and served in this capacity until his death 3 May 1713. He got his B.A. (1655) from Corpus Christi and his M.A. (1658) from Magdalen Hall, Oxford: *Fasti,* pt. 2:214, 248; *Alumni Oxonienses, 1500–1714,* ed. Joseph Foster, 4 vols. (Oxford and London: James Parker & Co., 1891-1892), 2:806. He also served as Master of Lord Leicester's Hospital in Warwick for forty-one years. One of his services was to hold a school in the hospital: *The Victoria History of the County of Warwick,* 8 vols. (London: Oxford Univ. Press, 1904–1969), 2:310 and 8:532, 549.

[52] Samuel DuGard to Walter Blandford, Bishop of Worcester, 26 January 1672 (Bodl., Tanner MS 44, fol. 282).

him that she would not love him half so much if he held a large estate (**22, 27**). By 1672, Samuel was getting desperate, for he believed he could not marry without a living: seldom in seventeenth-century households did sons marry without a means of support, remaining in their parents' household.[53] To return to a father's household after establishing independence was even rarer. However, Samuel turned out to be the exception, for in February 1672 Lydia wrote that even her aunt and uncle expected the wedding and that she and Samuel would live with the senior DuGards (**29**). Samuel, in fact, did not acquire his living until a year and a half after his marriage.

Lydia had a difficult time providing her share of the contract, too. The bride was expected to bring furnishings, capital, and skills to the marriage.[54] While her father had made provision for her portion in his will, there were complications in getting the money (**30, 31**), even though she had reached her twenty-first birthday in September of 1671. It is impossible to estimate the value of Lydia's inheritance; in addition to lands in Worcestershire and a house in London, she might well have inherited a part of her father's printing operation that had been taken over by Henry Lloyd (**31**).[55] Still, she implied that her estate was not large (**22**). The issue of her jointure was not a problem. Apparently Thomas DuGard was willing to agree to the wedding by March of 1672, for Lydia says, "as for Joynture, Ile leave it wholly to my Uncle. for I am confident heel deal handsomely by me" (**29**).

But one more problem stood in the couple's way. Samuel wanted to keep his marriage secret so that he could retain his fellowship as long as possible. Therefore, he wished to avoid the public calling of banns and to marry outside his own parish. To do this he needed to obtain a special license from the proper ecclesiastical authority. Lydia mentioned the problem on 25 March 1672 (**31**). The conditions for getting a license were listed in canon law: there must be no impediment of pre-contract, consanguinity, affinity, or other lawful cause; there must be no pending suit touching marriage of the couple; the couple must have the consent of parent or guardian if under the age of twenty-one; and the marriage would then still have to be celebrated publicly in the parish church or chapel where one of the two lived, between eight in the morning and noon unless the license specified otherwise.[56] Getting married by license was becoming more

---

[53] Macfarlane, *Marriage and Love*, 28, 91, 94–95; Houlbrooke, *The English Family*, 20.

[54] Macfarlane, *Marriage and Love*, 278.

[55] Plomer (1907) 119; Plomer (1922), 191. Henry Lloyd is listed as a printer in London, 1662–1675. Lloyd took over William DuGard's press in 1662 when DuGard died.

[56] Edmund Gibson, *Codex Juris Ecclesiastici Anglicani*, 2nd ed., 2 vols. (Oxford: Clarendon Press, 1761), 1:428.

popular in the seventeenth century.[57] These licenses had become a status symbol, since they were affordable only by the middle and upper classes. For Samuel and Lydia to be married by license, then, was not particularly unusual. However, getting the license was an additional hurdle, possibly delaying their wedding day. Samuel's insistence on one indicated his willingness to do something a bit suspect; he wanted to hide his marriage in order to keep drawing his salary.

By 20 March 1672, Lydia was certain that she and Samuel would manage to marry quite soon despite all the impediments (31). Within a few days Samuel came home to Barford, license in hand, and they got married on 18 April 1672, not in his father's church, but in the neighboring parish of Wasperton.[58] After the marriage, in order to protect Samuel's fellowship, Lydia did not mention the wedding in her letters, for she feared that someone might read them and she didn't want to be personally responsibly for his losing his fellowship (32). The news, however, did reach Oxford quickly, and in June 1672 Samuel lost his position at Trinity. Finally Lydia could sign her letters "your most afectionate and faithfull Wife" (33). With this closing the letters came to an end. Lydia and Samuel were happily married, and Samuel returned home to live with his wife.

Apparently she and Samuel lived with Samuel's family at least until August 1673, since Samuel was still corresponding with Thomas Barlow, Provost of Queen's College, using the Barford rectory as his return address.[59] And on 1 April 1673, Lydia gave birth to her first child, Thomas, who was baptized by his grandfather. In August 1673, Samuel finally was called to be rector of the church of All Saints in Forton, Staffordshire. Everyone must have been blissfully happy. He was ordained in his new church in October of 1673, and a year later Lydia gave birth to a second son, Richard, who was baptized on 29 September 1674 at All Saints by his own father.[60] Just less than a year later, on 20 August 1675, Lydia died in childbirth.[61] The child, a daughter, survived and was named Lydia after her mother

---

[57] Ronald A. Marchant, *The Church under the Law 1560–1640* (London: Cambridge Univ. Press, 1969), 20.

[58] The license was signed by John Rogers and Samuel DuGard; it explicitly stated that the marriage between Samuel and Lydia could take place in Barford or Wasperton, a village just south of Barford. John Rogers was a friend of Thomas DuGard and his wife, and rector of Hampton Lucy, a neighboring village; he was authorized by the Bishop of Worcester to issue marriage licenses (Hereford and Worcestershire County Record Office, Worcester, Ref. No. 797, 3A 2035/9 no. 3736).

[59] Samuel wrote to Thomas Barlow at Queen's College, Oxford, from Barford in August 1673, thanking him for his long letter (Queen's College, Oxford, MS 275, fol. 36).

[60] Richard DuGard, son of Samuel and Lydia DuGard, was baptized 29 September 1674 (Forton Parish Register, D4049/1/1, William Salt Record Office, Stafford).

[61] Lydia DuGard, wife of Samuel DuGard, died 20 August 1675; Lydia DuGard, daughter of Samuel and Lydia DuGard, was baptized 20 August 1675 (FPR, 4049/1/1). Audrey Eccles

and grandmother. So sadly, after all the waiting and planning, Lydia and Samuel had only three married years together; she left Samuel with three small children, Thomas, aged two, Richard, aged one, and the newborn Lydia.

A few more details complete the story. Three years after Lydia's death Samuel married Elizabeth Kimberley, his second cousin. This is the same Elizabeth Kimberley whose company Lydia enjoyed so much when she lived with the Ashbys in Worcester in 1671 (**8, 17, 24**). Samuel and Elizabeth had seven children,[62] and Samuel was inspired to write another short treatise entitled *A Discourse Concerning the Having Many Children* (1695).[63] Once again he defended his private actions in a public way. And one more piece of Samuel's personality fits into place. He loved the idea of having many children. From his will, dated 6 June 1696, it is clear that he looked after his children fairly and expected a great deal from them. When he died in 1697, he left behind ten children: Lydia's three and Elizabeth's seven. In his will he was careful to make provision for all of them, making sure that Lydia's children inherited the things that he and Lydia had prized.[64] Lydia's daughter, Lydia, married Daniel Cotton, ironmaster, of the Cotton family of Holmes Chapel, Cheshire, on 13 May 1704 in Tong, Shropshire. She was his second wife and for a very short while she was mother to his two small children, Sarah and Thomas. However, on 26 February 1705, she wrote her will (**35**), most likely because she knew the risks of her own pregnancy. As fate would have it, within a few days she gave birth to a son who was named Dugard Cotton, but sadly both mother and infant died on 3 March 1705.[65]

Lydia's letters make her come alive. Lydia has spark, intelligence, a sense of humor, compassion, and, most interestingly, a remarkable individual voice. She has a sense of agency, revealing that women as well as men seek their own happiness. Her words demonstrate that it was possible for a woman in the late

---

estimates that maternal mortality was about 25 per 1000 births: Audrey Eccles, *Obstetrics and Gynecology in Tudor and Stuart England* (London: Croom Helm, 1982), 125. Roger Schofield concluded that maternal mortality was 15.7 per thousand, as high as 23.5 per 1,000 in London, during the reign of Charles II: Roger Schofield, "Did the Mothers Really Die? Three Centuries of Maternal Mortality in 'The World We Have Lost'," in *The World We Have Gained: Histories of Population and Social Structure,* ed. Lloyd Bonfield, Richard M. Smith, and Keith Wrightson (Oxford: Blackwell, 1986), 231–60, here 232–33.

[62] Elizabeth, 18 February 1679; William, 5 October 1680; Hannah, 20 September 1682; Phebe, 21 May 1684; Samuel, 18 April 1686; Susanna, 14 March 1688; and Charles, 28 February 1691 (FPR, 4049/1/1).

[63] DuGard, *Polupaidia, or A Discourse Concerning the Having Many Children.*

[64] The will of Samuel DuGard, dated 6 June 1696, proved 29 April 1698, with an inventory of his goods dated 6 May 1697 (Lichfield Record Office, B/C/11, Lichfield).

[65] J. P. Earwaker, *History of Sandbach* (Manchester: E. J. Morten, 1972; first published 1890), 194–95.

seventeenth century to be strong and assertive while living within the norms of her society. Unfortunately many of her letters were not preserved and I can't help wishing for information that she does not provide. But these letters help us experience a young woman's life, what she was thinking about, and what she did. They are indeed a very special treasure.

These letters clearly show that by the 1670s the daughters of schoolmasters were capable of writing elegant, intimate letters and using them to their own advantage. While her story is indeed special, I would argue that her sensibilities and her skills are not. If Lydia is any indication, women by 1670 both were capable of writing informal, passionate letters and able to do so with ease and frequency. And letters, which exist in the multitudes in record offices throughout England waiting to be tapped, are a rich source for understanding women's lives.

THE EVERGREEN STATE COLLEGE

The Commonplace Book
of Sir John Strangways:
An Editor's View

THOMAS G. OLSEN

Historians of Parliament and specialists in seventeenth-century political history are reasonably familiar with Sir John Strangways, but since as a literary author he is unknown to almost everyone, I would like to begin with some biographical information. In situating him in an age and a set of historical circumstances, I think I can suggest the real reason that we have a commonplace book to discuss and I had a project of some complexity and interest that occupied me for several years.

I am persuaded that the commonplace book owes its existence to the fact that Strangways, a Royalist who took up arms against Thomas Fairfax's parliamentarian forces, was imprisoned in the Tower of London between 29 November 1645 and 15 May 1648 on charges of high treason. Apart from a short mock panegyric published in Coryate's *Crudities* (1611) and probably owing more to youthful enthusiasm than to creative ambitions, Strangways was not inherently a literary man.[1] Though he did have the advantages of a fine education and many opportunities that might have led him in a literary direction, he was not temperamentally cut out for imaginative writing. In fact, I sometimes wondered whether it was not precisely *because* he was so advantaged and comfortable in life that he

---

This paper was presented at the RETS Open Business Meeting held at the 2004 MLA convention in Philadelphia, PA, Arthur F. Kinney, University of Massachusetts, Amherst, presiding.

[1] Thomas Coryate, *Coryats Crudities hastily gobled up in five Moneths travells* (1611), d^v–d2.

turned to literary self-expression only after his fortunes changed so catastrophically in the 1640s.

Born into the upper gentry in 1585, Strangways was the younger son but eventual inheritor of the very considerable fortune of his father, John Strangways of Melbury, Dorset, who died in 1593.[2] His family was an established one that grew increasingly prosperous from farming and rents, and if they were typical of West-Country gentry of the period, they may also have augmented their income in the wool trade and sea transport. They were prominent members of the local landed gentry, and they slowly extended their influence by marrying with the gentry of neighboring counties.[3] Strangways's mother Joan (d. 1603) was the sister of Nicholas Wadham, the founder of Wadham College, Oxford, and in 1607 Strangways married Grace Trenchard, daughter of Sir George Trenchard, another prominent member of the Dorset gentry. By 1603, Strangways had already inherited a considerable part of the family estate (his elder brother dying of the plague), and in 1609 he succeeded to one-third of the lands in Somerset and Dorset of his uncle Nicholas Wadham.[4] He was knighted by 1608 and in 1611 he was offered but refused a baronetcy.

Not only socially and financially advantaged, Strangways was also well educated. He matriculated at Queen's College, Oxford in 1601, and in 1611 he was granted special admission to the Middle Temple.[5] Though there is no evidence that he took a degree, Strangways's poems and commonplace entries suggest a very good knowledge of the Latin authors typically read in the late Tudor and early Stuart curricula as well as a fondness for epigrams.[6] Perhaps more important, in the commonplace book there also runs a deep engagement with and understanding of the logic of English legal principles and precedents, as well as political theory. He was clearly doing more than just biding his time at Oxford and the Middle Temple.

---

[2] The best short biographical essays are those by Mary Freer Keeler, *The Long Parliament, 1640–41: A Biographical Study of Its Members* (Philadelphia: The American Philosophical Society, 1954), 353–54; and by David L. Smith in the *Oxford Dictionary of National Biography* (Oxford: Oxford Univ. Press, 2004), 53:21–23.

[3] J. P. Ferris, "The Gentry of Dorset on the Eve of the Civil War," *Genealogist Magazine* 15 (1965): 104–8, here 106, 108.

[4] See John Hutchins, *The History and Antiquities of the County of Dorset* (Westminster: William Shipp and James Whitworth Hodson, 1863), 2:662–63 for a complete genealogical survey of the family. See also Keeler, *Long Parliament*, 364, and J. P. Ferris, "Strangways, Sir John," in *The House of Commons*, ed. Basil Duke Henning, 3 vols. (London: Secker & Warburg, for The History of Parliament Trust, 1983), 3:498–99.

[5] Keeler, *Long Parliament*, 353; Ferris, "Strangways," 498.

[6] See Hoyt Hopewell Hudson, *The Epigram in the English Renaissance* (Princeton: Princeton Univ. Press, 1947), esp. chaps. 3–4.

In 1612, Strangways began a public career that would last half a century, serving as sheriff of Dorset, Justice of the Peace, and member of the lieutenancy. He served as MP for Dorset in 1614, 1621, 1624, and 1628–29, for Weymouth in 1625, and for Melcombe Regis in 1626, though it would appear that he resorted to a number of questionable strategies in order to secure what one local historian has termed a "sustained monopoly" in local elections.[7] In all, Strangways's early adult years and his entry into political life are rather typical of a member of the rural landed gentry in his era; little in his political career to about 1625 would have suggested that he would ever achieve renown, first as a vocal opponent of the king and later as one who suffered greatly in the service and the defense of the monarchy.

However, as we all know, the king's increasing isolation from his MPs and, eventually, his refusal to call a parliament at all changed many things. Strangways was certainly caught up in these events. During the period of the Personal Rule, he contended quite vigorously with the king in several ways, particularly over finances, the redress of grievances, and religious reform. But his most persistent and heartfelt criticism was reserved for what he considered Charles's indifference to English law. Before the Commons he proclaimed that "wee will trust the Kinge if he will *inable* us to," shrewdly placing the burden of making a first show of good faith on the shoulders of the monarch.[8] In parliament he also urged that "All kings that are not tyrants or perjured, will keep themselves within the bounds of the laws of the[ir] kingdoms."[9] These sentiments did not go unnoticed: in a letter signed by Charles I on 28 June 1626, Strangways is among those named as fomenters of "the Troubles of Parliament[,] of divers things tending much to our dishonour, and to the stirring up of the disaffection of divers of the members of both Houses for the furtherance of their prisonable ends."[10]

Strangways worked vigorously for the impeachment of Buckingham in 1626, eventually becoming one of the royal favorite's great enemies in Parliament; he

---

[7] The phrase is that of John K. Gruenfelder, in "Dorsetshire Elections, 1604–1640," *Albion* 10 (1978): 1–13, here 1. Gruenfelder demonstrates that Strangways used a fairly typical combination of social influence as well as strategic marriages and friendships to maintain power in, and to influence the outcomes of, local elections.

[8] Esther S. Cope and Willson H. Coates, eds., *Proceedings of the Short Parliament of 1640,* Camden Society, Fourth Series, 19 (London: Royal Historical Society, 1977), 171 (my emphasis).

[9] William B. Bidwell and Maija Jansson, eds., *Proceedings in Parliament, 1626,* 3 vols. (New Haven: Yale Univ. Press, 1991–1992), 3:370; quoted in David L. Smith, *Constitutional Royalism and the Search for Settlement, c. 1640–1649* (Cambridge: Cambridge Univ. Press, 1994), 58.

[10] BL Egerton MS. 2978, fol. 18.

opposed Ship Money, and he refused the Forced Loan of 1627, an action for which he was briefly taken into custody.[11] In 1637, he was brought up before the Star Chamber on charges of illegal gold exportation, and in 1639 he refused, for the second time, a loan to the king.[12]

As I came to understand my subject, I came to realize that Strangways's political behavior during the period of the Personal Rule grew less out of any particular animosity toward the king and more out of a deep, abiding commitment to the time-honored traditions of law and procedure that Charles I constantly sought to circumvent or suppress. The arguments of several historians—David Underdown and David L. Smith in particular—help us to understand the full import of a commonplace entry such as this, taken from Strangways's manuscript: "We do well know that our estates, lives, and fames are preserved by the laws, and that the King is bound by his laws."[13] In coming gradually to understand my subject, I came to see this position as the core concern, the real leitmotiv, of his entire project: the preservation of wealth, safety, and reputation through the stabilizing, even the sanctifying powers of English law. Significantly, in this entry Strangways also emphasizes that "the *King* is bound by his laws." Let me try to explain why this part of his formulation is so crucial.

In the opening months of the Long Parliament, before strict lines separating the king's party from the party of the parliamentarian cause were sharply drawn, Strangways's position was relatively moderate.[14] But as debate grew increasingly radical and sharp lines of demarcation emerged, he began slowly to ally himself with the king's party, no doubt more out of an abiding respect for the rule of law and traditional privileges than any deep devotion to the sovereign himself. For example, in February 1641 he argued openly with Cromwell over the political enfranchisement of the bishops, a debate that moved a group of radical MPs to urge that he be censured.[15] In November of that same year, he reported to the Commons that "hee last night was encompassed with above 200 sworded and

---

[11] Wallace Notestein, *The Journal of Sir Simonds D'Ewes* (New Haven: Yale Univ. Press, 1923), 63; David Underdown, *Fire From Heaven: Life in an English Town in the Seventeenth Century* (New Haven: Yale Univ. Press, 1992), 183–84; Robert C. Johnson, ed., *Commons Debates, 1628* (New Haven: Yale Univ. Press, 1977), 1:65.

[12] Keeler, *Long Parliament*, 353.

[13] David Underdown, *A Freeborn People: Politics and the Nation in Seventeenth-Century England* (Oxford: Clarendon Press, 1996), 84, quoting Strangways (p. 89 in my edition, but modernized in his citation); Smith, *Constitutional Royalism*, 3, 61, and *passim*.

[14] Conrad Russell, *The Causes of the English Civil War* (Oxford: Clarendon Press, 1990), 15.

[15] Anthony Fletcher, *The Outbreak of the Civil War* (New York: New York Univ. Press, 1981), 134, also 143.

staved [people who] told him they came to him for his vote for the putting down off the Bishops." The angry mob would soon identify him as "one off the greatest enemies wee have."[16] In March of the following year, he argued openly with John Pym—someone he had allied himself with in the 1620s—another sure sign that he was moving in a direction opposite that of the radical Junto that would soon command the Commons.[17]

Strangways returned to Dorset in the summer of 1642, apparently still committed, though no doubt with less optimism, to his own moderate designs for political reform based upon a centrist Protestantism and respect for legal and procedural traditions. But like nearly everyone in England, he was being pulled more and more deeply into a conflict he had hoped to avoid, a war very few wanted.[18] He was one of the first Royalist MPs to be disabled, on 6 September 1642. In July of that year, he was fined £4,000 by the Committee for the Advance of Money— the first of many fines and sequestrations he and his son Giles would incur, leaving the family something like £35,000 poorer by the time of the Restoration.[19] He would continue to lobby for negotiated peace until he finally took up arms in 1645, and, as his commonplace book repeatedly demonstrates, during his imprisonment he would continue to reflect extensively, even obsessively, upon his country's failures to achieve a peaceful solution to its political differences.[20]

The events of the mid-1640s are interesting in themselves, but space permits me to discuss only a few. Because of his participation in the Oxford Parliament of 1642, his name was included in a list of fifty-eight Royalist MPs who were not to be pardoned.[21] Meanwhile, events in the West Country had by this time also reached a point of crisis. Although Dorset saw no particularly significant battles, the region was strategically important to both sides in the growing conflict.[22] By March 1643, Strangways had entered with other Dorset Royalists into a pact of

---

[16] William Havelock Coates, *The Journal of Sir Simonds D'Ewes* (New Haven: Yale Univ. Press, 1942), 213n. Also see Edward Hyde, Earl of Clarendon, *The History of the Rebellion and Civil Wars in England*, ed. W. Dunn Macray, 6 vols. (Oxford: Clarendon Press, 1888; repr. 1958), 1:463–64n.

[17] Notestein, *Journal of Sir Simonds D'Ewes*, 493n.

[18] See the excellent discussion of the widespread will for neutralism and accommodation in Derek Hirst, *Authority and Conflict: England 1603–1658* (Cambridge, MA: Harvard Univ. Press, 1986), 223–30. On Strangways in particular, see Underdown, *Freeborn People*, 85–87.

[19] Hutchins, *History and Antiquities*, 2:664. And see *Journals of the House of Commons* (London, 1628–), 2:728–29, 754.

[20] Smith, *Constitutional Royalism*, 111–12.

[21] Hutchins, *History and Antiquities*, 2:664.

[22] Mrs. Edward Fripp, "Political History," in William Page, ed., *A History of Dorset*, Victoria History of the Counties of England 2 (London: Archibald Constable, 1907), 159.

mutual protection against any hostile forces that might enter the county.[23] Despite these preparations, however, when William Waller's forces advanced into Dorset, Strangways and his allies were forced to flee to Oxford, their defensive plans insufficient to protect (among others) Strangways's own estates, including his manor house at Abbotsbury.[24]

In late July 1645, after several years of skirmishes and campaigns in Dorset, Sir Thomas Fairfax and his army remained in the county in hopes of rooting out the remaining resistance there, principally among the Royalist-sympathizing Clubmen and a garrison of Royalists at Sherborne Castle under the command of Lewis Dyve, Strangways's son-in-law. The campaign against Sherborne Castle was evidently important enough for Fairfax to take an active role in overseeing the undermining and artillery operations and for Cromwell himself to visit the site of the siege.[25] After a council of war in late July, on 1–2 August Cromwell and Fairfax viewed the castle and settled on a strategy for its taking.[26] The castle was finally captured on 15 August, following the opening of "a breach that thirty men might enter abreast."[27]

The sequence of events leading to Strangways's eventual imprisonment is not entirely clear, but he certainly escaped capture during the siege itself. His son Giles was not so fortunate; parliamentary records confirm that on 29 August he was "brought to the Bar: And, kneeling there, Mr Speaker, by the Command of the House, acquainted him with the Greatness of his Crime": high treason, for which he was committed to the Tower.[28]

Lewis Dyve was committed at the same time, but Sir John was still a free man until late October. However, on 29 November he was, like his son before him, brought to the bar to hear his sentence:

> *Ordered*, that Sir *John Strangewaies* be forthwith sent for, and brought to the Bar by the Serjeant at Arms.
> *Resolved*, & c., That Sir *John* Strangewaies be forthwith committed Prisoner to the *Tower*, for committing High Treason against the Parliament and Kingdom.
> Sir *John Strangewaies* was brought to the Bar; and, kneeling there, Mr Speaker acquainted him with the horridness and Transcendency of his

---

[23] A. R. Bayley, *The Great Civil War in Dorset* (Taunton: Barnicott and Pearce, 1910), 63.
[24] Bayley, *Great Civil War in Dorset*, 65; and see Hutchins, *History and Antiquities*, 1:xvii.
[25] Bayley, *Great Civil War*, 281–82.
[26] Fripp, "Political History," 160.
[27] Bayley, *The Great Civil War*, 285.
[28] *Journals of the House of Commons*, 4:257.

Crimes and Treasons; and that he was, by Order of this House, committed Prisoner to the *Tower* for High Treason.[29]

Strangways's captivity was certainly not always spent under the strictest restraint, but this was a period nonetheless marked by many forms of duress and by his ongoing negotiations for his liberty and lands. He was permitted visits, even by MPs, and was one of the several Royalist recipients of King Charles's gift of two fat bucks for a feast in August of 1647.[30] During his imprisonment, he shared living space and no doubt political and moral ideas with a number of other captured Royalists. Among his fellow prisoners were, in addition to his son and son-in-law, John Paulet, Marquess of Winchester, and Thomas Coningsby, both of whom translated meditative works,[31] and Matthew Wren, Bishop of Ely. He reports that he was held in the same chamber in which Bishop Joseph Hall had been incarcerated—an association Strangways was happy to exploit to its fullest.[32]

After leaving the Tower in May 1648, Strangways returned to Dorset and spent the following twelve years removed from politics, no doubt bitter and wary. During this time the antiquarian William Dugdale praised Strangways for sharing with him what remained of the family's once-great archive, and in 1655 he was briefly imprisoned in the wake of Penruddock's Rebellion, though he seems to have had no hand at all in it.[33] It is my sense that he principally spent the 1650s trying to put his life and his estates back together.

At the Restoration Strangways was prominent in several ways. He and his son Giles signed a declaration of the knights and gentry of Dorset on 16 April 1660 and a declaration of thanksgiving on 12 June, delivered before the king at

---

[29] *Journals of the House of Commons*, 4:357–58.

[30] A contemporary pamphlet, however, suggests that, at least some of the time, the prisoners of the Tower did in fact lack the most basic provisions and amenities: see *A True Relation of the Cruell and Unparallel'd Oppression Which Hath Been Illegally Imposed Upon the Gentlemen, Prisoners in the Tower of London* (London, 1647). For reasons that I cannot explain, Strangways's name does not appear among the persons mentioned in this petition, though his son Giles's does. See also Thomas Wright, *Political Ballads Published in England During the Commonwealth* (London: C. Richards for the Percy Society, 1841), 88; *Journals of the House of Commons*, 4:431; and see Appendix 2 of my edition: *The Commonplace Book of Sir John Strangways (1645–1666)*, ed. Thomas G. Olsen, MRTS 275 (Tempe: Arizona Center for Medieval and Renaissance Studies in conjunction with Renaissance English Text Society, 2004), 259–60.

[31] Paulet translated Jacques Hugues Quarré's *Devout Entertainment of a Christian Soule* (1648) and Coningsby translated Boethius' *The Consolation of Philosophy* (1664).

[32] *The Commonplace Book of Sir John Strangways*, ed. Olsen, 129.

[33] *Commonplace Book*, 215, 221–25, 235–38.

Figure 1. Commemorative Medal Showing the Images of Sir
Giles Strangways and The White Tower.

Whitehall.[34] On 14 May, amid a spirited celebration lasting several days, Strangways read the king's proclamation and added his own commendations to the populace for their loyalty to the monarch's cause.[35] Sometime after his imprisonment his son Giles had a medal struck, which described his incarceration, the face showing his portrait and the reverse an image of the White Tower and the dates of his imprisonment (Figure 1).[36]

Strangways himself, his son Giles, and his grandson Thomas all sat as MPs in the first Restoration Parliament, Sir John representing Weymouth and Melcombe Regis. Apart from his participation in the celebrations at the Restoration and in the Cavalier Parliament, however, his advanced age—possibly combined with a lingering sense of political disappointment—seems to have made him prefer retirement to public life. A full-length portrait of him still hangs in Wadham College. It is dated 1663, "Aetatis. Suae: 78," and depicts a portly, alert man dressed in damask coat and broad-brimmed hat.[37] Three years later he died, on 30 December 1666, aged 82.[38]

The Commonplace Book

I have dwelt upon biographical details and political history because, as I hope to have demonstrated, Strangways's commonplace book really cannot be understood apart from its relation to its historical moment. I am sure that every commonplace book confirms this principle at some level,[39] but Strangways's particular circumstances as a prisoner and profoundly disappointed man, yet one

---

[34] *A Declaration of the Knights and Gentry in the County of Dorset* (London, 1660); and see Bayley, *The Great Civil* War, 387.

[35] *Mercurius Publicus* no. 21, 17–24 May 1660, 329, 331; and see David Underdown, *Revel, Riot and Rebellion: Popular Politics and Culture in England, 1603–1660* (Oxford: Oxford Univ. Press, 1987), 271–72.

[36] John Evelyn, *Numismata: A Discourse of Medals, Antient and Modern* (London, 1697), 114–15; Edward Hawkins, "Dorsetshire Numismatics; The Ancient Mints, with Notices of Some Medals Connected with the County," *Archaelogical Journal* 23 (1866): 126–28.

[37] Sir Thomas Graham Jackson, *Wadham College, Oxford, Its Foundation, Architecture and History, With an Account of the Family of Wadham and Their Seats in Somerset and Devon* (Oxford: Clarendon Press, 1893), 183; R. Lane-Poole, *Catalogue of Portraits in the Possession of the University, Colleges, City, and County of Oxford*, 3 vols. (Oxford: Clarendon Press, for the Oxford Historical Society, 1912–1926), 3:216–17. I am grateful to Cliff Davies of Wadham College, Oxford, for his help in locating information on the portrait.

[38] Hutchins, *History and Antiquities*, 2:679.

[39] See the helpful formulation of Peter Beal in "Notions in Garrison: The Seventeenth-Century Commonplace Book," in *New Ways of Looking at Old Texts: Papers of the Renaissance English Text Society, 1985–1991*, ed. W. Speed Hill (Binghamton, NY: Medieval & Renaissance

without particular literary ambition or skills, produced a document of almost unmitigated disappointment.

He opens the manuscript with the announcement, "A collection of some Notes for my owne private use, gathered out of severall authors as they have bin read by me: J Strangways: wherof most in the Tower—1645. During the Tyme of my sad imprysonment ther" (55). This description is somewhat misleading, however, for as it now stands, the commonplace book actually contains writings stretching from August 1645—before his incarceration—through 1665, the year before Strangways died. In fact, twelve of the 78 poems in the volume postdate his release.

A particular feature of the volume is that Strangways arranged the text in two sections, each one inverted and beginning at opposite ends—a relatively common arrangement variously called *tête-à-dos, dos-à-dos*, or *relieures jumelles*. Forty-two blank leaves separate the commonplace section, which contains 98 leaves of notes and observations, from the verse section, which includes a total of 78 original poems and versifications (or verse paraphrases) of biblical and meditative works. The writing is in a generally clear late secretary hand that becomes more compact and crabbed over time, especially in the poems from the 1660s. The volume is bound in a later, probably eighteenth-century, brown leather binding with some modest gold tooling.

In the course of studying the manuscript, I came to the conclusion that Strangways had it with him in the Tower during his incarceration. I devote several paragraphs of the Introduction to my rationale for this position,[40] but here let me explain why my conclusions matter. The commonplace section consists of forty-seven closely written leaves of numbered and unnumbered commonplace entries, generally in prose, sometimes quite randomly set down and sometimes arranged under a variety of topical headings, such as "Monies Raysed severall wayes never used in this Kingdome" and "The Severall Mottoes of the Severall Emperors ending with Ferdinand the second." Many, perhaps even a majority of them, amount to highly topical self-vindications of Strangways's political and moral positions: from "It is but a fancie of Inconciderate Spyritts to dreame That the Soule sleepeth till the day of Resurrection: For the clearing of this Trewth Concider three Arguments," to "That which David sayth in Hast Psal: 116:11: Saint Paul sayth in full deliberation: Every man is a Lyer: Rom: 3:4," to curt legal notations citing the parliamentary rolls, "Rot: Par: 11: R:2: Noe subsidy before the end of the parliament," or the basic morality of laws: "Oppressions may not be

---

Texts & Studies in conjunction with The Renaissance English Text Society, 1993), 131–47, here 133.

    [40] *The Commonplace Book of Sir John Strangways*, ed. Olsen, 49–50.

righted by violence but by Law: The redresse of Evill by a person unwarranted is Evill." It is vital to understand how closely Strangways's creative process as a poet was tied to his habits as a collector of commonplaces. Several of his poems began as commonplace entries—this pattern is evident in many places throughout the volume. In a very pure and evident way, his commonplace entries were indeed the raw materials he gathered, framed, and then sometimes drew upon to write many of his poems.[41]

This correspondence between the commonplace entries and the poems extends beyond merely borrowed subject matter or phrasing. The quintessentially moralistic and legalistic qualities of the commonplace section, his persistent interest in self-vindication and in the legal grounds for asserting the righteousness of his cause, carry over as well. Before beginning the project, I would have doubted that a poem could be derived from the contents of Coke's *Institutes* or the controversy over the Self-Denying Ordinance of 1645. Now I know that both are possible. The pragmatic, logical voice of the commonplace section, where the likes of Stamford, Coke, Foxe, and the chronicler Sir Richard Baker are recorded alongside Seneca and Saint Paul, sets the tone of the poetry: a vigorous public voice, serious and moralistic, generally free of ironic detachment or delight in exploring perspectives. If the poems typically lack great range in tone, subject matter, and technique, we can reasonably attribute at least some of these limitations to their genesis as gathered (and sometimes framed) moral propositions in the commonplace book of a man incarcerated, rightly fearing for his family's material well-being and quite possibly for his own life. Though the poems in general often read like versified commonplace entries, there are a few notable exceptions that achieve something beyond the merely topical. Let me cite just one, from about the eleventh month of his incarceration:

> Feare not (my Sonne) if that we be made poore
> And are inforc'd to beg from dore to dore:
> For if thou feare god thou aboundst in wealth
> Depart from sinne, and thou art sound in Health:
> Doe that which is, well-pleasing in his sight,
> Soe, thou shalt find great Burthens wondrous light.
> And having try'de thy patience, fayth, & Love

---

[41] See my discussion in my Introduction: *The Commonplace Book of Sir John Strangways*, 22–23, as well as various cross-references in my Commentary. Strangways's manuscript is thus both a commonplace book in the traditional sense of a repository of sentences and information and a verse miscellany (though one in which he kept only his own poems, not those he collected). See the discussion in Beal, "Notions in Garrison," 131–47.

He will from thee his punishments remove:
And in the end with Comfort will restore
To thee that good thou didst enjoy before.

per JS: 17° Octobris 1646:

One is left wondering: is this poem merely an exercise in convention, a page torn from the likes of Ralegh? Is it heartfelt and intimate?—one might well reach this conclusion, given the way that he and his son Giles suffered for their cause. Or is it an exercise in superfluous advice, given that Giles was living the real thing along with his father in the Tower? My own sense is that it is a bit of all three: conventional, as most of Strangways's verse was, because of his firm, often slavish obedience to forms; earnest because incarceration—as has often been said—has a way of focusing the mind; and entirely superfluous (though probably spiritually fortifying) to poor Giles.

Editorial Challenges and Solutions

Large sections of Strangways's manuscript offered no particular obstacles to the scholarly editor. Small ones, however, made up for lost opportunities. My fellow editors will have some understanding of and sympathy for what I mean.[42]

My two guiding principles in preparing this edition were, first, to reproduce the text as written, with as few editorial interventions as possible, and, second, to present a text with as few unnecessary impediments for modern readers as possible. As any editor will attest, these goals are frequently at cross-purposes. In order to achieve the one without forsaking the other I had to make a number of compromises. As a first principle, I tried to render all matters of spelling, capitalization, punctuation, and abbreviation as written. Wherever possible, I also maintained headings, section groupings, indentations, and Strangways's original spatial arrangements in order to convey a sense of how the manuscript was originally arranged; these I consider essential to conveying the unique qualities of this document and the thinking that went into it. Only where emendations

---

[42] I note with a feeling of sympathy that two of my fellow RETS editors open their essays with this point. See in *New Ways of Looking At Old Texts, III: Papers of the Renaissance English Text Society, 1997–2001,* ed. W. Speed Hill (Tempe, AZ: Medieval & Renaissance Texts & Studies in conjunction with The Renaissance English Text Society, 2004): Deborah Aldrich-Watson, "Notes on Editing The Verse Miscellany of Constance Aston Fowler: A Diplomatic Edition," 157–65, here 157; Jean Klene, "Working with a Complex Document: *The Southwell-Sibthorpe Commonplace Book,*" 169–75, here 169–70.

served the purpose of avoiding ambiguity or obscurity did I make the necessary adjustments.[43]

In preparing the edition I came to appreciate the flexible editorial principles of RETS, which imposes no fixed or artificial requirements upon their editors. I was permitted to decide that a clear-text approach made sense for my author—the same might not be true for projects that involve collation or must contend with important variants—and all matters of annotation were left to me and my very helpful editorial committee, consisting of Arthur F. Marotti, George W. Pigman III, Lois Potter, and especially its indefatigable chair, George Walton Williams. Trusting the good judgment and good sense of individual editors has, I think, been one of the signature characteristics of RETS editions and one reason they are all so useful in their own ways.[44] Frankly, I am not at all sure what I would have done with a section such as appears in pages 78–79 of my edition if I had had some editorial system imposed upon me (Figures 2a and 2b).

At the same time, I also came to concur with Michael Hunter's view that "the transfer of a text from manuscript to print entails an unavoidable degree of transformation" (as indeed it would have in the seventeenth century as well), and that "the production of an exact type facsimile of a manuscript document is . . . not a proper ambition, even were it feasible."[45] Hence readers will not find a page-for-page transcription, nor anything approaching a "type facsimile"—I was never trying to achieve this sort of edition. Instead, they will find, I hope, a book whose main texts are readable and uncluttered, but which also preserves almost everything that is distinctive about Strangways's traits as a writer of commonplaces and of verse.

Beyond the challenges of producing a transcription that is both accurate to the pen of Sir John Strangways and friendly to modern readers and their much different reading habits, I found that the greatest challenges in this project lay in putting together my Commentary. In its final form, the Commentary came to over thirty pages of fairly dense typography; it contains everything from the most perfunctory identifications of sources and analogues to the results of some of the most extraordinary scholarly wild-goose chases I have ever participated in.

---

[43] One consequence of this approach is that my Textual Notes are very extensive; they occupy almost twenty pages and constitute an extensive apparatus that allowed me to record all features of the original (cancellations, accidentals, editorial interventions, etc.), all the while keeping the main text quite clear.

[44] See the discussion of this principle in W. Speed Hill, "Editing Nondramatic Texts of the English Renaissance: A Field Guide With Illustrations," in *New Ways of Looking at Old Texts: Papers of the Renaissance English Text Society, 1985–1991*, ed. idem, 1–24, esp. 2–3.

[45] Michael Hunter, "How to Edit a Seventeenth-Century Manuscript: Principles and Practice," *The Seventeenth Century* 10 (1995): 277–310, here 287.

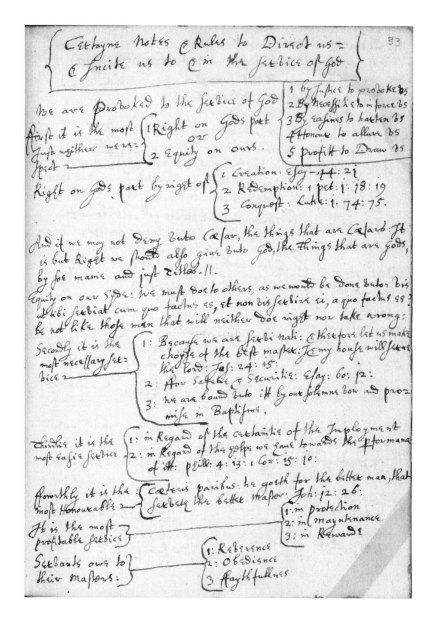

Figure 2a. An example of the Arrangement of Ideas in Strangways's commonplace section (MS pp. 33–34). See also Figure 2b.

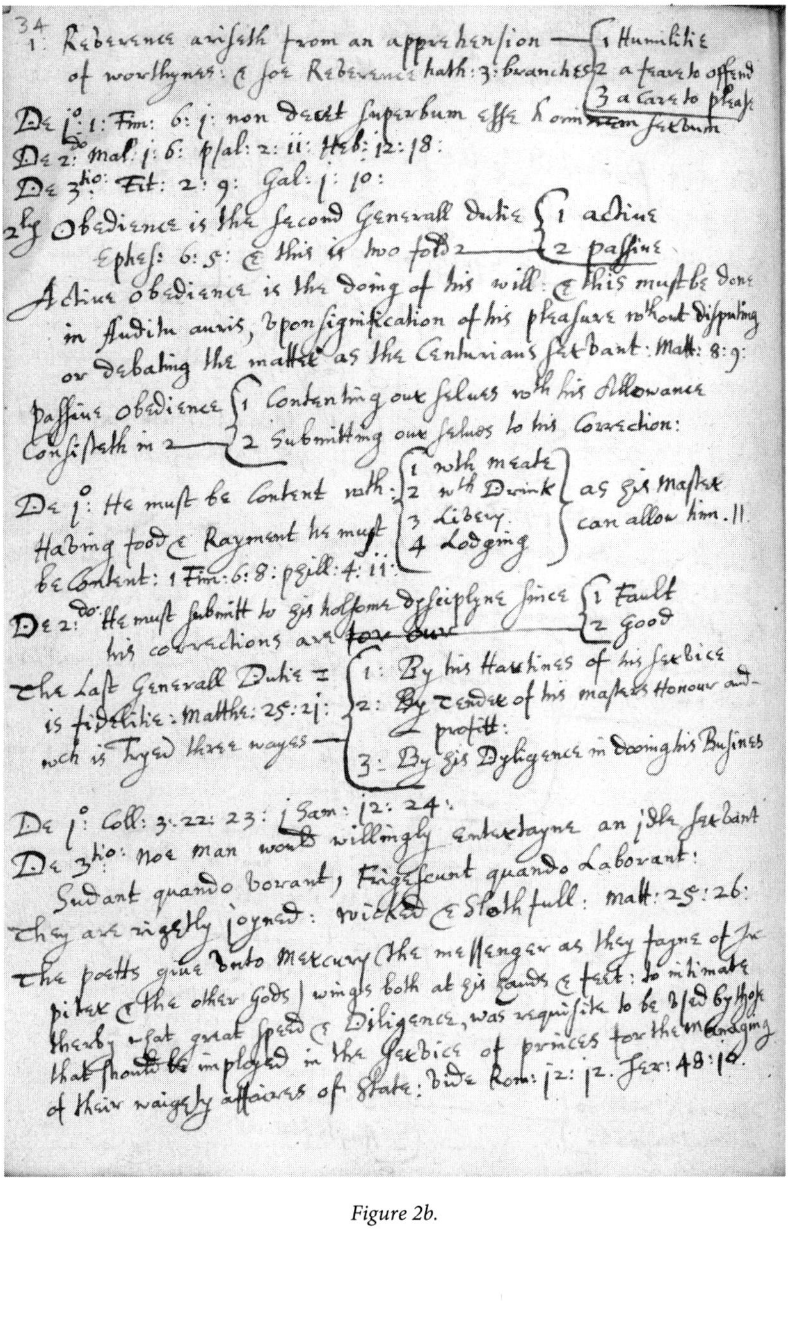

34
1: Reuerence arisith from an apprehension ⎰1 Humilitie
of worthynes: & for Reuerence hath: 3: branches⎱2 a feare to offend
⎱3 a care to please
De 1°: 1: Tim: 6: 1: non decet superbum esse hominem factum
De 2: Mal: 1: 6: psal: 2: 11: Heb: 12: 18:
De 3tio: Eph: 2: 9: Gal: 1: 10:

2ly Obedience is the second Generall Dutie ⎰1 actiue
Ephes: 6: 5: & this is two fold 2 ⎱2 passiue

Actiue obedience is the doing of his will: & this must be done
in auditu auris, vpon significacion of his pleasure without disputing
or debating the matter as the Centurians seruant: Mat: 8: 9:

Passiue obedience ⎰1 Contenting our selues with his Allowance
Consisteth in 2 ⎱2 Submitting our selues to his Correction:

De 1°: He must be Content with: ⎰1 with meate
Hauing food & Rayment he must ⎰2 with Drink ⎰as his master
be Content: 1 Tim: 6: 8: psal: 4: 11: ⎱3 Liberty ⎱can allow him. ‖
⎱4 Lodging

De 2do: He must submitt to his holesome disciplyne since ⎰1 Fault
his corrections are for our ⎱2 good

The Last Generall Dutie ⎰1: By his Hastines of his seruice
is fidelitie: Matthe: 25: 21: ⎱2: By tendre of his masters Honour and
which is tryed three wayes ⎱2 profitt:
⎱3: By his Dyligence in dooing his Busines

De 1°: Coll: 3: 22: 23: 1 Sam: 12: 24:
De 3tio: noe man would willingly entertayne an idle seruant
Sudant quando vorant, Frigescunt quando Laborant:
they are ryghtly joyned: wicked & Slothfull: mat: 25: 26:
the poetts giue vnto Mercury (the messenger as they fayne of Ju
piter & the other Gods) wings both at his hands & feete: to intimate
therby that great speed & Diligence, was requisite to be used by those
that should be imployed in the seruice of princes for the managing
of their waighty affaires of state: vide Rom: 12: 12. Ier: 48: 10.

Figure 2b.

For example, when Strangways wrote that we should not be spending our days "*busking* in the sunne," was he using a bit of West Country dialect, an unrecorded variant of the verb *to bask*, or (as I finally came to believe) did he merely make a slip of the pen, not fully closing his "a"? I spent more time than I care to think about trying to ponder the meaning of six or eight microns of white space.

I also learned that his learning was vast and (to me at least) sometimes quite arcane: matters of English common law and parliamentary procedure, and some nuances of theological controversy I found especially hard to comment upon helpfully, but in the Commentary readers will find a range of explanations based on figures from Pliny to Saint Paul, Richard II to Richard Hooker. As I reflect upon the task of writing a useful Commentary, I realize now that I labored far too anxiously in the shadow of some of the great editorial projects that inspired me: the works of Thomas More, the prose of John Milton, the Yale Parliamentary Papers. I was especially drawn to the high quality of the commentary in the *Complete Prose Works* of Milton, but also, I must say, constantly aware of the high standards set by previous RETS volumes and anxious not to change a tradition that I admire. Still, I would offer one bit of advice to future RETS editors: remember that you are an individual, not an editorial factory; seek the advice and expertise of others, but also know when to give up.[46]

Scholarly Opportunities

A consensus formed within my editorial committee that in Sir John Strangways we have found no new Milton or Marvell, no poetic voice poised to ring out loud and clear to the rapt attention of all, no figure destined for the pages of all the standard anthologies and survey courses. Nor did they foresee his becoming the subject of pitched battles among seventeenth-century specialists or the cynosure of any future Strangways Society. It should perhaps be the dull duty of this editor to defend his subject against charges of monotony of subject matter, narrowness of scope, and lameness of verse form. However, even after over twenty years of

---

[46] A second bit of advice to future RETS editors: against all these challenges to the lone editor stand the equanimity, patience, and knowledge of Bill Gentrup at the Arizona Center for Medieval and Renaissance Studies. At every stage he was accommodating and totally professional, while at the same time very much willing to let an editor's project be his or her own. Once your work is done and sits on his desk, you can count on a very pleasant collaboration indeed. In revising my paper for publication, I notice that the editor of the latest RETS volume came to the same conclusion (see G. Blakemore Evans, ed., *The Poems of Robert Parry* [Tempe: Arizona Center for Medieval and Renaissance Studies in conjunction with Renaissance English Text Society, 2005], viii).

thinking about Strangways, I am sorry to say that I cannot be his advocate on this point. His verse *is* almost uniformly pedestrian, narrow in both form and content, and in pretty much every way a far cry from even the most modest works of the great poets of his age.

After checking my transcription at an early stage of the project, a member of my editorial committee sent me the following comment: "Strangways turned out to have a few rewards, but not many. We did find ourselves touched at the strength of mind that kept him writing, perhaps to stay sane, while he was in prison, and at his churning out so much at the age of 80." I cannot help agreeing—both concerning my author's limitations as a creative mind and concerning his admirable energy and persistence.

Nonetheless, I do find a significant redeeming quality to his verse and have still more to say in favor of his commonplace entries. The poems have the distinction of being highly personal and genuine; they tell us more, in a way, about the realities of incarceration than some of the more polished, flamboyant, dazzling anthology pieces of the period—a gem such as Lovelace's "To Althea" comes to mind. For two-and-a-half years Strangways's life consisted of fear and tedium, mixed in probably always unsettled proportions, and I think his verses show us this reality. He hammered away at political, moral, and devotional poems because they must have been some of the few forms of solace he could look to. Why else would one undertake to versify the whole Epistle of James, the Ten Commandments (padded out to 349 lines), or Bishop Hall's prose meditation "The Free Prisoner" (769 lines)? Why else would one turn his energies to rewriting Luis de Granada's prose meditations as poems? I think in some respects Strangways's poems must have been jigsaw puzzles or solitaire games for the soul.

The commonplace entries have an integrity and directness all their own, too: earnest rehearsals of the righteousness of his cause culled from Coke and the statute books stand cheek by jowl with reports of monstrous births and prodigies culled from popular chronicle histories. The manuscript is a record of a particular kind of intellectual and creative process, but it is also a pristine, first-hand record of anxiety and boredom—a record of putting pen to paper in order to ward off tedium and fear. In this sense, we are very lucky to have such a document.

In the end, it was a project well worth doing, and I am very glad that RETS gave me the opportunity to bring his commonplace book to a wider audience. I would like to conclude with some concrete suggestions concerning what might be some future uses for this edition and the types of scholarly interest that, I hope, might await Strangways. First, I believe that his writings will be of interest principally to historians of seventeenth-century thought, religion, and politics, and only secondarily to scholars primarily interested in imaginative expression.

This said, however, in the last two decades or so many scholars of the period have rightly seen fit to read the cataclysmic historical changes of the mid-seventeenth century in terms of the age's discursive practices, and the era's literary output in terms of its historical moment. John King's *English Reformation Literature*, Nigel Smith's *Literature and Revolution in England*, and most recently Greg Walker's *Writing Under Tyranny* come to mind as important examples of such scholarship.[47] In all three, attention to the airy abstractions of literary "merit" is subordinated to a desire to understand literature's capacity to tell us about a time, a place, and a mental outlook. Strangways's Commonplace Book certainly does offer us this potential, for it is a text totally embedded in its moment, and in some respects its relative lack of sophistication may be one of its greatest merits. I see his Commonplace Book as a kind of funnel, into which the moral, political, and doctrinal concerns of the age rush headlong, blending together on their way to some reservoir of ideas that we might call a frame of mind or an outlook which we can hope to understand, if never wholly recover.

Future scholarship may look to this edition as a means of asking some good questions: 1) How did the disintegration of English political life—at least as people like Strangways saw it—affect those with a sure stake in it, but without a well-developed sense of how to write about it? Will a greater understanding of such types of literary production make a difference in how we understand and teach the Civil War period? 2) How do we explain the ideological about-face that Strangways and others (Marvell among them) made during the course of the 1640s and 1650s? Judging from his public comments in the 1620s and 1630s, and even from some of his entries in this manuscript, Strangways might well have embraced republicanism had some key events gone otherwise. What was the tipping point for him? For others? I am still not sure I know. 3) Why was such a well-educated man so utterly uninterested in the classical political theory that ignited his political rivals? 4) What is the relationship between the "stored timber" of the commonplace tradition and the finished goods of verse? Is there a pattern that can explain why some of Strangways's commonplace entries became poems, while most did not? Recent scholars such as Mary Thomas Crane and Ann Moss have done us all a great service by looking carefully at the commonplace tradition

---

[47] John N. King, *English Reformation Literature: The Tudor Origins of the Protestant Tradition* (Princeton: Princeton Univ. Press, 1982); Nigel Smith, *Literature and Revolution in England, 1640–1660* (New Haven: Yale Univ. Press, 1994); Greg Walker, *Writing Under Tyranny: English Literature and the Henrician Reformation* (Oxford: Oxford Univ. Press, 2005).

as a discursive practice that shaped generations of thinkers.[48] I think this edition might prove useful in instancing and demonstrating some of their findings.

While I am guardedly optimistic that the edition may prove useful for these and other kinds of inquiry, I do see an obstacle ahead as well. As Reid Barbour's very helpful recent review article in *ELR* demonstrates, there has been consistent interest in "literary republicanism" in the last several decades and a remarkable amount of this scholarship has been, to my mind, of the highest order.[49] But scholarship can tend to follow the course of least resistance—and it certainly tends to affirm the subject position of the scholar doing it. For these reasons, I feel that there has been, by and large, less recent interest in the conservative voices of the republican period: they do not, generally, affirm the position to which the great waves of historical process have carried us, nor were the conservatives as apt to seek out the medium of print until it was safe to do so. I wonder, for example, when can we expect an *ELR* review article on the subject of seventeenth-century literary anti-republicanism?

One principal reason for my optimism concerning this edition is this: in Strangways's Commonplace Book we have a body of political, doctrinal, and general cultural writings that lay, for better than three hundred years, undiscovered and unknown to those who can make the most of them. That is literally true: none of the nineteenth- or early twentieth-century historians I consulted seems to have had any inkling that Strangways kept a commonplace book; as far as I was able to determine, it was not until the 1980s, when it came to the Beinecke, that historians began to quote from it—obviously in the more cumbersome and relatively inaccessible form of a manuscript.

Among others, Raymond Anselment, Lois Potter, and James Loxley have made great strides in trying to theorize and explain the conjunction of Royalism and imaginative writing in the middle of the seventeenth century, but neither they nor anyone else can do this kind of scholarship without ready access to reliable texts.[50] I do not wish to make extravagant claims for Strangways as an

---

[48] Mary Thomas Crane, *Framing Authority: Sayings, Self and Society in Sixteenth-Century England* (Princeton: Princeton Univ. Press, 1993); Ann Moss, *Printed Commonplace Books and the Structuring of Renaissance Thought* (Oxford: Clarendon Press, 1996). See also the important earlier studies by Walter J. Ong, S. J., *Ramus, Method, and the Decay of Dialogue* (Cambridge, MA: Harvard Univ. Press, 1958) and Sister Joan Marie Lechner, O. S. U., *Renaissance Concepts of the Commonplaces* (New York: Pageant Press, 1962; repr. Westport, CT: Greenwood Press, 1974).

[49] Reid Barbour, "Recent Studies in Seventeenth-Century Literary Republicanism," *English Literary Renaissance* 34 (2004): 287–317.

[50] Raymond A. Anselment, *Loyalist Resolve: Patient Fortitude in the English Civil* War (Newark, DE: Univ. of Delaware Press, 1988); Lois Potter, *Secret Rites and Secret Writing:*

author or a creative mind, but I hope that this edition will allow many others to see what Sir John Strangways had to say. Then readers can decide for themselves what to make of him.

                    ∾   ∾   ∾

Author's Note: This essay was originally delivered as a paper at the RETS Open Meeting at the 2004 MLA convention. At that time my edition had not yet appeared, and so I made a conscious decision to deliver a paper introductory enough to be interesting to listeners who knew little or nothing of Strangways's life or circumstances, let alone his writings. To this end, I drew principally from several sections of my forthcoming introduction, especially in discussing Strangways's biography and historical circumstances. Though in revising it for publication in *New Ways IV* I have made a number of minor changes, I have not fundamentally revised the structure of what I originally presented, nor my approach. Now that the edition is published, however, I have changed all citations to refer to the edition, not the manuscript.

STATE UNIVERSITY OF NEW YORK, NEW PALTZ

Royalist Literature, 1641–1660 (Cambridge: Cambridge Univ. Press, 1989); James Loxley, *Royalism and Poetry in the English Civil Wars: The Drawn Sword* (New York: St. Martin's Press, 1997).

"Memorie shall attend thee": Past and Present in William Baspoole's The Pilgrime

KATHRYN WALLS

G UILLAUME DE DEGUILEVILLE WAS A CISTERCIAN MONK. HE WROTE THE first of his great trilogy of allegories, *Le Pèlerinage de la Vie Humaine*, in 1331. The *Vie* was faithfully translated into English in the early fifteenth century as *The Pilgrimage of the Lyfe of the Manhode*.[1] The work begins with the narrator's account of how—in a dream—he found himself with an overwhelming desire to reach the New Jerusalem. Having no sense of the direction he might take, he is met by the beautiful princess Grace Dieu, who urges him to enter her house (the Church). He passes through the moat surrounding it (baptism), and (once inside) views a series of events allegorizing the other six sacraments, and receives food for his journey (the host). He is then given his pilgrim's scrip (or satchel, standing for the creed) and staff (hope) by Grace Dieu. In a part of the story to which I shall return below, Grace Dieu also offers him a suit of armour (the virtues), which he finds too uncomfortable to wear. Setting forth as a pilgrim, he comes to a fork in his path. Taking the way attended by the damsel Idleness, he encounters each of the seven deadly sins (all monstrous hags) in turn, and loses his staff. He only retrieves it after offering the prayer to the Virgin that Chaucer translated as the "ABC" (Chaucer's translation was incorporated by the

---

This paper was presented at the RETS Open Business Meeting at the 2006 MLA convention in Philadelphia, PA, Arthur F. Kinney, University of Massachusetts, Amherst, presiding.

[1] For a conspectus of the basic information with sources, see Avril Henry, ed.,*The Pilgrimage of the Lyfe of the Manhode*, 2 vols., EETS 288, 292 (Oxford: Oxford Univ. Press, 1985, 1988), 1: xxvii.

later translator responsible for the prose *Lyfe*).[2] The pilgrim then undergoes experiences representing contrition, confession, and satisfaction (Grace Dieu begins the interlocking sequence by striking a rock that represents his own hardened heart). He continues on his way—only to be taken on a perilous skyward course by Youth (a damsel with feathered feet). He is brought back to earth (literally, of course, in this allegory) when he is attacked by Tribulation (a female blacksmith, who forges crowns on the backs of those wearing the doublet of patience). Grace Dieu advises him to take the safest route to his destination by boarding the Ship of Religion, which is inhabited by nine ladies representing aspects of the monastic life (Voluntary Poverty, Chastity, Prayer, etc.). Finally, having been attacked by Infirmity and Old Age, and visited by Misericorde (who feeds him from her bosom in an allegory of the last rites), he is executed by Death. At this point in his dream the narrator is woken up by the ringing of the bell for matins in his Abbey of Chaalit.

Deguileville's treatment of memory provides me with a valuable starting point. When, as I have already mentioned, the pilgrim finds the armour of the virtues too uncomfortable to wear, he has a notion that Grace Dieu will find someone to carry it for him. But he is humiliated when that person turns out to be a girl, and appalled to find that this girl has eyes in the back of her head (or rather her "haterel," l. 2630—the nape of her neck). Grace Dieu introduces her as Memory, one who "of *the* olde time . . . can wel speke" (l. 2663). Memory's assistance is, she says, "riht necessarie" to all who want to preserve knowledge and wisdom (ll. 2666–2667). She will follow the pilgrim as his beast of burden, his "soomeer."

This passage must have had particular appeal for William Baspoole, the Norfolk gentleman who, by about 1630, had got hold of two manuscripts of the Middle English *Lyfe* and was in the process of constructing his own version—*The Pilgrime*. What follows is Baspoole's rendering of the passage in the *Lyfe* that I have just outlined—and in this excerpt his rendering is faithful to the original:

> This wench hir name is **memory** which perceiues nothing of the tyme to come, but shee can tell thee all thats past. Of the ould tyme shee can speke ynough, and therfore are hir eyne behinde hir, shee is not dreadfull and hyddeous as thou weenest but shee is necessary to them of witt and scyence. Er this had clarkes of vniuersities fallen to greate pouertie, if their having

---

[2] Chaucer's "ABC" was also inserted into an English verse translation of Deguileville's second recension of the *Vie*, a verse translation normally attributed to John Lydgate. For this translation (which Baspoole seems not to have known) see F. J. Furnivall and K. B. Locock, eds., *The Pilgrimage of the Life of Man*, 3 vols., EETS e.s. 77, 83, 92 (London: K. Paul, Trench, Trübner & Co., 1899–1904), reprinted as one vol. (Millwood, NY: Kraus Reprint, 1973).

of learning be not kept which they gott before. Little worth are things gotten if after gotten lost, therefore she has the eye behinde, and therefore witt
well shee is Scyence, and grete wisdomes Treasurer, and therefore hould hir
not in despite (as thou hast done before) to call her wench fitt for nothing
but to carry potts . . . but rather dispise thy selfe that art no more worthy
(ll. 1781–1793).[3]

Baspoole probably saw himself as a "Memory" figure, a humble guardian or con-
servator of the important treasure represented by Deguileville's 300-year-old
work. He would have been well aware of the fact that such treasures had been
despised by the radical Protestant iconoclasts of the reign of Edward VI. In what
follows I want to survey the ways in which *The Pilgrime* represents itself as an
authentic text from the past—before going on to suggest something of how that
representation is, to a significant extent, misleading.

Anyone encountering the first fair copy of *The Pilgrime* (Magdalene College,
Cambridge, MS Pepys 2258) could not fail to note the date of Deguileville's original
work in the prominently displayed subtitle—which (on fol. 1r) not only describes
the text as "written in the yeare of Christ. 1331," but includes cross-references to
the pages on which this date is mentioned within the text. The text itself is free
of obvious anachronisms. Then there is its manuscript publication (the text was
hand-copied at least five times between c. 1630 and 1688), and (in the Pepys)
the coloured illustrations—both of which strongly project the work's medieval
origin.[4] Moreover, in the colophon to the 1655 MS (Cambridge University Library
MS Ff. 6. 30, fol. 124r) *The Pilgrime* is referred to as the "copy" of an "Originall"—
the "Originall" being Bodleian Library MS Laud Misc. 740, which evidently
found its way into the Bodleian after Baspoole had presented it to Archbishop
Laud, Chancellor of the University.[5] Finally, while Baspoole's modernization of
the medieval prose (in the interests of comprehensibility) makes it rather unlikely

---

[3] Transcribed from *The Pilgrime* by William Baspoole, ed. Kathryn Walls with Marguerite Stobo, MRTS 337 (Tempe: Arizona Center for Medieval and Renaissance Studies in conjunction with Renaissance English Text Society, 2008); Renaissance English Text Society, Seventh Series, vol. XXXI (for 2006). All subsequent references are to this edition.

[4] Although there are no illustrations in the Marsh's Library, Dublin MS Z3. 2. 9, frames
have been drawn for them. And although there are no illustrations in MS Cambridge University Library MS Ff. 6. 30 either, the colophon (fol. 124r) contains a note testifying to their importance: "*Desiderantur Emblemata/ad finem cujusque Capitis,/in Originali apposita.*"

[5] Baspoole had used what was to become the Laud manuscript as one of his sources for
The Pilgrime, smothering it with annotations of his own, some of them written in a quasi-
medieval hand. For a full discussion of Baspoole's treatment of the Laud MS, see my essay "'A
Prophetique Dreame of the Churche': William Baspoole's Laudian Reception of the Medieval
Pilgrimage of the Lyfe of the Manhode," in D. W. Doerksen and C. Hodgkins, eds., *Centered on*

that anyone could have regarded *The Pilgrime* as a "copy" in the strictest sense of that word, Baspoole does preserve many obsolete words ("hatrell" for "haterel" being one, l. 1753, cf. *Lyfe* l. 2630)—and he even introduces some archaisms of his own (like "merciable" for "merciful," l. 1809).[6]

Rosemond Tuve, without whose pioneering work my edition would not exist, clearly picked up on these cues. In her last work, *Allegorical Imagery: Some Mediaeval Books and Their Posterity* (published posthumously in 1966), Tuve was concerned to stress the survival into the sixteenth and seventeenth centuries of what we think of as distinctively medieval forms of thought and expression. One can imagine Tuve's delight when she discovered MS Pepys 2258. She saw it as incontrovertible evidence of the continuities she wished to stress. *The Pilgrime*, she believed, shows that Deguileville's early fourteenth-century allegory was as accessible in 1631 as it had been in 1331, that it was—as she puts it—"read as if it were simply an enjoyable and profitable book that happened to be handwritten after the invention of printing, and after the revolutionary changes in religion, taste, institutions and the arts which have always been thought [i. e. misguidedly] to constitute barriers seldom crossed by later men."[7] She claimed that Baspoole "does not cut or water-down allegory, and tempers no winds of outrageous imagery to seventeenth-century lambs."[8]

It transpires, however, that Tuve (a brilliant commentator on the *Lyfe*) was seriously mistaken about *The Pilgrime*. Baspoole revised the *Lyfe* to make it better reflect the values of Archbishop Laud, the man whose patronage he seems to have sought. True, he does not disguise the fact that his original was written by a fourteenth-century Catholic monk—indeed, the Marsh manuscript (of whose existence Tuve was unaware) was commissioned in 1688 by a devout Catholic, for presentation to Bishop Patrick Tyrrell, James II's Chief Secretary in Ireland.[9] This Catholic (a certain William Brian) clearly picked up on the same cues that had misled Tuve. While incorporating such cues, however, Baspoole consistently plays down those elements of Catholic doctrine that even Laudians continued to resist, while underlining material that seemed to anticipate Laudian values. Cuts, additions, and alterations all play their part. To take just one example: Monas-

---

the Word: Literature, Scripture and the Tudor-Stuart Middle Way (Newark, DE: Univ. of Delaware Press, 2004), 245–76.

[6] I discuss Baspoole's language in the Introduction (Section XI) of my edition: "Linguistic Features," 165–73.

[7] Rosemond Tuve, *Allegorical Imagery: Some Mediaeval Books and Their Posterity* (Princeton: Princeton Univ. Press, 1966), 204.

[8] Tuve, *Allegorical Imagery*, 195.

[9] Marsh's Library, Dublin MS Z3. 2. 9. For this information, see fol. 2r–v, transcribed in my Introduction to *The Pilgrime*.

ticism becomes the major theme of the *Lyfe* in the fourth and final Book (from l. 6700), when the pilgrim boards the "Ship of Religion" ("religion" being, of course, monasticism).[10] While Baspoole continues to call the ship by this name, he removes Deguileville's references to its superstructure (the "houses" of Cluny, Citeaux, etc.). He also reinterprets the large hoops that are said to hold the ship together (which in the *Lyfe* are the broad requirements of the Benedictine Rule) as the "x. Com*m*andments of allmightie god" (ll. 4996–4997). The ship thus becomes the Church in a general sense, Ecclesia. Moreover, Deguileville's word for the (sadly-decaying) wicker ties that are supposed to hold the larger hoops in position (and which represent the specific observances that embody obedience to the Rule), the word "osiers", is changed into "ouerseers" (l. 5012).[11] The "overseers" of Paul's commission in Acts 20:28 were traditionally identified with the bishops. Baspoole's consequent implication that the well-being of the Church depends on the strength of the bishops is entirely his own. Thanks to such changes, *The Pilgrime* is in fact a polemical text.[12]

As for Tuve's claim that Baspoole does not dilute Deguileville's allegory as such (Deguileville's allegory being emblematic to the point of being surrealistic, and not at all in the simpler "personification allegory" tradition of Langland and Bunyan), this claim too proves unfounded—Baspoole was uncomfortable with its ingenuity. A small instance of this discomfort may in fact be found in his treatment of Memory. As we have seen, Deguileville's Memory begins as a girl, but is finally described as a beast of burden, Grace Dieu advising the pilgrim: "*Thou* hast Memorie *th*i soomeer *th*at after *thee* shal come bihynde" (ll. 2697–2698). Baspoole eliminates the disconcerting notion of Memory as a kind of horse, reasserting the identity of the girl as a handmaiden by altering Grace Dieu's statement to "**Memorie** shall attend thee."[13] It should not, however, be thought that Baspoole is a duller writer than Deguileville. He intensifies the

---

[10] Deguileville's emphasis may be understood in the context of the vulnerability of the religious orders to the French crown in the early fourteenth century, a vulnerability that is analysed by William Chester Jordan in his recent study of Jacques de Thérines (abbot of Chaalit from 1310–1318): *Unceasing Strife, Unending Fear: Jacques de Thérines and the Freedom of the Church in the Age of the Last Capetians* (Princeton and Oxford: Princeton Univ. Press, 2005).

[11] Someone, probably Baspoole, has altered the word (spelled "ourseeres" in the Laud MS, fol. 118v) to match (adding an "e" to make the first and second syllables spell "ouer"), as Tuve was the first to note (*Allegorical Imagery*, 202).

[12] Cf. *The Pilgrime*, Introduction (Section IX), 91–122.

[13] L. 1799. The scribe uses a bold display hand to distinguish the maiden's name.

dramatic potential of the original text (writing with idiomatic vigour), and he invests his writing with greater biblical resonance.[14]

The Pilgrime is, then, most assuredly not a "copy" of the Lyfe. I do not think, however, that Baspoole would have conceded (even to himself) that he had in any way betrayed the noble function of Deguileville's damsel Memory. By presenting The Pilgrime in the 1630s as a replication of medieval material (while at the same time creating an "improved" version of this same material), Baspoole was actually promoting the notion that the past could make a contribution to the present. He thought, in other words, that without too many Catholic excesses and abuses to distract them his readers would realize how much the pre-Reformation Church had to offer. To approach the same point a little differently: As Grace Dieu tells the pilgrim (in Baspoole's version, that is), Memory is to carry the armour for a specific purpose—she will proffer it when he needs it, when he is most vulnerable: "**Memorie** shall attend thee with thyne armore, that in tyme of need thou mayst arme, and defend thee against thyne enemyes" (ll. 1799–1801, italics mine). The emphasis here is not so much on the inherent value of the armour, but on its usefulness in particular circumstances. It may be significant that the phrase "in tyme of need" is unique to The Pilgrime.

As Anthony Milton has shown, the Laudians, reacting against both orthodox Calvinists and separatist Puritans, believed that what the English Church needed was in fact greater continuity with its more immediate medieval past—the past that the Reformation had rejected (in favour, of course, of the more distant past of the Early Church).[15] The Laudians would have liked Deguileville's emphasis on the sacraments as vehicles of grace, on good works, on the responsibilities of bishops. At the same time, however, their enthusiasm for the past was selective. Generally speaking, at least, they did not want to revive practices such as the invocation of saints or prayers for the dead. As for the Papacy, they promoted the idea that the Church in England had been independent of the Papacy even before the Reformation.[16] Their notion of a virtually independent pre-Reformation Church in England seems to account for the fact that Baspoole, even though he was keen

---

[14] I demonstrate these points in "Medieval 'Allegorical Imagery' in c. 1630: Will. Baspoole's Revision of The Pilgrimage of the Lyfe of the Manhode," in M. J. Toswell and E. M. Tyler, eds., "Doubt wisely": Papers in Honour of E. G. Stanley, Studies in English Language and Literature (London and New York: Routledge, 1996), 304–22. See also The Pilgrime, Intoduction (Section X), 123–64.

[15] Anthony Milton, Catholic and Reformed: The Roman and Protestant Churches in English Protestant Thought, 1600–1640 (Cambridge: Cambridge Univ. Press, 1995), 370–421 et passim.

[16] Milton discusses the quasi-nationalism of the Laudians in Catholic and Reformed, 270–373.

to proclaim that *The Pilgrime* originated in 1331, at the same time suppressed all internal evidence of the fact that the *Lyfe* was originally a French text.[17] Baspoole might have seen his pilgrim in part as the English Church, an institution that—in his view—would do well to take more account of its own origins.

When reconstructing lost originals from present witnesses, scholarly editors try to serve the function of Deguileville's Memory in relation to their readers (although, it is to be hoped, without interpreting their role quite as Baspoole has done). In the case of *The Pilgrime*, however, I was in the fortunate position of having the first fair copy of the author's text (MS Pepys 2258)—a copy that has, moreover, been through his hands (quite literally in fact—it contains quite strikingly-presented marginal annotations entered by him). The two later manuscripts were therefore (strictly speaking) insignificant when it came to establishing the text (although they are of course important as evidence of the reception of it).[18] There were, nevertheless, some editorial challenges. The most interesting of these derive from the fact that the Pepys MS contains a number of alterations in a variety of non-scribal hands, some of which may have been entered by Baspoole, or on his authority. These alterations are generally minute (the writers were evidently concerned not to spoil the appearance of a beautiful manuscript) and it was quite impossible to categorise them with any confidence on the basis of scribal idiosyncrasies (as "Hands A, B, C," etc.). On the advice of the late D. F. McKenzie (who was at the time a senior colleague in the Department of English at the Victoria University of Wellington), I therefore decided to assess the validity of these alterations purely on the basis of their content. In my Textual Commentary, therefore, *all* alterations are subsumed under a single general heading "Pepys (b)"—while the original scribal reading is distinguished as "Pepys (a)." ("Pepys (b)" does not, I should emphasize, represent a single individual, authoritative or otherwise.) My task, then, was to assess the validity or otherwise of every Pepys (b) reading. In doing so, I was—at those points where Baspoole was remaining faithful to his medieval source—able to turn to the *Lyfe* for guidance. I was (at the risk of labouring my analogy) like the pilgrim himself, turning to evidence from the past in my times of need. In what follows, I want to explain my procedure from a selection of the more straightforward examples.

---

[17] Baspoole removes "In Frensch I haue set it" (Henry, *Lyfe* I, l. 12). He removes references to Deguileville's French monastery (Chaalit; *Lyfe* I, l. 18) and its twelfth-century prior (l. 2270). He also suppresses references to the French *Roman de la Rose* (ll. 5–8, 7298–7299). He introduces a reference to London, ll. 3953–3954.

[18] The later extant manuscripts are Marsh's Library, Dublin MS Z3. 2. 9 (copied directly from the Pepys manuscript in 1688), and Cambridge Univ. Library MS Ff. 6.30 (which is identified in a colophon as the fourth manuscript in a line of succession from the Pepys [counted as the first], and is dated 1655).

Before doing so, however, I need to explain a few relevant facts. The first is that the Middle English *Lyfe* has been scrupulously edited (from the six extant manuscripts) by Avril Henry for the Early English Text Society. (This allowed me to refer to the *Lyfe* by line numbers, and to consult her comprehensive account of substantive variants.) The second is that Baspoole did not, of course, have the advantage of Henry's edition. As I have already intimated, he used MS Laud Misc. 740 (a manuscript made in about 1420). Some of his misinterpretations and wordings are explicable in terms of this manuscript; many (though not all) of the illustrations in the Pepys manuscript are copied from illustrations in the Laud; and Baspoole's hand appears in the margins of the Laud manuscript just as it does in the Pepys. This meant that, in reconstructing Baspoole's source at any point, I needed to consult the Laud manuscript (which is referred to by Henry's abbreviation—"O" [for Oxford]—in my edition, and below). But the situation is a little more complicated. Baspoole clearly had access to a second medieval manuscript that is now lost. This is evident from the fact that while he often echoes the Laud MS, he sometimes echoes a rather different manuscript instead—a manuscript that has much in common with the Cambridge, St. John's College MS 189 (G. 21)—Henry's "J". It cannot, however, have been the St John's manuscript itself. This is partly because J is not illustrated, when we know that the second manuscript used by Baspoole must have contained a number of illustrations that complemented the models he found in the Laud manuscript (there being twenty-nine illustrations in the Pepys, twelve of which have no precedent in the Laud).[19] This lost manuscript was probably the immediate antecedent of the St John's, the antecedent hypothesized by Henry as "[ω]"—a manuscript that would have combined features of Henry's archetype along with some unique features (that were to be inherited by J). This manuscript may yet come to light—although it is possible that Baspoole defaced and destroyed it in the course of preparing his revised version (literally "cutting and pasting," perhaps).

According to the scribe of the Pepys MS of *The Pilgrime* (at l. 67), Grace Dieu—daughter of an emperor—describes herself as (according to the scribe) "dreadfull to all Folk." The word "dreadfull" has, however, been altered (in what is probably another hand) to read "needfull." Both readings make sense, as long as we remember that "dreadful" could mean "awe-inspiring" or "formidable"

---

[19] The twelve "extra" illustrations are in a tradition—a tradition that may be inferred from the set of illustrations in, for instance, Melbourne State Library of Victoria MS *096 G94 (although this manuscript was not one of Baspoole's sources either). For Henry's account of the Melbourne illustrations, see *Lyfe*, 1: xxxix–xli.

(*OED* dreadful, *a.* [*adv.* and *n.*] A. *adj.* 2. a.). In the *Lyfe*, however (at l. 169), all manuscripts have "needful." One can assume, therefore, that the alteration is correct, since it implies a knowledge of the original *Lyfe* that only Baspoole would have had. In this instance, my Textual Commentary reads:

needfull] *Pepys (b), Marsh, Camb.* [H 169]; dreadfull *Pepys (a)*

As I have already noted, by "Pepys (a)" I refer to an original reading, and by "Pepys (b)" I refer to any alteration to that reading (unless it is an obvious scribal self-correction)—Pepys (b) is not, I must reiterate, a single individual. The manuscript variants (the Cambridge and the Marsh) are listed, but I do not take them to have any authority.

At ll. 616 ff., Charity and Penitence are described as guarding the table (that is, the altar) in Grace Dieu's house. Charity holds Christ's "testament," by which he bequeaths his peace to mankind. According to the scribe, this is a "Testament *of* great Charter" (italics mine). But the scribal reading has been altered to read "a Testament *or* great Charter." The reading at the equivalent point in the *Lyfe* (l. 1091) does not anticipate either reading, but the fact that it places the words "a charter" in apposition to "a testament" ("a testament: a gret charter") confirms that "or" is the superior reading:

or] *Pepys (b)* [H 1091 a]; of *Pepys (a), Marsh, Camb.*

It looks as if the scribe who wrote "of" was expecting the phrase "of great *Charity*" here.

At ll. 1850 ff. (in a passage that follows closely on the account of Memory discussed above), the pilgrim ponders his inability to carry his armour for himself, given that he is not handicapped by any injury. Where the word for "injury" in the *Lyfe* (l. 2766) is "mayme," however, Baspoole's scribe has written "mayne," which is—as far as I have been able to ascertain—a meaningless word in the context. Here, although no correction has been entered, I emended the text accordingly (flagging the emendation as such with an asterisk):

*mayme] *Camb.* (maime), [H 2766]; mayne *Pepys, Marsh*

(I have not of course used "(a)" or "(b)" when there are no alternatives in the Pepys MS.) It will be apparent that in this instance my emendation was anticipated in the Cambridge manuscript.

The emendation of "mayne" to "maime" would, I think, have been obvious in the context. At l. 2345, however, the case is rather different. Reason tells the pilgrim that the body could not move without the soul. The relevant verb here is "stir." The scribe has written "stine":

*stire] [H 3303]; stine Pepys, Marsh; shine Camb.

Without the Lyfe (which has "stire") one might well have chosen the (probably incorrect) emendation incorporated in the Cambridge manuscript—given that Reason has just distinguished between the cloudiness of the body and "the brightnesse of the sowle within" (ll. 2320–2321).

The Laud manuscript was crucial when it came to a conflict at ll. 2100 ff., where Grace Dieu warns the pilgrim about the obstinacy of Rude Entendement (Ignorance). He is, she says (ll. 2109–2110), as hard as a diamond. The original scribe, however, wrote "as hard as Diamond"—the "a" before "Diamond" having been inserted in another hand. The equivalent passage in Henry's text of the Lyfe was no help, Reason saying that Rude Entendement is "as hard as ayemaunt other dyament" (as hard as adamant or diamond). But in the Laud MS (O) we find the variant reading "as hard as a dyamant," which suggests that the inserted "a" is correct:

as a Diamond] Pepys (b), Camb.[O 3065]; as Diamond Pepys (a) (line filler after "as"), Marsh

At ll. 4292–4293, the hag Lust boasts that she could have wiped out Virginity, if Virginity had not taken refuge in the House of Grace Dieu: "And had she not tooke the Howse of GD. for a Sanctuary to a fowle death ere now had she beene done." But the original scribal reading misses out the first "had", producing the awkward "And she not took [etc]." The "had" in "And had she" is an insertion in another hand. Henry's text of the Lyfe was suggestive ("Ne hadde she withdrawe hire [etc],") but the St John's manuscript, where the expression is "And had she not comen from [etc]," suggests that Baspoole must have found these very words in his second MS (probably Henry's [ω]):

And had she] Pepys (b), Marsh, Camb., [J 5648]; and she Pepys (a)

One would have chosen the above reading without the assistance of J. At ll. 3973–3974, however, a sentence without a verb remains uncorrected in the Pepys. Avarice describes her crook: "Of this Crook S Symond this hand called

Symony."[20] I suppose "is" would be the obvious word to insert before "called" (a conclusion reflected in the Cambridge MS), but there are other possibilities. Indeed, a whole line might have been skipped here. The St John's MS indicates, however, that Baspoole did indeed see a single missing "is" in his second medieval manuscript (Henry's [ω]). The crucial words in the St Johns manuscript read "is this hand called." Henry's text is probably less helpful here, reading "*th*is hand *hatteth*" (italics mine). My Textual Commentary reads:

> *is this hand called] *[J 5268]*; this hand called *Pepys, Marsh;* this hand is called *Camb.*

In the vast majority of cases in which I had to decide between alternative readings (at least of a substantive kind) I was able to turn to the *Lyfe* in this way. It appears, therefore, that it was when Baspoole was following the Middle English quite closely that his wording was most likely to become problematic, giving rise to unauthorized "corrections" in the Pepys.[21] Sometimes, of course, his problematic wording might have confused the scribe in the first place, causing error in Pepys (a) and necessitating some valid (*Lyfe*-based) corrections on his own part.

VICTORIA UNIVERSITY OF WELLINGTON

---

[20] (i) In this elliptical sentence the displayed long 's' seems to function almost as an interpolated illustration. The point, of course, is that the crook of Simony looks like "S" for the "Symond" for whom/which it is named. (ii) "Symond" may be (as in the *Lyfe*) Simon, cf. Acts 8: 9–24. But it may, alternatively, be a word for "cement"—Baspoole's own punning reference to the adhesive character of this particular instrument of avarice. Cf. *OED* simmon, n. 1

[21] I had to bear in mind the possibility that Baspoole himself might have revised his own original (and *Lyfe*-based) intentions when reading through the scribe's copy of his work.

INDEX

(Proper names and topics that appear in the text and cited *anywhere* in the notes are included. Proper names that appear *only* in the notes are omitted.)

RETS PANELS AND PAPERS
(printed in this volume)

The Josephine A. Roberts Forums, MLA

2005: *Legal, Paratextual, and Typographic Concerns in
Early Modern English Texts*
chair, Thomas Leland Berger

"Paternal Paratexts": Fathering Books in the Age of
Mechanical Reproduction (295)
DOUGLAS A. BROOKS

Typographic Nostalgia: Popularity and the Meanings
of Black Letter (279)
ZACHARY LESSER

2006: *Early Modern Women's Manuscripts*
chair, Margaret P. Hannay

Petitioning Power: The Rhetorical Fashioning of
Elizabethan Women's Letters (229)
ERIN A. SADLACK

"To take in hand the practice of phisick": Early Modern
Women's Signatures in Print Medical Texts (269)
REBECCA LAROCHE

'Saturn (whose aspects soe sads my soul)': Lady Hester
Pulter's Feminine Melancholic Genius (239)
ALICE EARDLEY

Open Business Meetings, MLA

2003: Cousins in Love (317)
NANCY TAYLOR

2004:The Commonplace Book of Sir John Strangways:
An Editor's View (339)
THOMAS G. OLSEN

2006:"**Memorie** shall attend thee": Past and Present in
William Baspoole's *The Pilgrime* (359)
KATHRYN WALLS

Renaissance Society of America

2002: *Editing Early Modern Women's Writing*
chair, Margaret P. Hannay

Chronicling Elizabeth Tyrwhit's *Morning and Evening
Prayers*: A Narrative of Devotional Reform (255)
SUSAN M. FELCH

2004: *Text and Image in Foxe's* Book of Martyrs
chair, Carolyn Kent

Saints, Martyrs, Murderers: Text and Context of
Foxe's Images (23)
MARGARET ASTON

Text and Image in Foxe's *Book of Martyrs* (39)
JOHN N. KING

Watching Women in *The Acts and Monuments* (49)
DEBORAH G. BURKS

2005: *Manuscript Miscellanies of the English Renaissance*
chair, Steven W. May

Women's Verse Miscellany Manuscripts in the
Perdita Project: Examples and Generalizations (141)
VICTORIA E. BURKE

2007: *Early Modern Women's Manuscripts I*
chair, Margaret P. Hannay

Petrarchan Love and Huguenot Resignation in an
Album Owned by Louise de Coligny (1555–1620) (193)
JANE COUCHMAN

"Let me say this one word vnto you":
Situating the Mother's Legacy in Manuscript
[Heare councill and receiue instruction] (207)
SUSAN E. HRACH

2007: *Early Modern Women's Manuscripts II*
chair, Elizabeth H. Hageman

Missing, Marginal, Mutilated: Reading the Remnant
of Women's Manuscripts (217)
SHARON CADMAN SEELIG

The Medieval Congress at Kalamazoo

2002: *Editing Early Modern Women*
chair, Margaret P. Hannay

Editing a Recent Mary Wroth Letter (103)
MARGARET J. ARNOLD

2007: *Early Modern Women's Manuscripts*
chair, Margaret P. Hannay

Faire Phillis, The Marchants Wife, and the Tailers
Wife: Representations of Women in a Woman's
Early Modern Manuscript Commonplace Book (155)
KATHRYN DEZUR

Reading the Stage Rubrics of Mary Wroth's
Folger Manuscript of *Pamphilia to Amphilanthus* (165)
SUSAN LAUFFER O'HARA

From Margin to Milieu: The Authorship of
Le tombeau de Marguerite de Valois, Royne de Navarre (179)
KRISTEN L. OLSON

Renaissance English Text Society

Officers and Council
2002–2006

President, Arthur F. Kinney, University of Massachusetts at Amherst
Vice-President, A. R. Braunmuller, University of California, Los Angeles
Secretary, Carolyn Kent, New York, N.Y.
Treasurer, Robert E. Bjork, Arizona Center for Medieval and Renaissance Studies
Membership Secretary, William Gentrup, Arizona Center for Medieval and Renaissance Studies
Past President, W. Speed Hill†, Lehman College and The Graduate Center, City University of New York
Past Publisher, Mario A. Di Cesare, Fairview, North Carolina

Robert C. Evans, Auburn University at Montgomery
Margaret Ezell, Texas A&M University
Susan Felch, Calvin College
Roy Catesby Flannagan, University of South Carolina, Beaufort
David Freeman†, Memorial University, Newfoundland
Elizabeth Hageman, University of New Hampshire
Margaret Hannay, Siena College
John King, Ohio State University
Ian Lancashire, University of Toronto
Leah Marcus, Vanderbilt University
Arthur F. Marotti, Wayne State University
Steven May, Georgetown College
G. W. Pigman III, California Institute of Technology
Nigel S. Smith, Princeton University
George Walton Williams, Duke University

Liaisons

Thomas L. Berger, St. Lawrence University, The Malone Society
Mary L. Robertson, Huntington Library
Heather Wolfe, Folger Shakespeare Library

International Advisory Council

The Renaissance English Text Society was established to publish literary texts, chiefly nondramatic, of the period 1475–1660. Dues are $35.00 per annum ($25.00, graduate students; life membership is available at $500.00). Members receive the text published for each year of membership. The Society sponsors panels at such annual meetings as those of the Modern Language Association, the Renaissance Society of America, and the Medieval Congress at Kalamazoo.

General inquiries and proposals for editions should be addressed to the president, Arthur Kinney, Massachusetts Center for Renaissance Studies, PO Box 2300, Amherst, Mass., 01004, USA. Inquiries about membership should be addressed to William Gentrup, Membership Secretary, Arizona Center for Medieval and Renaissance Studies, Arizona State University, Box 874402, Tempe, Ariz., 85287–4402.

Copies of volumes x–xii may be purchased from Associated University Presses, 440 Forsgate Drive, Cranbury, N.J., 08512. Members may order copies of earlier volumes still in print or of later volumes from xiii, at special member prices, from the Treasurer.

FIRST SERIES

VOL. I. *Merie Tales of the Mad Men of Gotam* by A. B., edited by Stanley J. Kahrl, and *The History of Tom Thumbe* by R. I., edited by Curt F. Buhler, 1965. (o.p.)

VOL. II. *Thomas Watson's Latin Amyntas*, edited by Walter F. Staton, Jr., and Abraham Fraunce's translation *The Lamentations of Amyntas*, edited by Franklin M. Dickey, 1967.

SECOND SERIES

VOL. III. *The dyaloge called Funus, A Translation of Erasmus's Colloquy (1534)*, and *A very pleasaunt & fruitful Diologe called The Epicure, Gerrard's Translation of Erasmus's Colloquy (1545)*, edited by Robert R. Allen, 1969.

VOL. IV. *Leicester's Ghost* by Thomas Rogers, edited by Franklin B. Williams, Jr., 1972.

THIRD SERIES

VOLS. V–VI. *A Collection of Emblemes, Ancient and Moderne*, by George Wither, with an introduction by Rosemary Freeman and bibliographical notes by Charles S. Hensley, 1975. (o.p.)

FOURTH SERIES

VOLS. VII–VIII. *Tom a' Lincolne* by R. I., edited by Richard S. M. Hirsch, 1978.

FIFTH SERIES

VOL. IX. *Metrical Visions* by George Cavendish, edited by A. S. G. Edwards, 1980.

SIXTH SERIES

VOL. X. *Two Early Renaissance Bird Poems*, edited by Malcolm Andrew, 1984.

VOL. XI. *Argalus and Parthenia by Francis Quarles*, edited by David Freeman, 1986.

VOL. XII. Cicero's *De Officiis*, trans. Nicholas Grimald, edited by Gerald O'Gorman, 1987.

VOL. XIII. *The Silkewormes and their Flies* by Thomas Moffet (1599), edited with introduction and commentary by Victor Houliston, 1988.

SEVENTH SERIES

VOL. XIV. John Bale, *The Vocacyon of Johan Bale*, edited by Peter Happé and John N. King, 1989.

VOL. XV. *The Nondramatic Works of John Ford*, edited by L. E. Stock, Gilles D. Monsarrat, Judith M. Kennedy, and Dennis Danielson, with the assistance of Marta Straznicky, 1990.

SPECIAL PUBLICATION. *New Ways of Looking at Old Texts: Papers of the Renaissance English Text Society, 1985–1991*, edited by W. Speed Hill, 1993. (Sent gratis to all 1991 members.)

VOL. XVI. *George Herbert, The Temple: A Diplomatic Edition of the Bodleian Manuscript (Tanner 307)*, edited by Mario A. Di Cesare, 1991.

VOL. XVII. Lady Mary Wroth, *The First Part of the Countess of Montgomery's Urania*, edited by Josephine Roberts, 1992.

VOL. XVIII. Richard Beacon, *Solon His Follie*, edited by Clare Carroll and Vincent Carey, 1993.

VOL. XIX. An Collins, *Divine Songs and Meditacions*, edited by Sidney Gottlieb, 1994.

VOL. XX. *The Southwell-Sibthorpe Commonplace Book: Folger MS V.b.198*, edited by Sr. Jean Klene, 1995.

SPECIAL PUBLICATION. *New Ways of Looking at Old Texts II: Papers of the Renaissance English Text Society, 1992–1996*, edited by W. Speed Hill, 1998. (Sent gratis to all 1996 members.)

VOL. XXI. *The Collected Works of Anne Vaughan Lock*, edited by Susan M. Felch, 1996.

VOL. XXII. Thomas May, *The Reigne of King Henry the Second Written in Seauen Books*, edited by Götz Schmitz, 1997.

VOL. XXIII. *The Poems of Sir Walter Ralegh: A Historical Edition*, edited by Michael Rudick, 1998.

VOL. XXIV. Lady Mary Wroth, *The Second Part of the Countess of Montgomery's Urania*, edited by Josephine Roberts; completed by Suzanne Gossett and Janel Mueller, 1999.

VOL. XXV. *The Verse Miscellany of Constance Aston Fowler: A Diplomatic Edition*, by Deborah Aldrich-Watson, 2000.

VOL. XXVI. *An Edition of Luke Shepherd's Satires*, by Janice Devereux, 2001.

VOL. XXVII. *Philip Stubbes: The Anatomie of Abuses*, edited by Margaret Jane Kidnie, 2002.

VOL. XXVIII. *Cousins in Love: The Letters of Lydia DuGard, 1665–1672, with a new edition of* The Marriages of Cousin Germans *by Samuel DuGard*, edited by Nancy Taylor, 2003.

VOL. XXIX. *The Commonplace Book of Sir John Strangways (1645–1666)*, edited by Thomas G. Olsen, 2004.

SPECIAL PUBLICATION. *New Ways of Looking at Old Texts, III: Papers of the Renaissance English Text Society, 1997–2001*, edited by W. Speed Hill, 2004. (Sent gratis to all 2001 members.)

VOL. XXX. *The Poems of Robert Parry*, edited by G. Blakemore Evans, 2005.

VOL. XXXI. *William Baspoole's 'The Pilgrime'*, edited by Kathryn Walls, 2006.

VOL. XXXII. *Richard Tottel's 'Songes and Sonettes': The Elizabethan Version*, edited by Paul A. Marquis, 2007.

VOL. XXXIII. *Cælivs Secvndus Curio: his historie of the warr of Malta: Translated by Thomas Mainwaringe (1579)*, edited by Helen Vella Bonavita, 2008.

SPECIAL PUBLICATION. *New Ways of Looking at Old Texts, IV: Papers of the Renaissance English Text Society, 2002–2006*, edited by Michael Denbo, 2008. (Sent gratis to all 2006 members.)